MW00535389

GOD THE RULER

WHAT THE BIBLE SAYS ABOUT

GOD THE RULER

By

Jack Cottrell

Wipf and Stock Publishers

150 West Broadway • Eugene OR 97401

2000

What the Bible Says About God the Ruler

By Cottrell, Jack

ISBN: 1-57910-524-6

Reprinted by *Wipf and Stock Publishers*
150 West Broadway • Eugene OR 97401

Previously published by College Press Publishing Company, 1984.

Table of Contents

Preface

> . . . To make God a momentary Creator, who once for all finished his work, would be cold and barren, and we must differ from profane men especially in that we see the presence of divine power shining as much in the continuing state of the universe as in its inception. . . . For unless we pass on to his providence—however we may seem both to comprehend with the mind and to confess with the tongue—we do not yet properly grasp what it means to say: "God is Creator." Carnal sense, once confronted with the power of God in the very Creation, stops there, and at most weighs and contemplates only the wisdom, power, and goodness of the author in accomplishing such handiwork. (These matters are self-evident, and even force themselves upon the unwilling.) It contemplates, moreover, some general preserving and governing activity, from which the force of motion derives. In short, carnal sense thinks there is an energy divinely bestowed from the beginning, sufficient to sustain all things.
>
> But faith ought to penetrate more deeply, namely, having found him Creator of all, forthwith to conclude he is also everlasting Governor and Preserver—not only in that he drives the celestial frame as well as its several parts by a universal motion, but also in that he sustains, nourishes, and cares for, everything he has made, even to the least sparrow . . . .[1]

John Calvin has thus rightly emphasized the necessity of moving on from the doctrine of creation to the doctrine of providence. That is what this book is all about. It is the second volume of a three-volume series which began with an explanation of the nature and work of God as Creator, published as *What the Bible Says About God the Creator* by College Press at the end of 1983. In this second volume we turn to the concept of providence, or the nature and work of God as Ruler over his creation. The third volume, planned for publication in early 1987, will deal with the nature and work of God as Redeemer.

I will remind the reader that all Scripture quotations have been taken from the New American Standard Bible except where noted. I have made the following modifications in the printed form, however. (1) The NASB prints much of the Old Testament in poetic form, but as a rule I have turned it into prose (without changing the words). (2) I have not used capital letters for the word *Lord* where it translates *Yahweh* in the original text. (3) I have not used all capital letters when citing

1. John Calvin, *Institutes of the Christian Religion*, I.xvi.1, ed. John T. McNeill, tr. Ford Lewis Battles (Philadelphia: Westminster Press, 1960), I:197-198.

passages from the New Testament which are quotations from the Old Testament.

I wish to thank my parents for all the help and encouragement they have given to me over the years. I gratefully dedicate this volume to my mother, Jewell Cottrell, and to the memory of my late father, Major Cottrell (1910-1984).

Chapter One

THE IDEA OF PROVIDENCE

Creation refers to that singular activity by which in the beginning God brought the universe into existence. *Providence* is a general concept that refers to the broad scope of God's continuing activity in relation to the on-going world.[1] This intimate and multi-formed relationship between God and the created universe began as soon as the latter was made to exist, and it continues unabated even now. Thus a study of God in his work of creation[2] is naturally followed by a study of God in his work of providence, which is what this book is about.

TERMINOLOGY

The English word *providence* is derived from the Latin *providentia*, the verb form of which is a combination of *pro* and *videre*, meaning literally "to see ahead," "to see beforehand," "to foresee." In common use the word meant "to see ahead and thus to make plans and preparations for what is thus anticipated," or as we would ordinarily say, "to provide." Thus the term *providence*, though it literally (etymologically) means "foresight," usually has the connotation of "forethought," "foreseeing care," "prudent management and oversight."

The Greek terms are practically equivalent to the above. The verb form is *pronoeō*, "to perceive in advance," "to foresee," "to take thought for or make provision for." The noun is *pronoia*, meaning "prior knowledge," "forethought," "provision," "care." The Greeks used these terms both for their gods and for men. *Pronoia* is found as early as Herodotus in reference to divine providence; the goddess Athene was also known by this name. In reference to men a leader or ruler was commonly praised for his *pronoia*.

The English word *providence* occurs only once in the King James Version, namely, in Acts 24:2. It translates the Greek *pronoia*, which is used only here and in Romans 13:14. The verb *pronoeō* occurs only three times in the New Testament, in Romans 12:17; II Corinthians 8:21; and I Timothy 5:8. One may be surprised that the terms are not found more often, given the significance of the idea of providence in Christian doctrine. But even more surprising is the fact that none

---

1. The activity of God most directly related to the salvation of sinners (specifically, the saving work of Christ and that of the Holy Spirit) is usually considered separately under the heading of *redemption*.

2. See Jack Cottrell, *What the Bible Says About God the Creator* (Joplin, Mo.. College Press, 1983).

of the above passages refers to the providence of *God;* they all refer to the care and foresight of men. For instance, in Acts 24:2 Paul's accuser Tertullus flatters the governor Felix by saying, "By your providence reforms are being carried out for this nation." In I Timothy 5:8 Paul condemns anyone who "does not provide for his own." The terms themselves are not used for divine providence.[3]

What this means is that the idea of providence is not really derived from any particular Biblical terminology. It is rather a doctrine or a concept that appears on nearly every page of Scripture, to which the term *providence* has been appropriately attached. Our understanding of providence comes from a thorough study of the teaching of Scripture as a whole, and not from the way a few words are used.

PROVIDENCE DEFINED

Exactly what do we mean, then, when we speak of the providence of God? Basically we are referring to how God is related to the on-going world. Whereas creation deals with the *origin* of the universe, providence has to do with its *history* after that point. Even non-theists must ask certain questions about this matter. What determines the course of events that occur day by day? How can we explain what happens? Is there a power other than or greater than man that fixes his destiny and shapes the general or even specific outcome of things? In theistic terms, what does God have to do with any of this? Does he care? Is he involved? Is any of it *his* doing? If so, to what extent is he involved? To what extent does God participate in the course of nature and in the affairs of men? This is the question of providence.

---

3. A couple of references to divine providence appear in the apocrypha. See Wisdom 14:3, which praises God's watchcare over a boat at sea: "But thy providence, O Father, governeth it; for thou has made a way in the sea, and a safe path in the waves." Wisdom 17:2 refers to "the eternal providence." Also, many references to God's *pronoia* are found in the early Christian writers. An example is Theophilus, who wrote, "Now we also confess that God exists, but that He is one, the creator, and maker, and fashioner of this universe; and we know that all things are arranged by His providence, but by Him alone" ("To Autolycus," III:9, tr. Marcus Dods, *The Ante-Nicene Fathers,* Volume II, ed. Alexander Roberts and James Donaldson; New York: Charles Scribner's Sons, 1913; p. 113). Clement of Rome comments that when seeds are sown, "the mightiness of the Master's providence raiseth them up" ("To the Corinthians," 24, *The Apostolic Fathers,* ed. J. B. Lightfoot and J. R. Harmer; Grand Rapids: Baker Book House, 1962; p. 24). For other references see J. Behm, "προνοέω, πρόνοια," *Theological Dictionary of the New Testament,* ed. Gerhard Kittel, tr. G. W. Bromiley (Grand Rapids: Eerdmans, 1967), IV:1010-1012, 1017.

Throughout Christian history the wording of the definition of providence has differed considerably, but the general idea or content has been quite consistent. This will be seen as we present a number of these definitions, beginning with this detailed statement from Luther's Small Catechism:

> I believe that God has created me and all that exists; that he has given and still preserves to me body and soul, eyes, ears, and all my limbs, my reason and all my senses; and also clothing and shoes, food and drink, house and home, wife and child, land, cattle, and all my property; that he provides me richly and daily with all the necessaries of life, protects me from all danger, and preserves and guards me against all evil; and all this out of pure paternal, divine goodness and mercy, without any merit or worthiness of mine; for all which I am in duty bound to thank, praise, serve, and obey him. This is most certainly true.[4]

The Reformed confessional documents usually contain definitions of providence. For instance, the Second Helvetic Confession of 1566 says, "We believe that all things, both in heaven and in earth and in all creatures, are sustained and governed by the providence of this wise, eternal, and omnipotent God."[5] In answer to the question, "What dost thou understand by the Providence of God?" the Heidelberg Catechism (1563) says,

> The almighty and every where present power of God, whereby, as it were by his hand, he still upholds heaven and earth, with all creatures, and so governs them that herbs and grass, rain and drought, fruitful and barren years, meat and drink, health and sickness, riches and poverty, yea, all things, come not by chance, but by his fatherly hand.[6]

The Westminster Larger Catechism (1648) answers a similar question this way: "God's works of providence are His most holy, wise, and powerful preserving and governing of all His creatures; ordering of them, and all their actions, to His own glory."[7] The Westminster Confession of Faith (1647) spells it out more completely:

> God, the great Creator of all things, doth uphold, direct, dispose, and govern all creatures, actions, and things, from the greatest even to

4. Martin Luther, "Luther's Small Catechism," *The Creeds of Christendom*, 4th edition, ed. Philip Schaff (New York: Harper and Brothers, 1919), III:78.

5. *The Creeds of Christendom*, III:839-840.

6. Ibid., III:316.

7. *The School of Faith: The Catechisms of the Reformed Church*, tr. and ed. Thomas F. Torrance (London: James Clarke and Co., 1959), p. 187.

> the least, by his most wise and holy providence, according to his infallible foreknowledge and the free and immutable counsel of his own will, to the praise of the glory of his wisdom, power, justice, goodness, and mercy.[8]

Theologians of the nineteenth century have similar definitions. William Sherlock says, "The general notion of Providence is God's care of all the creatures he has made, which must consist in preserving and upholding their beings and natures, and in such acts of government as the good order of the world and the happiness of mankind require."[9] Charles Hodge sums it up this way: "God's works of providence are his most holy, wise, and powerful preserving and governing all his creatures and all their actions. Providence, therefore, includes preservation and government."[10] In the words of A. A. Hodge, providence "includes generally the entire sum of all God's activities exterior to himself and subsequent to creation through all time."[11]

Coming into the twentieth century we find A. H. Strong giving this definition: "Providence is that continuous agency of God by which he makes all the events of the physical and moral universe fulfill the original design with which he created it."[12] The Roman Catholic theologian Joseph Pohle, following Thomas Aquinas, defines providence as "the all-regulating and stable plan by which God, as the Supreme Ruler of the universe, ordains all things."[13] In Wilbur Tillett's words, "Divine providence . . . has reference to the preservation, care, and government which God exercises over all things that he has created, in order that they may accomplish the ends for which they were created."[14]

Theologians of more recent decades have not varied the definition to any great extent. H. C. Thiessen says that "providence means that continuous activity of God whereby He makes all the events of the

---

8. *The Creeds of Christendom*, III:612.

9. William Sherlock, *A Discourse Concerning the Divine Providence* (Pittsburgh: J. L. Read, 1848), p. 21.

10. Charles Hodge, *Systematic Theology* (Grand Rapids: Eerdmans reprint, n.d.), I:575.

11. Archibald Alexander Hodge, *Popular Lectures on Theological Themes* (Philadelphia: Presbyterian Board of Publication, 1887), p. 35.

12. Augustus H. Strong, *Systematic Theology*, 3 vols. in 1 (Valley Forge: Judson Press, 1907), p. 419.

13. Joseph Pohle, *God: The Author of Nature and the Supernatural*, ed. Arthur Preuss (St. Louis: B. Herder, 1912), p. 91.

14. Wilbur Fisk Tillett, *Providence, Prayer and Power* (Nashville: Cokesbury Press, 1926), p. 6.

physical, mental, and moral phenomena work out His purposes; and that this purpose is nothing short of the original design of God in Creation."[15] With his usual precision Louis Berkhof says, "Providence may be defined as that continued exercise of the divine energy whereby the Creator preserves all His creatures, is operative in all that comes to pass in the world, and directs all things to their appointed end."[16] The Lutheran theologian Francis Pieper says that divine providence "means that God actually preserves and governs the universe and all individual creatures through His omnipresence and His omnipotence."[17] W. Carl Ketcherside gives this definition:

> . . . It is the bringing together of the forces of nature, or the ordering of events and circumstances, to achieve the divine purpose. And it is the doing of this by the power of the divine mind regulating and arranging these things.[18]

Similar definitions are given even by the less conservative theologians. Karl Barth says, "By 'providence' is meant the superior dealings of the Creator with His creation, the wisdom, omnipotence and goodness with which He maintains and governs in time this distinct reality according to the counsel of His own will."[19] He sums it up as "the lordship of God over world occurrence."[20] Emil Brunner speaks of providence as "the preservation of the world and the divine government of the world," or "that present activity of God in the world, which is only indirectly, not directly, related to the redemption of the world."[21] A final representative definition comes from Langdon Gilkey: "By Providence we refer to the rule of God over the events that make up the course of both nature and history," or "the purpose of God unfolding itself in the development of the cosmos and of human history."[22]

15. Henry C. Thiessen, *Introductory Lectures in Systematic Theology* (Grand Rapids: Eerdmans, 1949), p. 177.

16. Louis Berkhof, *Systematic Theology* (London: Banner of Truth Trust, 1939), p. 166.

17. Francis Pieper, *Christian Dogmatics*, tr. Theodore Engelder et al. (St. Louis: Concordia Publishing House, 1950), I:483.

18. W. Carl Ketcherside, "The Hand of God," *Christian Standard* (August 7, 1983), 118:10.

19. Karl Barth, *Church Dogmatics, Vol. III: The Doctrine of Creation, Part 3*, tr. G. W. Bromiley and R. J. Ehrlich (Edinburgh: T. & T. Clark, 1961), p. 3.

20. Ibid., p. 26.

21. Emil Brunner, *The Christian Doctrine of Creation and Redemption: Dogmatics, Vol. 2*, tr. Olive Wyon (Philadelphia: Westminster Press, 1952), p. 148.

22. Langdon Gilkey, "The Concept of Providence in Contemporary Theology," *The Journal of Religion* (July 1963), 43:171.

When we analyze this random sampling of definitions of providence, we see that they include four main elements. First, they refer to the *kind* of divine activity that is in view, namely, preserving and governing. Though other terms are sometimes used, these are used most often; and the others are either synonymous with or closely related to them. In reference to the divine activity of preservation God is said to sustain, maintain, uphold, protect, care for and provide for his creation. In reference to the divine government God is said to direct, order, dispose, ordain, regulate, arrange, and rule. This activity is continuous and not intermittent or occasional.

The second element is the *scope* of God's preserving and ruling. His activity is universal; it embraces the whole of creation. It includes all things or creatures, and all their actions. It includes every event and every circumstance, great or small, in both the realm of nature and the realm of history.

The third element of the definition of providence is the *means* by which God preserves and rules over all things. Mentioned most often is the omnipotence of God; but also included are references to his goodness, wisdom, mercy, omnipresence, and foreknowledge.

The final element of providence is its *purpose*. To what end does God preserve and govern his universe? Here of course the eternal purpose of creation itself comes into the picture. In his providence God is ordering and directing the world toward the fulfillment of his original plan and purpose, which is to share his goodness with his creatures for his own eternal glory.

In view of this analysis we may give the following definition: God's providence is his continuous activity of preserving and governing the whole of creation by his wisdom and goodness and power, for the fulfillment of his eternal purpose and for the glory of his name.

ACTIVE OR ABSENT?

The idea of providence, the concept of a God who is active in his world, will seem very natural to most Bible-believing Christians. This is simply the kind of God we have—a God who *acts*. As Jesus said in John 5:17, "My Father is working until now." Harry Blamires reminds us of this fact:

> When we say our prayers before getting into bed, are we deeply conscious of calling upon a God who acts? Not a God who can be occasionally and reluctantly stirred to action by the pressure of some distant yet

> persistent human appeal, but a God whose nature and whose joy it is to be ceaselessly, tirelessly active? . . .[23]

Blamires muses about what should happen when an intelligent Buddhist is first introduced to Christianity. What would strike him as the really novel aspect of the Christian God? "Not," says Blamires, "that this is a God of love: not that this is a God of self-sacrifice: but that this is a God who does things."[24]

We should note Blamires' characterization of our concept of an active God as a novelty. It is certainly true that in many religions and classic philosophies, God is absent from the world rather than active in it.[25] The anthropomorphic Greek gods and goddesses who dwelt on Mount Olympus basically kept to themselves, ultimately receding both from man and from nature. Cornford says, "The Olympians had passed beyond the reach of human needs and the touch of human emotion; they had even left their provinces in Nature, and it was found out that the business of the world could go forward without them."[26] The more sophisticated gods of the Greek philosophers were no more interested in the world than the Olympians. Aristotle's "Unmoved Mover" maintained an absolutely indifferent isolation from all mundane affairs. Epicurus' gods, made of some of the better atoms, dwelt undisturbed in tranquil bliss in the void between universes, "beautiful and happy and without thought of human affairs, eating and drinking and speaking Greek!"[27] This concept of an absentee God was a constant threat to the Christian thinking in the early centuries, with heretics such as Marcion and the Gnostics arguing that the physical creation was "no fit arena" for God's presence and activity.[28] A similar threat was posed by the English Deists of the seventeenth and eighteenth centuries.

Over against all such human speculations Biblical teaching has championed the idea of providence, the truth of a God who is active in nature and history,

---

23. Harry Blamires, *The Will and the Way* (London: S.P.C.K., 1957), p. 29.

24. Ibid.

25. See the discussion of exaggerated transcendence in Jack Cottrell, *What the Bible Says About God the Creator*, pp. 195ff.

26. F. M. Cornford, *From Religion to Philosophy* (New York: Harper Torchbook, 1957), p. 122. See pp. 115-119.

27. Frederick Copleston, *A History of Philosophy, Volume I: Greece and Rome, Part I*, new revised ed. (Garden City, N.Y.: Doubleday Image, 1962), p. 150.

28. Albert C. Outler, *Who Trusts in God: Musings on the Meaning of Providence* (New York: Oxford University Press, 1968), p. 33.

This Biblical truth has never been more severely challenged, however, than it is today.[29] Developments in modern western culture have forced us to ask once more, is God absent or active? Many are affirming the former with greater conviction than ever before. Modern man is suffering from what Thielicke calls "God's existentially experienced absence."[30] The world today, he says, regards itself "atheistically."[31] Thus there has never been a time that the doctrine of providence has been more needed, or more foreign to the prevailing views of the world. J. M. Boice remarks, "There is probably no point at which the Christian doctrine of God comes more into conflict with contemporary world views than in the matter of God's providence."[32] This agrees with Pollard: "Among the several key elements of the historic Christian faith which are difficult for the modern mind, there is none so remote from contemporary thought forms as the notion of providence." There is, he says, "a large measure of common agreement today that the very idea of providence is no longer tenable."[33] Outler sums up the crisis in this way:

> Thus, the root issue in the modern "problem of God" is the credibility of God's active "presence" *in this world*—personal and gracious—in the continuance of creation, in the vicissitudes of history, as the divine love in which we live and move and have our being. But *this* question is only another way of asking about divine *providence* . . . .[34]

This intensification of the sense of God's absence no doubt has many causes, but only two of them will be mentioned here. One has to do

---

29. Good discussions of this challenge may be found in the following: G. C. Berkouwer, *The Providence of God*, tr. Lewis B. Smedes (Grand Rapids: Eerdmans, 1952), ch. 1: "The Crisis of the Providence Doctrine in Our Century"; Langdon Gilkey, "The Concept of Providence in Contemporary Theology"; David E. Jenkins, *Guide to the Debate About God* (Philadelphia: Westminster Press, 1966), chs. 1 and 2; A. C. Outler, *Who Trusts in God*, chs. 1 and 2; William G. Pollard, *Chance and Providence: God's Action in a World Governed by Scientific Law* (New York: Charles Scribner's Sons, 1958), ch. 1: "The Problem of Providence in Contemporary Thought"; and Helmut Thielicke, *The Evangelical Faith, Volume One: Prolegomena, The Relation of Theology to Modern Thought Forms*, tr. and ed. Geoffrey W. Bromiley (Grand Rapids: Eerdmans, 1974), Part Two.

30. Helmut Thielicke, *The Evangelical Faith*, I:227.

31. Ibid., p. 222.

32. James Montgomery Boice, *Foundations of the Christian Faith, Volume I: The Sovereign God* (Downers Grove, Ill.: InterVarsity Press, 1978), p. 229.

33. William Pollard, *Chance and Providence*, pp. 17-18.

34. A. C. Outler, *Who Trusts in God*, p. 27.

with the question of God's active presence in nature; the other relates to his activity in history. They are, respectively, an acceptance of the all-sufficiency of natural science to account for the phenomena of nature, and a barrage of unprecedented episodes of evil.

Before the rise of modern science, natural processes were in a large measure mysterious, and a cause for awe and wonder. The theist was content to assume that God was controlling these forces for his own purposes, inscrutable or otherwise. If he sent a bountiful harvest, this was accepted with gratitude; if he sent a plague or a famine, this was accepted as chastisement or a lesson in trust. In any case it could all be explained as God's providential activity. But as scientific understanding increased, the "hand of God" as an explanation for what happens was gradually replaced by the "laws of nature." Of course, the Darwinian theory of evolution was especially significant in bringing about this transition. This is so not just because the concept of evolution replaced fiat creation as an explanation for the origin of individual species. It is true because it helped to shift man's attention and trust away from God and toward science in general. And science has not disappointed its inquirers. It has unveiled the role of bacteria, viruses and genetics in disease, along with the wonders of antisepsis and vaccination. It has described the role of wind currents and ocean currents and jet streams as factors in weather patterns. It has split the atom, put men on the moon, and invented an omnipotent technological panacea—the micro-chip. In short, science has shown that natural law can account for just about everything that happens in the world of nature, and we are assured that any remaining mysteries will soon be solved. As brain research continues at a rapid pace, some would say that even human behavior (and thus history itself) will soon be explainable in the same way that we explain why water freezes or gasoline burns. The universe thus takes on the appearance of a single vast network of intricately interlocking causes and effects, all operating according to immanent and self-sufficient laws which the human mind is capable of understanding and exploiting.

The result of all this seems to be that God is out of a job, or, as Outler puts it, he has fallen victim to automation.[35] A quotation from Pollard says this very well:

> . . . Time after time phenomena which had always before been baffling and mysterious have yielded to scientific analysis, and are now seen to

35. Ibid., p. 31.

> have a quite proper and expected place in the causal network of the natural world. There has seemed to be no limit to the capacity of science to inquire into any given situation and eventually to explain it completely as the inevitable consequence of the antecedents out of which it emerged and with which it is causally connected. The patient who believes he has been providentially delivered from sickness is refuted by his physician who explains the event in terms of well-understood physiological, biochemical, and bacteriological processes whose combined operation led unfailingly in accordance with universal laws of nature to an expected result. The farmer who believes rain to have been providentially provided for his crops finds his beliefs challenged by the meteorologist who explains it in terms of the physics of the atmosphere and the movement of air masses. The joy and gratitude which earlier filled the hearts of all in contemplating the manifold provision which God has made for His creatures in grain and fruit and flower, in the good earth and green pasture, in lofty forests and buried mineral treasure, have been replaced by a sense of marvel at the achievements of man in modern electronics, chemistry, agriculture, and medicine which have showered upon us a new abundance of man-made foods, materials, and devices.[36]

Berkouwer indicates how this omnipotent explanatory power of science has made the doctrine of providence obsolete in the minds of many:

> . . . As nature has been consistently reduced to natural causes, the "hypothesis" of God's preservation and rule of the world has been rendered less necessary. The enlightened scientific mind has come to look on the Providence doctrine more or less as a bromide convenient for pre-scientific naivete, but now rendered unpalatable by the "deeper insights" of the scientific method. The thought of a world locked up in natural cause has acted as a power of suggestion on the modern mind. Now that nature has given up her secrets and man has seen through what used to be called supernatural, the world has been relieved of God. . . .[37]

The most famous analysis of this problem is that of Dietrich Bonhoeffer, who coined a number of often-quoted phrases while imprisoned by the Nazis during World War Two. "God is being increasingly pushed

---

36. William Pollard, *Chance and Providence*, pp. 18-19. See also Adrio König, *Here Am I! A Christian Reflection on God* (Grand Rapids: Eerdmans, 1982), p. 112: "What has happened? In this view, God has lost his functions one by one. Gradually we have begun to provide for ourselves those things that previously we asked from him. In this way he has gradually disappeared from our world of experience and has been displaced by our scientific advances from the things that concern us."

37. G. C. Berkouwer, *The Providence of God*, p. 18.

out of a world that has come of age," he said.[38] "Man has learnt to deal with himself in all questions of importance without recourse to the 'working hypothesis' called 'God'."[39] "It is becoming evident that everything gets along without 'God'—and, in fact, just as well as before."[40] "God as a working hypothesis in morals, politics, or science, has been surmounted and abolished; and the same thing has happened in philosophy and religion."[41] "And we cannot be honest unless we recognize that we have to live in the world *etsi deus non daretur.*"[42]

Though Bonhoeffer himself did not fully accept the concept of an absent God, other theologians have embraced it completely, notably Rudolf Bultmann. The idea of a universe in which supernatural powers of any kind intervene is purely mythological and totally unacceptable in the light of modern science, he says.

> . . . This conception of the world we call mythological because it is different from the conception of the world which has been formed and developed by science since its inception in ancient Greece and which has been accepted by all modern men. In this modern conception of the world the cause-and-effect nexus is fundamental. Although modern physical theories take account of chance in the chain of cause and effect in subatomic phenomena, our daily living, purposes and actions are not affected. In any case, modern science does not believe that the course of nature can be interrupted or, so to speak, perforated, by supernatural powers.[43]

"Modern men take it for granted that the course of nature and of history, like their own inner life and their practical life, is nowhere interrupted

---

38. Dietrich Bonhoeffer, *Letters and Papers from Prison*, enlarged edition, ed. Eberhard Bethge, tr. Reginald Fuller et al. (New York: Macmillan, 1972), p. 341.

39. Ibid., p. 325.

40. Ibid., p. 326.

41. Ibid., p. 360.

42. Ibid. I.e., as if God were not given or not permitted. A. C. Outler sums up this attitude described by Bonhoeffer thus: "The world 'come-of-age' means man on his own in a cosmos that has no room and no need for God. And with this triumphant revelation, out goes the linchpin of traditional Christian doctrine: the belief in the providence of God as the ultimate environment of human existence" (*Who Trusts in God*, p. 6).

43. Rudolf Bultmann, *Jesus Christ and Mythology* (New York: Charles Scribner's Sons, 1958), p. 15.

by the intervention of supernatural powers."[44]

Thus we see what a devastating effect modern science has had on the concept of providence in the minds of many; we see how it has resulted in a sense of God's absence from the realm of *nature*. At the same time the idea of a God who is active in the sphere of *history* has also been lost, mainly because of a mounting number of incidents of inhumanity, suffering, and evil. Beginning with the second decade of this century we have witnessed a worldwide war, the Russian gulag, another worldwide war, the Jewish holocaust, the atomic destruction of two Japanese cities, the Korean and Vietnamese conflicts, the Cambodian holocaust, and multitudes of other atrocities on a lesser scale. In view of such events, how can anyone continue to say that an all-wise, all-loving, all-powerful heavenly Father watches over and guides the affairs of men? Even in times of relative calm in the world, there are enough suffering and death to raise serious questions about God's providential control. But in the twentieth century the situation seems to be much worse, and the presence of God in history is simply repudiated by many.

Langdon Gilkey points to "the almost violent irruption of evil" as one of the main causes of the "rather sudden disappearance of Providence" in our time. There may be other reasons, he says, why our generation shies away from the notion that God rules the objective events of history, "but surely this deep emotional sense of *unbelief* is central among them: how could he, it is all too horrible!"[45] With similar emotion Thielicke refers to the "much publicized statement that after Auschwitz it is no longer possible to praise the God 'who o'er all things so wondrously reigneth.' "[46]

Even from these brief comments we can understand why so many today have lost the sense of God's presence in nature and history, even within Christendom itself and within the circle of serious theologians. The doctrine of providence does not receive the attention it once did. Gilkey observes that "this concept of Providence is notable mainly in

---

44. Ibid., p. 16. In another place Bultmann says, "All our thinking to-day is shaped irrevocably by modern science." Also, "*man's knowledge and mastery of the world* have advanced to such an extent through science and technology that it is no longer possible for anyone seriously to hold the New Testament view of the world—in fact, there is no one who does." These quotations are from Bultmann's "New Testament and Mythology," *Kerygma and Myth: A Theological Debate*, ed. Hans Werner Bartsch, tr. Reginald H. Fuller (New York: Harper Torchbook, 1961), pp. 3-4.

45. Langdon Gilkey, "The Concept of Providence," pp. 175-176.

46. Helmut Thielicke, *The Evangelical Faith*, I:228.

its absence from theological discussion" today. It is "a rootless, disembodied ghost, flitting from footnote to footnote, but rarely finding secure lodgment in sustained theological discourse."[47] At the same time the alleged fact of God's absence has received considerable attention. The most sustained expression of this view was the "death of God" movement of two decades ago. While some of the theologians connected with this movement were actually expounding metaphysical theories,[48] others were simply trying to verbalize what has in fact been happening in Western culture as the result of the kind of influences discussed above.[49]

In a real sense the death-of-God phenomenon had a good result in that it called attention to what was taking place, namely, that a certain idea or certain ideas of God had in fact become obsolete. That is, God *as conceived of in a particular way* was dead. This led many to ask the question, "*Whose* God is dead?"[50] The point here is that only when God's nature has been misunderstood or when his relation to his world has been wrongly interpreted to begin with will there be any conflict between the idea of providence and *whatever* happens in nature or history. Only a false god can be crowded out of this world by any valid discovery of science; only a false god can be banished from history as inconsistent with even the foulest acts of human wickedness.

The god unthroned by modern science indeed was not the God of the Bible. There is no conflict between the true God and true science. In fact a principal impetus of modern science was the biblical doctrine of creation.[51] Unfortunately, however, at the very time science was gaining momentum, there existed a false view of God's relation to his

47. Langdon Gilkey, "The Concept of Providence," p. 171. He is speaking mainly about non-conservative theology.

48. For example, see especially Thomas J. J. Altizer, *The Gospel of Christian Atheism* (Philadelphia: Westminster Press, 1966).

49. For example, see Gabriel Vahanian, *The Death of God: The Culture of Our Post-Christian Era* (New York: George Braziller, 1961); and William Hamilton, *The New Essence of Christianity* (New York: Association Press, 1961). See also Hamilton's contributions to Thomas J. J. Altizer and William Hamilton, *Radical Theology and the Death of God* (Indianapolis: Bobbs-Merrill, 1966). Part Two of Helmut Thielicke's *The Evangelical Faith, Volume One: Prolegomena* is a lengthy discussion of this whole issue.

50. See for instance David H. C. Read, *Whose God Is Dead? The Challenge of the New Atheism* (Cincinnati: Forward Movement Publications, 1966).

51. See Jack Cottrell, *What the Bible Says About God the Creator*, pp. 147-150.

creation. It was mainly this false view of God to which Bonhoeffer was calling attention in his prison epistles. Only a "god of the gaps" (or God as a stop-gap), he said, or God as a *deus ex machina* has become superfluous.[52] This "god of the gaps" concept goes back to the time when natural processes were not understood and were simply attributed to God for lack of a better explanation. That is, God filled the gaps in man's knowledge. Because the processes were not understood, man did not know how to control them; thus he had to pray for God to act by sending rain or health or a good harvest. That is, God filled the gaps in man's ability. But as scientific knowledge and technology increased, the gaps in man's knowledge and ability decreased, thus making God's role in nature smaller and smaller. When science has closed all the gaps, God can retire altogether. The *deus ex machina* idea is smaller. The term means "a god from the machine," and is derived from the world of ancient Greek drama. In some of the plays the leading characters would be brought to such a precipice of danger or plot entanglement that there would seem to be no logical solution or denouement. But at the critical moment, by means of a mechanical device (*machina*) built into the stage, a god or goddess would suddenly appear on the scene and rescue the situation (like the cavalry in the old grade-B western movies). To say that God has been treated as a *deus ex machina* means that he has been given a role in the drama of life only when man has found himself in a situation that he could not handle on his own. But now that science has given man an unprecedented confidence in his own competence, there is no longer any need to call upon this problem-solver God.

In a similar way the god which is forced to abdicate in the face of human evils is not the true God. Berkouwer points out that since the latter part of the nineteenth century there was a growing perception of God as "mere optimistic love," a deity incapable of wrath.

> . . . But armed with such a milked concept of God, man could hardly erect a defence against the coming storms of the new era. It has become patent that the terrorizing world with its demonic appearance cannot be explained by an eternal, self-evident philanthropy, by this grace without judgment. Relations between this "god" and this world became increasingly strained. In times of quiet prosperity the rose-colored light of the providence of this "god" may have appeared to fall over the world. But in catastrophe, in the trenches, the caves, and the concentration

---

52. Dietrich Bonhoeffer, *Letters and Papers from Prison*, pp. 281, 311-312, 361.

> camps of this world, the eternal Philanthropist was exposed as a delusion. This was the beginning of the crisis of faith in our day. . . .[53]

How shall we respond to this "crisis of faith"? How shall we answer those who are proclaiming God's absence from nature and history today? First we must point out that the gods they have seen swept away by the currents of science and the torrents of evil were not the true God, the God of the Bible. Then we must explain the true nature of God as revealed in the pages of Scripture. Then we must show how our God is actually related to this world, how he is constantly and actively involved in every event of nature and history. He is indeed "the God who is there," the God who is present in his world, to his world, and for his world. As a popular song once put it, "He's got the whole world in his hands." This is providence.

A LIMITED PRESENCE?

I do not mean to imply that the idea of providence is in total eclipse in our day. Even though it may have lost considerable ground in our culture as a whole, it is still very much alive, particularly among conservative Christians and even among many who are not so conservative. Among those who definitely adhere to the idea of providence, however, there are a larger number who would disagree with one of the points emphasized in the last paragraph above. There it is affirmed that God "is constantly and actively involved in *every* event of nature and history." Many would judge this to be too extreme and would prefer to limit the scope of God's involvement in the world. They do not deny that God is active in the world, but only that he is involved in *everything* that happens.

This limitation of the scope of God's presence and activity in his world takes many forms. Some of them are among the most common ideas of providence to be found today. Most of the following examples will be immediately recognizable, and many readers may identify with one or the other of them. My point, though, is that these ideas of providence are inadequate because they are too limited, namely, they do not allow for God's involvement in the whole of his creation.

---

53. G. C. Berkouwer, *The Providence of God*, p. 26. See p. 28: "This genial Providence, this grace without judgment, this love without justice, this forgiveness without redemption, forms the background of the crisis of our century."

Nature Only

The first view of a limited providence is the idea that God is present in nature but not in history as such. God is seen as the creator of the world and as one who is still involved in its natural processes. He gives the sunshine and the rain and the harvest, and he cares for the birds and the flowers. He controls the movements of galaxies and atoms. But his relation to the world of men is more or less indirect, insofar as they benefit from or suffer from what happens in nature.

An example of this "nature-only" concept of providence is the person who never thinks of God or of God's involvement in his life except when he engages in a ritual "saying of grace" before a meal. God is thus acknowledged as a beneficent gardener. Another example is the "acts of God" concept usually associated with insurance policies. This usually attributes natural disasters to the hand of God, e.g., earthquakes, floods, and lightning.

History Only

Another limited view of providence is just the opposite of the above, namely, that God is active in history but not in nature. This idea usually arises as one response to the advance of modern science. That is, even if we do not need God any longer in order to explain and manipulate nature, he can still be involved in our personal lives. Pollard notes how this alternative usually divides creation into two domains.

> . . . The first domain of physical nature is then considered to be wholly determined and to be proceeding inexorably under its own power along the course which scientific law requires that it follow. Providence is then strictly confined to the second domain of which man is a part. Only this portion of creation is the object of His providential care and mercy and only within it does God act in redemption or in judgment.[54]

Pollard cites as an example of this the idea that one's religion is purely an individual matter, a private relationship between himself and his God. He may engage in personal prayer and meditation and communion with God, but he does not expect to encounter God anywhere on the "outside." Whatever takes place there, in business or politics or international life, is altogether in the hands of human beings. Other examples, not quite so extreme, would see God as active in human relationships

---

54. William Pollard, *Chance and Providence*, p. 31.

on a broader scope than this, including within God's providence the family and the church, and perhaps even the affairs of nations as well. All natural processes, however, especially in the realm of inanimate nature, are ruled by autonomous scientific law.[55]

Major Matters Only

Still another limited idea of providence is the notion that God cares about and attends to the major events of the universe but does not bother himself with the small and the trivial. Such a view may be the result of a too-limited understanding of God himself. If God is not omniscient or all-powerful, then he may not be able to keep track of every detail in the universe. More often, however, this notion comes from thinking of God as being too important or majestic to notice details. It is contended "that such activity would burden God too heavily and would give the trivial things of life undue prominence over against the great things."[56] A. H. Strong cites these examples from pagan writers: "The gods concern themselves with large things; the small things they ignore" (Cicero). "Even in kingdoms among men, kings do not trouble themselves with insignificant affairs" (also Cicero). "It is a shame to believe that God would hear the talk of men" (the ancient Cretans, who made an image of Jove without ears).[57] Even the Christian writer Jerome shared this view:

> . . . It is an absurd detraction of the majesty of God to say that God knows every moment how many gnats are born and how many die; how many bedbugs, fleas, and flies there are on earth, what number of fishes live in the water. We are not such fatuous sycophants of God that while we make His power concern itself with most insignificant creatures, we are unfair to ourselves by assuming a like providence extending over rational and irrational creatures.[58]

This is similar to the inadequate view of God which J. B. Phillips labels "Managing Director" in his book, *Your God Is Too Small*. We know that the managing director of a large corporation employing thousands of workers cannot possibly tend to all its details. Then when we think of the magnitude of the universe and the responsibility of God in taking care of it all, we say: "*I cannot imagine* such a tremendous

55. Ibid., pp. 31-32.
56. Francis Pieper, *Christian Dogmatics*, I:485.
57. A. H. Strong, *Systematic Theology*, p. 429.
58. Cited in Francis Pieper, *Christian Dogmatics*, I:485.

God being interested in small details." The problem here, says Phillips, is that people tend to model their concept of God upon what they know of man. "To hold a conception of God as a mere magnified human being is to run the risk of thinking of Him as simply the Commander-in-Chief who cannot possibly spare the time to attend to the details of His subordinates' lives."[59]

This view does not necessarily limit providence to either nature or history, but limits its extent in both.

Occasional Good Fortune

Perhaps the most common of the narrow views of providence is the idea that for the most part God is content to stand by and watch the world proceed in accordance with natural laws and human decisions, but that occasionally he decides to intervene to do someone a special favor. And *favor* is the appropriate word, since this view almost always associates God with good events and not bad ones. God is seen as dropping an occasional blessing here, answering a prayer there, providing an unexpected bit of income for a widow's bills, directing a traveler away from the scene of a sure accident, or bringing about a beneficial meeting between two individuals. These are the kinds of incidents that many people would describe as coincidence or at best "luck" or good fortune. But others would say, "No, that was surely the providence of God." Blamires gives an apt description of this view:

> . . . Perhaps no idea is so desperately in need of rehabilitation within Christendom as the idea of Divine Providence. Through the weakness of our faith, the idea of Providence has suffered a vulgarization which has all but robbed it of meaning. "The hand of Providence!" we say, when some remarkable event gives a new turn to circumstances after the eleventh hour has struck and some overwhelming tragedy seems imminent. Is not this the very error . . . of assuming that only on rare occasions of extremest urgency does God interfere in human affairs? "Providence has intervened," we say with a sigh, as a life is saved by inches in a road accident. No doubt Providence *did* act. But must we say *intervene* of a God whose hand is daily and hourly upon the affairs of men? Must we speak as though God only occasionally wakened up to the cries of human distress, to make a quick saving sally into the world of men—like a guerilla warrior operating in enemy territory—thence to retire immediately to his long sleep of neglect?[60]

---

59. J. B. Phillips, *Your God Is Too Small* (London: Epworth Press, 1952), pp. 39-43.
60. Harry Blamires, *The Will and the Way*, p. 43.

A. A. Hodge has similarly chastised those who hold this weak view of providence and has offered a typical illustration:

> . . . There prevails a very unintelligent and really irreligious habit among many true Christians of passing unnoticed the evidence of God's presence in the ordinary course of nature, and of recognizing it on the occasion of some event specially involving their supposed interests, as if it were special and unusual. They will say of some sudden, scarcely-hoped-for deliverance from danger, "Why, I think I may venture to say it was really providential." But would it have been any the less providential if they had been destroyed and not delivered? Would it have been any the less providential if they had not been in jeopardy at all and had needed no deliverance? The great Dr. Witherspoon lived at a country-seat called Tusculum, on Rocky Hill, two miles north of Princeton. One day a man rushed into his presence crying, "Dr. Witherspoon, help me to thank God for his wonderful providence. My horse ran away, my buggy was dashed to pieces on the rocks, and behold! I am unharmed." The good doctor laughed benevolently at the inconsistent, halfway character of the man's religion. "Why," he answered, "I know a providence a thousand times better than that of yours. I have driven down that rocky road to Princeton hundreds of times and my horse never ran away and my buggy was never dashed to pieces." Undoubtedly, the deliverance was providential, but just as much so also were the uneventful rides of the college president. God is in the atom just as really and effectually as in the planet. He is in the unobserved sighing of the wind in the wilderness as in the earthquake which overthrows a city full of living men, and his infinite wisdom and power are as much concerned in the one event as in the other.[61]

How many of us must admit that these quotations from Blamires and Hodge quite accurately describe what we think of as "divine providence"? This is indeed a prevalent view, held in all piety and sincerity. But as we shall see, it does not begin to do justice to the magnitude of God's involvement with his creatures.

Salvation History

The final view of a limited providence that will be mentioned here is the idea that God is actively involved in the affairs of this world only insofar as it is necessary to bring about man's salvation. For many this would include the whole scope of salvation history, beginning with the

---

61. A. A. Hodge, *Popular Lectures on Theological Themes*, pp. 38-39.

"mighty acts of God" in Old Testament times in connection with Abraham or Moses. This would include the work of Christ and the history of the church, as well as the religious experience of individuals. After all, the work of salvation would seem to be the most appropriate and natural thing for God to be concerned about.

As Outler points out, such a view is sometimes an expression of a "god-of-the-gaps" theology: "all we need of God is what we admit we cannot manage on our own," and that is our salvation.[62] Everything else we feel we can handle, but salvation does seem to be exclusively the responsibility of God. Thus we let him take care of that.

Others have pointed out, however, that this stunted view of providence is often the result of a particular theological methodology, especially one that tries to measure all of God's activity (and all our knowledge thereof) in terms of his salvation purposes in Jesus Christ. Richard Baepler includes in this category "the massive Christocentric theology" of Karl Barth, as well as the *heilsgeschichtliche* or "history of salvation" theology. While such views focus upon the redeeming acts of God in history and in the hearts of believers, they have difficulty in showing how God is active in events not within the history of salvation, says Baepler.[63] This same point is made in other terms by Langdon Gilkey in his article on the concept of providence in modern theology. The tendency in neo-orthodoxy, he says, is to derive all that can be known of God and his works from one's own subjective, existential encounter with God's Word and Spirit.[64] This is an example of what I have called in an earlier work "the Christological fallacy."[65]

CONCLUSION

Thus it would appear that the idea of God's providence has fallen upon hard times in the modern world. If not denied altogether, it has been truncated in one way or another so as to eliminate God's presence in some part of his creation. It therefore seems appropriate to call upon

62. A. C. Outler, *Who Trusts in God*, p. 32.

63. Richard Baepler, "Providence in Christian Thought," *The Caring God: Perspectives on Providence*, ed. Carl S. Meyer and Herbert T. Mayer (St. Louis: Concordia Publishing House, 1973), p. 64.

64. Langdon Gilkey, "The Concept of Providence," pp. 181ff. In an excursus on Karl Barth's doctrine of providence, Gilkey shows how Barth attempts to extend God's sovereign control over "all creaturely occurrence," but is forced into internal inconsistencies as a result of his methodology (pp. 186-190).

65. Jack Cottrell, *What the Bible Says About God the Creator*, pp. 166ff., 371ff.

Christendom to consider anew this glorious theme of the providence of God. This book is intended to be only a modest contribution to that end. Its thesis is that God is not only active in the world, but is active in *all* the world, in *everything* that happens (though not necessarily in the same way): the known and the unknown, the familiar and the mysterious, the trivial and the spectacular, the minute and the majestic, the sad and the joyful, the painful and the pleasant, the good and the evil. For this is the idea of providence: not that God is merely "on call" and *ready* to act if needed, nor that he is active only in the sunshine and not in the shadow, but that he is indeed a "God who acts"—always and everywhere. I agree with Outler, that "if there is one constant and relatively consistent theme throughout the Bible . . . , it is that God's business with creation embraces it all—the world at every level, existence in every form." The proper view of providence does not picture God as "fitting into" some kind of gap in this or that. "Rather, it recognizes and acknowledges God's sovereign providence in his appropriate relations to *every* conceivable level and category of creation: nature, history, spirit, or whatever."[66]

In order to accomplish our purpose we shall proceed as follows. The next chapter will present a survey of non-biblical alternatives to providence, both non-theistic and theistic. This will be followed by chapters on general providence and special providence, including a detailed discussion of the relation between divine sovereignty and human freedom. A brief chapter on miracles is next, followed by a chapter dealing with the nature of God as related to his providential workings. Particular attention will be given to the concepts of sovereignty and immanence and to the attributes of knowledge, power, wisdom, and goodness. This will be followed by chapters on specific topics related to God's providential control, namely, the will of God, predestination, prayer, and the problem of evil. A brief conclusion will emphasize the creature's proper response to the God who "so wondrously reigneth."

---

66. A. C. Outler, *Who Trusts in God*, pp. 32-33.

Chapter Two

ALTERNATIVES TO PROVIDENCE

As noted in the last chapter, providence has to do with the way God is related to the events of the on-going world. This biblical doctrine seeks to answer such questions as the following: How can we explain what happens? What determines the course of events that we call "history"? What forces or influences or causes are operating to bring about the events that take place in the lives of individuals and in the universe in general? Who or what initiates or controls the actions that begin and continue day by day? These questions may not be asked very often, but they are foundational for one's general world view. The answer one gives is vital for his interpretation and understanding of reality as a whole.

From one perspective we can distinguish three distinct causes or principles of action which may be operating within the universe. Any one of them may be viewed as the sole cause of what happens, or any two or all three may be seen as working together in particular combinations. These three possibilities are (1) God, (2) free-will creatures, and (3) impersonal law (such as the laws of nature). Of course, within various world views these elements will not always be interpreted in the same way. For instance, "natural law" means one thing to a humanist and quite another thing to an occultist; also, "God" does not mean the same thing for a Hindu as for a Bible-believing Christian. Nevertheless these are the variables with which one must work in constructing his view of providence or an alternative thereof.

Before we proceed to elaborate upon the biblical teaching concerning providence, it is our purpose in this chapter to survey the main non-biblical alternatives to the providence doctrine. By comparing the Christian view with its rivals we will better understand what is at stake in this whole issue. We will also be able to appreciate the uniqueness and the beauty of the biblical concept.

The alternatives to providence fall into three general categories. We may call them (1) *indeterminism* or chance, (2) *self-determinism* or limited human autonomy, and (3) *determinism*. Our discussion of them will proceed in this order.

INDETERMINISM

"What should mortals fear, for whom the decrees of Fortune are supreme, and who hath clear foresight of nothing? 'Tis best to live at random, as one may."[1] These words, put into the mouth of one of his characters by the Greek dramatist Sophocles, express a viewpoint held by numbers of people in all ages, namely, that whatever befalls us is a matter of fortune or chance (Greek, *tychē*). Luck or coincidence will either bless us or burden us; we will be either lucky or unlucky. Events occur at random; nothing is sure or determined.

Of course we must be careful not to understand this in an absolute sense as if everything that happens is occurring completely at random. That is, we should not expect water to put out a fire one minute and burst into flames the next. We should not expect a dropped book to fall downward one day and upward the next. We do not have to guess whether water or fingernail polish will come out of a faucet the next time we turn it on. In a chance system natural laws still operate; in fact, of the three variables mentioned above (God, free-will creatures, impersonal law), natural law is the dominant determining factor in the universe. Now, for many people this is a sure formula for determinism, as we shall see below. However, for the indeterminist natural laws are not of such a nature that they must produce one and only one result in every case. Rather, at the various levels at which such laws operate (e.g., sub-atomic, molecular, planetary), there are built-in factors that allow for variation in results. These variations may be very slight and infrequent in the application of a given law to a particular sequence of events. However, there are such an enormous multitude of sequences constantly interacting and acting upon one another that significant variations are always possible. For instance, the genetic material of two uniting reproductive cells from the same individuals does not always have to combine in exactly the same way, as the differences in siblings will attest. The over-all result is that nothing happens *necessarily* the way it does. With regard to any given event, it is possible that it might not have happened in just that way, or that it might not have happened at all.

This particular view of natural law is not uncommon, nor is it necessarily wrong. What makes it unique in this connection, i.e., the reason why it results in a *chance* world view, is that natural law operating thus is seen as the ultimate causative factor in the universe. There is no transcending force or power which is responsible for individual events or for the course of events as a whole. A chance system is non-theistic.

1. Cited in William Chase Greene, *Moira: Fate, Good, and Evil in Greek Thought* (Gloucester, Mass.: Peter Smith, 1968), p. 159.

It will not necessarily deny the existence of God or gods, but whatever deity may exist will not be involved in the affairs of our universe. The world and its laws are autonomous and self-sufficient. No higher power, personal or impersonal, is in control. Things just happen—by chance.

Chance and Causation

A precise definition of chance is difficult to formulate, and it has been understood in a number of different ways. In most cases, however, it is defined in reference to causation. For example, some think of a chance event as one which has *no cause*. The Heisenberg indeterminacy principle is sometimes cited as an example of this. This principle states that one can never know both the exact position and the exact speed of any atomic particle at the same time. Thus one can never predict the fact or the consequence of the collision of two such particles. Though this makes little practical difference on the level of ordinary living,[2] it has led to some interesting metaphysical conclusions. Jacques Monod cites it as an appropriate though not necessary foundation for this view of a chance universe.[3] Others think that it might mean that some events (on the sub-atomic level at least) are uncaused and are thus the very essence of chance.[4]

Another understanding of chance is that it is an event whose cause is *unknown*, usually because of its extreme complexity. This is how some would understand the Heisenberg indeterminacy principle.[5]

---

2. See William G. Pollard, *Chance and Providence: God's Action in a World Governed by Scientific Law* (New York: Charles Scribner's Sons, 1958), pp. 47-56. He says that with rare exceptions quantum indeterminacies have essentially no effect on large-scale macroscopic phenomena of our direct experience (p. 55). He also questions the propriety of using the indeterminacy principle as an argument for human free will (pp. 53-54). See also Donald M. MacKay, *The Clock Work Image: A Christian Perspective on Science* (Downers Grove, Ill.: InterVarsity Press, 1974), pp. 14-15.

3. Jacques Monod, *Chance and Necessity: An Essay on the Natural Philosophy of Modern Biology*, tr. Austryn Wainhouse (New York: Alfred A. Knopf, 1971), pp. 114-115.

4. See Stephen M. Cahn, "Chance," *The Encyclopedia of Philosophy*, ed. Paul Edwards (New York: Macmillan, 1967), II:73-74.

5. Ibid. This does not mean that some day, when our observational instruments are perfected, we *will* be able to determine both the position and the speed of an electron simultaneously. Such a determination is not just a practical impossibility but a theoretical one. See William Pollard, *Chance and Providence*, pp. 54-55. See also A. d'Abro, *The Rise of the New Physics* (New York: Dover Publications, 1952), II:671-673.

This is also the understanding of chance that is connected with ordinary probability theory, i.e., the calculation of the "odds" in such activities as throwing dice or flipping coins. As Pollard points out, if we knew with certainty all the factors involved in the tossing of a coin (e.g., the motion and speed of the tosser's fingers, air and surface friction), we would know whether a given toss would result in heads or tails. There would be no "chance." But in the absence of such knowledge of causes, we speak of the result as chance.[6]

A third concept of chance describes it as "the intersection of two totally independent chains of events."[7] The key word here is *independent*, i.e., there is no plan or purpose for the two causal chains to intersect. Otherwise it would be a single chain of events. But when the meeting is unpurposed, we say it happens by chance or coincidence. For instance, as an event in causal chain A, a brisk wind happens to be blowing a particle of dirt along at about five and one-half feet above the ground. At the same time, via causal chain B, I happen to be walking in that same vicinity with the result that my eye and the particle of dirt intersect the same space at the same time. Thus, by chance, I get dirt in my eye.

Still another understanding of chance is that it refers to *random* occurrences, i.e., to those occasions wherein the same cause or cluster of causes is capable of producing more than a single event. This is similar to the view of natural law described in our general introduction to indeterminism above. This is the way Pollard defines chance:

> . . . The case which is really typical of science is one in which the laws of nature first define several possible states which a system under consideration may occupy in full conformance to them, and, secondly, in which they determine the probabilities that in individual instances the system will choose each of those several possible states in response to a given set of forces or causes acting upon it. Thus, the typical situation is an indeterminate one involving alternatives and latitude. . . .[8]

That chance and accident are present in history, Pollard says, means that

> . . . history is open and pregnant with many possibilities. We see clearly that history objectively considered did not have to be the way it was.

---

6. William Pollard, *Chance and Providence*, pp. 41-42.

7. Jacques Monod, *Chance and Necessity*, p. 114. This view is attributed to Aristotle (Stephen Cahn, "Chance," p. 73).

8. William Pollard, *Chance and Providence*, p. 60.

> Innumerable other histories involving very different courses of events were just as possible and could just as well have happened as the history which did in fact occur. Objectively considered, it is a pure happenstance that the world has the history it does have and not any one of the others it could equally well have had.[9]

Any one of these definitions of chance is compatible with indeterminacy as a world view, though the second one is too weak a concept to satisfy most indeterminists. The definitions accepted most often are the first and the fourth, as the following examples will illustrate.

Examples of Indeterminacy

A classic example of indeterminacy is the philosophy of Epicurus (341-270 B.C.), who adopted the atomist physics of Democritus with one important exception. Democritus (following Leucippus) taught that the universe consists of an infinite number of eternally-existing atoms, eternally moving in an infinite void. As the result of their motion they often collide and sometimes combine with each other, thus forming objects and ultimately universes. Though the origin of the motion is unexplained, the fact that it exists means that whatever combinations of atoms occur do so of necessity. I.e., Democritus was a determinist. Now, Epicurus liked everything in this system except its determinism. To him it seemed to rule out freedom of the will and thus responsibility for one's actions, which in turn seemed to make the whole concept of morality meaningless. Thus Epicurus altered the system slightly. He accepted the idea of an infinite number of particles moving through an infinite void, but he added the idea that the particles are of a certain weight and thus are falling "downward" through the void. But since they are all falling at the same speed, no collisions would ever occur unless the atoms occasionally moved sideways out of their straight downward paths. This is exactly what happens, according to Epicurus. As they fall the atoms sometimes swerve out of their regular paths, thus creating the collisions and combinations necessary for universes such as ours.[10]

---

9. Ibid., p. 83. We should note that Pollard is here simply *defining* chance and not advocating it as the sole explanatory principle for reality.

10. See Frederick Copleston, *A History of Philosophy, Volume I: Greece and Rome, Part II,* new revised edition (Garden City, N.Y.: Doubleday Image, 1962), p. 149. See also Gordon H. Clark, *From Thales to Dewey: A History of Philosophy* (Boston: Houghton Mifflin Co., 1957), pp. 148-149.

The important part of this world view is the *swerve*; this is what provides for chance or indeterminacy. As Greene says, the Epicurean swerve is "unaccountable, contingent, practically causeless, and amounts almost to chance."[11] This is probably too conservative a description. Clark sees Epicurus as saying that the atoms swerve "at quite uncertain times and without any cause."[12] Cahn agrees that for Epicurus the swerves are entirely uncaused; thus he uses this as an example of chance as uncaused events.[13] The point is that any universe produced by collisions of swerving atoms is the result of pure chance. This applies likewise to all subsequent events in such a universe, including the activities of the mind, which is also composed of atoms. This is the basis for Epicurus' view of free will: the spontaneous swervings of mental atoms are conceived of as an act of the will.[14]

Thus the Epicurean creed was, "Chance, not wisdom, rules the life of men."[15] (We may remember that Epicurus did not deny the existence of gods, but he denied that they have anything to do with this or any other universe.)

A second and more recent example of indeterminacy is modern evolutionism. Not everyone who believes in evolution would be included here, such as those who see evolution as a God-directed process. Also we are not including here those who see it as a mechanistic, deterministic process. By evolutionism we mean in this context the view that this particular universe has evolved as the result of an accumulation of innumerable random events. These events did not have to happen the way they did; hence another totally different universe might have resulted if certain equally plausible alternatives had occurred instead. (In principle this is no different from the Epicurean theory; there is simply a greater and more accurate understanding of the workings of natural law.)

There are several classic examples of this view of a chance universe. First we may cite that of Bertrand Russell as expressed in his essay, "A Free Man's Worship."[16] Here he describes nature as "omnipotent

11. William Greene, *Moira*, p. 334.

12. Gordon Clark, *From Thales to Dewey*, p. 149.

13. Stephen Cahn, "Chance," pp. 73-74.

14. William Greene, *Moira*, p. 335.

15. This is a statement by the poet Chaeremon, quoted by Plutarch in his *Essay on Chance*, cited in William Greene, *Moira*, p. 369.

16. Bertrand Russell, "A Free Man's Worship," *Mysticism and Logic*, by Bertrand Russell (Garden City, N.Y.: Doubleday Anchor, n.d.), pp. 44-54. The article was originally published in 1903.

but blind," and as engaged in a "blind hurry . . . from vanity to vanity."[17] "Blind to good and evil, reckless of destruction, omnipotent matter rolls on its relentless way," a mighty "empire of chance."[18] Man himself "is the product of causes which had no prevision of the end they were achieving; . . . his origin, his growth, his hopes and fears, his loves and his beliefs, are but the outcome of accidental collocations of atoms."[19]

A similar example is that of Julian Huxley, who affirms that in the past evolution has occurred through "the blind and automatic forces of mutation and selection."[20] Concerning the universe as a whole he says,

> . . . Nowhere in all its vast extent is there any trace of purpose, or even of prospective significance. It is impelled from behind by blind physical forces, a gigantic and chaotic jazz dance of particles and radiations, in which the only over-all tendency we have so far been able to detect is . . . the tendency to run down.[21]

G. G. Simpson agrees that "the objective phenomena of the history of life" can be readily explained on the basis of "the mainly random interplay of the known processes of heredity."[22]

An elaborate defense of this view is presented by Jacques Monod in his book *Chance and Necessity*, in which he says that his thesis

> . . . is that the biosphere does not contain a predictable class of objects or of events but constitutes a particular occurrence, compatible indeed with first principles, but not *deducible* from those principles and therefore essentially unpredictable.[23]

In other words the universe and every element in it, especially the realm of living things, is the result of chance. It is an error to think of ourselves as "necessary, inevitable, ordained from all eternity."[24]

Monod concentrates on the molecular processes of proteins and uses their pure randomness as a model for the universe. In these

---

17. Ibid., pp. 46, 52.

18. Ibid., p. 54.

19. Ibid., p. 45.

20. Julian Huxley, *Evolution in Action* (New York: New American Library Signet Books, 1953), p. 72.

21. Ibid., pp. 11-12.

22. George Gaylord Simpson, *The Meaning of Evolution* (New Haven: Yale University Press, 1949), p. 343.

23. Jacques Monod, *Chance and Necessity*, p. 43.

24. Ibid., p. 44.

processes, "nothing but the play of blind combinations can be discerned."[25] This applies specifically to the transmission of the genetic code or DNA, which is subject to constant mutations.[26]

> We call these events accidental; we say that they are random occurrences. And since they constitute the *only* possible source of modifications in the genetic text, itself the *sole* repository of the organism's hereditary structures, it necessarily follows that chance *alone* is at the source of every innovation, of all creation in the biosphere. Pure chance, absolutely free but blind, at the very root of the stupendous edifice of evolution: this central concept of modern biology is no longer one among other possible or even conceivable hypotheses. It is today the *sole* conceivable hypothesis. . . .[27]

Man himself emerged out of the universe only by chance,[28] "the product of an enormous lottery presided over by natural selection, blindly picking the rare winners from among numbers drawn at utter random."[29]

Thus according to evolutionism, earth and its life forms—including man—exist purely by chance. It is assumed that the same processes at work here have probably produced a multitude of other kinds of intelligent life forms in other solar systems. An excellent cultural expression of such a chance universe is the *Star Wars* trilogy, with its Wookies and Ewoks and Hutts and other inhabitants of the galaxies. There could be no better tribute to the Huxleys and the Monods than the pub scene from "Star Wars" and Jabba the Hutt's royal court in "Return of the Jedi."

Implications of Indeterminism

Any indeterminist world view has several important implications that need to be noted. First, it apparently leaves room for the reality of free will in human beings. This is a main concern for many who adopt this view. As we saw above, Epicurus was anxious to avoid determinism so that freedom and thus morality might be preserved. With no overriding forces (e.g., God or Fate) manipulating puppet strings attached

---

25. Ibid., p. 98.
26. Ibid., pp. 108-112.
27. Ibid., pp. 112-113.
28. Ibid., p. 180.
29. Ibid., p. 138. Each new generation of men includes a trillion mutations, which is indeed a "gigantic lottery," he says (p. 121). For comments on Monod's work see Francis Schaeffer, *Back to Freedom and Dignity* (Downers Grove, Ill.: InterVarsity Press, 1972), pp. 10-16; James Houston, *I Believe in the Creator* (Grand Rapids: Eerdmans, 1980), pp. 264-265.

to our lives, we should be able freely to choose our own destiny. We need to ask, however, whether free choices in a world produced and controlled by chance are worth very much. For Epicurus, even man's thoughts and decisions are produced by random swerves of the atoms of the mind. There would seem to be very little relief or glory in such a concept, which is hardly more noble than Fate. Even when free-will choices are not considered as the product of random brain motion, a chance universe swallows them up just as the Sahara Desert swallows up individual grains of sand. As Carl Henry remarks, chance no less than determinism "implies the insignificance of human decision."[30] By sheer free will no one in such a system can decide to be anything more than an accident of blind evolution, or to avoid death, or to live again after death. Bertrand Russell's desperate protest that "in spite of Death . . . Man is yet free"[31] seems hollow. Man as the offspring of chance has about as much freedom as a larva within its cocoon, and he cannot even look forward to metamorphosis.

A second implication of indeterminism relates to ethics. Epicurus was correct in thinking that free will is necessary for morality or ethics to be a meaningful category. If man is not free, then he is not responsible for his deeds and thus can be neither praised nor blamed for them. The very concepts of right and wrong become irrelevant. But apparently Epicurus did not realize that more than freedom of choice is required in order to make ethics viable. One must also have some way of determining what is right and what is wrong. The problem is that in a chance universe there is absolutely (!) no reason to apply these labels to one thing or action rather than another. This is Francis Schaeffer's main criticism of Monod's view. "With such a position," he says, "there is nothing in the universe itself to which man can appeal in regard to values." How, then, shall he decide how to live? "Where will he get his moral principles? If there are no moral absolutes against which man can measure his actions, how then shall he understand what value is?" Schaeffer's answer is, "If man sees himself as Monod sees him, the values are up for grabs. Anything can become a value."[32] Each person's ethical system will have to be arbitrarily chosen and individually applied, which makes the whole concept of ethics meaningless.

---

30. Carl F. H. Henry, *God, Revelation and Authority, Volume VI: God Who Stands and Stays, Part Two* (Waco: Word Books, 1983), pp. 80-81.

31. Bertrand Russell, "A Free Man's Worship," p. 46.

32. Francis Schaeffer, *Back to Freedom and Dignity*, pp. 12, 14.

In the third place, indeterminism excludes any purpose or meaning for the universe as a whole or for any element within it, such as human life. In the previous volume it was pointed out that only the fact of creation can allow us to claim purpose and meaning for our existence.[33] But the concept of chance *ipso facto* rules out creation; thus there is no room at all for any signficant meaning. As G. G. Simpson acknowledges, "Evolution has no purpose; man must supply this for himself."[34] The idea is that man has (accidentally) acquired self-consciousness and thus is able to do things with a purpose and give meaning to his own actions. Nevertheless such a person cannot give meaning to *himself,* to his life, or to the life of mankind in general. Bertrand Russell's words keep ringing in our ears, i.e., that man's origin, growth, hopes, fears, loves, and beliefs are no more than "the outcome of accidental collocations of atoms." Trying to extract meaning from such a sterile beginning is equivalent to attempting an act of creation *ex nihilo,* something of which we finite beings are incapable.

A final implication of indeterminism is that there is no value that can be assigned to individual human life. Francis Schaeffer makes this point in his criticism of Francis Crick, who agrees with Monod that the evolutionary process is a matter of "chance events." Thus it is no wonder that he can advocate such things as abortion, euthanasia, and mandatory eugenics. "If man is what Francis Crick says he is, then he is only the product of the impersonal plus time plus chance; he is nothing more than the energy particle extended. And, therefore, he has no intrinsic worth."[35]

This, then, is the kind of universe we are living in if chance—uncaused or random occurrences—is the ultimate explanation of why things happen the way they do. A sharper contrast with biblical providence could hardly be imagined.

SELF-DETERMINISM

The second alternative to providence is called self-determinism because it gives autonomous man the reins of history and attributes to him the power of shaping his own destiny. Man is autonomous in the sense that no overruling power such as God or Fate intervenes in the

---

33. Jack Cottrell, *What the Bible Says About God the Creator* (Joplin, Mo.: College Press, 1983), p. 154ff.

34. G. G. Simpson, *The Meaning of Evolution,* p. 310.

35. Francis Schaeffer, *Back to Freedom and Dignity,* p. 23. See pp. 17-22.

historical process to turn man aside from his own goals. Of course such an autonomy is not absolute; man cannot do *everything* he wants just by willing it. For instance, without artificial means man cannot just decide to fly or go deep-sea diving; he cannot direct himself to swim non-stop across the Pacific Ocean or to stay awake for three months. In other words he is limited by natural law and must be content to work within its boundaries. Nevertheless man is supreme in that he is the principal agent of change; he determines himself and his future.

Three examples of self-determinism will be cited here. At first glance these three world views would seem to have almost nothing in common and would seem to be unlikely candidates for a single category. The fact is, however, that despite differences on other points they all agree in their explanation of how things happen in the on-going world. They all agree, against biblical providence, that man working within the boundaries of natural law is the dominant force in the universe. These three philosophies are humanism, occultism and Deism.

Humanism

The premier example of self-determinism is humanism, by which we mean the secular humanism which dominates the American Humanist Association and is expressed in the "Humanist Manifesto II" and the "Secular Humanist Declaration."[36] Humanists call themselves "non-theists" and assert that traditional theism is "an unproved and out-moded faith." There are no creation and no providence, no salvation and no after-life. "The human species is an emergence from natural evolutionary forces."[37]

There is a close relation between evolutionism presented in the last section and the humanism now under discussion. In fact they often form two halves of a single world view, with many of the same thinkers holding to both. This is true in the following way. Whereas chance is the primary factor for explaining the evolutionary *past* (at least until the emergence of man), human autonomy has now become the primary factor for explaining the *future*. The child of chance is himself the father of the future.

This is one of the main themes of the evolutionist Julian Huxley. Until man arrived on the scene, he says, nothing but blind, purposeless

36. *Humanist Manifestos I and II* (Buffalo: Prometheus Books, 1973); *A Secular Humanist Declaration* (Buffalo: Prometheus Books, 1980).

37. *Humanist Manifestos I and II*, pp. 13, 16-17.

chance was at work. But the presence of man has changed all that. Now there is someone who can act purposefully and set goals.

> In the light of evolutionary biology man can now see himself as the sole agent of further evolutionary advance on this planet, and one of the few possible instruments of progress in the universe at large. He finds himself in the unexpected position of business manager for the cosmic process of evolution. . . .[38]

G. G. Simpson likewise promotes man to this new Olympus: "Plan, purpose, goal, all absent in evolution to this point, enter with the coming of man and are inherent in the new evolution, which is confined to him."[39]

William Pollard discusses this same point and gives similar examples in a section of his book called "Secular alternatives to providence."[40] He cites, for example, a book by V. Gordon Childe presumptuously titled *Man Makes Himself* [41] He also quotes the geneticist H. J. Muller as saying that human beings must now "take over the reins from the genes, whose task in furnishing the directives by the process of mere trial and error is at last done, and to steer for themselves henceforth towards a future of ever greater understanding and achievement."[42] The whole point of Muller and the others, says Pollard, is that "man in his autonomy and sovereignty is quite capable of mastering fate and directing history to whatever goal he chooses for it."[43] "That is the illusion which secular man summons up out of the depths of his own autonomy to conceal the reality of his objective status, and give him an alternative to providence on which he can pin his hopes."[44]

In his book *The Abolition of Man* C. S. Lewis points out how this view leads ultimately to a planned evolution controlled by a scientific

---

38. Julian Huxley, *Evolution in Action,* p. 113. See also p. 31: the fact that man is the "sole agent" capable of leading evolution to new heights solves the old riddle of human destiny. See also his *Religion Without Revelation* (New York: New American Library Mentor Books, 1957), pp. 190-193.

39. G. G. Simpson, *The Meaning of Evolution,* pp. 344-345. See also p. 348: "It is another unique quality of man that he, for the first time in the history of life, has increasing power to choose his course and to influence his own future evolution."

40. William Pollard, *Chance and Providence,* pp. 173ff.

41. V. Gordon Childe, *Man Makes Himself* (New York: New American Library Mentor Books, 1951).

42. H. J. Muller, *Proceedings of the Eighth International Congress of Genetics* (Lund, 1948), p. 126; cited in William Pollard, *Chance and Providence,* p. 176.

43. William Pollard, *Chance and Providence,* p. 177.

44. Ibid., p. 173.

elite aptly called "the Conditioners."[45] The same picture is drawn boldly in fictional form by Aldous Huxley in *Brave New World*, where the kinds of specific individuals needed for the future are planned and prescribed by "the Predestinators," are artificially gestated on an assembly line under the watchful eye of "the Director of Hatcheries and Conditioning," and take their place in a programmed society run by "the Ten World Controllers."[46] In real life the mind-boggling advances in the fields of reproductive and genetic engineering are bringing the fantasy closer and closer to reality.[47]

The humanist philosophy of self-determinism has been formally expressed in all of the popular manifestos. The "Humanist Manifesto I" (1933) concluded with these words: "Man is at last becoming aware that he alone is responsible for the realization of the world of his dreams, that he has within himself the power for its achievement. He must set intelligence and will to the task."[48] The second manifesto (1973) declared, "We can discover no divine purpose or providence for the human species. While there is much that we do not know, humans are responsible for what we are or will become. No deity will save us; we must save ourselves." Our most effective instruments for accomplishing this are "reason and intelligence," including "the controlled use of scientific methods."[49] The "Secular Humanist Declaration" (1980) continues, "Secular humanism places trust in Human intelligence rather than in divine guidance. . . . Human beings are responsible for their own destinies."[50]

Occultism

There could be no stranger and more unwilling bedfellows than humanism and occultism. The humanists would particularly object to this grouping, since they consider all forms of the paranormal or supernatural to be irrational superstition that hinders rational solutions to world problems. There is good reason for this association, however. In the first place, many occultists would themselves reject the idea that they are dealing in the "supernatural." They would contend that the

45. C. S. Lewis, *The Abolition of Man* (New York: Macmillan, 1947), chapter 3.
46. Aldous Huxley, *Brave New World* (New York: Bantam Books, 1953), pp. 1, 6, 22.
47. See Jack Cottrell, *The Bible Says* (Cincinnati: Standard Publishing, 1982), chapter 10; J. Kerby Anderson, *Genetic Engineering* (Grand Rapids: Zondervan, 1982).
48. *Humanist Manifestos I and II*, p. 10.
49. Ibid., pp. 16-17.
50. *A Secular Humanist Declaration*, p. 24.

forces to which they are appealing are just as *natural* as the law of gravity, though they are not as widely known and understood. Also, humanists leave room for an expanded concept of nature: "Nature may indeed be broader and deeper than we now know; any new discoveries, however, will but enlarge our knowledge of the natural."[51] Finally, we are concerned here only with a similarity of form, not necessarily of content. Though humanists and occultists may not agree as to what is meant by "natural law," they do agree that natural law is the primary framework of the universe and that man is free to shape his own destiny by harnessing and using natural forces. Whether this be by means of science or by means of occult techniques, the assumption is that of a limited human autonomy as the key to history.

Occultists do not all share the same world view. Many would be true supernaturalists, believing in personal gods and/or goddesses who dispense supernatural banes and boons. Others would speak of gods or goddesses but only as personifications of natural forces. One of the more common occult concepts, and the one that is under consideration here, is that the natural world includes dimensions and powers that are largely unknown and which differ considerably from standard physics. These powers are neutral and impersonal, and when properly understood can be controlled and used by almost anyone. In this way man as autonomous agent can gain control of his destiny.

The primary example of this occult viewpoint is traditional witchcraft, also known as Wicca. Its basic world view is described well by a practicing witch and coven leader named Miriam Simos, who calls herself Starhawk. The key word is *energy* or *power*.

> The mythology and cosmology of Witchcraft are rooted in that "Paleolithic shaman's insight": that all things are swirls of energy, vortexes of moving forces, currents in an ever-changing sea. Underlying the appearance of separateness, of fixed objects within a linear stream of time, reality is a field of energies that congeal, temporarily, into forms. In time, all "fixed" things dissolve, only to coalesce again into new forms, new vehicles.[52]

This view of "the All as an energy field polarized by two great forces, Female and Male, Goddess and God, . . . is common to almost all traditions of the Craft."[53] These forces are available for our use: "Witches

51. *Humanist Manifestos I and II*, p. 16.

52. Starhawk, *The Spiral Dance: A Rebirth of the Ancient Religion of the Great Goddess* (San Francisco: Harper & Row, 1979), p. 18.

53. Ibid., p. 26.

conceive of the subtle energies as being, to a trained awareness, tangible, visible, and malleable."[54] They are malleable by means of magic, which is "the art of sensing and shaping the subtle, unseen forces that flow through the world, of awakening deeper levels of consciousness beyond the rational."[55] The various rituals, spells, and meditations of witchcraft are designed to make this power flow where the witch wants it to go. "Of all the disciplines of magic, the art of moving energy is the simplest and most natural. It comes as easily as breathing, as making sound. Picture the power in motion, and it moves. Feel it flowing, and it flows."[56] Through magic one can tap sources of energy that are unlimited but nonetheless natural. "Magic is part of nature; it does not controvert natural laws. It is through study and observation of nature, of the visible, physical reality, that we can learn to understand the workings of the underlying reality."[57]

In 1974 these beliefs were incorporated in a document called "Principles of Wiccan Belief," drawn up by the short-lived Council of American Witches. It reads in part as follows:

> 1. We practice Rites to attune ourselves with the natural rhythm of life forces . . . .
>
> 3. We acknowledge a depth of power far greater than that apparent to the average person. Because it is far greater than ordinary, it is sometimes called "supernatural," but we see it as lying within that which is naturally potential to all.
>
> 4. We conceive of the Creative Power in the Universe as manifesting through polarity—as masculine and feminine—and that this same Creative Power lives in all people . . . .
>
> 5. We recognize both outer worlds and inner, or psychological, worlds—sometimes known as the Spiritual World, the Collective Unconscious, the Inner Planes, etc.—and we see in the interaction of these two dimensions the basis for paranormal phenomena and magical exercises. We neglect neither dimension for the other, seeing both as necessary for our fulfillment. . . .

---

54. Ibid., p. 129.
55. Ibid., p. 13. This is "a natural potential inherent in each one of us" (p. 19).
56. Ibid., p. 129.
57. Ibid., p. 132. Another practicing witch, Paul Huson, sums it up by saying that a witch develops powers "by the observance of natural power tides within the framework of the universe, which constantly ebb and flow, and may be utilized to great advantage as indeed they always have been over the centuries by cultists and occultists alike" (*Mastering Witchcraft: A Practical Guide for Witches, Warlocks, and Covens;* New York: G. P. Putnam's Sons, 1970; p. 24).

> 7. We see religion, magick, and wisdom-in-living as being united in the way one views the world and lives within it—a worldview and philosophy-of-life which we identify as Witchcraft, the Wiccan Way.
>
> 8. Calling oneself "Witch" does not make a witch—but neither does heredity itself, or the collecting of titles, degrees and initiations. A Witch seeks to control the forces within him/herself that make life possible in order to live wisely and well, without harm to others, and in harmony with Nature.
>
> 9. We acknowledge that it is the affirmation and fulfillment of life, in a continuation of evolution and development of consciousness, that gives meaning to the Universe we know, and to our personal role within it. . . .
>
> 13. We acknowledge that we seek within Nature for that which is contributory to our health and well-being.[58]

The *Star Wars* fiction again provides us with a good example of this view of reality. It popularized the concept of "the Force," the impersonal universal energy which could be harnessed by evil men as well as good for either foul or benevolent purposes. The Jedi Knights were witches par excellence.[59]

Deism

The third example of self-determinism is the view known as Deism. Again at first glance Deism would seem to have almost nothing in common with either humanism or occultism. Indeed, there are many crucial differences, but not as many as one might think, especially in reference to humanism. The main difference is that Deism accepts the existence of a personal God, one who is the Creator of the universe and is distinct from it. But once we get past the point of creation, there is little difference between the secular humanist's understanding of history and that of the Deist. Both posit autonomous natural law and autonomous human reason as the factors responsible for what happens in the on-going world.

The very term *Deism* has come to be identified with a certain way in which God is related to the world. In the words of John Orr, the term *Deist* means "one who admits a Creator but does not admit that the Creator has interfered with the operation of natural laws since the

---

58. Margot Adler, *Drawing Down the Moon: Witches, Druids, Goddess-Worshippers, and Other Pagans in America Today* (Boston: Beacon Press, 1979), pp. 99-101.

59. See Norman L. Geisler and J. Yutaka Amano, *The Religion of the Force* (Dallas: Quest Publications, 1983).

creation, and who advocates a rationalistic religion of nature as against any religion based on special or supernatural revelation."[60] The key concept is non-interference. When God created the world he endowed it with everything necessary for its pilgrimage through time. Thus he declines to intervene in it, assuming the role of "First Mover" or "absentee God." It should be noted that the use of this term in this rather restricted sense is not exactly equivalent to the historical English Deism of the seventeenth and eighteenth centuries. Men such as Lord Herbert of Cherbury (d. 1648), John Toland (d. 1722), and Matthew Tindal (d. 1733) were for the most part committed to such a view of God, but their deistic philosophy included other equally-important tenets, such as an emphasis on moral religion and an elevation of human reason.

The deistic view of God arose in part because of the ascendancy of a new scientific outlook, particularly "the rise of the mechanical model of nature associated with the name of Newton."[61] The Newtonian physics made it easy to think of the world as a great machine pre-set to run with a beautiful regularity. Of course, like any machine, it should be so constructed that it is capable of running on its own, independent of its maker. In fact, as a general principle, it was thought that the more skilled the machine-maker was, the less attention and repair the machine would need. Now, since God is the infinite, all-wise and all-powerful Creator, *his* machine (the world) should be so perfectly constructed that it would need no further attention whatsoever. And indeed, this is just the way the Deist regarded it. The world had everything it needed from the beginning. This included a religion so perfect that no further revelation would be necessary.[62]

This view suggests a number of comparisons. For instance, A. H. Strong says that according to Deism, "God builds a house, shuts himself out, locks the door, and then ties his own hands in order to make sure of never using the key."[63] The most common figure, though,

60. John Orr, *English Deism: Its Roots and Its Fruits* (Grand Rapids: Eerdmans, 1934), p. 17.

61. E. Graham Waring, editor, *Deism and Natural Religion* (New York: Frederick Ungar Publishing Company, 1967), p. v.

62. This was one of the main emphases of the Deists. See John Orr, *English Deism*, p. 141: "Tindal's main line of argument is developed from his conception of God. God is perfect, therefore any religion he gives to men must be perfect and incapable of improvement. From this he concluded that no later revelation such as the Bible could improve on the religion given man at the creation."

63. Augustus H. Strong, *Systematic Theology*, 3 volumes in 1 (Valley Forge: Judson Press, 1907), p. 15.

is that of the machine. For the Deists themselves this analogy was not at all derogatory. Indeed, comparing God with a master machinist was a compliment. As Barth notes, "For the mechanically minded 18th century a clock assembled, wound and started once and for all was the perfect work, and God was thus compared to a great clock-maker whose work exalts its maker by no longer needing him." In fact God was seen as having achieved absolute perfection because he had created that elusive dream of all scientists—the perpetual motion machine.[64]

Thus Deists tended to deny the very concept of immanence or the presence of God in the world. God was given the role of spectator, having only a general interest in what goes on here. As Waring says, "The idea that the almighty sustainer of the world-machine should bother with the particularities of trivial finite beings seemed absurd and unworthy." Thus "the older sense of the divine concern for the creature and the divine purpose for history is gradually attentuated."[65]

The two elements that keep the world going are natural law and human reason. The natural laws are inflexible and unvarying; nature is thus endowed with a perfectly monotonous regularity and uniformity. But the true sovereign of the world-process is man himself with his all-sufficient rational powers. As Waring says, the age of Deism "saw man's reason as the instrument for his individual and corporate betterment. . . . It was believed that man can attack and overcome by educational and technical means, and good will, all the evils of life."[66] God is not needed; autonomous man is free to work out his own destiny by himself. Pohle sums it up somewhat sarcastically in these words: "The God of the Deists allows the mighty engine of the universe to run at rovers and permits the droll little creatures called men to disport themselves as they please."[67]

Implications of Self-Determinism

Each of the examples of self-determinism discussed in this section has significant implications in its own right. Our concern here, however,

---

64. Karl Barth, *Church Dogmatics, Vol. III: The Doctrine of Creation, Part 3,* tr. G. W. Bromiley and R. J. Ehrlich (Edinburgh: T. & T. Clark, 1961), p. 12.

65. E. Graham Waring, editor, *Deism and Natural Religion,* p. xiii.

66. Ibid., p. xiv.

67. Joseph Pohle, *God: The Author of Nature and the Supernatural,* ed. Arthur Preuss (St. Louis: B. Herder, 1912), p. 94.

is to set forth the implications derived from their common explanation of the on-going universe. The first is that *nature is a closed system;* nothing supernatural or divine can ever take place within it. We would expect this from the humanist and the occultist, since they do not grant the existence of a true supernatural in the first place. But this is also the assumption of the Deist: nature is totally self-contained and unperforated by God. This means that for the self-determinist almost all of the distinctive features of biblical faith must be either denied or given a naturalistic interpetation. This includes all miracles, revelation, and answers to prayer. It includes the incarnation, the atonement, and the resurrection of Christ. It includes the whole concept of providence.

The second implication is that *man alone is responsible* for his own destiny and in a large measure for the destiny of the whole universe. "He's got the whole world in his hands" applies to man, not God. This must put a tremendous burden on the heart of anyone who takes any of these views seriously. It helps us to understand the sense of urgency permeating a document such as the "Humanist Manifesto II," even if we disagree with most of its contents.

Finally we would note that the self-determinists operate with a *very high view of human nature*. They generally have a very optimistic view of man, assuming that he is both able and willing to tackle the task of securing the future of the world. The concept of sin and sinfulness is weak if not absent. For example the "Humanist Manifesto II" concludes with a call for human beings "to produce the kind of world we want. . . . We are responsible for what we are or will be. . . . We believe that humankind has the potential intelligence, good will, and cooperative skill to implement this commitment in the decades ahead."[68]

DETERMINISM

The third alternative to biblical providence is called determinism. According to this view, whatever happens *has* to take place the way it does—just that way and no other. It is the idea that "for everything that ever happens there are conditions such that, given them, nothing else could happen."[69] "An all-embracing, all-governing causality"[70]

68. *Humanist Manifestos I and II,* p. 23.

69. Richard Taylor, "Determinism," *The Encyclopedia of Philosophy,* ed. Paul Edwards (New York: Macmillan, 1967), II:359.

70. G. C. Berkouwer, *The Providence of God,* tr. Lewis B. Smedes (Grand Rapids: Eerdmans, 1952), p. 144.

is responsible for every event. A power that transcends and encompasses all particulars directs and controls the whole course of nature and history. This view is sometimes called causalism or pan-causalism[71] (whereas indeterminism is called casualism). It is also called fatalism, with the words *fate* and *destiny* occurring regularly in this context. Popular expressions of this philosophy are "*Que sera, sera*" ("Whatever will be, will be") and "When your time is up, you're gonna go."

Determinism says that no event or action "just happens," as in chance; nor is it self-caused, as in self-determinism. Every action is determined in some way by an outside force or an antecedent cause. This even includes—and here is the main thing at stake—human decisions. In other words, free will is ruled out. Freedom is an illusion. We may think we are acting freely and without constraint, but we are not.

We should point out that few deterministic systems are absolute. According to some, the general course of things and even the general course and character of a person's life may be inexorably determined, but there is still some room for that person to maneuver, at least enough to adjust his mental states to accept the inevitable. Others describe the general course of events as being determined—*unless* you have some inside information which enables you to side-step your fate. And even those whose philosophy calls for an all-encompassing, inescapable destiny are usually inconsistent and do not actually live as if this were the case. As Brunner remarks, "Never has a champion of pan-mechanism really regarded his fellowmen as mechanisms, nor has he treated them so. No one can evade the idea of responsibility and therefore of freedom."[72] Pollard refers to a "wonderful remark" by Dorothy Sayers, that "even the most thoroughgoing philosophic determinist will swear at the maid like any good Christian when the toast is burned."[73]

Quite a number of world views are deterministic in nature. We may group them into three categories: naturalistic, pantheistic, and theistic. These will be examined now in turn.

Naturalistic Determinism

The first type of determinism is called naturalistic because the force or power which dominates the universe is natural rather than supernatural

71. Emil Brunner, *The Christian Doctrine of Creation and Redemption: Dogmatics, Vol. 2,* tr. Olive Wyon (Philadelphia: Westminster Press, 1952), p. 164.

72. Ibid., pp. 164-165. See also Georgia Harkness, *The Providence of God* (Nashville: Abingdon, 1960), pp. 40ff.

73. William Pollard, *Chance and Providence,* p. 124.

or divine. It is impersonal, not personal. Built into the very existence of things is an unalterable, inexorable, necessary law or principle of development that makes the sequence of events inevitable.

Fate

Such a view takes several forms, the first of which is a belief in fate. This concept occurs in Greek literature as far back as Homer and was represented by the word *moira*. The idea was that of a fixed order of necessity, an impersonal law that overrules and overrides all other forces to bring about an inevitable end. William Greene's study shows that there was considerable ambiguity among the Greeks as to the exact relation between fate and the gods. Though basically an impersonal force, fate was sometimes identified with the will of the gods or the will of Zeus in particular.[74] On occasion the Olympic divinities were even depicted as overruling fate and necessity,[75] but this did not happen very often. More often it was seen as an order of necessity which stands above and behind the gods themselves, especially after Homer.[76] According to Simonides, not even the gods fight against necessity.[77] Aeschylus said that not even Zeus can avoid what is destined.[78] A. B. Bruce cites the following loose translation of a few lines from Euripides:

> A bow of steel is hard to bend,
>   And stern a proud man's will;
> But Fate, that shapeth every end,
>   Is sterner, harder still;
> E'en God within the indented groove
> Of Fate's resolve Himself must move.[79]

The "fates" were often spoken of in the plural. They were personified and given three names: Clotho, "the Spinner" (as the one who spins men's destiny); Atropos, "She who cannot be turned"; and Lachesis, "the Dispenser of Lots."[80]

---

74. William Greene, *Moira*, pp. 48, 111.
75. Ibid., p. 196. Greene is referring to Euripides' play, *Alcestis*.
76. Ibid., p. 16.
77. Ibid., p. 68.
78. Ibid., p. 124.
79. Alexander Balmain Bruce, *The Moral Order of the World in Ancient and Modern Thought* (London: Hodder and Stoughton, 1899), p. 102. Interestingly, this too is taken from the *Alcestis*. See footnote 75 above.
80. William Greene, *Moira*, p. 16. Gordon Clark describes them as "Clotho who spins the thread of life, Lachesis who measures its length, and Atropos who cuts it off" (*From Thales to Dewey*, p. 160).

Greene denies that the Greek writers were completely fatalistic.[81] In most cases they saw fate as dealing with the general course of things, drawing in the broad strokes of history while allowing mankind (and even the gods) to decide on some of the smaller lines and lighter colors. Though "Fate has indeed contrived all," a man is still able to assert himself to some extent according to his character.[82]

The idea of fate is a hardy perennial and still has a continuing appeal to the popular mind. A secular song from the middle of the twentieth century summed it up this way:

> When I was just a little girl,
> I asked my mother, "What will I be?
> Will I be pretty? Will I be rich?"
> Here's what she said to me:
>
> "*Que sera, sera!* Whatever will be, will be!
> The future's not ours to see. *Que sera, sera!*"

Whatever else this may be, it is not biblical providence.

Astrology

A second form of naturalistic determinism is astrology, which may be thought of as a very specific kind of fate. According to astrological theory the determining agents for world history and individual lives are the heavenly bodies, especially the sun, the moon, the planets, and even certain stars and galaxies. Their specific positions relative to each other and to the earth in general are responsible for the character and spirit of whole eras of our history. Their positions relative to the precise time and place where an individual is born determines his character and destiny. In other words, "The destinies of individuals, nations, and humanity in general is written in the Stars."[83] It has been summed up thus:

> Astrology, like all other systems of human thought, has its fundamental premises and purposes, or goals. The basic premise of popular astrology is this: From time immemorial certain celestial bodies have been sending

81. William Greene, *Moira*, p. 91.

82. Ibid., p. 156. See pp. 145-146.

83. Zolar, *The Encyclopedia of Ancient and Forbidden Knowledge* (Los Angeles: Nash Publishing, 1970), p. 238. On the supposed astrological ages (e.g., the "age of Aquarius"), see James Bjornstad and Shildes Johnson, *Stars, Signs, and Salvation in the Age of Aquarius* (Minneapolis: Bethany Fellowship, 1971), pp. 90ff.

> forth influxes, or influences, separately, and in various coordinations with each other, that tend to affect human personality, destiny, and earthly activities of various sorts. These influences are absorbed by each of us as we draw our first breath at birth, and this particular conformation of celestial influences forever determines what one popular astrologer says is up to 80 percent of our personality and destiny potentials.
>
> Throughout our lives, the premise continues, the celestial bodies continue to affect us in predictable patterns based on the original conformation.[84]

The key to an individual's destiny is the exact time and place of his birth. (Knowing the general "sign" under which one was born tells relatively little.) Using his chart of the heavens an astrologer can pinpoint the various planetary influences that were bearing down upon that spot at that particular moment. He then interprets what this means for that person's life and character. Using the same data in comparison with projected positions of the planets on a particular day yet to come, he then attempts to predict the fate in store for that individual on that day. Thus he can warn of impending danger, or give advice on personal or business decisions. The important thing is knowing one's birth data: "Everything in your life . . . seems to be subservient to the fact of the time and place of your birth."[85]

Astrology is not an absolute fatalism, however. Everyone has the potential for a limited freedom—*if* he takes advantage of the alleged predictive powers of his astrologist. One can master the stars rather than have the stars master him, *if* he knows their secrets. "Knowledge of the truth gives you immensely greater freedom of choice," says Goodavage.[86] For instance, if one's charts show that a particular day is full of danger for him, he can change his plans for the day and have a good chance of avoiding harm. He would certainly cancel all travel plans, and would probably just stay home all day.[87] Thus, as a popular

84. Owen S. Rachleff, *Sky Diamonds: The New Astrology* (New York: Hawthorn Books, 1973), p. 7. There is no unanimity as to *how* the heavenly bodies have their effect on us. Not all astrologers speak of "influxes" radiating from above. One says there is "absolutely no implication that the planets and luminaries which compose Nature's clock *affect us directly*" (Alexandra Mark, *Astrology for the Aquarian Age;* New York: Essandess, 1970; p. 20).

85. Joseph F. Goodavage, *Astrology: The Space Age Science* (New York: New American Library Signet Books, 1966), p. 201. This is why most individuals are different from one another in temperament and life experiences. Very few are born at the same time and place as someone else. See Zolar, *Encyclopedia*, p. 240.

86. Joseph Goodavage, *Astrology*, p. 204. Also, see Zolar, *Encyclopedia*, p. 374.

87. See Goodavage, *Astrology*, pp. 200ff.

song put it several years ago, you can "read your horoscope and cheat your fate."

This freedom applies only to specific events in a person's life, however. With regard to the general course of his life and with regard to the general destiny of the world, the "stars" are in control.

Mechanism

Although both fate and astrology are forms of naturalistic determinism, they are to some degree a bit mystical or esoteric. Astrology is even treated by many people as a branch of occultism. Our third example of naturalistic determinism, however, is simple, straightforward mechanism. According to this view matter or nature is all that exists, and it is completely controlled by ordinary natural laws. There is no mysterious power or influence permeating all things or bearing down upon us from the stars. The only influences are those with which science is familiar, such as the law of gravity, the laws of motion, the laws of thermodynamics and electromagnetism. These and other physical laws, *and these alone,* are the sole causative agents in the universe.

We have already seen that in a chance universe, natural law is taken to be the dominant factor, but there the understanding of natural law is somewhat different from that of mechanistic determinism. In a chance system the laws are generally dominant, but often there is room for more than one event or course of events to be produced by the operant causes. But this is not the case in mechanism, where the operation of natural law must produce a single specific effect and no other. The universe is seen as one giant interlocking machine, with every event following of necessity upon the one before it. History thus unfolds according to the working of impersonal universal laws immanent in nature; the world is completely determined within itself.[88] As the determinist understands it, "the whole universe must indeed really be a vast and intricate mechanism which at any moment has only one possible outcome."[89]

The essence of mechanism is very well expressed in Pollard's description of Laplace's demon:

> . . . The mathematician Laplace formulated this absolute and inescapable universality of the laws of classical mechanics in a particularly cogent

88. William Pollard, *Chance and Providence,* pp. 43, 72.
89. Ibid., p. 25.

> and impressive manner. Only make available to him, said Laplace, a being of infinite computational capacity, a mathematical demon of enormously greater capacity than even the most elaborate of present-day high speed electronic computers. With such a demon at his service, he would then ask only to be told the exact position and velocity of every particle in the universe at a particular instant of time. With this information and the universal laws of mechanics, Laplace asserted that he could then have his demon use it to specify precisely what the exact state of the whole universe would be at any desired time in the future. The impossibility of supplying the required mathematical demon is, of course, no argument against the power of this conclusion. It is sufficient to know that the world is constructed in such a way as to make such a statement possible to have a complete and thoroughgoing determinism.[90]

It is important to note that according to this view human thought and volition are no different from flowing water or falling objects. The laws of nature explain one just as completely as the other. As one mechanist is said to have put it, the brain secretes thought as the liver secretes bile. Thus the concept of free will is eliminated or else subjected to serious reinterpretation.

An early example of mechanism was the atomist philosophy of Leucippus and Democritus. Though they did not explain what caused the atoms to be moving about in the infinite void, they posited this movement as the sole cause of whatever happens in the universe. The moving and colliding atoms behave strictly according to the laws of mechanics; thus whatever happens is bound to happen. Leucippus explicity stated, "Nothing happens at random, but everything for a reason and by necessity."[91]

A more recent mechanist was Thomas Hobbes, who said that "all the effects that have been, or shall be produced, have their necessity in things antecedent."[92] This may sound at first like nothing more than the principle of sufficient cause, until we note the word *necessity.* For Hobbes, all causes are necessary causes, which means that the way things happen is the only possible way they *could* happen. This mechanistic determinism applies to the human sphere as well as to

90. Ibid., pp. 45-46.

91. G. E. R. Lloyd, "Leucippus and Democritus," *The Encyclopedia of Philosophy,* ed. Paul Edwards (New York: Macmillan, 1967), IV:448.

92. Cited in Frederick Copleston, *A History of Philosophy, Volume V: Modern Philosophy, the British Philosophers, Part I: Hobbes to Paley* (Garden City, N.Y.: Doubleday Image, 1964), p. 32.

any other.[93] "Whatever happens, whether in the realm of human behavior, human thought, or elsewhere is caused and hence causally determined by changes of material particles. Voluntary actions are therefore no less necessitated than anything else."[94]

A final example is Thomas Huxley, who tried to refute the charge that Darwinianism required a chance universe. In so doing he went to the opposite extreme:

> The whole world, living and not living, is the result of the mutual interaction, according to definite laws, of the forces possessed by the molecules of which the primitive nebulosity of the universe was composed. If this be true, it is no less certain that the existing world lay potentially in the cosmic vapour, and that a sufficient intelligence could, from a knowledge of the properties of the molecules of that vapour, have predicted, say the state of the fauna of Britain in 1869, with as much certainty as one can say what will happen to the vapour of the breath on a cold winter's day . . . .[95]

Marxism

The philosophy of Marxism is a fourth example of naturalistic determinism. Though its founders were thorough-going materialists, they objected to the concept of mechanistic materialism which was prevalent in the early nineteenth century. They preferred instead a view called dialectical materialism, formed by adapting Hegel's doctrine of historical development to their materialism. This enabled them to say that history is moving toward a particular goal, the ideal of a classless communistic society.

Dialectical materialism is a law or principle which says that the material universe is moving *necessarily* and *inevitably* toward its goal. It is as certain as the laws of motion themselves. In fact, it interprets history as having a kind of built-in law of motion all its own. All matter is active, moved from within by an inner necessity of its nature toward a goal which nothing can prevent. Marxists today refer to this as "autodynamism." It represents the "inherent Energy in matter, a *vital* Energy,

---

93. Ibid., pp. 32-33.
94. Richard Taylor, "Determinism," p. 364.
95. Thomas H. Huxley, *Life and Letters,* I:544-545; cited in John C. Gienapp, "Providentialism and Evolutionary Biology," *The Caring God: Perspectives on Providence,* ed. Carl S. Meyer and Herbert T. Mayer (St. Louis: Concordia Publishing House, 1973), p. 233.

containing within itself and inevitably bringing to actuality man and mind and human society and the perfection of human society."[96]

The reason why matter-in-motion will inevitably reach its goal is that it is governed by specific dialectical laws, originally formulated by Friedrich Engels as (1) the law of the unity of contradictory opposites, (2) the law of transformation from quantity to quality, (3) the law of the negation of the negation, and (4) the law of upward movement. These four causal laws "permeate and govern the progressive unfolding of the entire universe—of mathematics, geology, nature, science, logic, history (revolution), linguistics, society, economics, aesthetics, law, ethics, religion, philosophy (and even ideas)."[97]

The key word in Marxist philosophy is *inevitable*. The fact that the dialectical laws will inevitably produce a classless communistic society makes this a deterministic system. The fact that these laws are wholly immanent within nature makes it a naturalistic determinism.

Psychological Determinism

A final example of this alternative to providence is psychological determinism. This differs slightly from the other four in this category in that it is concerned only with human behavior and not with universal history as such. Its main point is that all human behavior can be completely explained by antecedent causes such as childhood trauma, heredity, or environmental stimuli. Francis Schaeffer's summary of behaviorism applies generally to this view:

> . . . Essentially, behaviorism declares that all of a person's behavior is the result of environmental conditioning, whether that conditioning occurred prior to birth and resides in the genes or subsequent to birth and resides in the external environment. . . . That is, all of an individual's actions are either predetermined by his heredity or immediately determined by his surroundings. . . .[98]

The immediate casualty of such a view, of course, is the concept of free will. Thinkers in earlier times, such as Leibnitz and J. S. Mill, had tried to reconcile determinism and free will by saying that a person's will is free (even if caused) as long as he is doing what he *desires* to do.

96. F. J. Sheed, *Communism and Man* (New York: Sheed and Ward, 1949), pp. 34-36.
97. Francis Nigel Lee, *Communist Eschatology* (Nutley, N.J.: Craig Press, 1974), pp. 39-40.
98. Francis Schaeffer, *Back to Freedom and Dignity*, pp. 32-33.

But psychological determinists claim that this explanation will no longer suffice. Philosophers such as John Hospers offer evidence that "our very desires, volitions, and even deliberations are the product of unconscious forces, compromises, and defenses which are not only not within our control but whose very existence is usually unsuspected by those—all of us—who are their victims."[99]

Sigmund Freud may be listed as one of the first psychological determinists. He concluded that certain kinds of abnormal adult behavior can be traced to childhood experiences. Ultimately even normal behavior was explained in this way. Alasdair MacIntyre points out the significance of these conclusions in references to determinism:

> . . . Freud's discovery of the causation both of neurotic symptoms and of normal character traits fatally weakened any attempt to maintain that human behavior was essentially exempt from explanation in causal terms or that the line between responsible rational behavior and nonresponsible irrational behavior could be drawn in terms of the applicability of the notion of cause. Later attempts to show that human actions cannot be caused . . . have had to ignore not only the fact of but even the logical possibility of psycho-analytic explanations of action in terms of predisposing childhood causes. . . .[100]

The behaviorist B. F. Skinner falls into the same category. In his book *Beyond Freedom and Dignity* he states his absolute views in almost the same words as MacIntyre: "Personal exemption from a complete determinism is revoked as a scientific analysis progresses."[101] He argues against the existence of any kind of autonomous "inner man" or spiritual center of man which is able to initiate or originate behavior.[102] We now know, he says, that the real causes for human actions lie in the external environment: "The autonomous agent to which behavior has traditionally been attributed is replaced by the environment."[103] Since environmental causes are observable and accessible, we are now able to manipulate and direct behavior as we will; we can even talk about a "technology of behavior."[104] Skinner sums up his view in comparison with the traditional view thus:

---

99. Richard Taylor, "Determinism," p. 368.

100. Alasdair MacIntyre, "Freud, Sigmund," *The Encyclopedia of Philosophy*, ed. Paul Edwards (New York: Macmillan, 1967), III:252.

101. B. F. Skinner, *Beyond Freedom and Dignity* (New York: Alfred A. Knopf, 1972), p. 21.

102. Ibid., pp. 14, 200.

103. Ibid., p. 184. See also pp. 16, 25, 205, 214-215.

104. Ibid., pp. 25, 201, 215. Chapter 1 is entitled "A Technology of Behavior."

> . . . In the traditional picture a person perceives the world around him, selects features to be perceived, discriminates among them, judges them good or bad, changes them to make them better (or, if he is careless, worse), and may be held responsible for his action and justly rewarded or punished for its consequences. In the scientific picture a person is a member of a species shaped by evolutionary contingencies of survival, displaying behavioral processes which bring him under the control of the environment in which he lives, and largely under the control of a social environment which he and millions of others like him have constructed and maintained during the evolution of a culture. The direction of the controlling relation is reversed: a person does not act upon the world, the world acts upon him.[105]

After all this Skinner has the boldness to protest, "Man is not made into a machine by analyzing his behavior in mechanical terms."[106]

Such views as these have long been accepted in the psychiatric profession. Richard Taylor declares that "contemporary psychiatrists are for the most part highly impatient with theories of human freedom," since they accept the fact that behavior is causally determined.[107] Francis Schaeffer testifies,

> Everywhere I go I find behaviorists completely committed to his [Skinner's] view. Man is accepted as a machine, and he is treated as a machine. Such professionals are there by the hundreds, some of them with understanding, some of them with power, some of them only in little places. In some places they control the educational process down into the earliest days of school. . . .[108]

It should be pointed out that the widely-used practice of *behavior modification* is the practical application of Skinner's determinism.

Pantheistic Determinism

In pantheistic determinism we encounter for the first time an alternative to providence that involves the concept of the divine as active in the processes of nature and history. We have seen that there are other

105. Ibid., p. 211.
106. Ibid., p. 202.
107. Richard Taylor, "Determinism," p. 368. For specific examples see the quotation from Edward Thorndike of a statement made in 1910, cited in William Pollard, *Chance and Providence*, p. 47. See also the citation from Robert P. Knight of a statement made in 1946, in Rousas Rushdoony, *The Mythology of Science* (Nutley, N.J.: Craig Press, 1967), p. 46.
108. Francis Schaeffer, *Back to Freedom and Dignity*, p. 42.

world views which do not deny the existence of deity as such (e.g., the Epicureans), or even God's role as creator (e.g., Deism); but none of these views relates God to the on-going world. In pantheism we find the opposite extreme in that God is not only related to everything that happens in the world but also is the sole cause of its happening.

The deity of pantheism is hardly the God of the Bible. The term comes from the Greek words for "all" and "God"; it means basically that God is essentially and substantially equivalent to all things. God and the world are identical in the extension of their being. The natural *is* the supernatural. God is not a separate being, distinct from the world; he is simply the sum total of all finite beings, including human beings. When speaking of the causes of particular events in history, we cannot distinguish between divine and natural causes, or primary and secondary causes. There is only one causal agent, and whether we call it natural or divine it is the same.

Despite this very unbiblical concept of God, pantheism at first glance would seem to be more acceptable at least than naturalistic determinism. At least we are able to bring some kind of God into the picture, so perhaps we are approaching something like the biblical concept of providence. Is this a valid conclusion? Unfortunately, no. There are two reasons for this. First, though pantheism may be a kind of theism, there is considerable ambiguity as to whether its "God" is personal or impersonal. In the many forms of pantheism some seem to tend toward a personal concept of God, while others (if not most) look upon the deity as impersonal. If the latter is the case, then it seems that there is very little difference between such a view and pure materialism. Whether we call the totality of impersonal being *God* or *matter* would seem to be just a question of semantics. But even when the pantheistic deity is seen as personal, this is usually needed for one reason, namely, to allow for the concept of some kind of purpose for the universe. Beyond this the personhood has little function.

The second reason why pantheism brings us no closer to biblical providence is that it is every bit as fatalistic or deterministic as naturalistic determinism. Whether blindly or purposefully, the omni-ontological deity causes all things to happen just the way they do; they could happen in no other way. All events proceed according to a law of absolute necessity.

In the rest of this section we will give a brief explanation of some of the more familiar forms of pantheistic determinism, namely, Stoicism, the Hindu concept of *karma,* and Spinozism. As we proceed it will be apparent that we are dealing with concepts quite alien to the Bible.

Stoicism

A proper classification of Stoicism is not a simple task, particularly since the Stoics themselves had some disagreements as to the relation between God and the world. Though some ambiguity remains, we can agree with Hartshorne and Reese that "Stoicism belongs on the whole under the pantheistic label."[109] An even greater ambiguity attaches to the question of whether the Stoics' God was in any sense personal. In one sense it is difficult to see how any pantheism could teach that God is personal, but the Stoics seemed to think in these terms. A. B. Bruce judges that they were personal theists,[110] and Gordon Clark points out that they attributed reason, wisdom, intelligence, and foresight to the deity.[111] In his "Life of Zeno" Diogenes Laertius said this of the Stoics: "They also say that God is a living being, immortal, rational, perfect, and intellectual in his happiness, unsusceptible of any kind of evil, having a foreknowledge of the world and of all that is in the world."[112]

The main reason for describing the deity as intelligent or personal is so that *purpose* can be ascribed to his acts. History moves with a fatalistic certainty, but it moves toward a goal.[113] Thus it is not exactly accurate to say, as Brunner does, that the Stoic determinism "is blind."[114]

It is, nevertheless, a determinism. Various Stoic writers agree, says Diogenes Laertius, that "all things happen by fate. Fate is an endless chain of causation or the reason by which the world is regulated."[115] Seneca stated it plainly:

---

109. Charles Hartshorne and William L. Reese, *Philosophers Speak of God* (Chicago: University of Chicago Press, 1953), p. 165. MacIntyre, on the other hand, says that Marcus Aurelius is the only one who should be called a pantheist (Alasdair MacIntyre, "Pantheism," *The Encyclopedia of Philosophy,* ed. Paul Edwards; New York: Macmillan, 1967; VI:32).

110. A. B. Bruce, *The Moral Order of the World,* pp. 112ff.

111. Gordon Clark, *From Thales to Dewey,* p. 161. The Stoics distinguished between the active and passive aspects of nature. The active part, the elemental Fire, the Logos, is the rational part which permeates the whole (ibid., pp. 158ff.).

112. Diogenes Laertius, "Life of Zeno," tr. C. D. Yonge, *Essential Works of Stoicism,* ed. Moses Hadas (New York: Bantam Books, 1961), p. 43.

113. Gordon Clark, *From Thales to Dewey,* p. 161. The goal itself is not specified; it is enough to know that there *is* one. Whatever it may be, it is not really significant. According to the Stoic doctrine, the course of world history occurs over and over again in the same way endlessly. See Hartshorne and Reese, *Philosophers Speak of God,* p. 165.

114. Emil Brunner, *The Christian Doctrine of Creation and Redemption,* p. 157.

115. Diogenes Laertius, "Life of Zeno," p. 44.

> . . . I know that all things proceed according to a law that is fixed and eternally valid. Fate directs us, and the first hour of our birth determines each man's span. Cause is linked with cause, and a long chain of events governs all matters public and private. Everything must therefore be borne with fortitude, because events do not, as we suppose, happen but arrive by appointment. . . .[116]

He adds, "We are all chained to Fortune. . . . All life is bondage."[117] According to Chrysippus, all is predestined and we are at best the agents of Fate.[118] Though the Stoics spoke of providence, it was just another word for fate. As Greene says, "Fate and Providence" were just "two faces of a single reality."[119] "The world, they thought, is the only possible world, and nothing in it could be different from what it is."[120]

Was the Stoic determinism absolute? The language sometimes suggests that it was. Hartshorne and Reese declare that for the Stoics "it meant that all events to the last detail are fixed in advance by the universal law."[121] Greene remarks that their initial assumption was "the absolute power of an all-inclusive Fate."[122] But, as Greene himself takes pains to point out, the Stoic philosophers were usually inconsistent and allowed for a slight measure of freedom.[123] It was indeed very slight, though, and consisted mainly in the interior freedom to accept one's fate or to fight against it (in vain). Some used the illustration of a dog tied to a moving wagon. The dog is free either to accept the situation and trot along, or to resist and be dragged. Either way he will go along. But man has the advantage over the dog in that he is a rational animal and can understand all this and intelligently surrender to fate.[124] As Marcus Aurelius said it, "Only to the rational animal is it given to follow voluntarily what happens; but simply to follow is a necessity imposed on all."[125] Marcus also advised, "Willingly give

---

116. Seneca, "On Providence," *The Stoic Philosophy of Seneca*, tr. Moses Hadas (Garden City, N.Y.: Doubleday Anchor, 1958), p. 41.

117. Seneca, "On Tranquility of Mind," *The Stoic Philosophy of Seneca*, p. 93.

118. William Greene, *Moira*, p. 347.

119. Ibid., p. 342.

120. Richard Taylor, "Determinism," p. 361.

121. Hartshorne and Reese, *Philosophers Speak of God*, p. 165.

122. William Greene, *Moira*, p. 350.

123. Ibid., pp. 340-341, 348-351.

124. See Frederick Copleston, *A History of Philosophy, Volume I: Greece and Rome, Part II*, pp. 134, 139-40; Gordon Clark, *From Thales to Dewey*, p. 164.

125. Marcus Aurelius, "To Himself," tr. George Long, *Essential Works of Stoicism*, ed. Moses Hadas (New York: Bantam Books, 1961), p. 186. This work is often called "Meditations."

yourself up to Clotho, allowing her to spin your thread into whatever things she pleases."[126] Epictetus has summed it up nicely:

> Lead me, O Zeus, and thou O Destiny,
> The way that I am bid by you to go:
> To follow I am ready. If I choose not,
> I make myself a wretch, and still must follow.
>
> But whoso nobly yields unto necessity,
> We hold him wise, and skilled in things divine.[127]

Thus the "stoical attitude" of endurance was not originally just the virtue of patience; it was the only reasonable way to respond to fate.

Karma

The Hindu religion is basically pantheistic. The Supreme Being is identical with all that is truly real. For some forms of Hinduism this means that the Supreme Being (God, Brahman) is one with the universe, "that Brahman transforms Himself into the ever blossoming and developing form of the external world. . . . The Supreme Being is the whole universe, animate and inanimate."[128] Other forms of Hinduism hold that the external universe is an illusion and that Brahman alone exists only in his pure oneness.[129] Within the wide scope of Hindu writings Brahman is represented sometimes as neutral and impersonal, and sometimes as a personal deity.[130]

Despite differences such as this the common element of pantheism remains, and imbedded within this is another concept which lies at the very heart of the Hindu concept of existence. It is the Hindu version of fate called *karma,* that eternal and unbending law which determines all the forms of human existence. Basically the word *karma* means "action" or "deed," but it has come to stand for the structure of cause and effect that links all human actions with their just consequences.

---

126. Ibid., p. 129.

127. Epictetus, "The Manual," tr. George Long, *Essential Works of Stoicism,* ed. Moses Hadas (New York: Bantam Books, 1961), p. 101.

128. Radhagovinda Basak, "The Hindu Concept of the Natural World," *The Religion of the Hindus,* ed. Kenneth W. Morgan (New York: Ronald Press, 1953), p. 83.

129. Ibid., p. 84; Satis Chandra Chatterjee, "Hindu Religious Thought," *The Religion of the Hindus,* ed. Kenneth W. Morgan (New York: Ronald Press, 1953), pp. 238-240.

130. Jitendra Nath Banerjea, "The Hindu Concept of God," *The Religion of the Hindus,* ed. Kenneth W. Morgan (New York: Ronald Press, 1953), pp. 48-49.

It is a law of causation, a law of actions and their retribution. It says that a person must reap what he sows, whether good or bad. "Every action of an individual inevitably leads to some results, good or bad, and the life of the individual who acts becomes conditioned by the consequences of those acts. . . . This is the inexorable law of karma."[131] This means that if someone does something good, it will rebound upon him with good consequences; his life will ultimately be better for it. If he does something evil, he will inevitably suffer some retribution. But this often does not occur within a single lifespan, thus the theory of rebirth or reincarnation is necessary for the sake of karma. Even though one does not usually remember his former lives, he can be sure that his present character and circumstances have been conditioned and determined by what he has done in them. As Dandekar explains,

> The present life of an individual is conditioned by the consequences of those acts done by him in his previous life which did not produce their results during that lifetime. The moral consequences of his past conduct are conserved and have their effect in the present life. His past acts, for instance, determine the kind of body which he assumes, the family, society, and position in which he may be born, and the acts which he may do in the present life. Every creature is the creation of his own past deeds. Nothing in this world, either physical or moral, happens as the result of mere caprice or blind chance. Everything which exists has come into being by the operation of an immutable law. Thus the otherwise inexplicable vicissitudes of life and the inequalties among human beings are explained by the doctrine of karma.[132]

Zaehner says, "Human *karma* is but a fraction of the *karma* of the whole universe, and this totality of *karma* adds up to fate, and fate itself is under the control of God."[133]

Some object that karma is not a deterministic, fatalistic concept;[134] but this is true only in a very limited sense. It is said, for instance, that it cannot be deterministic because everything that a person suffers (or enjoys) he actually brings upon himself by his past deeds, even if these were done in a previous life. Thus an individual is responsible for

131. R. N. Dandekar, "The Role of Man in Hinduism," *The Religion of the Hindus*, ed. Kenneth W. Morgan (New York: Ronald Press, 1953), p. 127.

132. Ibid., p. 128.

133. R. C. Zaehner, *Hinduism*, 2 edition (New York: Oxford University Press, 1966), p. 106.

134. Maha Thera U Thittila, "The Fundamental Principles of Theravada Buddhism," *The Path of Buddhism*, ed. Kenneth W. Morgan (New York: Ronald Press, 1956), p. 85.

his own happiness and misery, which is surely the very opposite of fatalism.[135] But this explanation is valid only in its form, not in its content. Formally the present individual may be the "same person" as the one in his previous lives, but the lack of a continuity of consciousness and even a continuity of personality makes this objection quite empty. The fact is that as far as this present conscious individual is concerned, he has no choice as to his life circumstances. They were shaped by forces as much outside his control as the law of karma itself.

But there is another sense in which karma is not completely fatalistic, and that is in a sense similar to the Stoic doctrine. A person's circumstances and lot in life are predetermined, to be sure, but he has some freedom as to how he will accept that lot and conform himself and his attitudes to it. He is even able to act contrary to his innate tendencies, which amounts to moral progress and thus karmic advance if those innate tendencies happen to be bad.[136] But as some have pointed out, this is only a relative freedom; the law of karma still creates boundaries beyond which an individual cannot pass.[137] In fact there is a suggestion that the Supreme Being himself *will not allow* a person to avoid his karma. In the Hindu Scriptures known as the *Bhagavad-Gita,* Krishna (an incarnation of the deity) instructs Arjuna (a soldier reluctant to enter into an impending battle) concerning the duty imposed upon him by his karma. R. C. Zaehner cites the following translation of a crucial passage in the *Gita:*

> "If you persist in hugging your ego," Krishna says to Arjuna, "and [obstinately] refuse to fight, vain is your resolve, for Nature will compel you. Bound by your own *karma,* you will be forced to do what, in your deluded state, you do not want to do. The Lord of all creatures stands in the heart of all, making them move hither and thither like cogs in a machine by means of his uncanny power (*mayā*)" (BG, 18.59-61).[138]

135. Ibid., pp. 87-88; R. N. Dandekar, "The Role of Man in Hinduism," pp. 128-129.

136. Maha Thera U Thittila, "The Fundamental Principles of Theravada Buddhism," pp. 90-91; R. N. Dandekar, "The Role of Man in Hinduism," pp. 129-130.

137. See Satis Chatterjee, "Hindu Religious Thought," p. 218.

138. R. C. Zaehner, *Hinduism,* p. 104. There are other translations which do not present quite as strong a concept of determinism. For instance, here is the one by A. C. Bhaktivedanta in *Bhagavad-gita As It Is* (New York: Collier Books, 1972), pp. 828-831: "If you do not act according to My direction and do not fight, then you will be falsely directed. By your nature, you will have to be engaged in warfare. Under illusion you are now declining to act according to My direction. But, compelled by your own nature, you will act all the same, O son of Kunti. The Supreme Lord is situated in everyone's heart, O Arjuna, and is directing the wanderings of all living entities, who are seated as on a machine, made of the material energy." This still reflects a strong determinism, however.

Zaehner summarizes it thus, that however wrong your duty appears to be, "you are none the less in duty bound to do it, and if you refuse, then Fate, that is, God's will, will take you by the forelock and make you."[139] The "primacy of fate over human effort" makes it futile to resist, but through "co-operation with fate" one pleases the Supreme Being and earns a favorable karmic result.[140]

Spinozism

A modern example of pantheistic determinism is the philosophy of Benedict Spinoza (d. 1677). His was a pure, impersonal pantheism and a thorough-going determinism that did not allow any room for freedom whatsoever. Not even the deity is free: he acts from the necessity of his nature. Everything about God and about the universe as the self-revelation of God is *necessary*.

> . . . What happens is always what must happen, in the strict sense of following from the immutable essence of God, which itself exists necessarily. And, since all events are thus inevitable, we should cease to fret over them and accept what in no case could have been otherwise.[141]

In Spinoza's own words, "Things could not have been produced by God in any other manner or order than that in which they were produced." Also, "All things must have followed of necessity from a given nature of God, and they were determined for existence or action in a certain way by the necessity of divine nature."[142]

Theistic Determinism

The final alternative to providence to be considered here is theistic determinism. In this category the concept of God will be much more acceptable to a Bible believer; indeed, some examples of theistic determinism occur within Christendom itself, with the biblical God being interpreted in this way. In any case the theistic understanding of God is that he is a personal Sovereign whose existence is separate from and distinct from that of the created universe. Though separate from it he is concerned about it and is immanently involved in its on-going

---

139. R. C. Zaehner, *Hinduism*, p. 103.
140. Ibid., pp. 106-107. Here the similarity with Stoicism is very apparent.
141. Hartshorne and Reese, *Philosophers Speak of God*, p. 190.
142. Cited in ibid., p. 193.

affairs. In fact, in most cases the theistic determinist will be able to accept the definition of providence which we gave above on page 14: "God's providence is his continuous activity of preserving and governing the whole of creation by his wisdom and goodness and power, for the fulfillment of his eternal purpose and for the glory of his name."

Why, then, do we treat this as an *alternative* to providence? Because of the way God's governing activity is understood, namely, in a deterministic manner. The view is that the eternal Sovereign absolutely and directly ordains or causes everything that happens, including the thoughts and actions of human beings. This means that God is the primary causative agent of everything that happens in the universe. Even when he works through so-called secondary causes, God alone is the originator of the action. As with any determinism, this calls into question the reality of human free will along with its corollary, moral responsibility. Thus, although it honors the concept of God's active involvement in his world, theistic determinism goes to the other extreme and robs the world of its God-given integrity as a created realm with its own relative independence.

Here we intend to set forth three examples of this type of determinism, namely, the philosophy of Leibnitz, the God of Islam, and Christian absolute foreordination.

Leibnitz

Gottfried Leibnitz (d. 1716) is well-known for his treaching that this universe is "the best of all possible worlds." How did he arrive at this conclusion? Basically through what is called the *principle of perfection*. Leibnitz denied the Spinozan concept that even God is under an absolute necessity to do the things he does. However, there is a certain kind of necessity which does constrain God, namely, a *moral* necessity. That is, God is morally bound to do the very best he can in whatever he does. In reference to the creation of the world, in his infinite knowledge God would have known all the *possible* worlds which he could have created. Thus, because he himself is infinitely wise and good and powerful and perfect, he certainly would have chosen to create the *best* of these possible worlds, according to the principle of perfection.[143]

143. James Collins, *God in Modern Philosophy* (Chicago: Henry Regnery, 1959), p. 82. See also Frederick Copleston, *A History of Philosophy, Volume IV: Descartes to Leibnitz* (Garden City, N.Y.: Doubleday Image, 1963), pp. 287ff.

This implies that God had it within his absolute power to create any possible world with any conceivable combination of events, acts, and decisions on the part of men. For instance, he could have chosen to create a world in which I would have decided to have a grapefruit for breakfast today instead of an orange; but he chose the one in which I would eat the orange. Or he could have created the possible world in which Adam chose not to sin, but he elected to create this one. All things considered, this one is the best. But in so decreeing to create this one, God in effect ruled out any alternative choices on the part of individuals. It is absolutely certain that every choice will be made just as it is and in no other way, just because this is the world God chose from the beginning. This is in a real sense a concept of absolute determinism. Leibnitz's theory that the universe is composed of an innumerable amount of self-contained and noninteracting monads created to relate to each other in a pre-established harmony is consistent with this concept of determinism.[144] The following analysis shows this very well:

> . . . The monads are forces, sometimes active, sometimes suspended, . . . governed by their own inherent tendencies, and without power of acting upon each other; but their separate actions are so foreknown on one side, and predetermined on the other, in the moment of creation, that their concurrent evolutions reciprocally correspond, and effectuate all the phenomena of the universe. . . . This preordination of concurrences, apt for each occasion, between monadic developments, . . . makes the whole endless series of change the realization of foreseen and prearranged correspondences. It is the continual evolution of the immeasurable plan entertained by the Creator before the beginning of the ages, and brought into act at the appointed time and in the appointed order, with mathematical precision, though beyond the calculation of mathematical devices. Certain fabrics are curiously woven with colors so arranged in the yarn that when the weaving is performed each color falls with exact propriety into its due place, and contributes accurately to form, to tint, to perfect the contemplated pattern. So, in the system of pre-established harmony, "the web of creation is woven in the loom of time," with threads prepared from the beginning to fall into the requisite connections, and to produce a foreknown design. Each concurrent movement arrives at the appropriate time and place in consequence of the whole antecedent series of changes in each case, for nowhere is there any solution of continuity, and the present is always the progeny of the past and the parent of the future. . . .[145]

---

144. Frederick Copleston, *A History of Philosophy, Volume IV: Descartes to Leibnitz*, pp. 312ff.

145. George F. Holmes, "Leibnitz," *Cyclopedia of Biblical, Theological, and Ecclesiastical Literature*, ed. John M'Clintock and James Strong (New York: Harper and Brothers, 1894), V:336.

It should be noted that Leibnitz's determinism was derived almost wholly by philosophical speculation rather than by the study of Scripture.

Islam

Islam's glory is its doctrine of God. He is Allah, the one and only, the eternal and almighty Creator. He is completely sovereign over all his creation; man's only proper response is submission to his all-encompassing will. (The word *Islam* means "to surrender, to submit.") The question is whether or not Allah is understood as absolutely foreordaining everything that comes to pass, thus making Islam a deterministic religion. The answer seems to be yes.

The Koran contains numerous passages which suggest that Allah is the sole cause of all that happens. He ordains the course of human lives: "It is he who hath created you of clay; and then decreed the term of your lives; and the prefixed term is with him" (6:2).[146] "No female conceiveth, or bringeth forth, but with his knowledge. Nor is anything added unto the age of him whose life is prolonged, neither is anything diminished from his age, but the same is written in the book of God's decrees" (35:11). A refrain that constantly recurs cites God's sovereignty over human actions: "God will lead into error whom he pleaseth, and whom he pleaseth he will put in the right way" (6:40). "Whomsoever God shall direct, he shall be rightly directed; and whomsoever he shall cause to err, thou shalt not find any to defend or to direct" (18:18). "But he whom God shall cause to err, shall have none to direct him: and he whom God shall direct, shall have none to mislead him" (39:35). God seals the hearts of unbelievers: "As for the unbelievers, it will be equal to them whether thou admonish them, or do not admonish them; they will not believe. God hath sealed up their hearts and their hearing" (2:6).[147]

Some passages of the Koran suggest that everyone is free to choose as he pleases. For instance, "The truth is from your Lord; wherefore let him who will, believe, and let him who will, be incredulous" (18:28). But these passages must be read in the light of others which suggest that God gives faith to those whom he selects. "But if thy Lord had pleased, verily all who are in the earth would have believed in general. Wilt thou therefore forcibly compel men to be true believers? No soul

146. Citations from the Koran are from the translation by George Sale (London: Frederick Warne and Co., 1890). Sale provides no verse divisions.

147. See also 7:100-101; 47:16, 23.

can believe but by the permission of God" (10:99-101). "And though we had sent down angels unto them, and the dead had spoken unto them, and we had gathered together before them all things in one view; they would not have believed, unless God had so pleased" (6:111). "Verily this is an admonition: and whoso willeth, taketh the way unto his Lord: but ye shall not will, unless God willeth; for God is knowing and wise. He leadeth whom he pleaseth into his mercy" (76:29-31). "And whomsoever God shall please to direct, he will open his breast to receive the faith of Islam: but whomsoever he shall please to lead into error, he will render his breast straight and narrow" (6:125).

In their interpretation of such passages the Islamic scholars took different views. The so-called rationalist school argued for free will, over against the orthodox.[148] Wolfson calls them the Predestinarians and the Libertarians.[149] The predestinarian view has been strongly held. Wolfson cites this popular story as an illustration:

> The Apostle of God . . . said: Adam and Moses disputed with each other. Said Moses: O Adam, it is thou, our father, who didst frustrate our destiny and eject us from Paradise; to whom Adam replied: It is thou, O Moses, whom God did especially favor with converse with Himself and for whom He traced lines of writing with His own hand—dost thou blame me for doing that which God predestined for me forty years before He created me? Therefore Adam got the better of Moses in the dispute.[150]

Robert E. Speer cites another Moslem writer, Al Berkevi:

> It is necessary to confess that good and evil take place by the predestination and predetermination of God, that all that has been and all that will be was decreed in eternity, and written on the *preserved table;* that the faith of the believer, the piety of the pious and good actions are foreseen, willed, predestined, decreed by the writing on the *preserved table;* produced and approved by God; that the unbelief of the unbeliever, the impiety of the impious and bad actions come to pass with the foreknowledge, will, predestination and decree of God, but not with His satisfaction and approval. Should any ask why God willeth and produceth evil, we can only reply that He may have wise ends in view which we cannot comprehend.[151]

---

148. Fazlur Rahman, "Islamic Philosophy," *The Encyclopedia of Philosophy,* ed. Paul Edwards (New York: Macmillan, 1967), IV:219.

149. Harry A. Wolfson, *The Philosophy of the Kalam* (Cambridge: Harvard University Press, 1976), pp. 601ff.

150. Ibid., pp. 605-606.

151. Robert E. Speer, *The Light of the World* (West Medford, Mass.: Central Committee on the United Study of Missions, 1911), pp. 206-207.

Some Islamic philosophers, such as Al Ashari, went so far as to exclude all secondary causes and make God the immediate cause of all things, including human acts. Thus such acts are not just predetermined but are also effectuated by God. "According to al-Ashari, God wills the unbelief of the unbeliever, creates it in him, and damns him for it, as truly as he creates the belief of the believer and . . . rewards him for it."[152]

There can be no doubt that Islam presents us with a deterministic view of God. The divine decree has predestined all things, and the divine will is the efficient cause of all that happens.

> . . . The strong conviction found in all parts of the Moslem World that all things have been determined by the will of Allah very often destroys initiative and the desire for improvement. For instance, parents often neglect to put a fence about the open pool of water which is found in almost every yard; and then when their children fall into the pool and are drowned, as often happens, they say, "It was the will of God." There have been various schools of thought in Islam which have fought against this fatalism (Kismet), but without much success. . . .[153]

Christian Absolute Foreordination

A third example of theistic determinism, and the final alternative to biblical providence to be considered here, is a form of Christian theology. It has no specific name, though some would call it Augustinianism or even Calvinism. It is better simply to describe it generically as the doctrine of absolute foreordination.

This doctrine begins with a view of God and creation that is basically biblical. God is infinite and eternal and personal; and he brought the universe into existence by an act of creation *ex nihilo*. Though it is essentially distinct from him, he continues to hold it in existence and to be intimately involved in its history. But here is where the problem arises. *To what extent* is God involved in the world of nature and the world of mankind? The answer, as with the other forms of theistic determinism, is that God and God alone decrees and ordains everything that happens. In fact, his all-encompassing, efficacious, and

---

152. George Foot Moore, *History of Religions, Vol. II: Judaism, Christianity, Mohammedanism* (New York: Charles Scribner's Sons, 1919), pp. 426-427. See also Harry Wolfson, *The Philosophy of the Kalam*, p. 607.

153. William McElwee Miller, "Islam," *Religions in a Changing World*, revised edition, ed. Howard F. Vos (Chicago: Moody Press, 1961), p. 70.

unconditional decree[154] was decided upon from all eternity. This means that everything is not just ordained by God, but is *fore*ordained by him. Even before the creation, God had already determined everything that would be coming to pass.

This doctrine is the result of a particular way of understanding two basic attributes of God, namely, his foreknowledge and his power. These are interpreted in such a way that God's relationship to the world is that of a causative agent. Even apart from a consideration of the power of God, the fact of his foreknowledge is seen as imparting a kind of fixity or necessity upon the course of world events. This is illustrated in the following conversation, which originally applied only to the predestination of the elect but is equally applicable to the foreordination of all things:[155]

> Two ministers met on a train and began to discuss the doctrine of predestination. One (Mr. A.) said to the other (Mr. C.), "I do not believe in predestination. I don't see how you or anyone else can."
>
> "Let me ask you a few questions," said Mr. C., "then perhaps you will understand."
>
> "Ask away!"
>
> Mr. C. then began, "Are you of the opinion that all sinners will be saved?"
>
> "By no means," said Mr. A.
>
> "But you have no doubt," added Mr. C., "that it will be finally and formally determined, at the day of judgment, who are to be saved and who are to perish?"
>
> "I am certainly of that opinion," replied Mr. A.
>
> "I would ask, then," continued Mr. C., "if the great God is under any necessity to wait until the last judgment in order to determine who are the righteous that are to be saved, and the wicked who are to perish?"
>
> "By no means," said the other, "for He certainly knows already."
>
> "When do you imagine," asked Mr. C., "that He first attained this knowledge?"
>
> Here Mr. A. paused, and hesitated a little; but he soon answered, "He must have known it from all eternity."
>
> "Then," said Mr. C., "it must have been fixed from all eternity."
>
> "But that does not necessarily follow," protested Mr. A.

154. These adjectives are applied to the decree by Louis Berkhof in his *Systematic Theology* (London: Banner of Truth Trust, 1939), pp. 104-105.

155. This conversation is recorded by John Kirk in his book, *The Cloud Dispelled: Or, The Doctrine of Predestination Examined* (New York: N. Tibbals & Co., 1860), pp. 27-30. I have revised it slightly.

> "Then it must follow," said Mr. C., "that He did not *know* from all eternity, but only *guessed*, and happened to guess right; for how can the omniscient God *know* what is only uncertain?"
>
> Here Mr. A. began to perceive his difficulty; and after a short debate, he confessed it should seem it must have been fixed from eternity.
>
> "Now," said Mr. C., "one question more will establish the truth of predestination. You have acknowledged, what can never be disproved, that God could not know from eternity who shall be saved, unless it had been fixed from eternity. If, then, it was fixed, I humbly request that you inform me *who fixed it*?"

This conversation is alleged to have converted Mr. A. through the force of the argument from foreknowledge, which is summed up by John Kirk thus: "Because it is admitted that God foreknows whatsoever comes to pass, and because He could not have foreknown it unless He had fixed that it should take place, therefore God foreordained every thing that comes to pass, and that from all eternity."[156]

Apart from this concept of foreknowledge, it is also assumed that the doctrine of God's omnipotence makes absolute foreordination necessary. How can God be all-powerful and sovereign over all if he has not *caused* everything? If any creature can be thought of as initiating action, then this would be something outside God's will and he would not be omnipotent. Sovereignty is thus seen as necessarily including causation. God may or may not work through secondary causes such as natural law or human agency; but even if he does, he causes them, too. In the final analysis, God is the sole causative agent in the universe.

In the most consistent forms of this doctrine, human free will is eliminated. Of course when men act they *feel* free, and they *are* free in the sense that they are not coerced into doing anything contrary to their own subjective willingness. But freedom in the sense of the ability to act otherwise is absent; every person must do what God from all eternity has foreordained that he shall do.

We will now give several specific examples of this view. Though its roots are usually traced to Augustine (d. 430), its most complete and consistent expressions are found in the great Reformation theologians and their followers. We begin with a few references from Martin Luther's classic work, *The Bondage of the Will.*[157] In this book Luther's

156. Ibid., p. 27.

157. Martin Luther, *The Bondage of the Will,* tr. J. I. Packer and O. R. Johnston (Old Tappan, N.J.: Fleming H. Revell Co., 1957). The original was published in 1525.

specific purpose is to deny that man's will is free, in response to a book affirming that point by Desiderius Erasmus. The denial of freedom takes two different forms based on two different grounds. In the first place, the *sinner's* will is bound as the result of the Fall and its legacy, total depravity. Thus for every sinner there is a "total inability to will good."[158] His will is bound so that he can only sin; God alone can cause him to believe and do what is right. This is the context for Luther's famous statement that man's will is like a beast standing between two riders.

> . . . If God rides, it wills and goes where God wills . . . . If Satan rides, it wills and goes where Satan wills. Nor may it choose to which rider it will run, or which it will seek; but the riders themselves fight to decide who shall have and hold it.[159]

In the second place, and in another sense, man's nature simply *as man* is not free, in this case simply because of the nature of God. This is the point that is relevant here.

For Luther, God's foreknowledge imparts necessity to all things. It is immutable:[160] "if God foreknows a thing, it necessarily happens."[161]

> It is, then, fundamentally necessary and wholesome for Christians to know that God foreknows nothing contingently, but that He foresees, purposes, and does all things according to His own immutable, eternal and infallible will.[162]

Likewise, because of his omnipotence God is the sole cause of all things, including everything relating to man's actions. Totally apart from God's working in the sinner's heart through grace, he

> . . . works all things in all men, even in the ungodly; for He alone moves, makes to act, and impels by the motion of His omnipotence, all those things which He alone created; they can neither avoid nor alter this movement, but necessarily follow and obey it . . . .[163]

This means that every action performed by man, outward or inward, is set in motion by God. This is true even of the wicked acts of sinful men—and of Satan himself. Even though Satan and the ungodly are wicked, they are still creatures and are

158. Ibid., p. 199.
159. Ibid., pp. 103-104.
160. Ibid., p. 80.
161. Ibid., p. 215; see p. 217.
162. Ibid., p. 80.
163. Ibid., p. 267.

> . . . no less subject to Divine omnipotence and action than all the rest of God's creatures and works. Since God moves and works all in all, He moves and works of necessity even in Satan and the ungodly. But He works according to what they are, and what He finds them to be: which means, since they are evil and perverted themselves, that when they are impelled to action by this movement of Divine omnipotence they do only that which is perverted and evil. . . .[164]

Thus even these "evil instruments . . . cannot escape the impulse and movement of His power." Divine omnipotence moves Satan; it also "makes it impossible for the ungodly man to escape the action upon him of the movement of God; of necessity he is subject to it, and obeys it."[165]

From this it is obvious that there can be no such thing as free will. In fact, says Luther, it "knocks 'free-will' flat, and utterly destroys it."[166] "This omnipotence and foreknowledge of God, I repeat, utterly destroy the doctrine of 'free-will'."[167] "Our will works nothing, but is rather the object of Divine working, else all will not be ascribed to God."[168] God's will thus imposes a necessity upon our wills.[169] Near the conclusion of his work Luther gives this summary statement:

> . . . For if we believe it to be true that God foreknows and foreordains all things; that He cannot be deceived or obstructed in His foreknowledge and predestination; and that nothing happens but at His will . . . ; then, on reason's own testimony, there can be no "free-will" in man, or angel, or in any creature.[170]

A second example of the concept of absolute foreordination is another Reformation theologian, Huldreich Zwingli. Berkouwer correctly notes that Zwingli saw "the absolute necessity of all human activity" as the logical corollary of "the Reformation God-concept."[171] This fact is clearly seen in the essay entitled "On the Providence of God." In this piece Zwingli affirms that God is the only real cause of anything that happens. "For there can be but one cause. For, as the origin of all

164. Ibid., p. 204.
165. Ibid., pp. 204-205.
166. Ibid., p. 80.
167. Ibid., p. 217.
168. Ibid., p. 79.
169. Ibid., pp. 80, 214-215.
170. Ibid., p. 317.
171. G. C. Berkouwer, *The Providence of God*, p. 147.

things is one, so must the cause be one."[172] "Divine Providence, when It created the world, foresaw and arranged things so that everything should take place in proper course and time. Things were bound to happen, therefore, according to the way Divine Providence had determined from eternity."[173] The so-called secondary causes are not properly called causes.[174]

This applies to man as much as to any other creature. "The sum total of the whole matter is that all things which have to do with man, either as to his body or as to his soul, are . . . completely from God as their only real cause."[175] "Thus whatever we do or think is of God, the Doer and Disposer of all things."[176] Speaking of Esau and Jacob, Zwingli says, "For before the creation of the world Divine Providence had just as much determined about their acts and life as about their creation and birth. . . . Life and activity, therefore, are just as much arranged by Divine Providence for every man as are his birth and generation."[177]

Even the sinful acts of man are completely caused by God. *All* things having to do with man "are so completely from God as their only real cause, that not even the work of sin is from any one else than God."[178] Even the first sins of angels and men were caused by God, since God knew that his own righteousness could not be properly appreciated by them unless there were unrighteousness with which to contrast it. Thus "the Deity is Himself the author of that which to us is unrighteousness, though not in the least so to Him." It is not unrighteousness to God because he is not under the law. "Therefore He sinneth not when He does in man that which is sin to man but not to Himself." Concerning these sins, God "wrought" them; "He makes the angel and man transgressors." He instigates the creatures to sin, and drives them to it.[179] Concerning the sinner, Zwingli affirms, "I grant that he was

172. Huldreich Zwingli, "On the Providence of God," *The Latin Works of Huldreich Zwingli*, Volume II, tr. Samuel M. Jackson, ed. William J. Hinke (Philadelphia: Heidelberg Press, 1922). This monograph was written in 1530.

173. Ibid., p. 208.

174. Ibid., p. 155.

175. Ibid., p. 203.

176. Ibid., p. 204.

177. Ibid., pp. 205-206.

178. Ibid., pp. 203-204.

179. Ibid., pp. 175-177; see p. 227. On the point that God is not bound by law, see p. 182: "One and the same deed, therefore, adultery, namely, or murder, as far as it concerns God as author, mover and instigator, is an act, not a crime, as far as it concerns man, is a crime and wickedness. For the one is not bound by the law, the other is even damned by the law."

forced to sin."[180] Thus man's will is not really free.[181] The champions of free will, who are the logical opponents of providence, are under a delusion.[182]

Absolute foreordination was also taught by John Calvin. As to why anything occurs, he says, "We must always at last return to the sole decision of God's will."[183] "Whatever happens proceeds from the Lord."[184] God's will is the cause of all things, and his providence the "determinative principle" for all.[185] "The will of God is the necessity of things," i.e., "what he has willed will of necessity come to pass."[186] The Heavenly Father "so holds all things in his power, so rules by his authority and will, so governs by his wisdom, that nothing can befall except he determine it."[187] "We acknowledge the will of God to be the ruling cause of all things," the "one principle and all-high *cause* of all things in heaven and earth!"[188]

Calvin recognized that foreknowledge as such does not determine the course of events. "Indeed, I will freely admit that foreknowledge alone imposes no necessity upon creatures, yet not all assent to this. For there are some who wish it also to be the cause of things." Calvin's approach was different. He declared that God foreknows all things *just because* he has determined them. God "foreknew because he so ordained by his decree."[189]

> . . . If God only foresaw human events, and did not also dispose and determine them by his decision, then there would be some point in raising this question: whether his forseeing had anything to do with their necessity. But since he foresees future events only by reason of the fact that he decreed that they take place, they vainly raise a quarrel over foreknowledge, when it is clear that all things take place rather by his determination and bidding.[190]

---

180. Ibid., p. 183.
181. Ibid., p. 137.
182. Ibid., p. 183.
183. John Calvin, *Institutes of the Christian Religion,* III.xxiii.4, ed. John T. McNeill, tr. Ford L. Battles (Philadelphia: Westminster Press, 1960), II:951.
184. Ibid., I.xviii.1 (I:230-231). The numbers in parentheses are the volume number and page numbers in the McNeill-Battles edition.
185. Ibid., I.xviii.2 (I:232); III.xxiii.2 (II:949).
186. Ibid., III.xxiii.8 (II:956).
187. Ibid., I.xvii.11 (I:224).
188. John Calvin, "A Defence of the Secret Providence of God," *Calvin's Calvinism,* tr. Henry Cole (Grand Rapids: Eerdmans, 1956), pp. 234, 246.
189. John Calvin, *Institutes,* III.xxiii.7 (II:955).
190. Ibid., III.xxx.6 (II:954-955).

We should emphasize the reference to "all things," since Calvin included *everything* in the one eternal decree. "The world is so governed by God, that nothing is done therein but by his *secret counsel and decree*."[191] "From this we declare that not only heaven and earth and the inanimate creatures, but also the plans and intentions of men, are so governed by his providence that they are borne by it straight to their appointed end."[192] This includes all the decisions and actions of human beings. "Men can accomplish nothing except by God's secret command, . . . they cannot by deliberating accomplish anything except what he has already decreed with himself and determines by his secret direction."[193] "Whatsoever men do, they do according to the *eternal will and secret purpose* of God."[194] "Of all things that are done, *the will of God* is therefore rightly considered to be the *first cause*, because He so rules at His pleasure the natures of all things created by Him, that He directs all the counsels and actions of men to the end which He had Himself preordained."[195]

> . . . Although men, like brute beasts confined by no chains, rush at random here and there, yet God by His secret bridle so holds and governs them, that they cannot move even one of their fingers without accomplishing the work of God much more than their own! But the faithful, who render unto Him their willing service, as do the angels, are to be considered, in a peculiar manner, *the hands* of God! . . .[196]

What of free will? "God, whenever he wills to make way for his providence, bends and turns men's wills even in external things; nor are they so free to choose that God's will does not rule over their freedom."[197] Also,

> . . . The internal affections of men are no less ruled by the hand of God than their external actions are preceded by His eternal decree; and, moreover, . . . God performs not by the hands of men the things which He has decreed, without first working in their hearts the very will which precedes the acts they are to perform.[198]

---

191. John Calvin, "A Treatise on the Eternal Predestination of God," *Calvin's Calvinism*, tr. Henry Cole (Grand Rapids: Eerdmans, 1956), p. 189.
192. John Calvin, *Institutes*, I.xvi.8 (I:207).
193. Ibid., I.xviii.1 (I:229).
194. John Calvin, "A Treatise on the Eternal Predestination of God," p. 205.
195. John Calvin, "A Defence of the Secret Providence of God," p. 247.
196. Ibid., p. 238.
197. John Calvin, *Institutes*, II.iv.7 (I:315).
198. John Calvin, "A Defence of the Secret Providence of God," p. 243.

Thus it would seem that men are not free either in their willing or in their doing.

There should be no dispute that God works all the godly motions in the hearts of his own people. "The great question is, whether He holds also in the hand of His power all the depraved and impious affections of the wicked, and turns them hither and thither, that they might desire to do that which He hath decreed to accomplish by their means?" The answer is yes. "What we maintain is, that when men act perversely, they do so . . . by the ordaining purpose of God."[199] "As far as men are concerned, whether they are good or evil, . . . their plans, wills, efforts, and abilities are under his hand; . . . it is within his choice to bend them whither he pleases and to constrain them whenever he pleases."[200] This includes Satan as well: "Satan and all the impious are so under God's hand and power that he directs their malice to whatever end seems good to him, and uses their wicked deeds to carry out his judgments."[201] "Satan performs his part by God's impulsion."[202]

Calvin applies this teaching to Adam's first sin with unabated vigor. In one place he says that Adam "fell solely by his own will."[203] But this statement is quite meaningless (at best) when compared with other things said on the same subject. Calvin says quite clearly that "God not only foresaw the fall of the first man, and in him the ruin of his descendants, but also meted it out in accordance with his own decision." Now, "the decree is dreadful indeed, I confess. Yet no one can deny that God foreknew what end man was to have before he created him, and consequently foreknew because he so ordained by his decree."[204] "I thus affirm that God did ordain the Fall of Adam."[205] We should point out that Calvin does not retreat into the idea of God's permissive will at this point. He does not like the distinction between God's doing and God's permitting; God is the *doer*![206] "How vain and fluctuating is that flimsy defence of the Divine justice which desires to make it appear that the evil things that are done, are so done, not by the will

---

199. Ibid., pp. 241-242.
200. John Calvin, *Institutes*, I.xvii.6 (I:218).
201. Ibid., I.xviii.1 (I:229).
202. Ibid., I.xviii.2 (I:232).
203. Ibid., I.xv.8 (I:195).
204. Ibid., III.xxiii.7 (II:955-956).
205. John Calvin, "A Treatise on the Eternal Predestination of God," p. 126.
206. John Calvin, *Institutes*, I.xviii.1 (I:228-229).

of God, but by His permission only."[207] Thus it is with the first man: "Adam fell, not only by the permission of God, but by His very secret counsel and decree."[208]

At this point Calvin introduces a qualification that is totally inconsistent with everything he has said, but which is no doubt forced upon him by his heart. Despite the repeated declarations that everything—men's sins, Satan's wickedness, Adam's fall—is the result of God's own decision and decree, Calvin in the end denies that God is the *author* of sin. "Although, therefore, I thus affirm that God did ordain the Fall of Adam, I so assert it as by no means to concede that God was therein properly and really the *author* of that Fall." God is only the ultimate cause, not the proximate cause. "But now, removing as I do from God all the *proximate cause* of the act in the Fall of man, I thereby remove from Him also all the *blame* of the act, leaving man alone under the sin and the guilt."[209] "Wherefore, when the wickedness of men proceeds thus from the Lord, and from a just cause, but from a cause unknown to us, although the first cause of all things be His will, that He is therefore the author of sin I most solemnly deny."[210] Thus Calvin refuses to draw the conclusion which his premise seems so obviously to require. Even the explanatory device used to justify his denial, i.e., the distinction between the first or remote cause and the proximate or secondary cause, points more reasonably in the other direction. It would seem that the first or ultimate cause of a thing should bear the real and true responsibility for it, while the proximate cause (itself caused) should be relieved of the blame. One can only conclude, as Brunner does, that Calvin is simply less logical than Zwingli on this point.

> . . . Although like Zwingli he conceives Providence as the absolute determination of all that happens, he tries to escape from the final conclusions, that even sin is inevitable and God becomes the Origin of Sin and Evil. Such an assertion seems to him—very naturally—to be blasphemy. Only we cannot see how he can avoid drawing this conclusion, save by a forcible act of will which refuses to admit a logical conclusion.[211]

Brunner calls this element of Calvin's thought "painful and dishonest."[212]

---

207. John Calvin, "A Defence of the Secret Providence of God," p. 244.
208. Ibid., p. 267.
209. John Calvin, "A Treatise on the Eternal Predestination of God," pp. 126-128.
210. John Calvin, "A Defence of the Secret Providence of God," p. 251.
211. Emil Brunner, *The Christian Doctrine of Creation and Redemption*, p. 171.
212. Ibid., p. 172.

These Reformation theologians have had many followers, but we will cite here only one contemporary example, namely, Gordon H. Clark. In his book *Biblical Predestination* Clark affirms that "God plans, decrees, and controls all events." Also, "the ultimate, original, and first cause is God."[213] God's foreknowledge as such is enough to make all things inevitable; "every event is foreordained because God is omniscient."[214] But the foreknowledge itself is the product of God's decree: God foreknows because he has decreed what shall come to pass.[215]

Since God decrees all events, it is obvious that he must determine human decisions. Though God works through men as instruments, we must remember that God is the cause of the instruments.[216] "The idea that a man can decide what he will do, as Pilate decided what to do with Jesus, without that decision's being eternally controlled and determined by God makes nonsense of the whole Bible."[217]

This includes even sinful acts. God knew ahead of time that Joseph's brothers would sell him into slavery.

> . . . This evil act was therefore inevitable. It could not not-happen. Foreknowledge implies inevitability. If Joseph's brothers had killed him, as they first thought of doing, then God would have been mistaken. The sale had to take place. Does this mean that God foreordains sinful acts? Well, it surely means that these acts were certain and determined from all eternity. It means that the brothers could not have done otherwise. Then who made those acts certain? The brothers could not have made them certain, for they were not yet born. . . . If God did not determine them, then there must be in the universe a determining force independent of God. . . .[218]

Of course, Clark rejects the existence of such a force, and he does not shrink from the implication. Since God determines men's choices, and some of these choices are evil, then the fact is that God causes evil.[219]

---

213. Gordon H. Clark, *Biblical Predestination* (Nutley, N.J.: Presbyterian and Reformed, 1969), pp. 53, 55.

214. Ibid., pp. 45, 63.

215. Ibid., p. 40. Here Clark quotes with approval from Stephen Charnock, *The Existence and Attributes of God* (Grand Rapids: Kregel reprint, 1958), pp. 189, 205 (1873 edition: I:415, 433).

216. Gordon Clark, *Biblical Predestination*, pp. 53ff.

217. Ibid., p. 64.

218. Ibid., p. 45.

219. Ibid., pp. 58-59.

Is there such a thing as free will? Clark does not fool around with misleading redefinitions of the term. It means, he says, what most people think it means: "the absence of any controlling power, even God and his grace, and therefore the equal ability in any situation to choose either of two incompatible courses of action."[220] Is there such a thing? "It is so obvious that the Bible contradicts the notion of free will that its acceptance by professing Christians can be explained only by the continuing ravages of sin blinding the minds of men."[221] Of course, the Bible often asserts that men will to do things.

> . . . But the question is not whether they will, or have a will, but whether God determines their will. The question is not whether a man chooses; but whether his choice had a cause or reason. The Calvinist does not deny will or volition; he denies that volition like all the rest of creation is independent of God.
>
> The Calvinist may even say that will is free, not absolutely, or free from God, but free from the laws of physics and chemistry. Indeed the Calvinist reacts strongly against behaviorist determinism. But he asserts divine predetermination, foreordination, predestination.[222]

We have called the view represented by Luther, Zwingli, Calvin, and Clark a form of theistic determinism. Many object strenuously to the use of this term for this view. Berkouwer says that "an identification of Christianity and determinism can lead only to immeasurable evil for the Church and theology. The Christian doctrines of predestination and Providence are actually something wholly other than determinism."[223] Carl Henry is likewise very concerned to distinguish this view from deterministic theories such as Stoicism or Islam.[224] It is true that there are some crucial differences between such views on the one hand and Christian absolute foreordination on the other. Some deterministic views are completely impersonal; that which determines is an impersonal force such as fate, rather than the personal God. This seems to be Berkouwer's point: determinism, he says, amounts to a "de-personalization of the God-concept."[225] In Henry's mind the term *determinism* conjures up thoughts of an arbitrary decree (as in Islam) or a necessary

220. Ibid., p. 113.
221. Ibid., p. 114.
222. Ibid., pp. 122-123.
223. G. C. Berkouwer, *The Providence of God,* p. 147.
224. Carl F. H. Henry, *God, Revelation and Authority,* VI:80-82.
225. G. C. Berkouwer, *The Providence of God,* p. 152.

decree (as in Leibnitz). Both are concerned that determinism excludes free will. As Berkouwer says, "Determination and freedom of the will are mutually exclusive. This is why Divine determining is utterly different from what is generally understood by determinism."[226]

While we recognize the important difference at stake here, we must conclude that the refusal to call the view now under discussion *determinism* is simply semantic quibbling. If all events take place as the result of the causal influence of an overruling force, so that it was impossible for these events to have happened any other way, this is determinism whether the force is personal or impersonal, free or bound, arbitrary or purposeful. And as we have already seen, those who represent this view are not reluctant to abandon human free will. Thus we agree with Brunner that this view is a "determinism from above."[227]

Implications of Determinism

We have examined three main forms of determinism. Though vastly different in detail, they all agree in the explanation of why things happen the way they do. They agree that there is a single controlling principle or power which is responsible for all things, which imparts to them a necessity to be that way and no other. We now conclude this section with a look at the main implications of a consistent determinism. We should keep in mind that some systems are less consistent than others, as they try to avoid some of these implications.

Man

First, there are several implications with regard to the nature of man. The most obvious is the elimination of free will in any significant sense of the term. Taylor is correct when he says, "Thus, if no man's destiny is in any degree up to him, if everything that he ever does is something he could never have avoided, then in the clearest sense it is idle to speak of his having a free will."[228] Berkouwer is also correct: determination and freedom of the will are mutually exclusive. This realization has resulted in at least three responses on the part of determinists. Some simply grant that freedom does not exist. Others attempt to define

226. Ibid., p. 151.
227. Emil Brunner, *The Christian Doctrine of Creation and Redemption*, pp. 170-171.
228. Richard Taylor, "Determinism," p. 360.

freedom in such a way that it can be preserved along with determinism, e.g., being able to act as one desires. Still others modify their determinism somewhat, making it somewhat less than absolute in order to leave room for at least a measure of freedom. All such maneuvering confirms the validity and the seriousness of this implication.

Another implication is that determinism tends to foster a sense of resignation on the part of man, resulting in inactivity or quietism. It takes away initiative. If "whatever will be, will be," why make any effort to accomplish anything, to avoid danger, or to change one's circumstances? This is usually just a practical problem, since the serious thinkers within the systems usually have an explanation as to why this quietism is not warranted.

A third implication has to do with the dignity of man. If everything we do is determined for us, and we are only acting out a role written by someone or something else, our integrity and worth as individuals seem to be brought into question. How can we any longer praise anyone for great discoveries and inventions, for acts of bravery and sacrifice, for outstanding physical and intellectual accomplishments? As MacKay says, even our criminals are robbed of the dignity of being blamed for their actions.[229] Men no less than clouds and weeds are cogs in the machine, or puppets, or pawns. Schaeffer objects to Skinner's behaviorism on this ground. He notes that Skinner declares that man is "not separate from his surrounding environment. Everything man is, everything man makes, everything man thinks is completely, one hundred percent, determined by his environment." According to Skinner, "The individual does not initiate anything." His view is that "all behavior is determined not from within but from without." Such a view robs man of his value and worth, says Schaeffer.[230] If we remove the word *environment* from the above critique and substitute the word *fate*, or the word *Allah*, or the word *God*, the result is the same.

Evil

In the second place, determinism has serious implications with regard to what is usually called the existence of *evil* in the world. Whether we speak of physical evils such as tidal waves and cancer, or of moral evils such as rape and murder, in a deterministic system the One Cause is

229. Donald M. MacKay, *The Clock Work Image*, pp. 17-18.
230. Francis Schaeffer, *Back to Freedom and Dignity*, pp. 34-35.

ultimately responsible for them. If the One Cause happens to be an impersonal force, this does not bother us very much. But in a theistic determinism, where the determining force happens to be an omnipotent personal deity, this raises all kinds of serious questions. The so-called "problem of evil" is difficult enough in any case, but theistic determinism makes it much worse.

Morality

Finally, deterministic world views have implications for the area of morality, which is undermined in two different ways. First, free will and moral responsibility seem to be inseparably linked. Thus, if there is no free will, then there is no such thing as moral responsibility. As Brunner says, "Pan-causalism, or determinism, is opposed to our moral knowledge of responsibility; if everything happens because it *must*, then there is no room for responsibility; responsibility can only be maintained by the aid of intolerable sophisms."[231] The concepts of wrong-doing and guilt likewise are called into question; and the propriety of punishment is denied. Berkouwer's remarks are incisive:

> One is reminded here, by way of parallel, of the war criminals who defended themselves by saying that they acted according to order: "A command is a command." A concept of absolute determining causality is sympathetic with this kind of talk. If a judge of law were to accept such a theory, he would have to excuse every delinquent from sentence. A criminal is only a non-responsible link in a causal chain. In determinism man is never responsible for a new act in a definite situation and, thus, can never be considered guilty regardless of which act he chooses to perform. Deterministic causality principally and consistently pronounces man morally free by denying him his volitional freedom.[232]

Second, morality is affected by determinism in the sense that it becomes difficult to distinguish any longer between good and evil. The One Cause is equally responsible for all things; the same power that produces the Hitlers also produces the Gandhis. That is to say, the things we are accustomed to calling "good" and "evil" are all related to the One Cause in the same way. A. A. Hodge makes this remark

231. Emil Brunner, *The Christian Doctrine of Creation and Redemption*, p. 171.
232. G. C. Berkouwer, *The Providence of God*, p. 145.

concerning pantheism, but it applies just the same to any determinism: "All evil, precisely as all good, comes immediately from God, and evil men are related to him precisely as are saints and angels."[233] There no longer seems to be a basis for distinguishing good from evil; it would seem that "whatever is is right."[234] Gordon Clark criticizes Stoic pantheism thus: "Now if right is defined as that which God does, then on this pantheistic basis our actions would be *ipso facto* right, and there would be no evil in the universe."[235] But we could say the same thing about *any* deterministic system, *especially* about a theistic determinism such as Clark's own. If what God does is right, and if God does everything, then everything is right. Zwingli is forced to acknowledge this when he says God is above the law or not bound by the law, and so is not guilty of wrong-doing even though he causes men to sin. His only inconsistency is in ascribing guilt and wrong-doing to the human instruments and calling their actions "sin." John Calvin tries to avoid this problem by saying, "We fancy no lawless god who is a law unto himself."[236] But when he is discussing how God causes the wills of evil men to sin, he declares that "all godly and modest folk" will readily agree with Augustine's words, "There is a great difference between what is befitting for man to will and what is fitting for God, and to what end the will of each is directed, so that it be either approved or disapproved. For through the bad wills of evil men God fulfills what he righteously wills."[237] What is this but a God who is a law unto himself? And where then is the proper distinction between good and evil? It disappears, as it does in any determinism.

CONCLUSION

Our purpose in this chapter has been to survey in a systematic way the variety of alternatives to biblical providence. We have seen that there are basically three of these: indeterminism, self-determinism, and determinism. The representatives of these various alternatives are for the most part not obscure and esoteric philosophies but will be recognized by most readers. We may marvel at the fact that the world seems to be disposed to accept almost *anything but* the biblical view.

---

233. Archibald Alexander Hodge, *Popular Lectures on Theological Themes* (Philadelphia: Presbyterian Board of Publication, 1887), p. 28.

234. Francis Schaeffer, *Back To Freedom and Dignity*, pp. 28, 40.

235. Gordon Clark, *From Thales to Dewey*, pp. 166-167.

236. John Calvin, *Institutes*, III.xxiii.2 (II:950).

237. Ibid., I.xviii.3 (I:234).

As we proceed now to set forth the biblical teaching concerning God's relation to the on-going world, we should be impressed with the uniqueness of the Christian doctrine of providence. On the background of this broad spectrum of alternatives, we should be able to appreciate the glory of God our Ruler, and the marvelous wisdom with which he rules over his creation.

Chapter Three

GENERAL PROVIDENCE

"The Lord has established His throne in the heavens; and His sovereignty rules over all" (Ps. 103:19). The Bible teaches very clearly that God's providential rule extends over all things. God rules over nature, or the realm of natural processes governed by natural law. He also rules over history, or the realm of human decisions, deeds, and destiny.

In our discussion of the providence of God we will distinguish three different ways in which God relates to the world. The first two may be properly thought of as providential activity, while the third extends beyond providence as such but must be discussed so that its relationship to providence may be made clear. The first way in which God relates to the world is called *general providence*. This includes primarily the realm of nature and refers mostly to the unvarying works of God in preserving the universe in existence and directing its natural processes according to the predictable patterns we call the "laws of nature." It also includes up to a point the lives and deeds of human beings. The second way God relates to the on-going world is called *special providence*. This refers to God's intervention into the regular course of things in order to produce a variation that would not have occurred otherwise but which does not violate the possibilities of natural law. Through special providence God exercises his rule over history, since this is his ordinary way of working out his special purposes for mankind. The third way that God relates to the world is through *miracles*, which are acts of God that are contrary to natural law.

These are the most common categories in the discussion of providence, although sometimes one or two others are distinguished. For instance, some would separate *preservation* from providence and discuss it separately.[1] Also, some would distinguish a *most special* providence from special providence, defining it as God's relation to believers as over against his relation to mankind in general.[2] Here we prefer to include the concept of preservation within the scope of general providence, and we prefer not to distinguish a most special from special providence.

---

1. For example, see Augustus H. Strong, *Systematic Theology*, 3 volumes in 1 (Valley Forge, Pa.: Judson Press, 1907), pp. 410ff.; Joseph Pohle, *God: The Author of Nature and the Supernatural*, ed. Arthur Preuss (St. Louis: B. Herder, 1912), pp. 62ff., 91ff.

2. For example, see Revere Franklin Weidner, *Theologia, or the Doctrine of God* (New York: Revell, 1902), pp. 93-94.

We should also note that all those who agree on the three categories mentioned above do not necessarily agree on the terminology used for them. For instance, A. A. Hodge calls them ordinary providence, grace, and miracle.[3] This is too narrow a term for the second category, however, since it includes works of judgment as well as works of grace. For another example, Carl Ketcherside refers to three levels of divine power which he calls natural, providential, and supernatural.[4] This seems to be misleading, however, since the first category is no less providential than the second, and since the second category also includes supernatural interventions from God. Indeed, it is most crucial to understand that God can work supernaturally without working miraculously. Thus we prefer to stay with our terms *general providence, special providence,* and *miracles.*

In this chapter we are concerned only with the first of these, general providence. As said earlier, this refers primarily to God's regular and uniform way of acting in the realm of nature. It has to do with God's general purpose for his world and for mankind, and it does not take account of any special human needs or of God's special purposes in reference to sin and salvation. It relates to all people alike, "for He causes His sun to rise on the evil and the good, and sends rain on the righteous and the unrighteous" (Matt. 5:45). As the divine power in which "we live and move and exist" (Acts 17:28), general providence is the fundamental description of our environment.

THE PRESERVATION OF NATURE

General providence means first of all that God *preserves* in existence all the things that he has created in both the invisible and visible realms. This work began as soon as the creation itself was accomplished. We must not think, in a deistic fashion, that God's work was finished when the creation was over. Genesis 2:2 says that God rested on the seventh day, but this means only that he rested from the work of *creating.* His providential preservation of the universe, a work begun as early as Genesis 1:1, did not cease then nor has it ceased since. As Jesus said, "My Father is working until now" (John 5:17).

3. Archibald Alexander Hodge, *Popular Lectures on Theological Themes* (Philadelphia: Presbyterian Board of Publication, 1887), p. 36.

4. W. Carl Ketcherside, "The Dynamic of God," *Christian Standard* (July 31, 1983), 118:12.

The doctrine of divine preservation is taught in Acts 17:28 in the statement that we *exist* (have our being) through God himself. We owe our very existence at this moment to God's power. Colossians 1:17, referring specifically to God the Son, says that "in Him all things hold together." In him the atomic particles adhere around their nuclei. In him the atoms cling together in their proper molecules. In him the molecules mesh into the elements. In him the various combinations of elements form individual substances and bodies. In him the gravitational pull of Earth causes us to stick to its surface. In him the planets revolve still around the sun. In him the galaxy maintains its identity as a wad of stars hurtling through space. The fact that Colossians 1:17 is talking specifically about God the Son does not exclude the Father and the Holy Spirit from this work; it is simply including the Son in this work and thereby affirming his identity as God. The same is true of another New Testament text, Hebrews 1:3. Here it is also said of God the Son that he "upholds all things by the word of His power."

The meaning of these verses is not just that God preserves us alive or preserves us from harm. Such a concept is taught in Scripture, as in Psalm 36:6, "O Lord, Thou preservest man and beast."[5] But the doctrine of preservation is much more than this. It is the idea that God preserves the universe as a whole in its very existence, i.e., he does not allow it to slip back into non-existence. We must remember that God created everything *ex nihilo*, that is, from nothing. Whatever has come into being from nothingness can also be caused to revert back to nothingness, to completely disappear, to be annihilated. And it would, if God were not actively holding it in existence by his power. Thus the most basic physical law, the first law of thermodynamics, the law of conservation of energy, remains constant and dependable only because of the providence of God.[6] As Karl Heim remarks,

> . . . God is God simply because He alone is eternal. All things or essences other than God are inherently temporal, and exist therefore only in the

5. We should note also that Nehemiah 9:6 probably falls into this category. Though the King James Version says, "Thou preservest them all," more recent versions understand this as "Thou dost give life to all of them" (NASB).

6. As an example of what could happen if God withdrew his upholding power, we may permit ourselves to ask what happened to the physical bodies (and clothing) assumed by God and by angels for the purpose of theophanies in the Old Testament era (as, for example, in Gen. 18:1-8; 32:24ff.). One possibility is that the bodies and clothing, created *ex nihilo* for their limited purposes, were allowed to revert to nothingness after those purposes had been accomplished.

> present moment. Their fate in the next moment is not yet decided. They have no power in themselves to endure from this moment into the next. Left to themselves, they would without God fall back into their non-existence. God, who *alone* has immortality, is able to hold temporal beings like ourselves over the Void, and carry us over from one moment to the next. . . .[7]

It is not necessary to speculate as to *how* God preserves his creatures in existence; we do not have any specific data on the matter. Some have suggested that it is a kind of "continuous creation," in the sense that God continues to create the universe anew *ex nihilo* each moment. One writer is quoted as saying, "We may say with justice that the universe, as it now appears, is created each instant out of nothing, just as in the first day of creation."[8] This concept is not acceptable, however. The Bible seems to confine God's creative work to the beginning (Gen. 1:1) and to look upon it as unique. Creation is a distinct act. Also, the continuous creation idea seems to undermine the integrity of the universe as an existing reality. Its very continuity as something that truly exists is weakened. This view posits an endless succession of universes, each existing for a moment, then going out of existence, then being replaced by a newly-created universe. Such a view seems highly speculative and inconsistent with Scripture.

It is enough simply to say, as Hebrews 1:3 does, that God upholds all things by the word of his power. Spiritual and material created beings stay in existence by the constant operation of the preserving power of God, by "the perpetual influx of power from the first cause."[9]

There is no justification for thinking that the existence-status of the creation is somehow in jeopardy, or that the "nothingness" whence it came is now some kind of enemy which threatens to overwhelm and

---

7. Karl Heim, *The Transformation of the Scientific World View,* tr. W. A. Whitehouse (New York: Harper and Brothers, 1953), pp. 29-30. See also Emil Brunner, *The Christian Doctrine of Creation and Redemption: Dogmatics, Volume II,* tr. Olive Wyon (Philadelphia: Westminster Press, 1952), p. 153: "Without the preserving will of God the world would fall into nothingness in a flash. The world is not so 'solid' and indestructible as it looks. . . . At every moment God 'upholds' the world above an abyss of nothingness, into which it could fall any moment, and into which it would fall, if God were not holding it."

8. Karl Heim, as cited in G. C. Berkouwer, *The Providence of God,* tr. Lewis B. Smedes (Grand Rapids: Eerdmans, 1952), p. 60.

9. William Sherlock, *A Discourse Concerning the Divine Providence* (Pittsburgh: J. L. Read, 1848), p. 23.

engulf it once more.[10] Karl Heim's statement concerning temporal things, that "their fate in the next moment is not yet decided," is not true. Their fate *is* decided, because God has committed himself to upholding them in existence. God's act of creation was a kind of promise or covenant—a covenant with being itself, to maintain it in existence. Psalm 148 invokes God's creatures to praise him: "Let them praise the name of the Lord, for He commanded and they were created. He has also established them forever and ever; He has made a decree which will not pass away" (Ps. 148:5-6). God has decreed that his creatures shall continue in existence, and in his faithfulness he will keep that promise. It is possible that the term "forever and ever" (*le'ōlam*) in verse 6 means only "until the end of the age," thus allowing for an annihilation of the universe at the second coming of Christ (II Peter 3:10-12). Some would take it to mean that God, having brought all things into existence, will keep them in existence literally forever. Thus the new heavens and new earth (II Peter 3:13) would be a kind of renovated universe. "Though God will dissolve this present frame of things, and, it may be, cast the world into a new mould, yet nothing that is made, neither matter nor spirit, shall be annihilated or reduced into nothing again."[11]

The key word for all creatures, then, is *dependence*. We constantly and completely depend upon the power of God for our very existence ("in Him we . . . exist"), and we confidently depend upon his faithfulness to keep us and not to drop us back into the abyss of nothingness. An awareness of this basic dependence causes us to realize just how potentially fragile and frail our existence is; but at the same time, an awareness of the fact that the almighty and faithful God is the one on whom we depend removes all our fears of non-existence. In view of such absolute dependence, our only attitude toward God our Ruler can be one of humility and trust.

THE PROCESSES OF NATURE

General providence includes not only God's continual preservation of the very being of his creatures, but also his constant and complete

10. Contrary to Karl Barth's treatment of nothingness (*das Nichtige*) in *Church Dogmatics, Volume III: The Doctrine of Creation, Part 3,* tr. G. W. Bromiley and R. J. Ehrlich (Edinburgh: T. & T. Clark, 1961), pp. 289ff.

11. William Sherlock, *A Discourse Concerning the Divine Providence,* p. 25. Sherlock believes this has implications for the question of eternal punishment (see pp. 25, 32ff.).

control of all the natural processes in the universe, from the motion of subatomic particles to the hurtling of galaxies through space, from inorganic chemical reactions to the beating of a baby's heart. "In Him we live and move" (Acts 17:28).

In this section our main purpose is to set forth the abundant biblical testimony to God's involvement in the processes of nature. We are not concerned at this point to discuss how God uses natural events to work out his special purposes for mankind; that is reserved for the next chapter. Here we just want to emphasize how God is at work in the ordinary, regular, and universal events of nature, from the commonplace to the spectacular.

We note first of all how the movements of the celestial bodies and their relation to the earth are the work of God. In Job 38 God is chastising Job for his presumptuousness by asking him, in effect, "Who do you think you are, anyway? Here is what *I* have done; can you do anything comparable to this?" One of his questions has to do with the heavens:

> Can you bind the chains of the Pleiades, or loose the cords of Orion? Can you lead forth a constellation in its season, and guide the Bear with her satellites? Do you know the ordinances of the heavens, or fix their rule over the earth? (Job 38:31-33).

It is God who does all these things. He moves the stars and the galaxies through their paths in space; he moves the earth on its axis and in its orbit around the sun, thus producing seasonal changes. "He made the moon for the seasons; the sun knows the place of its setting" (Ps. 104:19).

God's control of such things gives him control over light and darkness also. "He causes His sun to rise" (Matt. 5:45). God challenged Job with this question: "Have you ever in your life commanded the morning, and caused the dawn to know its place?" (Job 38:12). Nighttime also comes from God: "Thou dost appoint darkness and it becomes night, in which all the beasts of the forest prowl about" (Ps. 104:20). Again to Job, "Where is the way to the dwelling of light? And darkness, where is its place, that you may take it to its territory, and that you may discern the paths to its home?" (Job 38:19-20).

We also note how God controls the larger elements of our environment, such as the oceans: "Have you entered into the springs of the sea? Or have you walked in the recesses of the deep?" (Job 38:16). And rivers: "He sends forth springs in the valleys; they flow between the mountains" (Ps. 104:10). And geologic events such as earthquakes and volcanoes: "He looks at the earth, and it trembles; He touches the mountains, and they smoke" (Ps. 104:32).

In the next place we see that Scripture emphasizes God's personal concern for the animals which he created. Job 39 pictures God as a kind of universal shepherd who attends to the needs of mountain goats, deer, wild donkeys and oxen, ostriches, horses, hawks, and eagles. The Shepherd continues to challenge Job:

> Do you know the time the mountain goats give birth? Do you observe the calving of the deer? . . . Who sent out the wild donkey free? . . . Will the wild ox consent to serve you? Or will he spend the night at your manger? . . . Do you give the horse his might? Do you clothe his neck with a mane? Do you make him leap like the locust? . . . Is it by your understanding that the hawk soars, stretching his wings toward the south? Is it at your command that the eagle mounts up, and makes his nest on high? (Job 39:1, 5, 9, 19-20, 26-27).

A major theme in relation to animals is that God provides food and water for them. "Can you hunt the prey for the lion, or satisfy the appetite of the young lions . . . ? Who prepares for the raven its nourishment, when its young cry to God, and wander about without food?" (Job 38:39-41). Jesus answers this question: "Consider the ravens, for they neither sow nor reap; and they have no storeroom nor barn; and yet God feeds them" (Luke 12:24; see Matt. 6:26). God provides thus for all his animals:

> He sends forth springs in the valleys; . . . they give drink to every beast of the field; the wild donkeys quench their thirst. . . . He causes the grass to grow for the cattle . . . . The young lions roar after their prey, and seek their food from God. . . . They all wait for Thee, to give them their food in due season. Thou dost give to them, they gather it up; Thou dost open Thy hand, they are satisfied with good (Ps. 104:10-11, 14, 21, 27-28).

God gives food to all flesh (Ps. 136:25); he "makes grass to grow on the mountains. He gives to the beast its food, and to the young ravens which cry" (Ps. 147:8-9). "The eyes of all look to Thee, and Thou dost give them their food in due time. Thou dost open Thy hand, and dost satisfy the desire of every living thing" (Ps. 145:15-16). Even "the trees of the Lord drink their fill" (Ps. 104:16). The death of animals no less than their life is in God's hands: "Thou dost hide Thy face, they are dismayed; Thou dost take away their spirit, they expire, and return to their dust" (Ps. 104:29). Jesus reminds us, "Are not two sparrows sold for a cent? And yet not one of them will fall to the ground apart from your Father" (Matt. 10:29; see Luke 12:6).

We may note also that God makes similar provision for the needs of man, as he provides a bountiful harvest and fruitful seasons, filling our hearts with food and gladness (Acts 14:17).

> Thou dost visit the earth, and cause it to overflow; Thou dost greatly enrich it; the stream of God is full of water; Thou dost prepare their grain, for thus Thou dost prepare the earth. . . . Thou hast crowned the year with Thy bounty, and Thy paths drip with fatness. The pastures of the wilderness drip, and the hills gird themselves with rejoicing. The meadows are clothed with flocks, and the valleys are covered with grain . . . (Ps. 65:9-13).

See also Psalm 104:14-15, which says that the labor of man tills the earth but God causes the food to grow.

The natural processes most commonly attributed to God's providence are those having to do with the weather. Attention is centered upon God's gift of rain since it provides the essential substance of life. Lightning and thunder are also prominently mentioned since they provide an audio-visual display of God's majestic presence. The wind and clouds and even the evaporation process are also described as God's work. So are snow, hail, and ice, as well as dew and frost. Two or more of these weather-related processes are often mentioned together in the biblical texts cited below, even though our intention is to highlight only one at a time.

It is interesting that the vital though not easily detectable process of evaporation is specifically mentioned in Scripture as God's work. Psalm 135:6-7 says, "Whatever the Lord pleases, He does, in heaven and in earth, in the seas and in all deeps. He causes the vapors to ascend from the ends of the earth; Who makes lightnings for the rain; Who brings forth the wind from His treasuries." Job 36:27-28 puts it this way: "For He draws up the drops of water, they distill rain from the mist, which the clouds pour down, they drip upon man abundantly."

Closely associated with evaporation is the formation and movement of clouds, which are also attributed to God. "Can anyone understand the spreading of the clouds, the thundering of His pavilion?" (Job 36:29). God makes the clouds his chariot, says Psalm 104:3; he "covers the heavens with clouds" (Ps. 147:8). "Also with moisture He loads the thick cloud; He disperses the cloud of His lightning. And it changes direction, turning around by His guidance" (Job 37:11-12).

Thunder and lightning are also described as the works of God, with thunder often being represented as God's voice.

> . . . Listen closely to the thunder of His voice, and the rumbling that goes out from His mouth. Under the whole heaven He lets it loose, and His lightning to the ends of the earth. After it, a voice roars; He thunders with His majestic voice; and He does not restrain the lightnings when His voice is heard. God thunders with His voice wondrously, doing great things which we cannot comprehend (Job 37:2-5).
>
> . . . The voice of the Lord is upon the waters; the God of glory thunders, the Lord is over many waters. The voice of the Lord is powerful, the voice of the Lord is majestic. The voice of the Lord breaks the cedars; yes, the Lord breaks in pieces the cedars of Lebanon. . . . The voice of the Lord hews out flames of fire. The voice of the Lord shakes the wilderness; the Lord shakes the wilderness of Kadesh. The voice of the Lord makes the deer to calve, and strips the forest bare, and in His temple everything says, "Glory!" (Ps. 29:3-9).[12]

"When He utters His voice, there is a tumult of waters in the heavens, and He causes the clouds to ascend from the end of the earth; He makes lightning for the rain, and brings out the wind from His storehouses" (Jer. 10:13). "Behold, He spreads His lightning about Him, and He covers the depths of the sea. . . . He covers His hands with the lightning, and commands it to strike the mark" (Job 36:30, 32). God issues this rebuke to Job: "Can you send forth lightnings that they may go and say to you, 'Here we are'?" (Job 38:35).

The wind also is at his command: "Fire and hail, snow and clouds; stormy wind, fulfilling His word" (Ps. 148:8). "He walks upon the wings of the wind" and "makes the winds His messengers" (Ps. 104:3-4).

When Jesus said that God "sends rain on the righteous and the unrighteous" (Matt. 5:45), he was echoing a major theme of the inspired poets. God *does* send rain, as he emphasized to Job:

> Who has cleft a channel for the flood, or a way for the thunderbolt; to bring rain on a land without people, on a desert without a man in it, to satisfy the waste and desolate land, and to make the seeds of grass to sprout? Has the rain a father? Or who has begotten the drops of dew? . . . Can you lift up your voice to the clouds, so that an abundance of water may cover you? . . . Who can count the clouds by wisdom, or tip the water jars of the heavens . . . ? (Job 38:25-28, 34, 37).

---

12. Instead of "The voice of the Lord makes the deer to calve," the NIV text of verse 9 reads, "The voice of the Lord twists the oaks."

The answer, of course, is God, "Who provides rain for the earth, Who makes grass to grow on the mountains" (Ps. 147:8). "He waters the mountains from His upper chambers; the earth is satisfied with the fruit of His works" (Ps. 104:13). "Thou dost visit the earth, and cause it to overflow; Thou dost greatly enrich it; The stream of God is full of water; Thou dost prepare their grain, for thus Thou dost prepare the earth. Thou dost water its furrows abundantly; Thou dost settle its ridges; Thou dost soften it with showers" (Ps. 65:9-10).

We note finally that God is also the giver of moisture from heaven in its frozen forms. The hail and snow fulfil his word (Ps. 148:8). "For to the snow He says, 'Fall on the earth,' and to the downpour and the rain, 'Be strong.'" Indeed, "from the breath of God ice is made, and the expanse of the waters is frozen" (Job 37:6, 10). Once more Job is put in his place by God: "Have you entered the storehouses of the snow, or have you seen the storehouses of the hail, which I have reserved for the time of distress, for the day of war and battle? . . . From whose womb has come the ice? And the frost of heaven, who has given it birth? Water becomes hard like stone, and the surface of the deep is imprisoned" (Job 38:22-23, 29-30). The elements are swift to obey God's command:

> . . . He sends forth His command to the earth; His word runs very swiftly. He gives snow like wool; He scatters the hoarfrost like ashes. He casts forth His ice as fragments; who can stand before His cold? He sends forth His word and melts them; He causes His wind to blow and the waters to flow (Ps. 147:15-18).

Having set forth the biblical data, we may now emphasize several facts concerning the processes of nature and God's relationship to them. First, we must remember that we are dealing here with matters of general providence, not special providence. For the most part these are the regular, ordinary events of nature that affect everyone, good and evil alike, in the same way (Matt. 5:45). Some of the phenomena, such as hail or volcanoes, may be occasional or even rare, but they are still part of the natural course of things. Most of them are so familiar that we all but take them for granted: a cloud, a sunrise, a rainstorm, a bird flying, a gust of wind. These and all the other common occurrences of nature are the objects of God's general providence.

Second and most significant is the constant testimony of Scripture that the processes of nature are *the work of God:* he is the one who actually does these things! In God's great rebuke of Job (chapters 38 and 39) he asks a string of questions that leave no doubt as to what he is claiming about himself. Who has done this? Have you ever done this? Have you ever seen this? Where were you when this was done? Can you do this? Is it at your command that this happens? This is God's way of saying, "No! It is I and I alone who am responsible for these things! *I* have done them!" God *causes* the sun to rise; God *appoints* darkness. God feeds the birds; he gives all the animals their food. God causes evaporation; God makes lightning; thunder is his voice. He sends rain and gives snow. He issues commands to the clouds, and they go where he tells them (Job 37:12). He commands the lightning to strike its mark. Hail, snow, and wind do as he orders them. At his command the snow falls and the earth freezes; at his command it thaws again. There can be no mistake; the testimony is clear: God is the subject of these actions. They are his doing. "Stand and consider the wonders of God. Do you know how God establishes them?" (Job 37:14-15). We humbly confess that we do not know *how* God is the doer of these things, but we freely acknowledge *that* he does them.

A third point is that God has a complete and detailed *knowledge* of all the phenomena of nature, large and small. The same God who tends the galaxies (Job 38:31-32) and counts and names the stars (Ps. 147:4) also knows the very number of hairs on our heads (Matt. 10:30; Luke 12:7). He who counts the clouds (Job 38:37) also monitors the pregnancy of wild animals and watches over the birth of their offspring (Job 39:1-3). "I know every bird of the mountains," says God (Ps. 50:11). As Jesus reminds us, not one sparrow is forgotten before God (Luke 12:6), and he marks the death of every one of these creatures (Matt. 10:29).

This leads to a fourth observation, namely, that there seems to be a relationship of real intimacy between the Creator and his creation. We get the impression that God loves the world of nature and cares for it with a tenderness and concern that we might observe in a gardener caring for his prize roses. We can understand that the land of Canaan, the promised land, might be described as a "land for which the Lord your God cares; the eyes of the Lord your God are always on it, from the beginning even to the end of the year" (Deut. 11:12). But God also cares for land even where no people dwell; he sends it rain so that its seeds may sprout (Job 38:25-27). God pictures himself as walking "in the recesses of the deep," as if he enjoys watching the sea creatures he put there (Job 38:16; Ps. 104:25-26). Psalm 104 is a marvelous portrayal of the intimate relation between God and his world. He makes light his cloak (v. 2). He uses the clouds for chariots and rides on the wings of the wind (v. 3). He feeds and waters his animals, and even waters his trees (vv. 11, 14, 16, 27). He is even pictured as feeding them out of his hand (v. 28). Truly, "Let the glory of the Lord endure forever; let the Lord be glad in His works" (v. 31).

In this connection we may emphasize again that God's providence embraces *all* the phenomena of nature, large and small. God's care extends to the very least of his creatures. It has been expressed this way:

> Objects of the divine providence are all created things, none excepted, visible and invisible, living and lifeless, heaven, earth, and sea, and all that is in them. As He has created all things, so also His providence extends over all. He preserves . . . not alone man, the noblest creature, but also all irrational animals. . . . God cares not only for the genus of birds, but for every species, storks, swallows, and sparrows, and even for every single individual of every species, for every single stork, swallow, and sparrow. He not only takes care that the trees grow and are preserved, but He provides for every single tree and branch and leaf. . . . The smallest, most insignificant, and most useless thing is under God's government and providence. . . . As the light of the sun does not disdain the lowliest worm, so also God's providence does not turn away from it. We should well note this, that God's providence extends to the lowliest things. God does not rule like an earthly king, who provides by a general edict for all and every one of his subjects in general, though there are thousands whom the king does not know. God knows the smallest and provides for it . . . . If it is not improper for God to create them, why should it be improper for Him to preserve them? . . . The power of God is no less evident in the creation of a gnat than in that of an elephant; and the same applies to His providence. . . . Finally, it does not overburden God, as one might think. His infinite intellect knows no weariness.[13]

Another apt statement says, "He is God of the small. He is God of the mite, the morsel, the mote and the molecule; He is God of the particle and the pittance. To Him insignificant is significant, and there are no secrets."[14]

A final emphasis that emerges from the biblical data on general providence is God's *total sovereignty* over nature. This is evident throughout. He issues a command, and the elements obey it. He touches a mountain,

---

13. Cited in Francis Pieper, *Christian Dogmatics*, tr. Theodore Engelder et al. (St. Louis: Concordia Publishing House, 1950), I:486-487.

14. Ruth Glover, "Lilliputian or Leviathan," *Christian Standard* (June 10, 1984), 119:15.

and it smokes. He but looks at the earth, and it shakes. Indeed, "I know that the Lord is great, and that our Lord is above all gods. Whatever the Lord pleases, He does, in heaven and in earth, in the seas and in all deeps" (Ps. 135:5-6). "The Lord sat as King at the flood; yes, the Lord sits as King forever" (Ps. 29:10). There is none who compares with him. His challenge to Job is summed up in these words: "Do you have an arm like God, and can you thunder with a voice like His?" (Job 40:9).

PROVIDENCE AND NATURAL LAW

We must now attempt to deal with one of the most difficult questions regarding general providence, namely, the nature of the relationship between God's providential activity and natural law. In other terms, what is the relation between the First Cause and his created secondary causes?[15] Mascall has well remarked "that intractable problems arise in the reconciliation of divine omnipotence with the reality of secondary causes."[16] Another writer expresses similar doubts as to whether these problems can be resolved: "The mystery of the relation between the almighty, ever-present efficiency of God and the imparted quasi-independent forces of nature and of will, is not to be solved by any faculty of man."[17] This is probably true, but nevertheless in the following discussion we shall at least come to understand the nature of the problem and a suggested approach to an answer.

The Reality of Natural Law

In light of our discussion of the Bible's emphasis on God's role in nature, one might be tempted to ask whether we should abandon the concept of natural law. The temptation should definitely be resisted. The reality of physical laws or laws of nature cannot be denied. Such things as the laws of gravity, motion, physics, chemistry, and thermodynamics are well-established and are an essential part of our ordered existence. From moment to moment we depend upon the regularity

15. The only so-called secondary causes under consideration here are those in the area ot natural law. How human wills relate to divine causation will be discussed later.

16. E. L. Mascall, *Christian Theology and Natural Science* (New York: Ronald Press, 1956), p. 199.

17. William Burt Pope, *A Compendium of Christian Theology*, 3 ed. (Cleveland: Thomas amd Mattell, n.d.), I:439.

and predictability of the natural processes. God should never be thought of as a threat to their reality. In fact, the opposite is the case.

But exactly what *are* the "laws of nature"? There is no uniformly accepted answer to this question, but the two preferred possibilities usually center around *sequence* and *force*. Charles Hodge says that the "laws of nature" concept "either means an observed regular sequence of events, without any reference to the cause by which that regularity of sequence is determined; or it means a uniformly acting force in nature."[18] Mascall notes that science itself has vacillated between the concept of natural law as a kind of metaphysical causality of things and natural law as simply the invariable sequence of things.[19] It is easy to see that the regular and uniform sequence of things is an essential part of natural law. Some would say, however, that that is the extent of it. The so-called "laws of nature" are descriptive devices, not explanatory. They are merely the formalized results of our observations of what happens in nature. They only describe the orderly sequence of events in nature; they do not explain *why* things happen the way they do. But others would say that there is more to it than this. They see physical laws as providing a causal explanation of why things happen. The material universe is invested with certain forces such as gravity and electro-magnetism which cause matter to act in certain regular and predictable ways. The invariable sequences that we observe are the result of the operation of these causal forces.

It seems to me that the concept of uniform sequence is inadequate as the sole explanation of natural law. The concept of causality or force must also be included. It is not at all necessary that this lead to a view of physical determinism, though some have drawn such a conclusion.[20] Also, the "laws of nature" themselves are not equivalent to the causal forces; they are simply the verbalized descriptions of the way these forces act, or of the orderly results of the operation of these forces.

Even if we acknowledge that there are causal forces underlying the laws of nature, this is not the complete picture. We must still ask, why should there be such forces in the first place? What is their origin? What causes the causes? This leads to the next section.

---

18. Charles Hodge, *Systematic Theology* (Grand Rapids: Eerdmans reprint, n.d.), I:607.

19. E. L. Mascall, *Christian Theology and Natural Science*, pp. 197-198.

20. Ibid., p. 198.

Classical Theistic Explanations

Within the general scope of theism, several main views have been advanced as to how God is related to natural law. At one extreme is Deism. As this view is generally understood, God in the beginning created the universe and endowed it with the appropriate physical forces. Being a master craftsman, he made these forces self-sufficient and self-perpetuating. Thus after the initial creation God withdrew from the world, leaving the laws of nature to operate autonomously and without any further interference from him. These laws are thus the sole cause of what happens in the natural world. The biblical data concerning God's causal involvement in nature are seen as a poetic acknowledgement of his creatorship but nothing more.

At the opposite extreme is the view that God is the sole cause of the natural processes. There are no other forces at work; nature is animated by the power of God alone. The usual representative of this view is most versions of pantheism. In Stoicism, for example, the physical world as we observe it is the passive side of God's nature; but it is infused with the active side of his nature (the Primal Fire, the *logos*), which is the sole source of its motion. Other representatives of this view are sometimes found among theists themselves. John Wesley, in suggesting that God alone is the "true author of all the *motion* that is in the universe," declared, "All matter, of whatever kind it be, is absolutely and totally inert. It does not, cannot, in any case, move itself; and whenever any part of it seems to move, it is in reality moved by something else." Regarding the sun, moon, and stars, for example, "none of these move themselves: they are all *moved* every moment by the Almighty hand that made them."[21] If this view is held consistently, then all secondary causes are omitted and, as Mascall puts it, "what seems to be the activity of finite beings is, when we get behind the curtain, the lonely activity of God."[22]

A third view, one that has found general acceptance within many Protestant circles, is called concurrence (or sometimes concursus). This is the view that the processes of nature are fully (though not equally)

---

21. John Wesley, "Sermon LXXXII—Spiritual Worship," *Sermons on Several Occasions* (New York: G. Lane & C. B. Tippett, 1845), II:178-179. In an interesting echo of Stoicism, Wesley attributes all motion to the "ethereal fire" intermixed with everything, the fire itself being moved by the Universal Mind. See H. Orton Wiley, *Christian Theology* (Kansas City, Mo.: Beacon Hill Press, 1940), I:483.

22. E. L. Mascall, *Christian Theology and Natural Science*, p. 199.

caused by both God and natural laws. God as the primary cause is completely responsible for natural occurrences; but at the same time he works through natural laws as secondary causes, which may also be considered as fully responsible for what happens "naturally." This view is summarized in the following quotation:

> The same effect is produced not by God alone, nor by the creature alone, nor partly by God and partly by the creature, but *at the same time by God and the creature*, as one and the same total efficiency,—by God as the universal and first cause, and by the creature as the particular and second cause.[23]

As stated by Berkhof, concurrence means that "each deed is in its entirety both a deed of God and a deed of the creature." Though secondary causes are real, "God is immediately operative in every act of the creature." Everything that happens "is determined from moment to moment by the will of God." According to Berkhof, "In every instance the impulse to action and movement proceeds from God."[24] Francis Pieper, another representative of this doctrine, says this:

> . . . The operation of the means is not coordinate with the operation of God, but subordinate to it, and subordinate to that extent that the means work only that which God works through them, and they work only as long as God works.[25]

What creatures do "naturally," they do because of a continuous influx of God's power into them. Thus "the so-called 'laws of nature' are not something which differs from God's will and operation, but are God's will and operation itself in its relation to the existence and operation of the creatures."[26]

Though other views besides these have been suggested, these three are the principal ones and will give an adequate idea of how this whole issue of God's relation to natural laws has been approached. We will now proceed to an evaluation of these views and an attempt to

23. Revere Franklin Weidner, *Theologia, or the Doctrine of God*, p. 95. The quotation is actually from the seventeenth-century Lutheran theologian J. A. Quenstedt and is found (in the original Latin) in the 1715 Leipzig edition of his *Theologia*, I:760.

24. Louis Berkhof, *Systematic Theology* (London: Banner of Truth Trust, 1939), pp. 171-173. Though he is mainly discussing human beings as secondary causes, his comments represent his view of secondary causes as such.

25. Francis Pieper, *Christian Dogmatics*, I:487.

26. Ibid., I:487-489.

set forth what seems to me to be the understanding most consistent with biblical teaching.

The Relative Independence of Natural Laws

Regarding the views presented above, orthodox Christendom has generally been united in rejecting the first two, i.e., the extreme views that only God or only natural law is working efficiently in nature. The third view, however, has found wide acceptance. Indeed, it does embody a truth that must be firmly held, that "in their different modes of primary and secondary causality respectively, both God and created agents are active in all the processes of nature."[27] In my opinion, however, the doctrine of concurrence must be questioned because however much emphasis it puts on the reality of natural laws, these secondary causes are engulfed by and negated by the Primary Cause. Emil Brunner has called this doctrine "valueless and extremely doubtful," for one reason because it does not do justice to the independence of God's creatures.[28] W. B. Pope speaks of it as "only the shadow" of the continuous creation theory.[29]

These assessments seem valid to me. Though the advocates of concurrence take great pains to insist that the secondary causes are real causes and that their operations are genuine, their affirmations have a hollow sound and lead one to suspect, "Methinks thou dost protest too much." If no creature can act until God acts upon it, if "nothing created can originate action,"[30] if every natural process is determined each moment by the divine will, then how is this view really different from the second view mentioned above, i.e., that God is the sole cause of natural events? As the doctrine of concurrence is explained, there would seem to be no need of second causes at all *in the sense of causes*. It would seem more appropriate to speak of instruments or means, since an instrument is simply a tool in the hand of a user and need not contribute anything on its own. If we are going to do justice to the concept of cause in relation to laws of nature, if they are truly

27. E. L. Mascall, *Christian Theology and Natural Science*, p. 199.

28. Emil Brunner, *The Christian Doctrine of Creation and Redemption*, pp. 153-154.

29. W. B. Pope, *A Compendium of Christian Theology*, I:447. He says that the view is more acceptable "outside the sphere of moral action," i.e., when applied only to nature and not to human agents. In a later chapter we will discuss how the doctrine of concurrence relates to free will.

30. Charles Hodge, *Systematic Theology*, I:598.

going to be second *causes*, then the concept of concurrence will have to be rejected or at least modified considerably. We agree with Berkhof, of course, that "God is immediately operative in every act of the creature," but in what sense? Is it necessary for God to be the determining cause of every act or event, in order for him to be operative in it? Could his operation or influence be indirect rather than direct? Could the reality of God's role as creator and his role as preserver be a sufficient basis for calling natural processes God's deeds? Does his infinite and immediate *knowledge* of all these processes qualify him as being "immediately operative" in them? Could it be that the concept of concurrence is necessitated only by the doctrine of absolute foreordination?

As an alternative to the doctrine of concurrence I would suggest the idea of *relative independence* for nature and the forces which work within it. I am relating this concept only to the processes of nature, and not to its preservation (as will be explained below). That is, God's creatures are relatively independent in their actions but not in their being. In the very beginning God endowed his creatures with certain built-in laws or forces or (in the case of animals) instincts that enable them to function without his having to determine their every move. As Mascall says, "There is an order of nature in which real beings exert real activity, even though those beings and their activity depend wholly upon the incessant creative and conserving action of God."[31] This seems to be what W. B. Pope is getting at when he speaks of "the imparted quasi-independent forces of nature."[32] Miner Raymond says it specifically: "We conceive of God as having, in the beginning, invested matter with its natural forces and fixed the laws by which these forces are and must be regulated; so that the formula, 'God governs the world by general laws,' expresses a truth."[33] As Brunner says, "Nowhere does the Bible question the reality of the world as an independent reality which has been established by God."[34]

Lest there be those who are beginning to think that this sounds a lot like Deism, let me hasten to point out that we are talking about only a *relative* independence for the laws of nature. We are not saying that they "have efficiency in and of themselves" as if God had nothing

31. E. L. Mascall, *Christian Theology and Natural Science*, p. 199. I would not apply the word *incessant* to God's creative action.

32. W. B. Pope, *Compendium of Christian Theology*, I:439.

33. Miner Raymond, *Systematic Theology* (Cincinnati: Walden and Stowe, 1877), I:510-511.

34. Emil Brunner, *The Christian Doctrine of Creation and Redemption*, p. 153.

at all to do with their origin and operation. God is very much actively involved in nature. The natural processes are without a doubt the very works of God, as the many Bible texts discussed above have confirmed. As Sherlock says, "It is impossible to give any tolerable account of such texts as these, without confessing that God keeps the direction and government of natural causes in his own hands."[35] Most of these texts may be in the poetic books of the Bible, but poetic statements are not untrue statements. They express poetically what is profoundly true, that the works of nature are the works of God.

Now, specifically in what senses can we say that the works of nature are the works of God? There are three: (1) They are God's works in the sense that God is the Creator of the whole system of nature with its dependable forces and uniform processes. (2) They are God's works in the sense that he is the one who preserves the very being of nature. (3) They are God's works in the sense that he exercises a constant and intimate control over everything that happens.

First, God is the one who created the whole realm of nature. In his infinite wisdom he designed the highly versatile atomic structure of matter including the basic electro-magnetic forces that govern its operations. By his almighty power he brought it all into existence in completed detail, with the principle of order built therein. Natural law is thus God's own idea. He thought it, he decreed it, he created it. Thus, as Ramm says, "The laws of Nature are the laws of God."[36]

In this connection we may note a very interesting statement by Brunner, that "God has given the world its 'orders'."[37] This can be taken in two senses. On the one hand, via created natural laws, God has endowed the world with order and regularity. The constancy, reliability, and stability of nature, as Brunner points out, are an expression of the faithfulness of God.[38] The uniformity of nature was not just a discovery of modern science but has been a part of biblical teaching from the beginning, as Ramm notes.[39] Genesis 1 records that God made living creatures to reproduce their young according to their various orders or kinds (vv. 11, 12, 21, 24, 25). He made the sun and the moon to relate to the earth in such a way that there are orderly

35. William Sherlock, *A Discourse Concerning the Divine Providence*, p. 39.

36. Bernard Ramm, *The Christian View of Science and Scripture* (Grand Rapids: Eerdmans, 1956), p. 85.

37. Emil Brunner, *The Christian Doctrine of Creation and Redemption*, p. 154.

38. Ibid.

39. Bernard Ramm, *The Christian View of Science and Scripture*, p. 85.

times and seasons (Gen. 1:14-18; see 8:22). Jeremiah 31:35-36 refers to the "fixed order" which God established from the beginning: "Thus says the Lord, who gives the sun for light by day, and the fixed order of the moon and the stars for light by night . . . : 'If this fixed order departs from before Me, . . . then the offspring of Israel also shall cease from being a nation before Me forever.'" In Jeremiah 33:20 God speaks of his covenant for the day and his covenant for the night, so that day and night may have their appointed times.[40] These "orders" or natural laws that God has established are a kind of covenant with mankind that his creation will operate according to fixed patterns on which we can depend.

But, to go back to Brunner's statement, there is another sense in which "God has given the world its 'orders.'" He has ordered it or commanded it to do certain things, and he calls upon it to follow the orders which he has laid down for it. For instance, God has issued a decree to the sea, that it shall stay within its bounds (Jer. 5:22). He said to it, "Thus far you shall come, but no farther; and here shall your proud waves stop"! (Job 38:11; see Ps. 104:5-9). When the snow and hail fall and the wind blows, they are but fulfilling the decree of God (Ps. 148:8). When animals act according to their marvelous instincts, they are carrying out the commandments laid down for them by God (Job 39-41; see 39:27).

Thus the works of nature are the works of God because he created the system in the first place and gave the "orders" which are now being obeyed by his creatures. But this much could perhaps be said by a Deist; so we go on to the second sense in which the works of nature are the works of God, namely, he is the one who preserves the natural world in existence moment by moment, as was discussed at the beginning of this chapter. Here the world has no independence, relative or otherwise; it *absolutely* depends upon God for its being. If there is a "constant influx" of power from God to his creatures, this is where it will be found. In this sense "God is *world ground* of all things."[41] This absolutely rules out any deistic notion of God's withdrawal from nature once he has created it. Thus nature and natural law can never be completely autonomous, even in their on-going processes. John Macquarrie's statement must be totally rejected: "Science has shown us that the world can get along as a self-regulating

40. See ibid., p. 86, for a discussion of these passages.

41. Ibid., p. 84.

entity and we do not need to posit some other being beyond it."[42] Earlier we referred to Miner Raymond's statement that God invested matter with natural forces in such a way that the statement "God governs the world by general laws" expresses a truth. But then he says that this does not give the *whole* truth, "for we also conceive of God as everywhere present, and by an active agency 'upholding all things by the word of his power'; so that, in a sense, the formula, 'God does all that is done in the material world,' also expresses a truth."[43] With this statement we fully agree. We should note that God's preservation of the universe includes not only the upholding of the material stuff in existence, but also the preservation of the order of natural law itself. In preserving the world he preserves it as a world governed by the laws which he has ordained. God thus is the sustaining cause of the forces which cause the natural processes. Thus here is another sense in which the works of nature are the works of God.

Finally we would say that the works of nature are God's works because he exercises a continuous and intimate control over the whole of his creation, from the largest to the smallest detail. Through his omnipresence and omniscience he has a complete knowledge of all things. We might even say that Heisenberg's indeterminacy principle shatters itself against the infinity of God's knowledge, since God *can* discern at the same time both the speed and the location of an atomic particle—indeed, of *all* atomic particles! God not only knows everything that is happening; he cares about it. He watches not with indifference but with interest. In this sense he actually participates in the processes of nature. But the word *control* implies more than just knowledge and care. It implies a *superintending* care, to use W. B. Pope's term.[44] It implies the ability to interrupt and to change and to overrule. And this is exactly the case in God's relation to natural processes. He has given them a relative independence, and he permits them to flow according to the natural patterns which he has established; but he reserves the right to intervene in and to overrule those patterns if he so desires. In a sense everything that happens "has God's permission" to happen; he could prevent it if he wanted to. This is the true nature of his control even over natural processes, and such control is the essence of sovereignty.

---

42. John Macquarrie, *Principles of Christian Theology* (New York: Charles Scribner's Sons, 1966), p. 106.

43. Miner Raymond, *Systematic Theology*, I:511.

44. W. B. Pope, *A Compendium of Christian Theology*, I:449.

All of these factors together should make it very clear that whatever happens in nature is the work of God, even though nature itself has been granted a measure of independence. How this is so might be illustrated by two or three analogies, the limitations of which should be kept fully in mind. One very simple analogy is that of a person who sets a top or gyroscope spinning on a surface before him, with the option of nudging it or moving it as he wills. Another analogy comes from a completely different theological context but seems to have a comparable application here. It is the picture of the well-trained horse, usually used to illustrate the nature of inspiration. Here is one version of it:

> . . . You draw the lines to the right or the left as you see that the horse needs guidance; you check him when he would go too fast, and urge him forward when he would go too slow; but he usually keeps the road and maintains the desired gait and speed of his own accord; still your hand is ever on the lines, and its pressure on the bit is constantly felt, so that you are controlling the horse's movements when he is going most completely at his own will. Indeed, the horse is all the time going very much at his own will, and yet he is never without the control of the driver.[45]

A third and perhaps most appropriate analogy is that of a dedicated gardener. The gardener carefully prepares his ground, then he plants his seeds—flowers, vegetables, perhaps a few sunflowers just for the birds. He eagerly watches the tiny sprouts as they first break through the surface of the soil. He watches them grow and bud and bloom, and he keeps an eye on the tiny vegetables forming on his plants and vines. For the most part he can let nature take its course, but occasionally he must help the garden along. With a cultivator he keeps the soil loose. He chops out the weeds. He may even water it occasionally. He sprays a little here, and pulls off a bug there. He sticks some poles near the beans so the vines won't flow along the ground. He puts straw under the tomatoes and strawberries so they won't rot in contact with the soil. Then finally, when he presents a bouquet or a basket of vegetables to a friend, he is asked, "My, how nice! Did you grow these yourself?" And the gardener says, quite truthfully, "Yes, I did."

The world is God's garden. He planted it, and he is lovingly tending it as it grows. For the most part he, too, can "let nature take its course,"

---

45. J. W. McGarvey, *Evidences of Christianity* (Nashville: Gospel Advocate reprint, 1956), second section, p. 213.

though occasionally he must move something around here or there for special purposes, i.e., via special providence. But with regard to any part of it at any time, if anyone should ask, "Is God doing this?" we can truthfuly say, "Yes, he is."

A quotation from Miner Raymond sums up this point:

> . . . We conclude, then, as to God's government of the material world and of irresponsible beings—that is, as to what is called the natural government of God—that he governs by general laws, so that the conception of an investment of matter with certain forces operating under fixed laws is warranted by the facts in the case; and the supposition that, in a sense, with modifications, the machinery of the universe was so started in the beginning that it runs on of itself is a conception not wholly unwarranted. At the same time, God's will is sole originating force, and he is always every-where present, actively engaged in superintending, controlling, and subordinating to his will all the forces he has put in operation; so that we may truthfully conceive of him as doing whatever is done. He sends the rain, he clothes the field with grass, he gives strength to the sparrow's wing, and man goes forth to the labors of life in the strength that God giveth him. He holds the oceans in the hollow of his hand, and the winds obey his mandate. The brightness of the sun and the beauty of the moon are his. The mote that floats in the air, and the worlds that revolve in space, move as they are moved by his power—all things are subject to his will.[46]

The Value of This View

Some may wonder whether this issue is worth this much discussion, or whether it matters if we accept the concept of concurrence or not. Perhaps we should just forget natural laws altogether and say, with Tillett, that they are "meaningless and impotent, except as they are an expression of the uniform mode, according to which God preserves and governs the world."[47] It would be much simpler to agree with Ketcherside:

> Because of the continuity of nature there has grown up an idea that God placed it under certain laws which operate inexorably. But in Hebrews 1:3 Jesus is said to uphold all things by the power of His Word. . . . It is possible that Jesus may bring His power to bear upon

46. Miner Raymond, *Systematic Theology*, I:514-515.

47. Wilbur Fisk Tillett, *Providence, Prayer and Power* (Nashville: Cokesbury Press, 1926), p. 55.

> all things with consistency and unvarying application so that it *appears* to our human awareness as being governed and regulated by laws.[48]

We may recognize these statements by Tillett and Ketcherside as approaching the extreme view that God is the sole cause of everything that happens in nature. I will say at this point that if I had to choose between this view and the doctrine of concurrence, I would opt for the former. At least I can understand this view, whereas the concept of concurrence appears to me to be unintelligible. But the fact is that neither view does justice to the integrity of God's created order with its divinely bestowed (and thus relative) independence.

There are two specific advantages to viewing the natural world as being relatively independent and not the object of an absolute, all-determining foreordination. The first has to do with the way sin in the moral order has affected the natural order. The Bible teaches that sin's entrance into the world had a corrupting effect on the whole creation (Romans 8:20-22). It also teaches that there are times when, with God's permission, Satan himself manipulates the processes of nature. In Job 1:19 he brings a great wind that destroys Job's family. In Job 2:7 he is pictured as the one who "smote Job with sore boils from the sole of his foot to the crown of his head." Satan is also able to empower his followers with miracle-working ability, says II Thessalonians 2:9. Now, if God is the sole cause, or even the concurrent cause, of every natural process, it is very difficult to assimilate this data into the total picture. But if nature has been given a relative independence, it is more easily understood how it could be corrupted by sin and perverted by Satan.

A second advantage of this view is that it helps us to understand how the special providence of God is truly *special,* that is, how it is really different from his general providence. If we accept the concept of relative independence, then we can understand general providence as allowing the laws or forces of nature to function as the immediate cause of the natural processes. The Creator continues to preserve his creation, and to exercise a "superintending care" over it, but he does not immediately intervene. But at the same time God is *free* to intervene and to use the forces of nature by deflecting them or redirecting them in ways that accomplish his more specific purposes. This is special providence. He is free even to bypass these forces altogether, as in the case of a miracle. As Ramm says, "The God of the Bible is not manacled to the causal laws, nor is He a prisoner in his own creation."[49]

---

48. W. Carl Ketcherside, "The Dynamic of God," p. 12.
49. Bernard Ramm, *The Christian View of Science and Scripture,* p. 84.

As the sovereign ruler of nature he is free, and his freedom is the key to understanding providence. As Mascall says, "While conferring a certain degree of autonomy upon his universe and giving his creatures a certain freedom in sharing out that autonomy between them, God has reserved to himself the final decision as to whether a specified event occurs or not."[50] He can permit it to happen according to his established laws, or he can intervene to prevent it and cause another event to occur instead. Nature is relatively free, but God is absolutely free in this respect.

GENERAL PROVIDENCE AND HUMAN BEINGS

In this chapter we have concentrated primarily on God's general relationship to the on-going processes of nature. We have dealt very little with how providence relates to his moral creatures. The reason is that most of God's significant relationships with human beings fall under the heading of special providence and will be discussed in the next two chapters. Two brief comments must be made at this point, however.

First, God's general providence as discussed in this chapter does relate to human beings because and insofar as they are a part of nature. Since we are creatures, not only our bodies but also our spirits are preserved in existence by the hand of God. Also, the physical processes of our bodies, such as fetal growth (Ps. 139:13-16), cardio-vascular activity, and digestion, are governed by natural laws as outlined above. We should also remember that our general needs for nourishment and other necessities are usually provided by the normal operation of the system of nature (e.g., the rain, the sun, the seasons, the harvest).

Second, general providence also embraces in part the free-will decisions and actions of human beings. The reason for this is that the principle of *relative independence* applies to God's moral creatures in their exercise of free will just as much as, if not more than, it applies to the operation of physical laws in the realm of nature. In many if not most cases God permits human beings to make their own choices and chart their own courses without any special intervention. Of course he remains at all times in complete control and can intervene via special providence whenever he chooses, in ways consistent with the free will given to his creatures. This will be discussed in detail in chapter five.

---

50. E. L. Mascall, *Christian Theology and Natural Science*, pp. 200-201. I do not agree with the way Mascall proceeds to develop this thought. See the next footnote.

CONCLUSION

Our discussion of general providence makes it quite clear that biblical teaching stands in sharp contrast with the non-biblical views presented in the preceding chapter. Determinism is ruled out by the Creator's gift of relative independence to the natural world. God himself does not absolutely determine all events in the course of nature, but allows them to develop in accordance with physical laws. These physical laws themselves do not impose a determinism either, since God remains free to overrule them at any time.

Also excluded is Deism (the only relevant form of self-determinism, since theism is affirmed). This has been made very clear throughout the chapter.

Indeterminism is also excluded. God's creation of this specific world and his continuing superintendence of it are related to a specific goal and a particular purpose. A personal God rules the world, not impersonal chance. The view of natural law presented by Pollard (and even Monod) seems to be correct, namely, that even when natural law is allowed to operate without interference, it does not follow a rigid and necessary path but instead confronts many "forks in the road" where two or more alternatives are possible. The alternative taken may then be considered to be, in a sense, a matter of chance.[51] This by no means warrants a Monodian chance-universe, however, since God is in control and can always specify, if he wishes, which alternate pathway will be followed. Also, with regard to every event that actually takes place in the natural world, we must say that our sovereign God could have prevented it if he had wished. Thus there is no such thing as chance or luck or fortune in the strict sense of these words (i.e., "pure chance" or "blind luck"). References to luck, such as "Good luck!" or "Just lucky, I guess," are completely out of place in view of biblical providence.[52]

---

51. William Pollard, *Chance and Providence: God's Action in a World Governed by Scientific Law* (New York: Charles Scribner's Sons, 1958), pp. 60-61. Mascall presents a similar view of natural law, but suggests that at *every* such "fork in the road," God intervenes and makes the choice (*Christian Theology and Natural Science*, pp. 200-202). Such a view does not seem necessitated by biblical truth, however.

52. Ecclesiastes 9:11 says that "time and chance overtake them all." This is in no way a divine endorsement of a chance universe. It could be simply presenting the point of view of a cynical human being, which Ecclesiastes often seems to do. Or the word *chance* here could mean simply "occurrence," with the emphasis being on *evil* occurrence, just as the word *time* often signifies time of judgment. See verse 12; see also I Kings 5:4. See H. C. Leupold, *Exposition of Ecclesiastes* (Grand Rapids: Baker reprint, 1966), pp. 219-220.

It does not seem appropriate to close this chapter on such an academic note, and a negative one at that. A study of the biblical teaching concerning God's general providence, coupled with an even ordinary awareness of the wonders of the natural world, should fill our hearts with awe and praise. We should be completely overwhelmed by the thought of the wisdom and the greatness of the Sovereign Ruler of this amazing universe. Our worship and adoration are well expressed in the words of many hymns, two of which are as follows.

I sing the mighty power of God that made the mountains rise,
That spread the flowing seas abroad and built the lofty skies.
I sing the wisdom that ordained the sun to rule the day;
The moon shines full at His command, and all the stars obey.

I sing the goodness of the Lord that filled the earth with food;
He formed the creatures with His word and then pronounced them good.
Lord, how Thy wonders are displayed where'er I turn my eye:
If I survey the ground I tread or gaze upon the sky!

There's not a plant or flower below but makes Thy glories known;
And clouds arise and tempests blow by order from Thy throne;
While all that borrows life from Thee is ever in Thy care,
And everywhere that man can be, Thou, God, art present there.

—*Isaac Watts*

This is my Father's world, and to my listening ears
All nature sings, and round me rings the music of the spheres.
This is my Father's world! I rest me in the thought
Of rocks and trees, of skies and seas—His hand the wonders wrought.

This is my Father's world—the birds their carols raise;
The morning light, the lily white, declare their Maker's praise.
This is my Father's world! He shines in all that's fair;
In the rustling grass I hear Him pass—He speaks to me everywhere.

—*Maltbie D. Babcock*

Chapter Four

SPECIAL PROVIDENCE AND GOD'S PURPOSES

If we believed that natural law and human free will were the only forces operating to produce the events of the on-going world, our view would be little different from Deism in its practical effect. But our view does not have this limitation. We believe that there is a third force at work, one which controls and directs the others, namely, the direct action of God in the world. At times God's direct action bypasses his natural laws altogether and produces results that are usually called *miracles*. Much more often, however, God intervenes by acting upon natural laws and influencing human decisions so as to cause results that would not have occurred without the intervention but which are still within the possibilities of natural law itself and which do not violate the integrity of free will. This action is called *special providence*.

God's work of general providence is the same everywhere and at all times. All people, good and evil alike, are equally subject to it (Matt. 5:45). On the other hand, special providence differs from time to time and from place to place. It treats one group or person one way, and another group or individual in an entirely different way. Or it may affect the same people in different ways at different times.

The reason for this variation and this selectivity has to do with the purposes of God. In one sense God's primary purpose never changes, namely, to glorify his name in all things. This is the principal goal of creation itself, as well as of general and special providence. But on a secondary level God's purposes are not uniform and constant, mainly because they have to do with free will creatures such as human beings. This is all the more true now that sin has been introduced into the world. Though God's overall purpose for his creation remains the same, the manner in which he will accomplish it has been affected by the sin factor. God now has special purposes for certain groups and individuals, and special purposes call for special providence. Because God sovereignly rules all things through his special providence, we can have confidence that his purposes will not be thwarted, even though sin has entered. We need not fear, "for the Lord has both purposed and performed" (Jer. 51:12).

The goal of this chapter is to set forth the biblical data concerning God's providential accomplishment of his purposes. First we will briefly state his general purpose for the world in terms of the Kingdom of God. Then we will examine his providential control of men and nations as he worked out his purpose for the nation of Israel. Next we will see whether God has any special providence and purpose for individual believers as distinct from unbelievers. Finally we will look at the relation between special providence and natural law.

GOD'S PURPOSE FOR THE WORLD

The very concept of creation implies purpose. When one makes something, he usually has in mind a purpose for it. If he makes a cake, he usually intends for it to be eaten; and he proceeds to see that this purpose is carried out. If he makes a bookcase, he usually plans to fill it with books; thus he uses it in this way. When God created the universe, he did so for the purpose of manifesting his glory in and among his creatures and being glorified by them.[1] "For from Him and through Him and to Him are all things. To Him be the glory forever. Amen" (Rom. 11:36).

This fact is seen most clearly in the biblical teaching concerning the *kingdom of God,* a theme that appears prominently from the beginning of the Bible to its end. The Hebrew and Greek terms that are usually translated "kingdom" sometimes refer to the realm over which the king reigns, but most often and primarily they refer to his *reign* as such. Other English words that carry this meaning are *rule, royal power, dominion, kingship, lordship.* To stress the kingdom of God is to proclaim that God alone is ruler over the whole earth, that his lordship is supreme. To glorify God is to make him king in our own lives (Matt. 6:33) and to bring others to acknowledge his kingship.

Kingship and Creation

God's absolute and inalienable right to assert his kingship over all things is grounded in his *ex nihilo* creation of them. It is not the result of some kind of conquest over opposing powers, as if it were merely a case of "might makes right." No, God's lordship is based on the fact of creation: "The earth is the Lord's, and all it contains, the world, and those who dwell in it. For He has founded it upon the seas, and established it upon the rivers" (Ps. 24:1-2). His ruling authority is built into the very structures of existence; there is no way to alter the fact while anything exists.

---

1. See Jack Cottrell, *What the Bible Says About God the Creator* (Joplin, Mo.: College Press, 1983), pp. 124ff.

While absolute kingship belongs to God and always will by right of creation, God has created man in his own image so that he might exercise a kind of delegated authority over the rest of the material world. At the creation God said, "Let Us make man in Our image, according to Our likeness; and let them rule over the fish of the sea and over the birds of the sky and over the cattle and over all the earth." Then when God made them, male and female, he gave them this mandate: "Be fruitful and multiply, and fill the earth, and subdue it; and rule over the fish of the sea and over the birds of the sky, and over every living thing that moves on the earth" (Gen. 1:26-28). Thus man is "king of the earth," though he is a vassal of the Great King of all things.

We can say, then, that God reigns over the earth, but in a sense he reigns over it *through man*. When God delegated authority to man and commissioned him to rule, he was to a limited degree placing the future of the earth in the hands of man. And by giving him free will, God thus determined that man's rule would be genuine and not a sham. In a sovereign act of self-limitation God thus limited the way in which he would exercise his own authority over the world.

Kingship and the Fall

According to God's plan and purpose as established in the creation, his kingship over his creation and over man himself is best exercised through man's free and faithful service as God's vassal. This includes, of course, the vassal's complete acknowledgement of and submission to the absolute authority of God. But shortly after the inauguration of this arrangement, man came to the point where he no longer acknowledged the sovereignty of God. Instead he attempted to establish his own independent lordship, to "be like God" (Gen. 3:5). This was the Fall.

As a consequence of the Fall, there is a real sense in which God's own rule over man and therefore over the whole earth is interrupted (see Rom. 8:20). This is not the case in an absolute sense, of course, for in terms of inherent right and authority, God is always supreme. But it is true insofar as God's appointed vassal refuses to confess and submit to his supremacy. And by virtue of man's exalted position as king of the earth, God's relationship to the entire earth is affected by this refusal. Though man wants to be free from all authority and thinks he is free, he is actually a bondservant of sin (II Peter 2:19), a slave of death (Rom. 5:14, 17; Heb. 2:15), and a vassal of Satan. Thus in a real sense, by subverting man, Satan the usurper has now become prince or god of this world (John 12:31; 14:30; II Cor. 4:4).

Kingship and Redemption

As Absolute Ruler God could have asserted his kingship at the Fall in terms of sheer power in judgment and destruction. He has done this on several occasions since that time, but never on a completely universal scale,[2] since a universal destruction of all sinners would defeat his very purpose in creation. Thus God determined in eternity that his creation purpose would have to be worked out by means of *redemption* through Jesus Christ. The work of Jesus included atonement for man's rebellion against the sovereignty of God; and it included a crushing defeat of the usurpers—sin, death, and Satan—and a reestablishment of his own lordship through his resurrection from the dead.

Through Christ's redemptive work a way is thus opened for sinners to be restored to their intended relationship with the Sovereign Ruler in a free acknowledgement of his kingship. But now this acknowledgement and submission are directed not just to God as Creator, but to God as Creator and Redeemer in the person of Jesus Christ, God the Son. As the risen and conquering king he is the bearer of all authority (Matt. 28:18); he is our Lord and our God (John 20:28). It is the desire of the Father that all people should confess Jesus as Lord and thus fulfill the purpose of creation, to glorify God (Phil. 2:11). This is why the church's principal confession is (or should be) "Jesus is Lord."

Kingship and Consummation

Though the deity and lordship of Christ are sufficiently established in his resurrection, they are veiled in the incarnation and thus remain hidden to a degree throughout the church age. Thus during this age there are two groups: those who freely acknowledge his kingship and those who do not. These two groups co-exist now, as weeds and wheat exist together in a field (Matt. 13:30). But a day will come when God

2. The flood came close to this, but eight persons were saved by grace.

will reveal and establish his lordship in a final, miraculous, irresistible way, in the day of the revelation of Jesus Christ. At this time, in an act of judgment, he will establish his kingship by force over those who have not acknowledged it freely. At the same time those who have freely confessed and submitted to his kingship will finally enter into all the blessings of the unhindered reign of God (Rev. 11:15), while the created universe as a whole is cleansed and restored to its proper role in God's scheme of things (Rom. 8:21-23).

Kingship and Providence

Although it is not recognized by everyone, the fact is that God is the Sovereign Ruler and Lord of all. In the words of Hezekiah's prayer, "O Lord, the God of Israel, who art enthroned above the cherubim, Thou art the God, Thou alone, of all the kingdoms of the earth" (II Kings 19:15). King David blessed God with these words:

> Thine, O Lord, is the greatness and the power and the glory and the victory and the majesty, indeed everything that is in the heavens and the earth; Thine is the dominion, O Lord, and Thou dost exalt Thyself as head over all. Both riches and honor come from Thee, and Thou dost rule over all, and in Thy hand is power and might . . . (I Chron. 29:11-12).

He says in Psalm 22:28, "The kingdom is the Lord's, and He rules over the nations." Psalm 47:2 says, "For the Lord Most High is to be feared, a great King over all the earth." "The Lord reigns"; he is "the Lord of the whole earth," and "the Lord Most High over all the earth" (Ps. 97:1, 5, 9). "The Lord has established His throne in the heavens; and His sovereignty rules over all" (Ps. 103:19). "They shall speak of the glory of Thy kingdom, and talk of Thy power; to make known to the sons of men Thy mighty acts, and the glory of the majesty of Thy kingdom. Thy kingdom is an everlasting kingdom, and Thy dominion endures throughout all generations" (Ps. 145:11-13).

Because of his sovereign lordship God is able to work out his purpose for man and through men even when they are not aware of it. God's hand and God's purpose will prevail (Acts 4:28). Through his special providence he controls kings and kingdoms: "And it is He who changes the times and the epochs; He removes kings and establishes kings" (Dan. 2:21); "the Most High God is ruler over the realm of mankind, and . . . He sets over it whomever He wishes" (Dan. 5:21). His special providence also is in control of the smallest of events: "The lot is cast into the lap, but its every decision is from the Lord" (Prov. 16:33).

Thus there has never been any question that God will work out his purposes for his kingship, because his kingship itself is the very surety of it.

GOD'S PURPOSE FOR ISRAEL

The focal point of God's kingdom purpose is Jesus Christ. Because of sin's presence in the world, God chose to establish his kingship through the personal presence of the incarnate Logos, the Logos' atoning death, and his triumphant resurrection. Thus the coming of Jesus into the world was the hub of history, an event of such magnitude that no casual preparation for it would do. So what did God do to get the world ready for his coming? He chose one people from all the nations of the earth, and he worked with that people for century after century until there was a sufficient background and a sufficient expectation for the event itself.

Here, of course, we are talking about Israel. God's purpose for Israel, from the time he called Abraham until the time he called Mary, was to prepare for the first coming of Jesus into the world. Everything that happened to this nation from beginning to end was calculated and measured for this one thing: preparation. Practically all of the Old Testament, and the bulk of the Bible as a whole, are centered around this one theme: how God prepared the world for the coming of Christ.

God's dealings with Israel provide us with a massive amount of data concerning the way God is able to work in the world through special providence. This is true not just because the largest portion of Scripture deals with Israel, but also because of the special quality of God's relationship with his chosen people. Thus in this section the reader may begin to feel overwhelmed at the sheer bulk of references to God's control over the history of Israel and its neighbors. They are all included here, though, for that very reason: we *need* to be overwhelmed by the Old Testament's constant and unceasing testimony to the sovereignty of God in history. It is easy for us to ignore this part of Scripture altogether; and even when we read it we are apt to miss or take for granted this theme which runs like a connecting thread through every section of its literature—history, poetry, and prophecy alike.

This section will proceed as follows. First we will emphasize the fact of God's providential control over nations and individuals connected with Israel, including Israel itself. Then we will show how God's providential intervention, while directed toward the general purpose of preparing for the coming of Christ, has the more specific purposes of blessing on the one hand and punishing on the other. Finally we will stress the uniqueness of God's providential dealing with Israel.

God's Providence in Israel's History

In order to bring Israel to its appointed end it was necessary for God to exercise control not only over Israel but also over the nations around her. Sometimes this was done through miraculous means, as in the exodus from Egypt, but mostly it was accomplished through special providence. That God is able to do this cannot be doubted: "For the kingdom is the Lord's, and He rules over the nations" (Ps. 22:28). "The Lord nullifies the counsel of the nations; He frustrates the plans of the peoples" (Ps. 33:10). The following Bible references show how this was true throughout Israel's history. (The only passages used here are those which specifically refer to God's controlling hand in the events cited.)

First we may refer to the period of the conquest, when God enabled the people of Israel to conquer and drive out all the tribes of people inhabiting Canaan. As Nehemiah 9:24 addresses God, "So their sons entered and possessed the land. And Thou didst subdue before them the inhabitants of the land, the Canaanites, and Thou didst give them into their hand, with their kings, and the peoples of the land, to do with them as they desired." Joshua reminded the people that God had given them the land: "For the Lord has driven out great and strong nations from before you; and as for you, no man has stood before you to this day. One of your men puts to flight a thousand, for the Lord your God is He who fights for you, just as He promised you" (Josh. 23:9-10). An example of this is when God helped Israel to defeat the five kings of the Amorites with their armies by sending a lethal hailstorm: "And it came about as they fled from before Israel, while they were at the descent of Beth-horon, that the Lord threw large stones from heaven on them as far as Azekah, and they died; there were more who died from the hailstones than those whom the sons of Israel killed with the sword" (Josh. 10:11). (We are reminded of Job 38:22-23, when God asked Job, "Have you seen the storehouses of the hail, which I have reserved for the time of distress, for the day of war and battle?")

During the period of the Judges God's providence alternately favored Israel and abandoned her to her enemies, according to her faith or faithlessness. Nehemiah 9:27-28 says,

> . . . Therefore Thou didst deliver them into the hand of their oppressors who oppressed them, but when they cried to Thee in the time of their distress, Thou didst hear from heaven, and according to Thy great compassion Thou didst give them deliverers who delivered them from the hand of their oppressors. But as soon as they had rest, they did evil again before Thee; therefore Thou didst abandon them to the hand of their enemies, so that they ruled over them. When they cried again to Thee, Thou didst hear from heaven, and many times Thou didst rescue them according to Thy compassion . . . .

This pattern is repeated over and over in the book of Judges: "And Judah went up, and the Lord gave the Canaanites and the Perizzites into their hands" (Judg. 1:4). But then "the anger of the Lord burned against Israel, and He gave them into the hands of plunderers who plundered them; and He sold them into the hands of their enemies" (Judg. 2:14). But it did not so remain. As Ehud said in rallying Israel for battle, "Pursue them, for the Lord has given your enemies the Moabites into your hands" (Judg. 3:28). But then "the Lord sold them into the hand of Jabin king of Canaan" (Judg. 4:2), and later he "gave them into the hands of Midian" (Judg. 6:1). After seven years God chose Gideon to deliver Israel, and told him and his small army, "I will deliver you . . . . Arise, go down against the camp, for I have given it into your hands" (Judg. 7:7, 9). Nor was this the end of the cycle: see Judges 10:7; 13:1.

During the period of the monarchy Israel's situation was much improved, thanks to the providence of God. One of Saul's first acts was to lead his army against the Ammonites, concerning which he said, "Today the Lord has accomplished deliverance in Israel" (I Sam. 11:13). Perennial foes during this period were the Philistines, but God gave Israel dominance over them. As he said to David, "Arise, go down to Keilah, for I will give the Philistines into your hand" (I Sam. 23:4). On another occasion this exchange took place: "Then David inquired of the Lord, saying, 'Shall I go up against the Philistines? Wilt Thou give them into my hand?' And the Lord said to David, 'Go up, for I will certainly give the Philistines into your hand'" (II Sam. 5:19). On the other hand there were times when the situation was reversed. As the spirit of Samuel told the disobedient Saul, "Moreover the Lord will also give over Israel along with you into the hands of the Philistines . . . . Indeed the Lord will give over the army of Israel into the hands of the Philistines" (I Sam. 28:19). But during the time of David and Solomon God's providence gave peace so the temple could be built without distraction. As David told his people, "Is not the Lord your God with you? And has He not given you rest on every side?

For He has given the inhabitants of the land into my hand, and the land is subdued before the Lord and before His people. . . . Arise, therefore, and build the sanctuary of the Lord God" (I Chron. 22:18-19).

The period of the divided monarchy was mostly a time of tragedy for God's people. God himself brought about the division: "This thing has come from Me," he said (I Kings 12:24; see II Kings 17:21). On occasion he made both kingdoms vulnerable to outside enemies. He gave Judah over to Shishak of Egypt: "Thus says the Lord, 'You have forsaken Me, so I also have forsaken you to Shishak'" (II Chron. 12:5). Later he gave them to other enemies: "Then the Lord stirred up against Jehoram the spirit of the Philistines and the Arabs who bordered the Ethiopians; and they came against Judah and invaded it" (II Chron. 21:16-17). The Lord also gave Judah and King Ahaz into the hands of the Syrians (II Chron. 28:5, 9). Nor did the northern tribes escape: "So the anger of the Lord was kindled against Israel, and He gave them continually into the hand of Hazael king of Syria, and into the hand of Ben-hadad the son of Hazael" (II Kings 13:3). He even gave them over to their brethren to the south: "And when the men of Judah raised the war cry, then it was that God routed Jeroboam and all Israel before Abijah and Judah. And when the sons of Israel fled before Judah, God gave them into their hand" (II Chron. 13:15-16).

There were times when God gave the victory to his people. When Asa, king of Judah, faced a huge Ethiopian army, he prayed this prayer of faith in God's providence: "Lord, there is no one besides Thee to help in the battle between the powerful and those who have no strength; so help us, O Lord our God, for we trust in Thee." In response, "The Lord routed the Ethiopians before Asa and before Judah" (II Chron. 14:11-12). God also came to Uzziah's aid at times: "And God helped him against the Philistines, and against the Arabians who lived in Gur-baal, and the Meunites" (II Chronicles 26:7).

The northern tribes were finally abandoned by God to the Assyrians. "'Therefore, I will make you go into exile beyond Damascus,' says the Lord" (Amos 5:27). "'For behold, I am going to raise up a nation against you, O house of Israel,' declares the Lord God of hosts, 'and they will afflict you from the entrance of Hamath to the brook of the Arabah'" (Amos 6:14). And thus it happened as Amos prophesied: "So the Lord was very angry with Israel, and removed them from His sight; none was left except the tribe of Judah. . . . And the Lord rejected all the descendants of Israel and afflicted them and gave them into the hand of plunderers, until He had cast them out of His sight" (II Kings 17:18, 20).

But God was not through with Assyria yet. He later brought them against Judah itself, though not with the same finality as against Israel. Isaiah prophesied to Ahaz,

> . . . The Lord will bring on you, on your people, and on your father's house such days as have never come since the day that Ephraim separated from Judah, the king of Assyria. And it will come about in that day, that the Lord will whistle for the fly that is in the remotest part of the rivers of Egypt, and for the bee that is in the land of Assyria. . . . In that day the Lord will shave with a razor, hired from regions beyond the Euphrates (that is, with the king of Assyria), the head and the hair of the legs; and it will also remove the beard. . . . (Isa. 7:17-20).

"Now therefore, behold, the Lord is about to bring on them the strong and abundant waters of the Euphrates, even the king of Assyria and all his glory" (Isa. 8:7). God likened Assyria to an axe or a club that he was wielding in his hand (Isa. 10:15); "the rod of My anger and the staff in whose hands is My indignation," he called them (Isa. 10:5). The fact is recorded in II Chronicles 33:11, "Therefore the Lord brought the commanders of the army of the king of Assyria against them, and they captured Manasseh."

But God did not let Assyria escape; his providence brought about their destruction, too. After using them against Judah he says,

> "I will punish the fruit of the arrogant heart of the king of Assyria and the pomp of his haughtiness." For he has said, "By the power of my hand and by my wisdom I did this . . . ." Therefore the Lord, the God of hosts, will send a wasting disease among his stout warriors; and under His glory a fire will be kindled like a burning flame. . . . And it will burn and devour his thorns and his briars in a single day (Isa. 10:12-17).

"My anger will be directed to their destruction," God says (Isa. 10:25).

The same pattern was repeated with Babylon and the southern tribes. God warned them about what he was going to do: "Behold, I am bringing such calamity on Jerusalem and Judah, that whoever hears of it, both his ears shall tingle. . . . And I will abandon the remnant of My inheritance and deliver them into the hand of their enemies" (II Kings 21:12, 14). "Behold, I bring evil on this place and on its inhabitants," he said (II Kings 22:16). When Habakkuk cried out to God about the wicked conditions within Judah, God replied that he was devising a remedy: he was bringing the Chaldeans (Babylonians) against the land. "Look among the nations! Observe! Be astonished! Wonder! Because I am doing something in your days—you would not believe if you were told. For behold, I am raising up the Chaldeans" (Hab. 1:5-6). He gave this same message to the people through

Jeremiah: "Behold, I am bringing a nation against you from afar . . . . And they will devour your harvest and your food; they will devour your sons and your daughters" (Jer. 5:15, 17). "I will send to Nebuchadnezzar king of Babylon, My servant, and will bring them against this land, and against its inhabitants, and against all these nations round about; and I will utterly destroy them" (Jer. 25:9). Babylon is called "a golden cup in the hand of the Lord" by which he intoxicated all the earth (Jer. 51:7). God says to Babylon, "You are My war-club, My weapon of war; and with you I shatter nations, and with you I destroy kingdoms" (Jer. 51:20). Ezekiel brings the same warning: "Mountains of Israel, listen to the word of the Lord God! Thus says the Lord God to the mountains, the hills, the ravines and the valleys: 'Behold, I Myself am going to bring a sword on you, and I will destroy your high places" (Ezek. 6:3). "Behold I will arouse your lovers against you, from whom you were alienated, and I will bring them against you from every side: the Babylonians and all the Chaldeans . . . . And I shall commit the judgment to them, and they will judge you according to their customs. . . . I will give you into the hand of those whom you hate" (Ezek. 23:22-24, 28).

God's providence brought these things to pass, as is recorded in II Kings 24:2-3:

> . . . And the Lord sent against him bands of Chaldeans, bands of Syrians, bands of Moabites, and bands of Ammonites. So He sent them against Judah to destroy it, according to the word of the Lord, which He had spoken through His servants the prophets. Surely at the command of the Lord it came upon Judah, to remove them from His sight . . . .

II Chronicles 36:17 says, "Therefore He brought up against them the king of the Chaldeans . . . ; He gave them all into his hand." When the people were carried off into Babylon God said, "I have sent you into exile" (Jer. 29:4, 7). But he promised to bring them back:

> . . . For thus says the Lord, "When seventy years have been completed for Babylon, I will visit you and fulfill My good word to you, to bring you back to this place. . . . And I will be found by you," declares the Lord, "and I will restore your fortunes and will gather you from all the nations and from all the places where I have driven you," declares the Lord, "and I will bring you back to the place from where I sent you into exile" (Jer. 29:10, 14).

Just as surely as God delivered Israel from captivity, so did he punish the captors: "Then it will be when seventy years are completed I will punish the king of Babylon and that nation . . . for their iniquity, and the land of the Chaldeans; and I will make it an everlasting desolation" (Jer. 25:12; see verses 13-14). "The Lord has opened His armory and has brought forth the weapons of His indignation, for it is a work of the Lord God of hosts in the land of the Chaldeans" (Jer. 50:25).

> Thus says the Lord: "Behold, I am going to arouse against Babylon and against the inhabitants of Leb-kamai the spirit of a destroyer. And I shall dispatch foreigners to Babylon that they may winnow her and may devastate her land . . . . For this is the Lord's time of vengeance; He is going to render recompense to her (Jer. 51:1-2, 6).

The specific nation to be used against Babylon is named by the prophets: "Behold, I am going to stir up the Medes against them" (Isa. 13:17). "Sharpen the arrows, fill the quivers! The Lord has aroused the spirit of the king of the Medes, because His purpose is against Babylon to destroy it; for it is the vengeance of the Lord, vengeance for His temple" (Jer. 51:11).[3]

Thus we see that when God has a purpose to fulfill, he can control the fortunes of nations according to his will. This is amply demonstrated in the history of the nation Israel and of the nations that surrounded her. But one point that needs to be emphasized now is that nations are composed of individuals; and usually a few key individuals, such as kings, make the decisions that affect whole nations. So it would seem that if God is going to use nations, he must be able to influence and control individuals. And that is exactly what God does, according to the testimony of Scripture. The Bible teaches that God exercises a general control over individual men and women. He gives life: "He Himself gives to all life and breath and all things" (Acts 17:25). "In Him we live" (Acts 17:28). He can also take a life if he desires: "The Lord kills and makes alive" (I Sam. 2:6). "If He should determine to do so, if He should gather to Himself His spirit and His breath, all flesh would perish together, and man would return to dust" (Job 34:14-15). It happened, for example, that "the Lord struck the child that Uriah's widow bore to David, so that he was very sick," and on the seventh day he died (II Sam. 12:15, 18). That is why we should always say, "If the Lord wills, we shall live" (James 4:15).

Not only are our very lives in God's hand, but so also are all our deeds. James 4:15 says that we should say, "If the Lord wills, we

3. Other nations specifically mentioned as the objects of God's providence are Egypt (Isa. 19:2, 12) and Tyre (Ezek. 28:7), though Tyre was not actually a nation but a city.

shall live *and also do this or that*" (italics added). Acts 17:28 says, "In Him we live *and move*" (italics added). God is the one "in whose hand are your life-breath and your ways" (Dan. 5:23). "Righteous men, wise men, and their deeds are in the hand of God," says Ecclesiastes 9:1. The life and experiences of Job are an extended example of this truth. The ways God prepared great men for service to him are also examples, e.g., Moses (Ps. 105:26), David (Ps. 139:16), Jeremiah (Jer. 1:5), and Paul (Gal. 1:15). If he wants to he can "seal the hand of every man" (Job 37:7) and thus prevent him from carrying out his intended plan. "He breaks in pieces mighty men without inquiry, and sets others in their place" (Job 34:24). "The Lord makes poor and rich; He brings low, He also exalts" (I Sam. 2:7). "But God is the Judge; He puts down one, and exalts another" (Ps. 75:7). "The Most High God is ruler over the realm of mankind"; therefore "He sets over it whomever He wishes" (Dan. 5:21). "The king's heart is like channels of water in the hand of the Lord; He turns it wherever He wishes" (Prov. 21:1).

We can see how this general teaching of Scripture is illustrated again and again in the history of Israel. Going all the way back to the infancy of the nation, we see God's hand at work in the life of Joseph. We are told that "the Lord was with him; and whatever he did, the Lord made to prosper" (Gen. 39:23; see 39:2-3, 21). In his own suffering and exaltation Joseph discerned the providence of God at work to preserve his people from the danger of famine. From his exalted station in Egypt he addressed his guilt-stricken brothers as follows (Gen. 45:5-9):

> . . . And now do not be grieved or angry with yourselves, because you sold me here; for God sent me before you to preserve life. For the famine has been in the land these two years, and there are still five years in which there will be neither plowing nor harvesting. And God sent me before you to preserve for you a remnant in the earth, and to keep you alive by a great deliverance. Now, therefore, it was not you who sent me here, but God; and He has made me a father to Pharaoh and lord of all his household and ruler over all the land of Egypt. Hurry and go up to my father, and say to him, "Thus says your son Joseph, 'God has made me lord of all Egypt; come down to me, do not delay. . . .'"

Commenting on their own evil treatment of him, Joseph said, "And as for you, you meant evil against me, but God meant it for good in order to bring about this present result, to preserve many people alive" (Gen. 50:20).

At the Exodus and afterward God was able to accomplish his purposes by "hardening the heart" of various individuals. This is stressed with regard to Pharaoh: "Then the Lord said to Moses, 'Go to Pharaoh, for I have hardened his heart and the heart of his servants, that I may perform these signs of Mine among them.' . . . But the Lord hardened Pharaoh's heart, and he did not let the sons of Israel go" (Exod. 10:1, 20).[4] God also hardened the hearts of the Egyptian army so that they would pursue the Israelites through the Red Sea, to their doom (Exod. 14:17). Later Moses reminds the people that God had had his way with another king: "But Sihon king of Heshbon was not willing for us to pass through his land; for the Lord your God hardened his spirit and made his heart obstinate, in order to deliver him into your hand, as he is today" (Deut. 2:30). Concerning the Canaanite kings at the time of the conquest Joshua 11:20 says, "For it was of the Lord to harden their hearts, to meet Israel in battle in order that he might utterly destroy them, that they might receive no mercy, but that he might destroy them, just as the Lord had commanded Moses."

Later on when God wanted to use the surrounding nations to chastise Israel, his providence touched their kings in other ways. Judges 3:12 says that "the Lord strengthened Eglon the king of Moab against Israel, because they had done evil in the sight of the Lord." Then, from time to time, "The Lord raised up judges who delivered them from the hands of those who plundered them" (Judg. 2:16). He also promised to "raise up for Myself a faithful priest" to replace the corrupt sons of Eli (I Sam. 2:35).

As the period of the monarchy dawns God says, "I will send you a man" for your first king, namely, Saul (I Sam. 9:16). Later God rejected Saul from being king over Israel (I Sam. 15:26; 16:1; 28:17). Instead, God told Samuel, "I have selected a king for Myself" from among the sons of Jesse, namely, David (I Sam. 16:1). He told David, "I took you from the pasture, from following the sheep, that you should be ruler over My people Israel" (II Sam. 7:8; see I Sam. 13:14). For King Solomon's rule, the Lord gave him "a wise and discerning heart" (I Kings 3:12); he gave him "wisdom and very great discernment and breadth of mind" (I Kings 4:29). Nevertheless God told Solomon that because of his sin, "I will surely tear the kingdom from you, and will give it to your servant" (I Kings 11:11; see verses 31, 35). He raised up adversaries against Solomon (I Kings 11:14, 23).

4. Other references to God's hardening Pharaoh's heart are Exodus 4:21; 7:3; 9:12; 10:27; 11:10; 14:4, 8.

When the kingdom divided God was still in control. He said to the first king of the northern tribes, Jeroboam, "I exalted you from among the people and made you leader over My people Israel, and tore the kingdom away from the house of David and gave it to you" (I Kings 14:7-8). Still God declared that he would overthrow Jeroboam and raise up another king (I Kings 14:14). Later he said to one of Jeroboam's successors, Baasha, "I exalted you from the dust and made you leader over My people Israel" (I Kings 16:2). At another time God permitted a deceiving spirit to entice King Ahab into battle, where he perished (I Kings 22:19-35). God later dealt in a similar way with Sennacherib, king of Assyria, in order to deliver Judah from his hand: "Behold, I will put a spirit in him so that he shall hear a rumor and return to his own land. And I will make him fall by the sword in his own land" (II Kings 19:7; see verses 36-37). Here are God's words to Sennacherib: "Because of your raging against Me, and because your arrogance has come up to My ears, therefore I will put My hook in your nose, and My bridle in your lips, and I will turn you back by the way which you came" (I Kings 19:28). Some years earlier God had "stirred up the spirit of Pul, king of Assyria, even the spirit of Tilgath-pilneser king of Assyria," to go against the northern kingdom (I Chron. 5:26).[5]

In the book of Daniel we read how God was in control of the monarchy of Nebuchadnezzar, king of Babylon. "The Most High God granted sovereignty, grandeur, glory, and majesty to Nebuchadnezzar" (Dan. 5:18). But in order to tame the king's pride, God took away his kingship and gave him a peculiar madness for a fixed period:

> King Nebuchadnezzar, to you it is declared: sovereignty has been removed from you, and you will be driven away from mankind, and your dwelling place will be with the beasts of the field. You will be given grass to eat like cattle, and seven periods of time will pass over you, until you recognize that the Most High is ruler over the realm of mankind, and bestows it on whomever He wishes (Dan. 4:31-32).

It worked, too. When the king was restored to his normal mind, he acknowledged the Most High as the Sovereign Ruler of all (Dan. 4:34-37).

A final example of God's providential work in the lives of individuals is perhaps the most remarkable of all, namely, his use of Cyrus, the king of Persia who conquered Babylon and permitted the Jews to

5. Some translations spell this name Tiglath-Pileser.

return to their homeland. Over 150 years before Cyrus' reign God had specifically named him as his instrument for the restoration and the rebuilding of Jerusalem. He prophesied through Isaiah,

> . . . "It is I who says of Cyrus, 'He is My shepherd! And he will perform all My desire.' And he declares of Jerusalem, 'She will be built,' and of the temple, 'Your foundation will be laid.'" Thus says the Lord to Cyrus His anointed, whom I have taken by the right hand, to subdue nations before him, and to loose the loins of kings; to open doors before him so that gates will not be shut: "I will go before you and make the rough places smooth . . . . For the sake of Jacob My servant, and Israel My chosen one, I have also called you by your name; I have given you a title of honor though you have not known Me. . . . I will gird you, though you have not known Me; that men may know from the rising to the setting of the sun that there is no one besides Me. . . . I have aroused him in righteousness, and I will make all his ways smooth; he will build My city, and will let My exiles go free, without any payment or reward," says the Lord of hosts (Isa. 44:28—45:13).

In fulfillment of this prophecy "the Lord stirred up the spirit of Cyrus king of Persia" so that he sent out a proclamation permitting the Jews to return to Jerusalem to rebuild the city and the temple (Ezra 1:1-3).[6]

This concludes the survey of God's providence in Israel's history. The point has been to emphasize the fact that God is the one whose will is being worked through these events. *God* is the one who has done these things. God speaks in the first person singular: "I will deliver you . . . I will give the Philistines into your hand . . . this thing has come from me . . . I will make you go into exile . . . I am going to raise up a nation against you . . . I am about to remove you from the face of the earth . . . I Myself shall war against you with an outstretched hand and a mighty arm . . . I send it . . . I will punish the king of Assyria . . . I am going to make an end of them by the sword, famine and pestilence . . . I am bringing calamity on Jerusalem . . . I bring evil on this place . . . I am doing something . . . I am raising up the Chaldeans . . . I will send to Nebuchadnezzar . . . I am bringing a nation against you . . . I shatter nations . . . I destroy kingdoms . . . I Myself am going to bring a sword on you . . . I will bring them against you . . . I have sent into exile . . . I will bring you back . . . I shall dispatch foreigners to Babylon . . . I am going to stir up the Medes against them . . . I will put My hook in your

6. After the work of rebuilding had begun, God "turned the heart of the king of Assyria toward them to encourage them in the work" (Ezra 6:22), and he put it in Artaxerxes' heart to help them also (Ezra 7:27).

nose . . . I have selected a king . . . I will tear the kingdom from you . . . I have done it . . . I am doing it . . . I will do it."

The biblical writers and others likewise attribute the action to God. "You meant evil against me, but God meant it for good. The battle is not yours but God's." God killed Saul and gave the kingdom to David.[7] God sent Joseph.[8] God sent Moses.[9] God gives and God takes away.[10] God drives out great nations. God gave Israel into their enemies' hands. God struck David's child. God hardened Pharaoh's heart. God desired the death of Eli's sons. It is a work of the Lord God of Hosts. God did it. God is doing it. God will do it.

Cyrus is God's shepherd; he will do what God desires. Babylon is God's warclub, God's weapon for shattering nations. Assyria is God's razor, God's staff, the rod of God's anger. God uses people and nations to bring about his purposes for Israel. His sovereignty as Ruler over all of history is thereby demonstrated and magnified.

The Immediate Ends of Providence

The ultimate goal of all of God's works is the glory of his name. His specific purpose for Israel was to prepare for the coming of the King of Glory, Jesus. In the accomplishment of these more comprehensive purposes, God's works of special providence regarding Israel were directed toward more immediate or proximate ends. These may be summed up under two headings, i.e., either blessing or punishment.

Of course, God's general providence is a constant source of blessing, as he does good and gives rain from heaven and fruitful seasons, filling our hearts with food and gladness (Acts 14:17). But his special providence gives special blessings, as in the case of Israel. Sometimes God gave blessing in answer to prayer. He had closed Hannah's womb (I Sam. 1:5), but Hannah prayed fervently that he would give her a son (I Sam. 1:10ff.). "And the Lord remembered her," and she conceived and gave birth to Samuel (I Sam. 1:19-20). In the midst of a fatal illness King Hezekiah prayed for healing, and God answered: "I have heard your prayer, I have seen your tears; behold, I will add fifteen years to your life" (Isa. 38:1-5).

7. I Chronicles 10:14.
8. Psalm 105:17.
9. Psalm 105:26.
10. Job 1:21.

Quite often God's special blessings were a reward for faithful living. This was true in the lives of individuals. God blessed the household of Obed-edom for sheltering the ark of the covenant (II Sam. 6:11). He told Solomon he would prolong his days if he walked in God's ways and kept God's commandments (I Kings 3:14). Such conditional blessings were also offered to the nation as a whole. Prior to their crossing over the Jordan River into the promised land, God told the Israelites:

> . . . And it shall come about, if you listen obediently to my commandments which I am commanding you today, to love the Lord your God and to serve Him with all your heart and all your soul, that "I will give the rain for your land in its season, the early and late rain, that you may gather in your grain and your new wine and your oil. And I will give grass in your fields for your cattle, and you shall eat and be satisfied" (Deut. 11:13-15).

This basic promise is expanded in Deuteronomy 28:1-14. On the condition of their obedience God promised to give the children of Israel abundant prosperity, protection from their enemies, and a position of prominence among the nations.

In a similar way, blessings were sometimes bestowed as the result of a proper response to chastisement, namely, repentance. The return from exile in Babylon is a primary example of this (Jer. 29:10, 14). Another example is the promise of relief from the locust plague and famine described in Joel's prophecy. In anticipation of his people's repentance God promised to remove the locusts and renew the land.

> . . . So rejoice, O sons of Zion, and be glad in the Lord your God; for He has given you the early rain for your vindication. And He has poured down for you the rain, the early and latter rain as before. And the threshing floors will be full of grain, and the vats will overflow with the new wine and oil. Then I will make up to you for the years that the swarming locust has eaten, the creeping locust, the stripping locust, and the gnawing locust, My great army which I sent among you. And you shall have plenty to eat and be satisfied, and praise the name of the Lord your God, who has dealt wondrously with you; then My people will never be put to shame (Joel 2:23-26).

At times God blessed his people simply because it furthered his purposes to do so. For this reason God was with Joseph and caused him to prosper (Gen. 39:2-3, 23). Nehemiah perceived that the hand of God was with him and was favorable toward him in his project of rebuilding the walls of Jerusalem (Neh. 2:8, 18). "The God of heaven will give us success," he said (Neh. 2:20). God frustrated the plans of those who tried to interfere (Neh. 4:14); "they lost their confidence; for they recognized that this work had been accomplished with the help of our God" (Neh. 6:16).

The theme that occurs more frequently in the Old Testament is the exercise of special providence for the purpose of punishment. Sometimes the punishment is pure retribution, but always it is designed to chastise and to correct. Even if those receiving the punishment do not receive correction thereby (as in the case of those put to death), those who hear of it may do so.

We know that God chastens, disciplines, or corrects his people for their own good. Proverbs 3:11-12 says, "My son, do not reject the discipline of the Lord, or loathe His reproof, for whom the Lord loves He reproves, even as a father, the son in whom he delights." Solomon knew this principle well, for God had already said concerning him, "I will be a father to him and he will be a son to Me; when he commits iniquity, I will correct him with the rod of men and the strokes of the sons of men" (II Sam. 7:14). This, I believe, refers to some of the ways God uses special providence for the purpose of correction; he also uses natural elements to this end. There are numerous examples of these in the life of Israel. When the children of Israel needed to be taught the error of their ways, the prophet Samuel said to them,

> . . . "Is it not the wheat harvest today? I will call to the Lord, that He may send thunder and rain. Then you will know and see that your wickedness is great which you have done in the sight of the Lord by asking for yourselves a king." So Samuel called to the Lord, and the Lord sent thunder and rain that day; and all the people greatly feared the Lord and Samuel (I Sam. 12:17-18).

At other times God withheld rain as a stimulus to repentance: "Therefore the showers have been withheld, and there has been no spring rain. Yet you had a harlot's forehead; you refused to be ashamed" (Jer. 3:3). In Amos 4:4-11 the prophet Amos lists a number of ways in which God tried to bring his people to repentance, but the people were stubbornly rebellious. "I gave you also cleanness of teeth . . . and lack of bread"—famine, "yet you have not returned to Me," says the Lord. I withheld the rain in some of your cities, "yet you have not returned to Me." I smote you with scorching wind, mildew, caterpillars, and plague, "yet you have not returned to Me." I almost overthrew you like Sodom and Gomorrah, "yet you have not returned to Me," declares the Lord.

The Babylonian captivity was a lesson to the nation of Israel—a harsh and severe lesson, but a lesson nonetheless. As Jeremiah reflected on the ruins of Jerusalem, he concluded that God "does not afflict willingly, or grieve the sons of men"; but still he knew that God had brought it about: "Who is there who speaks and it comes to pass, unless the Lord has commanded it? Is it not from the mouth of the Most High that both good and ill go forth?" (Lam. 3:33, 37-38). Then he exhorts his people to learn their lesson and repent: "Why should any living mortal, or any man, offer complaint in view of his sins? Let us examine and probe our ways, and let us return to the Lord" (Lam. 3:39-40).

Following their return from captivity, when reconstruction of the temple had been interrupted by the selfish pursuits of the people, God sent them many messages that went unheeded until Haggai came with personal rebuke:

> . . . You have sown much, but harvest little; you eat, but there is not enough to be satisfied; you drink, but there is not enough to become drunk; you put on clothing, but no one is warm enough; and he who earns, earns wages to put into a purse with holes." Thus says the Lord of hosts, "Consider your ways! Go up to the mountains, bring wood and rebuild the temple, that I may be pleased with it and be glorified," says the Lord. "You look for much, but behold, it comes to little; when you bring it home, I blow it away. Why?" declares the Lord of hosts, "Because of My house which lies desolate, while each of you runs to his own house. Therefore, because of you the sky has withheld its dew, and the earth has withheld its produce. And I called for a drought on the land, on the mountains, on the grain, on the new wine, on the oil, on what the ground produces, on men, on cattle, and on all the labor of your hands" (Hag. 1:6-11).

The people finally saw the point and proceeded to rebuild the temple.[11]

In quite a number of cases it seems that God's providence was for punishment in the strict sense of the word; God brought disaster on sinners because they deserved it. This is seen most clearly where God punished the wicked with death. The evil sons of Eli died in battle against the Philistines, "for the Lord desired to put them to death" (I Sam. 2:25; 4:11). Nabal was an enemy of David; "it happened that the Lord struck Nabal, and he died" (I Sam. 25:38). The Lord gave a disobedient prophet to a lion, which tore him and killed him (I Kings 13:26). When rowdy youths taunted Elisha, he called for a curse from

11. Two cases of special providence for correction outside Israel are Nebuchadnezzar (Dan. 4:25-37) and Egypt (Isa. 19:1-22).

the Lord upon them. "Then two female bears came out of the woods and tore up forty-two lads of their number" (II Kings 2:24). To Hananiah, another disobedient prophet, the Lord said, "Behold, I am about to remove you from the face of the earth. This year you are going to die, because you have counseled rebellion against the Lord" (Jer. 28:16).

Sometimes the Lord punished a sinner by bringing death and disaster on those under his care. David's sin with Bathsheba was punished by the death of the child: "Then the Lord struck the child that Uriah's widow bore to David" (II Sam. 12:15). In addition God said, "Behold, I will raise up evil against you from your own household; I will even take your wives before your eyes, and give them to your companion, and he shall lie with your wives in broad daylight. . . . I will do this thing" (II Sam. 12:11-12). Because of his great wickedness Elijah told King Jehoram, "Behold, the Lord is going to strike your people, your sons, your wives, and all your possessions with a great calamity; and you will suffer severe sickness, a disease of your bowels, until your bowels come out because of the sickness, day by day." And so it happened, after being overrun by his enemies and after two years of sickness, Jehoram died in great pain (II Chron. 21:13-19). The sins of kings often brought punishment upon their entire households, as in the case of Jeroboam (I Kings 14:10ff.), Baasha (I Kings 16:3-4), and Ahab (I Kings 21:29).

On quite a number of occasions God saw fit to punish the whole nation through his special providence. Twice this happened because of the king's sin. God sent a three-year famine "for Saul and his bloody house, because he put the Gibeonites to death" (II Sam. 21:1). A sin by David brought a pestilence upon Israel in which seventy thousand perished (II Sam. 24:15). More often, though, a common guilt brought a common punishment. Even before they entered the promised land Moses warned the people what was in store for them if they violated their covenant with God and became disobedient. "The Lord will send upon you curses, confusion, and rebuke, in all you undertake to do, until you are destroyed and until you perish quickly, on account of the evil of your deeds, because you have forsaken Me" (Deut. 28:20). The catalogue of potential horrors included famine, drought, locusts, worms, and crickets (Deut. 28:17-18, 22-24, 38-42). It included all kinds of pestilence and disease: "The Lord will make the pestilence cling to you until He has consumed you from the land . . . . The Lord will smite you with consumption and with fever and with inflammation" (Deut. 28:21-22). "The Lord will smite you with the boils of Egypt and with hemorrhoids and with the scab and with the itch, from which you cannot be healed. The Lord will smite you with madness and with blindness and with bewilderment of heart" (Deut. 28:27-28). "The Lord will bring extraordinary plagues on you and your descendants, even severe and lasting plagues, and miserable and chronic sicknesses" (Deut. 28:59; see verses 35, 60-61). Also the Lord would cause them to be defeated by their enemies (Deut. 28:25) and ultimately to suffer the punishment of siege and exile with their unmitigated humiliation and suffering (Deut. 28:48ff.).[12]

All of these disasters were sent upon God's people at one time or another, culminating in their ultimate defeat and exile at the hands of their enemies. This was unquestionably a matter of punishment for their sins. Concerning the exile of the northern tribes it is written, "In the ninth year of Hoshea, the king of Assyria captured Samaria and carried Israel away into exile . . . . Now this came about, because the sons of Israel had sinned against the Lord their God" (II Kings 17:6-7). The same is true of the southern kingdom. Jeremiah's "horrible decree" concerning the Babylonian onslaught makes this clear:

> . . . "Behold, I am bringing a nation against you from afar, O house of Israel," declares the Lord. "It is an enduring nation, it is an ancient nation, a nation whose language you do not know, nor can you understand what they say. Their quiver is like an open grave, all of them are mighty men. And they will devour your harvest and your food; they will devour your sons and your daughters; they will devour your flocks and your herds; they will devour your vines and your fig trees; they will demolish with the sword your fortified cities in which you trust. . . . And it shall come about when they say, 'Why has the Lord our God done all these things to us?' then you shall say to them, 'As you have forsaken Me and served foreign gods in your land, so you shall serve strangers in a land that is not yours.' . . . Shall I not punish these people?" declares the Lord, "On a nation such as this shall I not avenge Myself?" (Jer. 5:15-19, 29).

"I am bringing such calamity on Jerusalem and Judah," God says, "because they have done evil in My sight" (II Kings 21:12, 15; see 22:16-17). And thus it happened: because the people sinned continually against God, "therefore He brought up against them the king of the Chaldeans who slew their young men with the sword in the house of

12. See I Kings 8:33ff. for another general list of providential disasters which could be brought upon the people because of their sin. See Deuteronomy 11:16-17 for another general warning. See also Psalm 107:33-34.

their sanctuary, and had no compassion on young man or virgin, old man or infirm; He gave them all into his hand" (II Chron. 36:17).[13]

We must not forget that such punishment upon Israel, though severe, was all directed toward the goal of preparing for the coming of Christ into the world. The seedbed into which the Seed of Abraham was to be sown had to be worked and reworked and weeded and purified and pulverized in order to make it a ready receptacle for the sowing. And even beyond this purpose was the ultimate purpose of God, to glorify his name in all things. God's special providence, whether for blessing or cursing, was a demonstration that he alone is God. When captivity comes, says Ezekiel 24:24, "then you will know that I am the Lord God." When the surrounding nations mock God's people because of their captivity, God will judge them also. For instance, "Thus I will execute judgments on Moab, and they will know that I am the Lord" (Ezek. 25:11). His purpose is summarized thus: "And I shall magnify Myself, sanctify Myself, and make Myself known in the sight of many nations; and they will know that I am the Lord" (Ezek. 38:23).

The Uniqueness of Old Testament Israel

We have been confronted with a wealth of information concerning God's providential dealings with Israel as a nation. Now we will surely be confronted with the temptation to systematize this data and to draw conclusions about how God works with nations in general. This temptation must be resisted. The reason for this is the fact that God's dealings with Old Testament Israel were unique, because his purpose for her was unique. The role of preparer for the Messiah was a role that could be played by one nation only, and God chose Israel for that privilege. The miracles and special providence by which God guided her history were all aimed at the accomplishment of that purpose. There is no reason to think that in some other part of the world at that time, such as Australia or East Asia, God was dealing with other nations in similar ways.

More importantly, there is no reason to think that God is working with any nation or nations in the Christian era, including today, as he worked with Israel and her neighbors in Old Testament times. Since Israel's purpose was to prepare for the first coming of Christ, that

13. God also brought providential punishment on pagan nations because of their sin: the Amalekites (I Sam. 15:2ff.); Assyria (Isa. 10:5ff.); and Babylon (Jer. 25:12-14; 51:12).

purpose must be seen as fulfilled once Christ has come and as having no parallel in our time. The *second* coming of Christ is of an entirely different order, and the preparation for that coming is likewise different. It does not require the nursing of a specific nation and the manipulation of her neighboring nations. Therefore we cannot assume that God is dealing with nations today after the pattern of the Old Testament. The promises and warnings that applied to Israel cannot be carried over and applied to modern countries such as the United States of America without violating basic hermeneutical principles. This applies to such grand promises as II Chronicles 7:14, "If . . . My people who are called by My name humble themselves and pray, and seek My face and turn from their wicked ways, then I will hear from heaven, will forgive their sin, and will heal their land." This is a promise to "My people," namely, Old Testament Israel. It cannot be generalized to apply to nations today.

Most important of all is the fact that not even modern-day Israel as a political nation nor even the Jews as a race are equivalent to Old Testament Israel. God chose Israel to prepare for the first coming of Christ, and she has served that purpose and fulfilled her destiny. The promise made to the fathers has been fulfilled in Jesus, specifically in his resurrection from the dead (Acts 13:32-34). God no longer distinguishes Jews from Greeks or Gentiles (Gal. 3:28; Eph. 2:11ff.). Someone may want to remind us of such statements as the one in I Chronicles 17:21-22:

> . . . And what one nation in the earth is like Thy people Israel, whom God went to redeem for Himself as a people, to make Thee a name by great and terrible things, in driving out nations from before Thy people, whom Thou didst redeem out of Egypt? For Thy people Israel Thou didst make Thine own people forever, and Thou, O Lord, didst become their God. . . .

Here and in other places (such as II Samuel 7:24) God's relationship with Israel is described by a term that is often translated in English as "forever." This is a misleading translation. The Hebrew word, *'ôlām,* does not have the inherent meaning of "forever." It *can* mean this in certain contexts, but it can also mean "perpetual" or "age-lasting." Allan MacRae says that it does not in itself contain the idea of endlessness, but means instead "indefinite continuance into the very distant future" and refers to "a long age or period."[14] In many cases in the

14. Allan A. MacRae, "*'ôlām,*" *Theological Wordbook of the Old Testament,* ed. R. Laird Harris et al. (Chicago: Moody Press, 1980), II:672-673.

Old Testament it means precisely this, i.e., lasting to the end of the Old Testament age itself. See, for example, references to the priests' clothing and washings (Exod. 28:43; 30:21), the priests' portion of the temple sacrifices (Exod. 29:28), the priesthood itself (Exod. 40:15), the Day of Atonement (Lev. 16:29, 31), the Sabbath (Exod. 31:16-17), the Levites as custodians of the ark (I Chron. 15:2; 23:13), and Solomon's temple (I Kings 8:13; 9:3). The point is that there is *no* modern-day parallel to Old Testament Israel on a national level; thus God's providential dealing with nations today does not necessarily take the form of the Old Testament pattern. What the biblical data show is what God can do and will do with reference to nations, if his purposes so require. There is no indication in the Bible that there is such a requirement in our time.[15]

Old Testament Israel does have a New Testament successor, but not a parallel. The successor is the *new* Israel, the church of Jesus Christ, which is constituted on a spiritual basis rather than a physical or national one. Its purpose is different from that of the old Israel. It is commissioned to preach the gospel of the already-come Christ, to evangelize, to bring the world to a saving knowledge of Christ and his spiritual blessings. To accomplish this purpose the church requires providence of a different kind, what might be called spiritual providence, or providence that aids in the spreading of the gospel. Much of what is involved here, such as the gift of the indwelling presence of the Holy Spirit, falls more properly under the general heading of redemption. In order to show the contrast, however, between the way God dealt with old Israel and the way he deals with the new Israel, we will present briefly three examples of God's special (spiritual) providence in reference to the church's purpose.

First we may mention the concept of God's "opening doors" for the spreading of the gospel. In II Corinthians 2:12 Paul says, "Now when I came to Troas for the gospel of Christ . . . a door was opened for me in the Lord." In Colossians 4:3 he asks for prayer "that God may open up to us a door for the word, so that we may speak forth the mystery of Christ." In the latter case, since he is writing from prison, we may assume that Paul is wanting the Lord to arrange for his release

15. For a fuller treatment of this issue see the following: William Hendriksen, *Israel in Prophecy* (Grand Rapids: Baker Book House, 1968); Philip Mauro, *The Hope of Israel* (Swengel, Pa.: Reiner Publications, 1970); Louis A. DeCaro, *Israel Today: Fulfillment of Prophecy?* (Nutley, N.J.: Presbyterian and Reformed, 1974); Jack Cottrell, "The Jews in Prophecy," *Christian Standard* (October 14, 1979), 114:22-24.

in some (providential) way. In any case he is firmly convinced that God is in control of the circumstances of his life to such a degree that opportunities for proclaiming the gospel can be provided by divine providence. In a somewhat similar situation he prays earnestly for the opportunity to go to Thessalonica to edify the brethren there. He is not in prison, but in some other way Satan has thwarted his plans for such a visit (I Thess. 2:18; 3:10). But he is confident that God can solve the problem: "Now may our God and Father Himself and Jesus our Lord direct our way to you" (I Thess. 3:11).

A second example of spiritual providence to help the church in its mission is the concept of God's "opening hearts" or convicting hearers of their needs as sinners and of Christ's power to meet those needs. We are told on one occasion, in reference to Lydia, that as Paul was preaching the gospel "the Lord opened her heart to respond to the things spoken by Paul" (Acts 16:14). Such convicting work is done mainly by the Holy Spirit (John 16:7-11) through the inspired message which he gave to the Apostles and others (John 16:12-15). It may also be accomplished through what Alexander Campbell calls "special providences."[16] Understanding from our study of the Old Testament what God *can* do for purposes of correction, we may affirm the *possibility* that he does similar things today to open hearts and minds to the truth of the gospel. Natural disasters, "accidents," or personal sickness may be sent by God to serve such a purpose. "Near misses" or "close calls" sometimes work in the same way. Such seemingly chance occurrences as tuning in a certain song on the car radio, or the preacher's selecting a particular topic for his sermon, may be the design of providence. By keeping certain thoughts in the sinner's consciousness—thoughts of a convicting word or song or look; thoughts of a loving spouse's example and prayer (I Peter 3:1-2)—God may open his heart. While neither the preached word nor such providential activity is irresistible (Acts 7:51), it is a significant example of God's desire to help the church carry out the purpose which he has assigned to it.

A third example of spiritual providence is the concept of God's "opening the word" to our understanding. God may help either the sinner or the Christian to a better understanding of the Bible by providentially causing him to cross paths with someone who can teach

---

16. Alexander Campbell and N. L. Rice, *A Debate on the Action, Subject, Design and Administrator of Christian Baptism* (Lexington, Ky.: A. T. Skillman & Son, 1844), p. 614. He says there is no objection to the cooperation of secondary causes in convincing and persuading sinners—including "the doctrine of special providences."

him. Or he may aid in the study of Scripture by sharpening our mental processes, helping us to think clearly, clearing our preoccupied minds, helping us to concentrate, or helping us to put the right ideas or concepts together. I would suggest such providential activity as an alternative to the doctrine of "illumination" which is so prevalent among Protestants.[17]

These examples are given to show how different the purpose and needs of the church are, as compared with those of Old Testament Israel. The totally different context means that God's providential activity today will be different from what it was in pre-Christian times. This should not be taken in any way as diminishing the majesty and awesomeness of God's special providence for Israel. In every way it is a remarkable display of his power and sovereignty over men and nations. It shows us that our God is indeed the Ruler of all things.

GOD'S PURPOSE FOR BELIEVERS

We turn now to a consideration of God's special providence for individual believers. This is a question often asked: Does God pay special attention to his people? Are there certain blessings and promises that are guaranteed for them but not for unbelievers? Is there a special providence for the righteous? Is it God's purpose that they should all experience total health and material prosperity in this life? Or is his special purpose confined to spiritual blessings? What can a believer expect from God's special providence?

The general principle seems to be quite clear: God *does* promise special favors for his people. There *is* a special providence for believers. Azariah states the principle in addressing King Asa: "The Lord is with you when you are with Him. And if you seek Him, He will let you find Him; but if you forsake Him, He will forsake you" (II Chron. 15:2). This is stated in another way by Hanani the prophet: "For the eyes of the Lord move to and fro throughout the earth that He may strongly support those whose heart is completely His" (II Chron. 16:9). Psalm 5:12 says, "For it is Thou who dost bless the righteous man, O Lord, Thou dost surround him with favor as with a shield." Romans 8:28 promises, "And we know that God causes all things to work together for good to those who love God." Paul adds this promise in Philippians

17. We may note that it is not improper to ask God for such providential aid to help us understand texts other than the Bible, e.g., a mathematics textbook or a theological treatise.

4:19, "And my God shall supply all your needs according to His riches in glory in Christ Jesus."

These are wonderful promises and a cause for great rejoicing to every believer. But we should be aware of one thing: though the general principle applies to all of God's people alike, the specific application can and does vary, particularly in the transition from old Israel to new Israel, the church. As we have already seen, God's purposes in the Old Testament were tied very closely to the physical fortunes of Israel. Thus it was proper for the Israelites to expect a material fulfillment of these promises. For instance, when we read concerning King Uzziah that "as long as he sought the Lord, God prospered him" (II Chron. 26:5), we quite naturally understand this as referring to physical prosperity. For another example, David in Psalm 37:39-40 speaks of protection from one's enemies: "But the salvation of the righteous is from the Lord; He is their strength in time of trouble. And the Lord helps them, and delivers them; He delivers them from the wicked, and saves them, because they take refuge in Him." An example of this protection is related by Ezra, who tells us how God protected the Jews from their hostile neighbors while they were rebuilding the temple: "But the eye of their God was on the elders of the Jews, and they did not stop them" (Ezra 5:5). He also guarded a caravan bringing a veritable treasure from Babylon for use in the temple service: "And the hand of our God was over us, and He delivered us from the hand of the enemy and the ambushes by the way" (Ezra 8:31).

But we must remember that God's purposes for the church are not the same as for Old Testament Israel, and that his special providence does not necessarily give us everything that was necessary for national Israel. Specifically, the emphasis has now shifted to the higher level of spiritual blessings, i.e., protection from spiritual enemies, not physical ones; spiritual prosperity, not physical; spiritual wholeness, not physical health. This will now be discussed in more detail.

Protection

The promise of special protection for the Lord's people occurs constantly in the Psalms. "The eyes of the Lord are toward the righteous, and His ears are open to their cry" (Ps. 34:15). "The salvation of the righteous is from the Lord . . . . He delivers them from the wicked, and saves them, because they take refuge in Him" (Ps. 37:39-40). "He keeps the feet of His godly ones, but the wicked ones are silenced in darkness" (I Sam. 2:9). The Lord will protect the righteous and keep him alive, and will not deliver him over to the desire of his enemies (Ps. 41:1-2). "The Lord keeps all who love Him; but all the wicked, He will destroy" (Ps. 145:20). "The Lord preserves the faithful" (Ps. 31:23). Thus David expresses his confidence that God alone can protect him: "But as for me, I trust in Thee, O Lord, I say, 'Thou art my God.' My times are in Thy hand; deliver me from the hand of my enemies, and from those who persecute me" (Ps. 31:14-15). "Thou art my hiding place; Thou dost preserve me from trouble; Thou dost surround me with songs of deliverance" (Ps. 32:7; see Ps. 31:20). "Thou art my rock and my fortress; for Thy name's sake Thou wilt lead me and guide me. Thou wilt pull me out of the net which they have secretly laid for me" (Ps. 31:3-4). "Even though I walk through the valley of the shadow of death, I fear no evil; for Thou art with me; Thy rod and Thy staff, they comfort me" (Ps. 23:4). Over and over the Psalms refer to God as a rock, a fortress, a refuge, a stronghold, a shield, and a deliverer. "The Lord is my rock and my fortress and my deliverer, my God, my rock, in whom I take refuge; my shield and the horn of my salvation, my stronghold" (Ps. 18:2).[18] Psalm 121:1-8 praises God for the overall protection of his providence:

> I will lift up my eyes to the mountains; from whence shall my help come? My help comes from the Lord, who made heaven and earth. He will not allow your foot to slip; He who keeps you will not slumber. Behold, He who keeps Israel will neither slumber nor sleep. The Lord is your keeper; the Lord is your shade on your right hand. The sun will not smite you by day, nor the moon by night. The Lord will protect you from all evil; He will keep your soul. The Lord will guard your going out and your coming in from this time forth and forever.

"God is to us a God of deliverances" (Ps. 68:20), for "many are the afflictions of the righteous; but the Lord delivers him out of them all" (Ps. 34:19). No wonder David could affirm his peace of mind: "In peace I will both lie down and sleep, for Thou alone, O Lord, dost make me to dwell in safety" (Ps. 4:8).

When David and the other Psalmists wrote these words of trust, they no doubt had in mind such enemies as the Philistines and the Moabites. David certainly would be thinking of King Saul. This does not mean that they limited their thoughts to their physical foes, but they would certainly have been included. But how do we as Christians

---

18. See also Psalms 46:1, 2, 7; 57:1; 62:2, 6-8; 144:2.

understand these promises of protection? Does this aspect of providence still apply to us? It most certainly does, but in terms of spiritual enemies. The New Testament makes it very clear that we cannot expect to escape physical harm from God's enemies. "Blessed are those who have been persecuted for the sake of righteousness," says Jesus (Matt. 5:10). He told his apostles to expect persecution (Matt. 10:16-24). "In the world you have tribulation," he told them (John 16:33). Paul warns, "And indeed, all who desire to live godly in Christ Jesus will be persecuted" (II Tim. 3:12). Peter's first letter addresses this theme throughout, but the Apostle gives this comfort: "To the degree that you share the sufferings of Christ, keep on rejoicing" (I Peter 4:13).

What kind of protection *can* we expect? Protection from spiritual enemies: "Greater is He who is in you than he who is in the world" (I John 4:4). Jesus has bound the strong man, Satan (Matt. 12:29; see Revelation 20:1-6). "The Lord will deliver me from every evil deed," says Paul, "and will bring me safely to His heavenly kingdom" (II Tim. 4:18). God "knows how to rescue the godly from temptation" (II Peter 2:9); he "will not allow you to be tempted beyond what you are able, but with the temptation will provide the way of escape also, that you may be able to endure it" (I Corinthians 10:13). He will "deliver us from evil" (Matt. 6:13).

It would be a wonderful thing to be able to say that because we are Christians, we will never have to suffer physical harm at the hands of men. The Apostle Paul certainly would have preferred this, instead of the many persecutions that he in fact suffered (II Corinthians 11:23-28). The thousands upon thousands of Christian martyrs would surely have been grateful for deliverance from the fire and wild beasts. But this is not the kind of protection God offers to us in this life. He promises now to guard us from those enemies that "wage war against the soul" (I Peter 2:11). Total peace is not promised until heaven itself. For those who are persecuted Jesus says, "Rejoice, and be glad, for your reward in heaven is great" (Matt. 5:12).

Prosperity

In any discussion of special providence the subject of material blessings will certainly arise. The very word *providence* suggests the word *provide,* and for many this means primarily providing for our physical needs. After all, our God is "Jehovah Jireh," or "The Lord Will Provide" (Gen. 22:14).[19] Also, we know that "every good thing bestowed and

19. The Hebrew literally means "Jehovah sees," but this is usually taken in the sense that the Lord sees our needs and provides for them.

every perfect gift is from above, coming down from the Father of lights" (James 1:17). Just how far can this be pressed? Can we expect to have our needs met? Can we expect more than this? Can we expect abundance and wealth to be ours as a reward for our faith?

There are a number of advocates of what is called the "gospel of health and wealth," who teach that God wants every true believer to have lots and lots of money and an abundance of the very best quality material possessions. "God wants you rich," is their message. Now we ask, is this a biblical teaching? The answer is no, absolutely not. There is no such promise anywhere in the New Testament. It is a fact of course that some Christians will be wealthy. This is not wrong (see III John 2), but neither is it the norm. Jesus commented, "The poor you have with you always" (Matt. 26:11). There were poor among the saints at Jerusalem (Rom. 15:26). What was Paul's command concerning these poor? Did he exhort them to pray and grow rich? No, instead he exhorted the rich and anyone who had more than he needed to *share* with the poor so that their needs could be met (I Cor. 16:1-3). Indeed, according to Scripture the main responsibility of the wealthy is to give from their abundance to help those in need. Paul says to instruct those who are "rich in this present world . . . to do good, to be rich in good works, to be generous and ready to share" (I Tim. 6:17-18). God permits some to prosper so that they might exercise the gift of giving (Rom. 12:8). "God is able to make all grace abound to you, that . . . you may have an abundance," says Paul, but he provides an "abundance *for every good deed*" (II Cor. 9:8; italics added). When God gives to us in abundance, this is like giving seed to someone to be sown elsewhere; he enriches for the purpose of liberality (II Cor. 9:10-11).

What does the Bible say to those who are seeking wealth? It warns very strongly against materialism, against laying up treasures on earth (Matt. 6:19). It warns about the danger of riches: "But those who want to get rich fall into temptation and a snare and many foolish and harmful desires which plunge men into ruin and destruction. For the love of money is a root of all sorts of evil, and some by longing for it have wandered away from the faith" (I Tim. 6:9-10). Jesus says, "Beware, and be on your guard against every form of greed; for not even when one has an abundance does his life consist of his possessions" (Luke 12:15). Jesus taught us to pray for our daily bread, not a Mercedes and a vacation home (Matt. 6:11). The apostle Paul sets the norm for us when he says, "I have learned to be content in whatever circumstances I am. I know how to get along with humble means, and I also know how to live in prosperity; in any and every circumstance I have learned the secret of being filled and going hungry, both of having abundance and suffering need" (Philippians 4:11-12).

But let us not overlook what God *does* promise in the way of physical blessings. Though he has not promised that every believer shall be wealthy in this world's goods, he *has* promised that our basic needs will be met. Psalm 33:18-19 declares, "Behold, the eye of the Lord is on those who fear Him, . . . to keep them alive in famine." David said, "The Lord is my shepherd, I shall not want" (Ps. 23:1). We are worth much more to God than birds (Matt. 6:26; 10:31); so if God feeds the birds and clothes the grass of the field with blossoms, "will He not much more do so for you?" asks Jesus (Matt. 6:26-30). Then he makes this promise: "But seek first His kingdom and His righteousness; and all these things shall be added to you" (Matt. 6:33). "All these things" refers to food and clothing—the necessities of life. This is what God promises to believers. He will supply all our *needs* (Philippians 4:19). He will cause us to have *all sufficiency* in everything; anything beyond this is an extra blessing to be used to meet other Christians' needs (II Cor. 9:8ff.).

We may note that God *does* have riches in store for every believer. He promises spiritual riches in this life, "the unfathomable riches of Christ" (Eph. 3:8). We are offered "the riches of His kindness and forbearance and patience" (Rom. 2:4) and "the riches of His grace" (Eph. 1:7). And for those who think it would be nice to have an abundance of the other kind of riches, perhaps these are included in the "riches of the glory of His inheritance in the saints" (Eph. 1:18) in the life to come, in the new heavens and new earth. Jesus promised that the meek and gentle "shall inherit the earth" (Matt. 5:5). For this present time it is our duty to respect God's priorities and God's timetable, and to rejoice that our needs are supplied by his providence.

Health

Another question regarding God's special providence for believers has to do with sickness and health. Some sincerely believe that on the cross Jesus took away not only our sins but also our sickness. They refer to Isaiah 53:4-5 and Matthew 8:16-17. Others have incorporated physical health into the larger package of "health and wealth" which they say is part of the essence of the gospel. What shall we say concerning this? Is it God's purpose that all believers should be free from illness and infirmities of all sorts? Does the Christian have the right to claim physical healing as part of the benefits offered by Christ through his atoning blood? Is it right to pray for healing? Is this a part of God's providence for believers?

Sickness and death are certainly not normal; they were not a part of the world that God created in the beginning. God's original purpose for man did not include them. They are part of the results of sin's entrance into the world. Since that first sin they have permeated and devastated the human race. They are man's enemies; they are unnatural.

In the midst of sickness God's people have always cried out to him for healing and deliverance, and God has always been ready to hear their prayers. Concerning the righteous person Psalm 41:3 says, "The Lord will sustain him upon his sickbed; in his illness, Thou dost restore him to health." James 5:14-16 says,

> Is anyone among you sick? Let him call for the elders of the church, and let them pray over him, anointing him with oil in the name of the Lord; and the prayer offered in faith will restore the one who is sick, and the Lord will raise him up, and if he has committed sins, they will be forgiven him. Therefore, confess your sins to one another, and pray for one another, so that you may be healed. The effective prayer of a righteous man can accomplish much.

The Apostle John prayed that his friend Gaius would "prosper and be in good health" (III John 2). In those eras when God gave miraculous powers, healing of the sick was always one way in which they were used.

Does all of this mean that healing and health are now standard gifts offered to all believers in relation to all sicknesses? This cannot be the case. It is true that God can and often does answer prayers for healing by exercising his special providence on our behalf. And we believe that he will do so, unless there is an overriding purpose that is served by the sickness itself. It may be that God in his wisdom determines that developing spiritual prosperity (e.g., patience, sympathy) is more important than health, or it may be that the illness is a means of correction and must be endured. Only God knows when such purposes apply; we simply trust his wisdom and goodness as we continue to pray for healing.

That physical healing is not guaranteed to believers would seem to be shown by the cases of sickness among Christians mentioned in the New Testament. Paul's "thorn in the flesh" was not removed, thus serving the higher spiritual purpose of teaching him humility (II Cor.

12:7).[20] Epaphroditus was apparently sick for a long time, and almost fatally so (Phil. 2:25-27). A gospel of guaranteed health should have brought him around much sooner than this. Also, Paul had to leave one of his co-workers, Trophimus, sick at Miletus (II Tim. 4:20). Why was he not healed instead? We are also told that Dorcas, a Christian woman who abounded with deeds of kindness and charity, "fell sick and died" (Acts 9:36-37). Did the gospel somehow fail her?

But what about the idea that Jesus' atonement brought physical healing for all who believe? This is true, but there is a fundamental fallacy at work here. Jesus' atonement did overcome all the effects of sin, including physical sickness and death. But the fallacy is in thinking that we are supposed to have all these effects removed immediately, in this life. This is not the case. If this were true, not only would every true believer always be healed; he would never even get sick. Nor would he ever die. And this would have applied to believers in Old Testament days, too, since the spiritual benefit of forgiveness (justification) was surely applied then. But of course none of this has happened, simply because the redemption of the body and of the physical universe as a whole does not take effect until the second coming (Rom. 8:18-23). Only the new body is incorruptible and immortal (I Cor. 15:42-44, 54). That the old one gets sick and stays sick and dies is no reflection upon the efficacy of the atonement, which has earned for us a new body. *This* is where guaranteed health is provided for us, not in this life.[21]

What *is* guaranteed to us by the gospel in this life is *spiritual* healing, the cleansing of the soul from the disease of sin. The heart is renewed and regenerated (Ezek. 36:26; Titus 3:5); the spirit is given new life in Christ Jesus (Rom. 6:3-4; Eph. 2:5). God is bestowing this kind of health and life now, even though the body is still subject to disease and death (Rom. 8:11).

The conclusion is that we should pray for bodily healing, because God's special providence is able to give it to us. But we should at the same time trust in God's wisdom. If he sees a reason why he should not restore us, we can remember the promise of Romans 8:28, "that God causes all things to work together for good to those who love God." Complete health may not be ours now, but we know that it surely will be in the day of resurrection and for eternity.

---

20. That it was probably a physical ailment is suggested by his calling it a thorn in the *flesh*.

21. For a critique of the view that physical healing was included in the atonement, see Stephen Nash, "Is Physical Healing an Intended Benefit of the Atonement?" *The Seminary Review* (September, 1981), 27:111-121.

Correction

The chastening or correction of his children has always been one of the purposes behind God's providential activity. Proverbs 3:11-12 puts down this principle: "My son, do not reject the discipline of the Lord, or loathe His reproof, for whom the Lord loves He reproves, even as a father, the son in whom he delights." Hebrews 12:5-6 cites this statement in the midst of a passage encouraging us to accept such discipline from God, and adds, "It is for discipline that you endure; God deals with you as with sons; for what son is there whom his father does not discipline? . . . He disciplines us for our good, that we may share His holiness." We are "trained by it" (Heb. 12:3-11).

As we have already seen in the history of old Israel, God's correction can take many forms, including bad weather, disease, and afflictions of all sorts. God can teach lessons by all such means. Job 33:13ff. mentions some of the ways God teaches and chastens. Sometimes he speaks in ways that we ignore (verse 14), such as dreams (verses 15-16). It may be that dreams at times embody the voice of conscience. "Man is also chastened with pain on his bed, and with unceasing complaint in his bones" (verse 19). Sometimes he is brought near to death itself (verse 22), but God delivers him (verses 23-28). "Behold, God does all these oftentimes with men, to bring back his soul from the pit, that he may be enlightened with the light of life" (verses 29-30). This passage suggests that sometimes God sends specific afflictions that are meant to convict us concerning certain sins in our lives, in which case the affliction would somehow be related to the sin. For example, sickness may be a warning concerning the sin of self-sufficiency, or of pride, or of workaholism.

Job 37:11-13 is another passage that specifically teaches how God's providence is used for correction. Since God is in control of the weather, a thunderstorm can go wherever God decides that it should go. "It changes direction, turning around by His guidance, that it may do whatever He commands it on the face of the inhabited earth" (verse 12). And for what purposes may God give a thundercloud special instructions? "Whether for correction, or for His world, or for lovingkindness, He causes it to happen" (verse 13). Sometimes for lovingkindness: to give a good harvest, or to answer the prayers of saints. Sometimes for his world: just because God himself enjoys seeing the deserts bloom and the waterfalls flow (see Job 38:25-27). But sometimes for *correction*: perhaps a flood to curtail greed, or a lightning strike to teach dependence upon him, or a tornado to shake us out of complacency and to awaken neighbor-love in our hearts.

In I Corinthians 11:17ff. Paul admonishes the church at Corinth for their abuse of the Lord's Supper, which was apparently quite severe. Because of their sins in relation to the Supper, Paul says, "many among you are weak and sick, and a number sleep" (I Cor. 11:30). This is understood by many to mean physical sickness and even death—chastening from God to teach his people to overcome carnality.

Without an apostle or a prophet to give us an inspired interpretation of our afflictions, we will not know for sure the divine purpose behind a particular affliction, nor if there is one. But every affliction is nevertheless an occasion for self-examination and for learning, and is one more reason to be grateful that "God causes all things to work together for good to those who love God" (Rom. 8:28).

In conclusion to this section we may summarize by saying that God's purposes for his people include protection from spiritual enemies but not necessarily physical harm, the meeting of our needs but not necessarily wealth, ultimate healing for our bodies but not necessarily in this life, and correction through affliction. This means that Christians are subject to persecution, poverty, illness, and disaster. These considerations should help to eliminate what Brunner calls "that dangerous popular misunderstanding of Providence, nourished by certain phrases in the Psalms, which seem to suggest that those who trust in God 'will always escape disaster.'"[22] Brunner continues,

> . . . Certainly *ultimately* this is what is intended and real trust in God is based upon this conviction. But this does not mean that penultimately, within this world of space and time, even the most Christian people will not have to face the worst disasters! . . . The Good Shepherd does permit His sheep to go through the Dark Valley. The just man must suffer much. . . .[23]

But along with this we must not forget the many times God's providence *does* protect us from harm, or supply us with a superabundance of this world's goods, or heal our sicknesses, or teach us God's lessons in not-so-painful ways. Nor must we forget the really special blessings which God has for his people, namely, the spiritual riches and wholeness and defense. Truly we can say with the Psalmist, "How great is Thy goodness, which Thou hast stored up for those who fear Thee,

---

22. Emil Brunner, *The Christian Doctrine of Creation and Redemption: Dogmatics, Vol. II*, tr. Olive Wyon (Philadelphia: Westminster Press, 1952), p. 158.
23. Ibid.

which Thou hast wrought for those who take refuge in Thee" (Ps. 31:19).

SPECIAL PROVIDENCE AND NATURAL LAW

In this chapter we have seen that the Sovereign Ruler of the universe can do and has done remarkable things in order to work out his purposes in this world. This is true especially in the way he controlled nations and individuals in connection with the history of Israel, but it is no less true in his special providence for the church and individual believers today. Now, those who know that God is a God of miracles may not find anything remarkable in the way God moved Israel and her neighbors around like pieces on a chessboard, or brought famines and pestilence at will. "Ho hum, just another miracle," they may be tempted to say. It is true that at times miracles were involved, especially during the period of the exodus from Egypt and the ministry of certain prophets such as Elijah and Elisha. But in most of the incidents cited in this chapter there is no suggestion of any miraculous activity on the part of God. Sometimes those who were carrying out God's will were not even aware that God was working and had entirely different purposes in their own minds. As Joseph said to his brothers, "You meant evil against me, but God meant it for good" (Gen. 50:20). God used Assyria to punish his people: "I send it against a godless nation and commission it against the people of My fury," he says; but as for Assyria's own conception of the matter, "it does not so intend nor does it plan so in its heart, but rather it is its purpose to destroy, and to cut off many nations" (Isa. 10:5-7). Likewise God used Cyrus, though Cyrus did not even know God (Isa. 45:4). Now the problem is *how* God is able to do what he does in these and similar cases without resorting to miracle. Surely he must be working in some way that is more intense and more direct than general providence. Indeed he is, and this is just what special providence is: a work of God in the world that lies somewhere between miracle and general providence.

One way to explain special providence, and to explain how God can work his purposes through it, is to see how it relates to natural law. We have seen that God has given the natural processes a relative independence, so that under his general providence they operate according to fixed patterns (natural laws) without further direct interference from God. But we have also seen that the Creator remains immanent in these natural processes and maintains control over them, so that he *can* intervene and alter them if he so chooses. And this is exactly what happens in the case of special providence. We are not talking about activity that is contrary to natural laws or which bypasses them in any way; that is the essence of miracle. No, special providence stays within the boundaries or the possibilities of natural law, but nevertheless brings about a result that might not have happened via general providence alone. This is possible because, as we saw in the last chapter, the laws of nature do not operate with such an iron-clad necessity that one and only one result can come about from a particular set of causes. Sometimes two or more possibilities may be equally viable for some natural events, e.g., the direction of a storm-cloud or the combination of the genetic materials of two reproductive cells. And herein lies the possibility of special providence. What determines the particular direction of the cloud or the actual combination of the genes? Sometimes it may be a causal factor that has just an infinitesimal edge over another. Sometimes it may be close to what we would call "chance." But at other times it may be *and is* the command of God. In this way the natural laws are at God's disposal, to serve the purposes of his special providence. Over a century ago William Sherlock summed this up well:

> For as God does not usually act without nature, nor against its laws, so neither does nature act by steady and uniform motions without the direction of God. But while everything in the material world acts necessarily and exerts its natural powers, God can temper, suspend, direct its influences without reversing the laws of nature. As, for instance, fire and water, wind and rain, thunder and lightning, have their natural virtues and powers, and natural causes, and God produces such effects as they are made to produce by their natural powers. He warms us with fire—invigorates the earth by the benign influences of the sun and moon, and other stars and planets; refreshes and moistens it with springs and fountains and rain from heaven—fans the air with winds, and purges it with thunders and lightnings and the like. But then when and where the rains shall fall and the winds shall blow, and in what measure and proportion, times and seasons, natural causes shall give or withhold their influences, this God keeps in his own power, and can govern without altering the standing laws of nature; and this is his government of natural causes in order to reward or punish men as they shall deserve. . . .[24]

---

24. William Sherlock, *A Discourse Concerning the Divine Providence* (Pittsburgh: J. L. Read, 1848), p. 38.

Sherlock also says,

> The sum is this, that all natural causes are under the immediate and absolute government of Providence—that God keeps the springs of nature in his own hands, and turns them as he pleases. For mere matter, though it be endowed with all the natural virtues and powers which necessarily produce their natural effects, yet it having no wisdom and counsel of its own, cannot serve the ends of a free agent without being guided by a wise hand. . . . And if God have subjected nature to human art, surely he has not exempted it from his own guidance and power.[25]

The purpose of all this is that "God does in some measure govern the moral by the natural world."[26] Through his control of nature, he controls men.

In this chapter we have already seen many examples of this. We have seen, for instance, how God punishes and rewards and corrects through his manipulation of the weather. By ordering a heavy snow or rain, "He seals the hand of every man, that all men may know His work" (Job 37:7). He can cause the storm-cloud to change direction, "that it may do whatever He commands it on the face of the inhabited earth" (Job 37:12). "For by these he judges peoples," says Job 36:31. Or as the NIV translates this verse, "This is the way he governs nations." For example, "The Lord hurled a great wind on the sea and there was a great storm on the sea" when he purposed to turn Jonah around and thereby save the city of Nineveh (Jonah 1:4). When he wanted to speed up the rebuilding of the temple he withheld the rain and "called for a drought on the land" (Hag. 1:11). But if he has no special purpose in view, he just lets nature take its course.

Another example of the use of natural law to serve the ends of special providence is God's control of the natural processes of the body in relation to disease and healing. The one in whom we have our very being would have no difficulty at all in varying our level of resistance or manipulating our immune mechanisms or giving us a bit of a chemical imbalance. This last option could possibly suffice to produce the change in Nebuchadnezzar's behavior (Dan. 4:25). A plague might be set off by a divinely-orchestrated proliferation of disease-carrying pests. Such a control of disease is also the control of death. God struck David's son with a sickness that, by design, produced his death (II Sam. 12:14-18). On the other hand, the control of disease is also the control of healing. If God can cause diseases, he can also heal them.

25. Ibid., pp. 39-40.
26. Ibid., p. 37.

An example similar to the one above is God's control of the musculature of the body. The significance of this is seen in a passage such as Proverbs 16:33, "The lot is cast into the lap, but its every decision is from the Lord." Why the lot lands the way it does (or the flipped coin, or a pair of dice) is mostly a matter of muscular movements in the hand, arm, and fingers. The difference between heads and tails may be due to a variation too subtle or minute for any of us to detect. But such a variation would be a small thing for God, and an extra impulse to a particular finger muscle to achieve the decision *he* wants is just routine special providence. So when the lot fell on Jonah (Jonah 1:7), this was just as God had ordered. The death of Ahab can be explained in a similar way. God had decreed that he would fall in battle at Ramoth-gilead (I Kings 22:20, 23, 28). Ahab, perhaps hoping to avoid God's sentence against him, disguised himself before entering the fight. This could have worked, since the enemy force was looking specifically for Ahab the king (I Kings 22:30-31). But the design of God's providence would not be thwarted: "Now a certain man drew his bow at random and struck the king of Israel in a joint of the armor. So he said to the driver of his chariot, 'Turn around, and take me out of the fight; for I am severely wounded.'" In fact, he died (I Kings 22:34, 37). How is it that a "random" arrow should find just the right person and strike at just the right spot? At least part of the answer is that God is able to provide the archer with just the right touch and strength to make the arrow go to the target God selects.

A possible modern example of special providence through the control of musculature is the intriguing account of a missionary's experience at the hands of Communist tormentors shortly after the take-over of China. After being arrested he was subjected to repeated attempts to cause him to doubt and to deny his faith. Then the interrogation took a nasty turn.

> The prisoner was taken into the inner precincts of the temple and tied to a chair. Kept awake by injection and immoral stimulation he was mercilessly questioned and accused by a succession of inquisitors, one starting before the other had finished.
>
> Mental blackouts were his salvation from complete destruction. Upon regaining consciousness, he would be assailed again and again. All the time his mind would throw back the answers, often in the words of Scripture.
>
> A knife was placed before him. He was tempted to take his life, but back came the answer, "My times are in Thy hands." The screaming

> voice of the interrogator demanded to know where the words came from and he threw a Bible before his victim. The sacred volume fell open at Psalm xxxi and, as the missionary read aloud each verse, the tension rose to breaking point in that hellish atmosphere.
>
> Here was a description of the present situation in detail. Here was the cry of the prisoner to his God for deliverance and, last of all, here was the very verse previously quoted. This was too much for the still superstitious inquisitor who fled from the room.[27]

Psalm 31 does indeed portray that scene very well, and verse 15 says, "My times are in Thy hand." The missionary was released by his captors, and was able to leave the country.

Was it just a coincidence that the Bible fell open at Psalm 31 on that occasion? Or was it a case of God's controlling the muscle movements of the interrogator in just the precise way required to cause it to open at that point? Certainly the latter is possible, and many prefer to believe that this is exactly what happened.

A final example of the use of natural law to bring about the purposes of providence is God's control of the animal kingdom. The Lord warned the Israelites that their disobedience would bring about plagues of locusts and worms (Deut. 28:38-39). This actually came to pass, with the locusts (Joel 1:4ff.) and with caterpillars (Amos 4:9). How could God accomplish this within the bounds of natural law? Possibly by granting the species extraordinary reproductive success, or by causing an imbalance in the food chain in their favor. Also with slight effort God could arrange for a ram to be caught in a thicket at just the right time (Gen. 22:13), or for a lion to be at a certain road just as a certain prophet was going that way (I Kings 13:26).

These last examples illustrate an aspect of special providence that deserves brief mention before we close this section on natural law. This is the idea that what some people call *chance*—the crossing of two distinct causal chains at just the right point to produce a significant but unexpected result—is a method by which God works providentially. Pollard calls this *accident* rather than chance and describes it as "situations in which two or more chains of events which have no causal connection with each other coincide in such a way as to decide the course of events."[28] Examples are the lion and the prophet meeting

27. "One Man with God," *The Presbyterian Journal* (December 28, 1966), p. 10.

28. William G. Pollard, *Chance and Providence: God's Action in a World Governed by Scientific Law* (New York: Charles Scribner's Sons, 1958), pp. 73-74. See also William Sherlock, *A Discourse Concerning the Divine Providence*, pp. 41ff.

as they did, or the arrow and King Ahab crossing the same bit of space at the same time. God's control of natural processes enables him to arrange such meetings if he so desires. For instance, we may speculate as to how the caravan of traders from Gilead just happened to arrive on the scene while Joseph's brothers were debating on how to get rid of him (Gen. 37:25ff.). A delaying sandstorm or a stubborn camel could easily have provided the proper timing. A modern example of the kind of thing we are talking about here is the following news article with the headline, "Mail Carrier Rescues Boy."

> Faint cries of "help me" led a mail carrier to the rescue of a six-year-old boy, trapped inside an abandoned refrigerator and near unconsciousness.
>
> The carrier, Armand Sequin, 59, revived Leonard Roy with artificial respiration and the lad walked away feeling well.
>
> Sequin said he had started on his route five minutes early Tuesday and was ahead of schedule. Had he been on time, Sequin said, the child likely would have been dead of suffocation.[29]

I have no idea whether this was actually an instance of special providence. I include it as an example of what God is able to do if he so wishes. It is the kind of thing—though of infinitely lesser significance—that Ketcherside speaks of after discussing the circumstances that brought Joseph to Egypt and Jesus' mother to Bethlehem: "And that was providence—the ordering or arranging of disconnected events in such a manner that they come into focus at a given historical point by the power of God."[30]

CONCLUSION

In this chapter we have attempted to present the biblical data concerning special providence and to show how God works in this way to carry out his specific purposes for the world in general, for Israel in particular, and for individual believers. The data considered demonstrate without question that God is indeed the Sovereign Ruler of history.

We have noted that one way in which God exercises control over men and nations is through his control of natural processes, i.e., using natural law in the interests of special providence. But this does not

29. The bibliographical data for this story are unavailable.

30. W. Carl Ketcherside, "The Hand of God," *Christian Standard* (August 7, 1983), 118:11.

explain everything, because much if not most of God's special providential activity can be accomplished only through *specific human decisions* which produce the result designed by God. Sometimes God's manipulation of nature is itself intended to influence human decisions toward a certain end, e.g., famine conditions to induce the completion of the temple (Hag. 1:5ff.). But sometimes the decisions themselves seem to be the very instruments of God's providence, e.g., Cyrus' permitting the Jews to return to their homeland in the first place. This raises what is perhaps the most serious question related to the subject of providence, namely, the freedom of the will. How does God work through free human decisions to accomplish his own purposes? This is the subject of the next chapter.

Chapter Five

SPECIAL PROVIDENCE AND FREE WILL

The point to be discussed in this chapter is the relationship between the sovereignty of God and the freedom of the human will. If God is absolutely sovereign, he must be in complete control of his creation. Does this mean that he must *cause* or in some other sense *determine* everything that happens? If so, does this include the choices and decisions of human wills? But if God determines every decision of our wills, does this not destroy our freedom? Does not such sovereignty rule out freedom of the will? On the other hand, if we really are free to make our own choices, does this mean that God has somehow lost control of the world? Is his sovereignty diminished? Does this make man a kind of co-creator alongside of God? In short, is it really possible to maintain divine sovereignty and human freedom at the same time?

This question has been debated extensively in the history of both philosophical and theological thought. It is probably one of the most difficult and most controversial issues that we have to face. One thing that makes it difficult is the problem of defining exactly what we mean by sovereignty and by free will. Another problem is sorting out the logical connections between the two. But for the Christian the most important aspect of the issue is the explanation of the biblical teaching about God's relationship to human thoughts, attitudes, decisions, and actions. This is a part of the more general topic of special providence, and we saw in the last chapter that the Bible pictures God as in complete control of the events and destinies of nations and therefore of history in general. We saw the extent of this control as it often includes and depends upon God's government of the lives and actions of individuals themselves. This is the point that will be explored in more detail in this chapter. What can we learn from the teaching of Scripture about God's special providential control over the very thoughts and decisions of individual men and women?

We have already set forth much of the biblical teaching relating to special providence, but we have deliberately reserved a discussion of the most specific and pertinent passages until now. Thus in this chapter we will begin with a look at scriptural references to the divine control over human decisions. Then we will see how Christian determinists use these passages to construct their doctrines of sovereignty and freedom. Next we will attempt to set forth an understanding of these doctrines that is more faithful to all the relevant biblical teaching. Finally we will point out some of the more serious problems in the determinists' view.

BIBLICAL DATA

In this section our plan is to set forth without comment the most pointed biblical data relating to God's sovereign control of human thoughts and actions. While some of the data may have been mentioned in the last chapter, most of it was not. We begin with some general references from the book of Proverbs: "The plans of the heart belong to man, but the answer of the tongue is from the Lord" (Prov. 16:1). "The mind of man plans his way, but the Lord directs his steps" (Prov. 16:9). "Many are the plans in a man's heart, but the counsel of the Lord, it will stand" (Prov. 19:21). "The king's heart is like channels of water in the hand of the Lord; He turns it wherever He wishes" (Prov. 21:1). Psalm 33:15 says that God "fashions the hearts of them all." Jeremiah 10:23 adds, "I know, O Lord, that a man's way is not in himself; nor is it in a man who walks to direct his steps." Philippians 2:13 tells believers that God "is at work in you, both to will and to work for His good pleasure." Anyone who makes plans ought to say, "If the Lord wills, we shall live and also do this or that," says James 4:15. Such passages as these suggest that God is in control of our thoughts, our words, and our deeds.

Examples of Control

For specific examples of the general statements given above, we may begin with references to the fact that kings' hearts may be turned wherever God wishes. After Saul was anointed as king, I Samuel 10:9 says that "God changed his heart." According to I Kings 3:12, God gave to Solomon "a wise and discerning heart." When the time was right for the final judicial destruction of the northern kingdom of Israel to begin, God brought the Assyrian armies against his people. How did he do this? "The God of Israel stirred up the spirit of Pul, king of Assyria . . . , and he carried them away into exile" (I Chron. 5:26). Later in a judicial act against the southern kingdom of Judah, God "stirred up against Jehoram the spirit of the Philistines and the Arabs" (II Chron. 21:16). The kings are not specifically mentioned, but we can assume that their decisions would be the crucial ones. After the southern kingdom had been taken into captivity by Babylon, God arranged for their release by stirring up the Medes against the Babylonians (Isa. 13:17). "Behold, I am going to arouse against Babylon . . . the spirit of a destroyer," says God (Jer. 51:1). Specifically it is said that "the Lord has roused the spirit of the kings of the Medes, because His purpose is against

Babylon to destroy it" (Jer. 51:11). One of these kings served a double purpose, as later we read that "the Lord stirred up the spirit of Cyrus king of Persia" to allow God's people to return to their homeland to rebuild Jerusalem and the temple (Ezra 1:1). The cooperation of other kings was secured by God's providential touch. After the people returned, God "turned the heart of the king of Assyria toward them to encourage them in the work of the house of God" (Ezra 6:22). He also put it into the heart of King Artaxerxes to help them (Ezra 7:27).

In all of these passages we see God accomplishing his purposes by "stirring up" or "turning" the hearts of kings. It is not explained *how* he did it; the Bible simply says that he did it.

Other references speak of God's controlling the *attitudes* of other nations toward Israel. When the people were ready to leave Egypt, "the Lord had given the people favor in the sight of the Egyptians, so that they let them have their request" for silver, gold, and clothing (Exod. 12:36).[1] On the other hand, God promised to make the nations of Canaan afraid of Israel to make the conquest easier. "I will send My terror ahead of you, and throw into confusion all the people among whom you come, and I will make all your enemies turn their backs to you" (Exod. 23:27). "This day I will begin to put the dread and fear of you upon the peoples everywhere under the heavens, who, when they hear the report of you, shall tremble and be in anguish because of you" (Deut. 2:25; see 11:25).

In other passages God is described as moving the hearts of the Israelites themselves. After the people had given a huge offering toward the construction of the temple, David prayed for them thus: "O Lord, the God of Abraham, Isaac, and Israel, our fathers, preserve this forever in the intentions of the heart of Thy people, and direct their heart to Thee; and give to my son Solomon a perfect heart to keep Thy commandments" (I Chron. 29:18-19). Solomon's prayer in I Kings 8:57-58 had a similar point: "May the Lord our God be with us, . . . that He may incline our hearts to Himself, to walk in all His ways and to keep His commandments." According to Haggai 1:14, God "stirred up the spirit" of Zerubbabel and of Joshua and of the remnant of the people, so that they would complete the rebuilding of the temple.

Other Old Testament references to God's working in the hearts of his people probably look forward to the time of the New Covenant, as

1. See Genesis 39:21, which says that God gave Joseph "favor in the sight of the chief jailer."

Carson notes.[2] Some of them may have a double reference, including within their scope both the remnant returning from Babylon and the New Testament Christians. One such passage is Jeremiah 24:7, "And I will give them a heart to know Me, for I am the Lord; and they will be My people, and I will be their God, for they will return to Me with their whole heart." Also, "I will give them one heart and one way, that they may fear Me always, . . . and I will put the fear of Me in their hearts so that they will not turn away from Me" (Jer. 32:39-40). Ezekiel 11:19-20 says, "And I shall give them one heart, and shall put a new spirit within them. And I shall take the heart of stone out of their flesh and give them a heart of flesh, that they may walk in My statutes and keep My ordinances" (see also Ezekiel 36:26-27).

In the New Testament itself God is spoken of as acting on the hearts of people, especially in relation to conversion. The NASB version of Acts 13:48 reads, "As many as had been appointed to eternal life believed," leading some to infer a direct work of God on the heart. Acts 14:27 says that God "opened a door of faith to the Gentiles," leading to the same inference. Acts 16:14 specifically says that God "opened" Lydia's heart "to respond to the things spoken by Paul." Acts 18:27 speaks of those who "believed through grace." Jesus says, "No one can come to Me, unless the Father who sent Me draws him" (John 6:44); "no one can come to Me, unless it has been granted him from the Father" (John 6:65). "'I will have mercy on whom I have mercy, and I will have compassion on whom I have compassion,'" says the Lord. "So then it does not depend on the man who wills or the man who runs, but on God who has mercy" (Rom. 9:15-16).

Special Providence and Sinful Deeds

The Bible passages that cause the most consternation in this connection are those which seem to picture God as in some way inducing men to have sinful attitudes and perform sinful deeds. In many cases of providential control as seen in the last chapter, God's purposes are accomplished by actions that have to be thought of as sinful on the part of individuals and even whole nations. In these and other cases God is specifically said to be behind these deeds, using them to do what he desires to be done.

---

2. D. A. Carson, *Divine Sovereignty and Human Responsibility: Biblical Perspectives in Tension* (Atlanta: John Knox Press, 1981), p. 29.

This seems to be true of the much-debated "hardening of hearts," which in most cases resulted in a spirit of opposition to God's stated purposes. This is definitely true of Pharaoh. After his resistance had been broken down by individual plagues, God would harden his heart so that he would refuse once again to let the people go. See Exodus 10:20, 27; 11:10; 14:8. The hardening and continuing resistance allowed God to add more plagues, thus making an everlasting impression on both Israel and the nations. "For this very purpose I raised you up," God said to Pharaoh, "to demonstrate My power in you, and that My name might be proclaimed throughout the whole earth" (Rom. 9:17). God hardened King Sihon's heart so that he refused to let the Israelites pass through his land, so that he would fight against Israel and be destroyed (Deut. 2:30ff.). See also Joshua 11:20. Concerning his enemies Jeremiah said, "Thou wilt give them hardness of heart, Thy curse will be on them" (Lam. 3:65). The Israelites themselves were not spared, as Isaiah 63:17 shows: "Why, O Lord, dost Thou cause us to stray from Thy ways, and harden our heart from fearing Thee?" In Romans 11 the Apostle Paul declares that the whole nation of Israel (except the remnant) was hardened, for "God gave them a spirit of stupor, eyes to see not and ears to hear not" (verses 7ff.; see verse 25). As a kind of general principle Paul says, "So then He has mercy on whom He desires, and He hardens whom He desires" (Rom. 9:18).

In another type of incident God is said to send an evil spirit or to allow an evil spirit to instigate sinful thoughts and deeds. Judges 9:23 says, "Then God sent an evil spirit between Abimelech and the men of Shechem; and the men of Shechem dealt treacherously with Abimelech." King Saul was particularly the object of such an evil spirit's work. "Now the Spirit of the Lord departed from Saul, and an evil spirit from the Lord terrorized him" (I Sam. 16:14). On one occasion this "evil spirit from God came mightily upon Saul, and he raved in the midst of the house," and attempted to murder David (I Sam. 18:10ff.). The same thing happened another time (I Sam. 19:9ff.). The prophet Micaiah tells of a vision in which he saw the Lord sending a spirit to deceive Ahab and entice him into battle, where he would be killed (I Kings 22:19-22). Micaiah then said to Ahab, "Now therefore, behold, the Lord has put a deceiving spirit in the mouth of all these your prophets; and the Lord has proclaimed disaster against you" (I Kings 22:23). See also II Kings 19:7.

We will now list some specific examples of evil deeds that were part of God's providential plans. One that receives much attention is the conduct of Joseph's brothers—their jealousy, hatred, murderous thoughts, and man-stealing which brought Joseph into Egypt. Indeed, they meant evil against Joseph. But at the same time, God meant it for good (Gen. 50:20). Joseph tells them that "it was not you who sent me here, but God" (Gen. 45:8). Somehow God was working through the brothers' evil choices to accomplish his purposes.

Another example is more direct. It involves the attitude of the Egyptians toward the Israelites. We have already noted how God gave his people favor in the eyes of the Egyptians. But even before that, "He turned their heart to hate His people, to deal craftily with His servants" (Ps. 105:25). Another example is Samson's request, contrary to God's stated law, that his father secure him a pagan wife from among the Philistines. Samson's parents naturally were reluctant to do this, but they "did not know that it was of the Lord, for He was seeking an occasion against the Philistines" (Judg. 14:1-4). This appears to say that Samson's lust for a pagan woman was "of the Lord." There is a more explicit example of this in II Samuel 12, when Nathan announced God's punishment against David for his sin against Uriah and Bathsheba. "Thus says the Lord, 'Behold, I will raise up evil against you from your own household; I will even take your wives before your eyes, and give them to your companion, and he shall lie with your wives in broad daylight. . . . I will do this thing before all Israel'" (verses 11-12). What did God do? He brought it about that David's own son, Absalom, violated his father's concubines on the roof of his own house (II Sam. 16:21-22).

In another incident involving David, "The anger of the Lord burned against Israel, and it incited David against them to say, 'Go, number Israel and Judah'" (II Sam. 24:1). It is not clear why numbering the people was such a great sin; nevertheless God punished the whole land with a pestilence that killed seventy thousand (II Sam. 24:15). Here it seems that God's providential working led the people into a sin which was then punished by another work of providence.

Solomon's son, Rehoboam, after he became king ignored his people's pleas and his elders' advice to lighten the burden of government on the people. This caused the ten northern tribes to rebel against Rehoboam and divide the kingdom. But this was God's will, as a punishment against Solomon and the people for their idolatry (I Kings 11:9-11). "So the king did not listen to the people; for it was a turn of events from the Lord, that He might establish His word" (I Kings 12:15). Was Rehoboam's harshness part of this "turn of events from the Lord"?

One other Old Testament example is Jeremiah 19:9, which prophesies concerning the conduct of the people of Jerusalem during the imminent siege by Babylon: "And I shall make them eat the flesh of their sons and the flesh of their daughters, and they will eat one another's flesh in the siege and in the distress with which their enemies and those who seek their life will distress them." So in some sense God "made" the people to engage in the evil practice of cannibalism.

The outstanding example of a sinful act being incorporated into God's providential plan is Judas' betrayal of Jesus. According to the Apostle Peter, Jesus was "delivered up by the predetermined plan and foreknowledge of God" and "nailed to a cross by the hands of godless men" (Acts 2:23). Indeed, says Peter, both Herod and Pilate, along with the Gentiles and the Jews, gathered together against Jesus, "to do whatever Thy hand and Thy purpose predestined to occur" (Acts 4:27-28). See Luke 22:22. Does this mean that God predestined Judas to commit the crime of the ages?

On other occasions it seems that God is responsible for deception, or for causing people to believe falsehoods or disbelieve truth. We have already noted the "deceiving spirit" which God sent to lure Ahab into battle (I Kings 22:22-23). And we have seen that it was "from the Lord" that Rehoboam ignored good advice in favor of bad. A similar example is that of Absalom, who announced that the advice of Hushai is better than that of Ahithophel. "For the Lord had ordained to thwart the good counsel of Ahithophel, in order that the Lord might bring calamity on Absalom" (II Sam. 17:14). In John 12:39-40 we are told that many in Jesus' audience "could not believe, for Isaiah said again, 'He has blinded their eyes, and He hardened their heart; lest they see with their eyes, and perceive with their heart, and be converted, and I heal them." II Thessalonians 2:11 refers to the time of the last days, when the man of sin arrives on the scene to deceive those who do not love truth. "And for this reason God will send upon them a deluding influence so that they might believe what is false."

A final example of God's providential control of men's sinful hearts and deeds is seen in the several occasions where God raised up a nation to go against another nation militarily, usually as a judicial punishment for sin. We have seen this to be the case in Assyria against Israel ("I am going to raise up a nation against you"—Amos 6:14; see I Chron. 5:26); the Philistines and Arabs against Judah ("The Lord stirred up" their spirit—II Chron. 21:16); the Assyrian nation against Judah ("I send it"—Isa. 10:6); and Babylon against Judah ("I am raising up the Chaldeans" —Hab. 1:6). To be sure these were judicial acts wherein God was meting out punishment deserved by the victims. Nevertheless, from the point of view of these conquering nations, they were engaging in aggressive warfare of the most greedy and cruel sort. God himself calls attention to the fierceness, cruelty, and arrogance of the Babylonians after announcing his plan to use them against Judah (Hab. 1:6-11). They must have broken every one of the ten commandments in their devastation of Judah (see Deut. 28:49ff.; II Chron. 36:17ff.). Yet God says, "I am doing this." In addition, the sins of both Assyria and Babylon were so great that God providentially arranged for *their* judicial destruction (see Isa. 10:16-17; Jer. 25:12).

The Problem

The incidents and events presented in this section are the most intense examples of God's special providence to be found in Scripture. They raise serious questions not only about the integrity of man's free will, but also about the integrity of God himself, insofar as he seems to incorporate even sinful deeds into his providential designs. The problem now is to come to some kind of coherent understanding of this data, to see if it is possible to harmonize the sovereign power of God with the freedom of the will.

THE DETERMINIST SOLUTION

The biblical data presented above and in the last chapter have been interpreted in a number of ways. Those who do not accept the inerrant authority of the Bible have the simplest solution, namely, to declare that many of the assertions concerning God's providential control either are just false or are pious exaggeration. Here, however, we are concerned mostly with those who accept the truth of the Bible's assertions. Within this category, one of the most commonly-accepted systematizations of the above data is that of the Christian determinists who hold to the view of absolute foreordination as discussed in chapter two above.[3] These include most Calvinists and some Thomists. At one point, as we shall see, they are joined by some secular philosophers.

While all such determinists will not agree on every detail, it is still possible to put together a composite picture of this view that should be acceptable to most of them. That is what we are attempting to do in this section.

---

3. See pp. 71-83 above.

The key word for these determinists is *sovereignty*, the sovereignty of God. Their main concern—a noble one, to be sure—is to guard the concept of divine sovereignty from any possible threats of erosion, particularly from the standpoint of human free will. Thus free will is either denied or is redefined to make it consistent with a specific concept of sovereignty. We shall see how this is true in three distinct ways, i.e., in reference to the sovereign decree, sovereign foreknowledge, and sovereign grace.

The Sovereign Decree

The cornerstone of the Christian determinist's doctrine of divine sovereignty is the eternal decree. As the Westminster Shorter Catechism (question 7) describes it, "The decrees of God are his eternal purpose according to the counsel of his will, whereby, for his own glory, he hath fore-ordained whatsoever comes to pass."[4] The Westminster Confession of Faith (III:1) gives a more detailed explanation:

> God from all eternity did, by the most wise and holy counsel of his own will, freely and unchangeably ordain whatsoever comes to pass; yet so as thereby neither is God the author of sin, nor is violence offered to the will of the creatures, nor is the liberty or contingency of second causes taken away, but rather established.[5]

Modern statements of this doctrine usually follow the wording of these documents, as illustrated by Bavinck: "God's decree is his eternal purpose whereby he has foreordained whatsoever comes to pass. Scripture everywhere affirms that whatsoever is and comes to pass is the realization of God's thought and will, and has its origin and idea in God's eternal counsel or decree."[6]

Characteristics of the Decree

The decree is called *eternal* because it was made in eternity past, before the actual creation and existence of anything outside of God. The decree is thus a detailed blueprint of everything that is going to happen. By means of the decree everything is predestined or ordained

4. *The Creeds of Christendom*, 4 edition, ed. Philip Schaff (New York: Harper and Brothers, 1919), III:677.
5. Ibid., p. 608.
6. Herman Bavinck, *The Doctrine of God*, ed. and tr. William Hendriksen (Grand Rapids: Eerdmans, 1951), p. 369.

in advance. History, or providence, is simply the execution of the decree which was fixed in eternity.

The decree is also *comprehensive*. "Whatsoever comes to pass" leaves no exceptions. Chafer says, "Whatever was to transpire in time was decreed from eternity, whether good or evil, whether great or small, whether wrought directly by God or indirectly through agencies."[7] In the case of things wrought indirectly, God decrees not only the end but also the means or causes for achieving them.[8] "That the decree of God can be regarded as suspended upon conditions which are not themselves determined by the decree is evidently impossible."[9]

God's eternal decree is also *efficacious*, which means "that what He has decreed will certainly come to pass; that nothing can thwart His purpose."[10] With reference to the universe, "this divine decree is both 'efficient' and 'exemplary' cause. . . . The final answer to the question why a thing is and why it is as it is must ever remain: 'God willed it,' according to his absolute sovereignty."[11] Though they speak of the decree as efficacious, many Christian determinists do not like to press the word *cause* too far, just because it sounds too much like determinism (which is usually repudiated by that name). Berkouwer tries to distinguish the Reformed view of providence from "rigorous determinism," asking, "Is it possible to avoid determinism once we accept God's sovereign rule over all things?"[12] Determinism, he says, is grounded in "the idea of an all-embracing, all-governing causality."[13] He recognizes that much Protestant thinking sounds very much like this: "Does not the idea of causality, which plays such an important role in determinism, have significant, even decisive place in Christian thought?"[14] But because he knows that divine causation negates free will[15] and that identifying Christianity as a determinism would be an

---

7. Lewis Sperry Chafer, *Systematic Theology* (Dallas: Dallas Seminary Press, 1947), I:232.

8. Louis Berkhof, *Systematic Theology* (London: Banner of Truth Trust, 1939), p. 105; Archibald Alexander Hodge, *Outlines of Theology* (New York: Robert Carter and Brothers, 1876), p. 165.

9. A. A. Hodge, *Outlines of Theology*, p. 167.

10. Louis Berkhof, *Systematic Theology*, p. 104.

11. Herman Bavinck, *The Doctrine of God*, p. 371.

12. G. C. Berkouwer, *The Providence of God*, tr. Lewis B. Smedes (Grand Rapids: Eerdmans, 1952), p. 141.

13. Ibid., p. 144.

14. Ibid., p. 147.

15. Ibid., pp. 144-145.

"immeasurable evil" for the church,[16] he decides that "the Reformed confession of Providence does not reason from the idea of causation."[17] He declares, "The living God rules here! We cannot explain the sequences of history with an all devouring system of causation."[18] The idea of "Christian determinism" is a contradiction of terms, he says.[19]

Berkhof is getting at the same point when he says that "the divine decree only brings certainty into the events, but does not imply that God will actively effectuate them" by his own direct action. Thus we are left with a comprehensively efficacious decree which does not necessarily effectuate everything. This definitely sounds like a contradiction of terms, but Berkhof must assert it in order to leave room for human free agency.[20]

Despite these word games it would appear that an efficacious decree casts God in the role of cause. Reformed theologians thus have not been reluctant to speak of God as "first cause" or "ultimate cause" as over against all second or proximate causes. Boettner, referring to the idea that all things are "fixed and settled," says that "nothing can have fixed and settled them except the good pleasure of God,—the great first cause,—freely and unchangeably foreordaining whatever comes to pass."[21] Also, there seems to be little reluctance to use the word *determine*. Berkhof says, "Reformed theology stresses the sovereignty of God in virtue of which He has sovereignly determined from all eternity whatsoever will come to pass."[22] Pink asserts, "He has determined in Himself from all eternity everything which will be."[23] God's decree "determines the certain occurrence of all things that ever come to pass," says A. A. Hodge.[24] Some would find it difficult to

16. Ibid., p. 147.

17. Ibid., p. 152.

18. Ibid., pp. 153-154. This whole section in Berkouwer is very weak, and he certainly does not succeed in his attempt to repudiate causation. He points out quite correctly that the essential difference between determinism and Christianity is that one proceeds from an impersonal power and the other from a personal power (pp. 151-152). But this in itself does not exclude causation. Thus there is a *non sequitur* in the implied connection between these statements, "The living God rules here!" and "We cannot explain the sequence of history with an all devouring system of causation."

19. Ibid., p. 153.

20. Louis Berkhof, *Systematic Theology*, p. 106.

21. Loraine Boettner, *The Reformed Doctrine of Predestination* (Grand Rapids: Eerdmans, 1932), p. 46.

22. Louis Berkhof, *Systematic Theology*, p. 100.

23. Arthur W. Pink, *The Sovereignty of God*, revised ed. (London: Banner of Truth Trust, 1961), p. 75.

24. A. A. Hodge, *Outlines of Theology*, p. 165.

give a clear distinction between cause and determination. Perhaps Gordon Clark is most consistent when he says simply that God "decrees and causes" all things.[25] The suggestion that God only permits some things to happen and does not actually cause them, says Clark, "ignores God's omnipotence and sovereignty. It presupposes that there is some force in the universe independent of God; no doubt God could counteract this force, but he does not; and the force or agent causes some event entirely apart from God's causation."[26] If there is something not caused by God, "there must be a cause external to and independent of God. In other words, God has ceased to be God."[27]

A final point is that the decree is *unconditional* or absolute.[28] This means that nothing in the decree has been conditioned by anything outside of God; God did not include anything in the decree as a response to or reaction to something. "God initiates all things";[29] what he decrees and does in no way depends upon the creature. This is the only way God can be sovereign. "A conditional decree would subvert the sovereignty of God and make him . . . dependent upon the uncontrollable actions of his own creatures."[30] This point is usually asserted over against the idea that God foreknows the free acts of his creatures, in which case some of God's knowledge would be derived from the creatures and even some of his decisions would be based on what he foresees in them. Such an idea, says Chafer, "places God in the unworthy position of being dependent upon His creatures."[31] Thus the decree is unconditional. This rules out the idea of conditional election, or the predestination of anyone to heaven on the basis of foreseen faith. The same God who predestines the end (heaven) also predestines the means (faith). The same is true of prayer. If God decrees an answer to prayer, this means that he has decreed the prayer also.[32] Everything is derived from the decree itself.

---

25. Gordon H. Clark, *Biblical Predestination* (Nutley, N.J.: Presbyterian and Reformed, 1969), p. 53. He is speaking specifically of human choices.

26. Ibid.

27. Gordon H. Clark, "The Sovereignty of God," *The Trinity Review* (November-December 1982), p. 4.

28. Louis Berkhof, *Systematic Theology*, p. 105. Another term is *independent* (see Herman Bavinck, *The Doctrine of God*, p. 370).

29. A. W. Pink, *The Sovereignty of God*, p. 158.

30. A. A. Hodge, *Outlines of Theology*, p. 168.

31. Lewis S. Chafer, Systematic Theology, I:230. It should be noted again that the item which is at stake is the free will of man.

32. William G. T. Shedd, *Dogmatic Theology* (Grand Rapids: Zondervan, 1969 reprint of 1888 edition), I:405.

The starting point, then, for Christian determinism is the eternal, comprehensive, efficacious, unconditional decree. This is seen as essential for maintaining the sovereignty of God.

Foreknowledge and the Decree

Since God's decree is unconditional, even his foreknowledge of future events is unconditional. That is, his foreknowledge is in no way dependent upon or derived from the events themselves. What *is* the relation between foreknowledge and the decree, then? Obviously since God is omniscient, he does know all future events with an infallible knowledge. If this knowledge is not derived from the events, whence is it derived? The answer is that it depends upon the decree itself. God foreknows all future events because and only because he has foreordained them. Otherwise he would not be able to know them.

This is the standard view of Christian determinists. Shedd says, "The Divine decree is the necessary condition of the Divine foreknowledge. If God does not first decide what shall come to pass, he cannot know what will come to pass."[33] Strong agrees: "No undecreed event can be foreseen." Thus "God cannot foreknow actualities unless he has by his decree made them to be certainties of the future. . . . He foreknows the future which he has decreed, and he foreknows it because he has decreed it."[34] Pink says emphatically, "Is it not clear that God foreknows what will be *because He has decreed what shall be*? . . . Foreknowledge of future events then is founded upon God's decrees, hence if God foreknows everything that is to be, it is because He has determined in Himself from all eternity everything which will be."[35]

In this connection Acts 2:23 is taken as implying a causal connection between predetermination and foreknowledge. It refers to the fact that Jesus was "delivered up by the predetermined plan and foreknowledge of God." The King James Version uses the term "determinate counsel." In referring to this passage Clark says, "Note that *foreknowledge* is dependent on determinate counsel."[36]

---

33. Ibid., pp. 396-397.

34. Augustus H. Strong, *Systematic Theology*, 3 vols. in 1 (Valley Forge: Judson Press, 1907), p. 357.

35. A. W. Pink, *The Sovereignty of God*, pp. 74-75.

36. Gordon H. Clark, "The Sovereignty of God," p. 4. Those who try to follow this suggestion will search the text in vain for any such reference to dependence.

Free Will Acts and the Decree

Since the decree is comprehensive and includes "whatsoever comes to pass," it must necessarily include all human thoughts, choices, decisions, and actions. In this regard human beings are no different from any other part of the creation.

> In biblical theology everything that God does is the outworking of his sovereign decree. In this respect man is no different from the stars or from the sands of the sea; that humans stand at a definite place in history is no more an accident than that the planets move in their orbits and that the nations have their given bounds.[37]

Man's free will acts are said to be both determined and free. The eternal decree "determines the free act through the free will of the free agent," says A. A. Hodge.[38] Thomistic theory declares, "In spite of freewill, . . . the influence which God exerts on His rational creatures is irresistible because it proceeds from an absolute and omnipotent Being whose decrees brook no opposition. What God wills infallibly happens." Also, "The Divine Omnipotence not only makes the action possible, but likewise effects it by moving the will from potentiality to actuality. . . . Free-will is predetermined by God before it determines itself."[39]

It is no wonder that most Christian determinists are somewhat uncomfortable with such language as it stands, sensing some kind of apparent contradiction. Thus a modification of the terms is usually indicated. We can see why some want to exclude the idea of causality from the determining decree. Usually it is said that the decree determines all things by rendering them certain or making them certain. "To predestinate voluntary action is, to *make it certain*"; to *force* voluntary action would be a contradiction, says Shedd.[40] Strong explains that God decrees free acts "in the only sense in which we use the word decreeing, *viz.*, a rendering certain, or embracing in his plan."[41]

---

37. Carl F. H. Henry, *God, Revelation and Authority, Volume VI: God Who Stands and Stays, Part Two* (Waco: Word Books, 1983), p. 78.

38. A. A. Hodge, *Outlines of Theology*, p. 169.

39. Joseph Pohle, *Grace Actual and Habitual*, ed. Arthur Preuss (St. Louis: B. Herder Book Co., 1949), pp. 233-234.

40. W. G. T. Shedd, *Dogmatic Theology*, I:413.

41. A. H. Strong, *Systematic Theology*, p. 358. We have already pointed out how difficult it is to exclude the idea of causation from a sovereign decree.

The Nature of Free Will

It might seem that the easiest course for a Christian determinist is simply to deny that there is such a thing as free will, as some have done.[42] But most Christian determinists are *compatibilists,* that is, they believe that free will (in some sense) is compatible with or can be reconciled with determinism in some way.[43] Their view is that "there is no logical inconsistency between free will and determinism, and that it is possible that human beings are free and responsible for their actions even though these actions are causally determined."[44] Thus they assert free will or free agency or at least full responsibility[45] in the strongest of terms, as illustrated in this quotation from A. A. Hodge: "This matter of free-will underlies everything. If you bring it to question, it is infinitely more than Calvinism. . . . Everything is gone if free-will is gone; the moral system is gone if free-will is gone."[46]

Though free will is freely asserted, it must be carefully defined in order to be compatible with deterministic sovereignty. The one definition that is ruled out on every hand is freedom as the power of contrary choice, that is, the ability to choose to do something as well as not to do it, or the ability to choose not to do something as well as to do it. This is the kind of freedom that is regarded as inconsistent with sovereignty. It is the kind Boettner has in mind in the following statement:

> Furthermore, if we admit free will in the sense that the absolute determination of events is placed in the hands of man, we might as well spell it with a capital F and a capital W; for then man has become like God, —a first cause, an original spring of action,—and we have as many semi-Gods as we have free wills. Unless the sovereignty of God be given up, we cannot allow this independence to man. . . .[47]

---

42. See in chapter two above, pp. 75-79, 82.

43. Ronald Nash, *The Concept of God* (Grand Rapids: Zondervan, 1983), p. 53.

44. William Hasker, *Metaphysics: Constructing a World View* (Downers Grove, Ill.: InterVarsity Press, 1983), p. 33. Italics omitted.

45. Even when reluctant to verbalize "free will," the determinist will emphasize *responsibility.* Pink says, "Two things are beyond dispute: God is sovereign, man is responsible." "The Scriptures set forth both the sovereignty of God and the responsibility of man" (*The Sovereignty of God,* pp. 9, 11). See the title of D. A. Carson's *Divine Sovereignty and Human Responsibility.*

46. A. A. Hodge, *Evangelical Theology* (London: Thomas Nelson and Sons, 1890), p. 157; cited in D. A. Carson, *Divine Sovereignty and Human Responsibility,* p. 207.

47. Loraine Boettner, *The Reformed Doctrine of Predestination,* p. 222.

It "tears the reins of government out of the hands of God, and robs Him of His power."[48]

What, then, *is* the nature of free will, according to the compatibilist view? Basically it is the ability to act *voluntarily,* choosing one's course of actions freely and without coercion in accord with one's character, inner motivation, and rational consideration. As Carson says, it means "the power of unconstrained, spontaneous, voluntary . . . choice."[49] As so defined, a person may have only one course of action open to him and still be free. "For example, a man may be locked in a room, but not want to get out. He therefore cannot get out (that is certain), but equally he does not want to get out (he is not there against his will)."[50] Thus even though the divine decree has foreordained that every single choice one makes will be that way and no other, every choice is still free because God has foreordained that each one will be made voluntarily. Here is Carl Henry's explanation (or rather, assertion):

> . . . What defines human nature is not the power of arbitrary decision and unpredictable action, but rather man's ability to act in view of reason and motive and hence in accord with character. . . . Responsible free agency consists in rational self-determination. To be morally responsible man needs only the capacity for choice, not the freedom of contrary choice. . . . Human beings voluntarily choose to do what they do. The fact that God has foreordained human choices and that his decree renders human actions certain does not therefore negate human choice.[51]

Such action is considered free because nothing outside a person is exerting any force on him to compel him to act that way and no other. Rather the choice is based upon his own inner desires, motives, and character. A person takes account of these, consciously or not, and then chooses to act in whatever way he desires to act. Thus "the *immediate cause* of the action is a psychological state of affairs internal to the agent—a wish, desire, intention or something of the sort."[52] Nash calls this the *"liberty of spontaneity,"* or "the ability to do whatever the person wants to do." Whether he has the ability to do otherwise is irrelevant; "the key question is whether he is able to do what

48. Ibid., p. 218.
49. D. A. Carson, *Divine Sovereignty and Human Responsibility,* p. 207.
50. Ibid.
51. Carl F. H. Henry, *God, Revelation and Authority,* VI:84-85.
52. William Hasker, *Metaphysics,* p. 34.

he most wants to do."[53] As Enoch Pond says, freedom "implies a proper natural ability to choose and act as the subject pleases."[54]

The key words here are *desire* and *motive.* One is free as long as he is able to choose according to his desires and motives. Chafer says that freedom is "the power of acting according to the prevailing inclination, or the motive which appears strongest to the mind."[55] "*What is it* that determines the will?" asks Pink. "We reply, The strongest motive power which is brought to bear upon it."[56] "Free agency is the power of self-determination in view of motives."[57]

This all seems innocent enough until we ask the question, What is the origin of the desires and motives? We must remember that the sovereign decree is comprehensive, and that it foreordains not only the ends God seeks but also all the means necessary for achieving those ends. Thus if God has predetermined that a person will act in a specific way at a specific time, *and* that he will so act voluntarily and without compulsion, all he has to do is to foreordain that his heart will possess the appropriate desires and motives at that time. Thus God can infallibly guarantee that all people will always choose just as he wants them to choose, even though they choose freely, because he controls the stuff out of which these choices are made. As Boettner says, "God so governs the inward feelings, external environment, habits, desires, motives, etc., of men that they freely do what he purposes." Also,

> . . . The comprehensive decree provides that each man shall be a free agent, possessing a certain character, surrounded by a certain environment, subject to certain external influences, internally moved by certain affections, desires, habits, etc., and that in view of all these he shall freely and rationally make a choice. That the choice will be one thing and not another, is certain; and God, who knows and controls the exact causes of each influence, knows what that choice will be, and in a real sense determines it. . . .[58]

Chafer argues similarly:

> When exercising his will, man is conscious only of his freedom of action. He determines his course by circumstances, but God is the author

53. Ronald Nash, *The Concept of God*, p. 54.

54. Enoch Pond, *Lectures on Christian Theology* (Boston: Congregational Board of Education, 1867), p. 304.

55. Lewis S. Chafer, *Systematic Theology*, I:243.

56. A. W. Pink, *The Sovereignty of God*, p. 96.

57. A. H. Strong, *Systematic Theology*, p. 360.

58. Loraine Boettner, *The Reformed Doctrine of Predestination*, pp. 214-215.

> of circumstances. Man is impelled by emotions, but God is able to originate and to control every human emotion. Man prides himself that he is governed by experienced judgment, but God is able to foster each and every thought or determination of the human mind. God will mold and direct in all secondary causes until His own eternal purpose is realized. . . .[59]

As Pond says, "God governs the moral world by motives."[60]

One way of describing how this might happen is to picture God as having in his mind every possible world that could be created. These would include worlds similar in every respect with the exception of one slightly different motive in one person in one of the worlds. They would include a different world for each possible combination of desires and motives for that person. They would include a different world for every possible combination of all possible persons. Though the number of possible worlds would thus be unimaginable to us, God knew them all perfectly—including possible worlds where the people had free will and where they did not. Now, out of all these possibilities, God decided —decreed—to create just one. He made the selection, therefore he determined precisely what combination of details would eventuate throughout the course of history. He did determine to create one of the worlds in which man has free will; but since he has selected one and only one of those possibilities, the world will unfold in precisely the way God has predetermined it, with the precise combination of free will choices that he desired. Thus even though we may always choose freely, it is impossible that we could choose anything other than what we do. This view is given by Pond in the following paragraph:

> In the order of nature, then, we are, first of all, to conceive of the Divine Being himself, in the possession of his essential and eternal attributes,—among which is *omniscience*. In the possession of omniscience, he looks out upon the whole range and compass of possible things. But everything, at this state, is barely *possible*. "I can adopt this plan, that, or the other,—anything, everything, within the range of possibility." As yet nothing is fixed, nothing determined on . . . . But among all the possible plans of operation presented to the Omniscient Mind, instantly and intuitively, the *best* plan is discovered, and instantly it is preferred or adopted. It is adopted in all its branches and particulars,—in all its endless ramifications. Everything embraced in this plan (and everything *is* embraced in it) is now settled and certain . . . .[61]

---

59. Lewis S. Chafer, *Systematic Theology*, I:241.
60. Enoch Pond, *Lectures on Christian Theology*, p. 284.
61. Ibid., pp. 185-186. See also Lewis S. Chafer, *Systematic Theology*, 8:230; A. H. Strong, *Systematic Theology*, pp. 356-358.

Here, then, is the determinists' concept of free will. Neither the power nor the possibility of alternate choice is essential to this view. It is only necessary that a man voluntarily choose his acts in accord with his own desires and motives; it matters not that God has sovereignly foreordained those desires and motives, along with the choices themselves.

Concurrence

In the chapter on general providence we discussed the concept of concurrence as it applies to natural processes. It should be noted that those who hold this doctrine, principally Christian determinists, apply it also to the acts of moral creatures. Thus every act of man has two causes, a primary cause which is God himself, and a secondary cause which is the person's own will. "In a very real sense the operation is the product of both causes."[62] The secondary cause (man) is never able to act in and of itself but can only act when energized by God. "So God also enables and prompts His rational creatures, as second causes, to function, and that not merely by endowing them with energy in a general way, but by energizing them to certain specific acts."[63]

The main point of the doctrine is to guard the sovereignty of God against the threat of the idea of some kind of independent action on the part of man. Carson prefers the term *ultimacy* to *concurrence*, because he thinks the latter is open to "synergistic overtones." That is, someone might be tempted to give too much weight to man's part in the tandem. He is not willing to give up the idea of man as second cause, but he diminishes it considerably.[64]

The fact is that it is very difficult for compatibilists to maintain the integrity of the human side of the concurring causes. In their efforts to do so they offer some creative expressions, such as Shedd's idea of "decreed self-determination,"[65] and A. A. Hodge's combination of God's "directive energy" with man's "spontaneity."[66] It is not too farfetched to think that such straining would not be worth the effort if

62. Louis Berkhof, *Systematic Theology*, p. 173.

63. Ibid.

64. D. A. Carson, *Divine Sovereignty and Human Responsibility*, pp. 210ff. See Chafer's comment that God's "sovereign power and purpose are working through and over all human forces and secondary causes" (*Systematic Theology*, I:242).

65. W. G. T. Shedd, *Dogmatic Theology*, I:404.

66. Archibald Alexander Hodge, *Popular Lectures on Theological Themes* (Philadelphia: Presbyterian Board of Publication, 1887), p. 49. He speaks of God's "immanent working within their will, whereby his directive energy becomes confluent with their own spontaneity."

it were not for the fact that some of man's acts are sinful. Hence a measure of freedom must be maintained in order to divert any blame for sin from God to man.

Sinful Acts and the Sovereign Decree

Perhaps the most difficult problem faced by Christian determinists is why the sovereign decree should have included sin in the first place. Since the decree is comprehensive it does include sin; and since the decree is efficacious God must in some sense have determined it; and since the decree is unconditional he must have decided to include sin in the decree of his own sovereign choice. Such considerations as these lead Chafer to wonder what *purpose* God saw for decreeing sin. He concludes that there are some desired ends that "are wholly dependent for their fruition upon the presence of sin in the world." Thus we must trust that God knew what he was doing by decreeing sin.[67]

But is there a more specific way to explain it in relation to divine sovereignty? Shedd considers the main possibilities that have been set forth and judges them all inadequate. He only knows that in whatever way God is related to the origin of sin, "it must be by a method that does not involve his causation."[68]

One explanation is that God causes the "matter" but not the "form" of sin.[69] That is, he determines the act itself but not the sinful part of it. The formal element is basically the sinful intention or motive behind the act. In terms of the doctrine of concurrence, God concurs in the act as such but not in the intention. This view is accepted by Pohle[70] and by Pieper, who does not really like the distinction but says it is the best we can do until we get to heaven.[71]

The most common method of explaining this problem is to say that with respect to sin, the sovereign decree is permissive rather than efficacious. The concept of permissive decrees is necessitated only by the imperative to account for sin. "The permissive decrees embrace

---

67. Lewis S. Chafer, *Systematic Theology*, I:235-236.

68. W. G. T. Shedd, *Dogmatic Theology*, I:411-412.

69. Ibid., p. 412.

70. Joseph Pohle, *God: The Author of Nature and the Supernatural*, ed. Arthur Preuss (St. Louis: B. Herder, 1912), pp. 68-69.

71. Francis Pieper, *Christian Dogmatics*, tr. Theodore Engelder et al. (St. Louis: Concordia Publishing House, 1950), I:490.

only moral features which are evil," says Chafer.[72] This means that God rendered all sinful acts certain, but he does not effectuate them or actively promote them as he does good acts.[73] Not everyone is comfortable with this distinction, however, including John Calvin. Noting the extreme difficulty of explaining the sovereign God's relation to wicked deeds, Calvin comments that some try to "escape by the shift that this is done only with God's permission, not also by his will; but he, openly declaring that he is the doer, repudiates that evasion."[74] Carl Henry finds that "the distinction between permissive will and efficient will is not very helpful."[75] Nevertheless it is commonly accepted, though with the qualification that we are not talking about "mere" or "bare" permission.

The mechanics of permission within a sovereign decree are not easy to comprehend, but some attempt to offer an explanation. It is basically the same as the one used to explain free will in general, i.e., in terms of God's sovereign control over the motives and circumstances that motivate us to act as we do. The omniscient God knows what circumstances and what motives will infallibly produce a free will decision to sin. Through his sovereign foreordination of these he renders our sins certain without being responsible for them. For example, speaking of sinful acts A. A. Hodge says, "Yet God's permissive decree does truly determine the certain futurition of the act; because God knowing certainly that the man in question would in the given circumstances so act, did place that very man in precisely those circumstances that he should so act."[76] Boettner agrees and says this is why we should never speak of "a bare permission, for with full knowledge of the nature of the person and of his tendency to sin, God places him or allows him to be in a certain environment, knowing perfectly well that the particular sin will be committed."[77] Berkhof cites with approval a statement by R. L. Dabney which explains this point well:

> This, then, is my picture of the providential evolution of God's purpose as to sinful acts; so to arrange and group events and objects around free

72. Lewis S. Chafer, *Systematic Theology*, I:236. See W. G. T. Shedd, *Dogmatic Theology*, I:406: "The permissive decree relates only to moral evil. Sin is the sole and solitary object of this species of decree."

73. Ibid.; Louis Berkhof, *Systematic Theology*, p. 105.

74. John Calvin, *Institutes of the Christian Religion*, I:xviii.1, ed. John T. McNeill, tr. Ford Lewis Battles (Philadelphia: Westminster Press, 1960), I:229.

75. Carl F. H. Henry, *God, Revelation and Authority*, VI:86.

76. A. A. Hodge, *Outlines of Theology*, p. 170.

77. Loraine Boettner, *The Reformed Doctrine of Predestination*. p. 229.

agents by his manifold wisdom and power, as to place each soul, at every step, in the presence of those circumstances, which, He knows, will be a sufficient objective inducement to it to do, of its own native, free activity, just the thing called for by God's plan. Thus the act is man's alone, though its occurrence is efficaciously secured by God. And the sin is man's only. . . .[78]

Sovereign Foreknowledge

A second determinist approach to the relation between sovereignty and free will is derived from a particular view of foreknowledge. This view is presented and discussed in two separate contexts, in philosophical theology as well as biblical theology. It is a view usually cited in passing by Christian determinists in reply to those theists who object to their reasoning concerning the foreordaining decree. The determinist says, in effect, "So you don't like the idea of the sovereign decree, do you? You think that the idea of foreordination is inconsistent with human freedom? Well, what about fore*knowledge*? You do believe in foreknowledge, don't you? Well, let me tell you something. Everything that you object to in reference to the decree is true also by virtue of foreknowledge alone! You don't have to accept the decree if you don't want to, but your precious concept of freedom is no more secure with foreknowledge than with foreordination." As Strong says, "The decrees are, like foreknowledge, an act eternal to the divine nature, and are no more inconsistent with free agency than foreknowledge is."[79]

Why this is so can be stated very simply. If God foreknows all things, even the free choices of human beings, then all these things are *certain*, since God's knowledge cannot be wrong. As Strong says, "Even foreknowledge of events implies that those events are fixed."[80] In the final analysis, then, man has no choice when it comes to his actions. They have been certain to occur since eternity, hence freedom seems

---

78. Robert L. Dabney, *Syllabus and Notes of the Course of Systematic and Polemic Theology*, 5 ed. (Richmond, Va.: Presbyterian Committee of Publication, 1871), p. 288; cited in Louis Berkhof, *Systematic Theology*, pp. 175-176.

79. A. H. Strong, *Systematic Theology*, p. 359. See the statement in Enoch Pond, *Lectures on Christian Theology*, pp. 190-191: "It will be perceived, also, that the objections commonly urged against the universal purposes of God lie with equal weight against this theory of universal foreknowledge. As remarked above, the former is no more inconsistent with human freedom than the latter. If universal foreknowledge can be reconciled with the unembarrassed free agency of man, universal decrees can be reconciled just as well, and after the same manner."

80. A. H. Strong, *Systematic Theology*, p. 359.

to be a chimera. Swinburne sums it up thus: "If God is omniscient then he foreknows all future human actions. If God foreknows anything, then it will necessarily come to pass. But if a human action will necessarily come to pass, then it cannot be free."[81]

This then raises another question. If foreknown future events are fixed and certain, who or what made them that way? The answer is that God must have, since he was the only one who was around when his foreknowledge rendered the events certain. "Foreknowledge implies fixity, and fixity implies decree," says Strong.[82] Boettner says the same thing: "Foreknowledge implies certainty, and certainty implies foreordination."[83] In Bavinck's words, "'God's foreknowledge' is of such a character that its object is foreknown with absolute certainty, and then it is identical with predestination."[84] Thus whether we accept the sovereign decree or only the sovereign foreknowledge, the result is said to be the same with regard to free will. "Foreknowledge on the part of God carries with it, of necessity, all the force of a sovereign purpose," says Chafer.[85]

Now, if the objector acknowledges the force of the argument from sovereign foreknowledge, he has only two choices. He may become a determinist, or may deny the reality of the foreknowledge of future contingent events (free will decisions in particular). Many have opted to do the latter. One example is Swinburne, who presents "a modified account of omniscience."[86] Omniscience means that God knows of every true proposition that it is true, he says. But if future free decisions have not been actualized yet, then statements about them are neither true nor false. Thus God's lack of knowledge about these events does not diminish his omniscience, because there is nothing there to know in the first place.[87] Another example is Steuer, who rejects foreknowledge simply because it is incompatible with free choice.[88]

Most Christian determinists find this alternative appalling, of course. They no more want to limit the sovereign foreknowledge of God than

81. Richard Swinburne, *The Coherence of Theism* (Oxford: Clarendon Press, 1977), p. 167.

82. A. H. Strong, *Systematic Theology*, p. 356.

83. Loraine Boettner, *The Reformed Doctrine of Predestination*, p. 44.

84. Herman Bavinck, *The Doctrine of God*, p. 377.

85. Lewis S. Chafer, *Systematic Theology*, I:237.

86. Richard Swinburne, *The Coherence of Theism*, pp. 172ff.

87. Ibid., p. 174. See the brief discussion of this view in William Hasker, *Metaphysics*, pp. 51ff.

88. Axel D. Steuer, "The Supposed Incoherence of the Concept of God," *Is God God?*, ed. Axel D. Steuer and James W. McClendon, Jr. (Nashville: Abingdon Press, 1981), p. 101.

the sovereign decree. And from either perspective, the concept of freedom must be either rejected or modified.

Sovereign Grace

A final and more limited determinist approach to the problem of free will is the argument from sovereign grace. The idea here is that sinful man is not free to do anything whatsoever toward his salvation, else the freedom and sovereignty of God's grace are jeopardized. Those who hold to this view usually subscribe to the doctrine of the sovereign decree as well as to the doctrine of total depravity, but the latter is an entirely separate line of thought and as such is only one aspect of the total problem of human free will for the determinist. In fact it is not even the primary aspect of the problem, for the limitations placed on the human will by the sovereign decree are much more basic than those derived from human depravity. The great Reformation theologians knew this, of course, and they accepted both kinds of limitation. Thus Berkouwer is wrong to declare that "Calvin's entire view of the bondage of the will" depended on his view of the fall of Adam; and that the Reformers "did not attack the creaturely freedom which God had created in human life, for this creaturely freedom did not compete with the omnipotent activity of God."[89]

In any case the argument from sovereign grace is a distinct perspective and deserves to be discussed in its own right. Some discussions of sovereignty tend to focus mostly on the limitations imposed by sin, thus avoiding some of the more difficult philosophical problems. Examples are Pink's book, *The Sovereignty of God,* and Arthur Custance's *The Sovereignty of Grace.*[90] In this connection the limitation on man's will began with the fall of Adam, which resulted (according to the view) in a state of total depravity for every natural member of the human race. The essence of total depravity is the total inability to do anything truly good in the sight of God, especially the total inability to do anything toward receiving salvation. Another term for

89. G. C. Berkouwer, *The Providence of God,* pp. 150, 152. In a strict sense Berkouwer could argue that he is right, since the "creaturely freedom" *as defined by the Reformers* did not compete with omnipotence. His statements leave the impression, however, that their whole discussion of human freedom revolved around the doctrine of total depravity, which is not the case.

90. Arthur C. Custance, *The Sovereignty of Grace* (Phillipsburg, N.J.: Presbyterian and Reformed, 1979).

this inability is *bondage of the will.* Man's will is bound in the sense that it is wholly inclined toward evil and impotent with respect to good. Here is where the rejection of freedom as the power of contrary choice is really stressed. The determinist strenuously denies that the sinner is free either to sin or not to sin, that he is free either to do good or to do evil. Freedom in this sense does not exist. But "free will" is not denied as such; it is simply redefined in accordance with the definition cited earlier in this chapter, namely, the ability to choose and to act in accordance with one's desires and character. But of course, since the sinner is totally depraved, he has only wicked desires and a wicked character to inform his will. Hence he always chooses sin, but he does so freely.

Starting with this concept of the bondage of the will, the determinist then argues that salvation must be *all of God* in every respect. God must choose who will be saved (since no depraved person would ever choose it for himself); this is unconditional predestination. And of course God must decide the time and the place for his sovereign bestowal of salvation on the chosen individual in an act of irresistible grace. And then the new believer's continuing sanctification and security are totally in God's hands, as he brings his chosen to glory. Thus given the doctrine of total depravity, the concept of sovereign grace seems to be a moral necessity if not a physical one. How else would the sinner ever be saved?

But at this point most determinists interject another element into the discussion which is not strictly dependent upon the fall and total depravity. The sinner is prevented from making any effort toward his salvation—even believing—not just by his condition of inability but by the demands of sovereignty as such. The idea is that if man is allowed to make just one move in the direction of salvation, even a passive one, then the honor and the glory of God's grace are somehow called into question. So in order for God to safeguard his sovereignty in the bestowal of grace, he must be allowed to do everything and initiate everything relating to man's salvation and good works. This is the concept of sovereign grace. It is often called monergism, a word which means that only *one person* is working in the process of salvation, namely, God. At the same time there is a rejection of synergism, the idea that man works with God to some degree in coming to salvation. This "working with God" is taken to include such basic decisions as believing and repenting; even these cannot be allowed as free choices if God is to remain sovereign. Thus he gives faith and repentance to those whom he chooses. This is the determinist explanation of such passages of Scripture as John 6:44; Acts 13:48; and Acts 16:14.

Arthur Custance's energetic defense of the sovereignty of grace is a good example of this point of view. In addition to the standard presentation of total depravity, irresistible grace, and the rest, Custance mounts an unrelenting attack on synergism as such. His last chapter, "The Leaven of Synergism," could stand as a rejection of human freedom totally apart from the consideration of total depravity. His concluding page includes these comments:

> . . . If man contributes any essential part towards his salvation, he effectively becomes his own saviour, even if that contribution takes no more concrete form than that of merely allowing God to act by non-resistance.
>
> There is here a clear point of demarcation. It is all of God or it is no good news at all. If man is free to resist, God is not free to act, for He is bound by man's freedom. If God is to be free to act, man must be bound by the will of God. . . .
>
> In truth there is no "Gospel" that is not entirely rooted in the sovereignty of God's grace in salvation, which is the sum and substance of Calvinism. . . . The crucial issue is the sovereignty of God's grace in the most absolute sense, a pure unabashed Monergism.
>
> The only defence against Synergism is an unqualified Calvinism ascribing all the glory to God by insisting upon the total spiritual impotence of man, an Election based solely upon the good pleasure of God, an Atonement intended only for the elect though sufficient for all men, a grace that can neither be resisted nor earned, and a security for the believer that is as permanent as God Himself.[91]

It should be noted also that it is God who works every good work in the believer, "both to will and to work for His good pleasure" (Philippians 2:13). The fact that God thus energizes the believer for good works preserves his sovereignty.

Conclusion

In this section we have seen how the determinist view of divine sovereignty has led to an attenuated view of free will in three different

91. Ibid., p. 364.

ways. First, by his sovereign decree God foreordains all things which come to pass, including human free acts. Thus freedom has to be redefined to make it compatible with predetermination. Second, God's sovereign foreknowledge in and of itself is said to have the same effect as the decree, with the same limiting result for human free will. Third, the sovereign grace of God does not allow the depraved sinner to make any free choices toward his own salvation; thus his will *must* be bound if God's grace is to remain sovereign.

This is the systematic framework within which Christian determinists explain the numerous biblical passages set forth earlier in this chapter as well as in the last chapter. Everything happens the way it does, the sinful things as well as the saving things, because God's sovereignty makes it so. After we present an alternative to this view in the next section, we will make some critical comments on the determinist approach in the last section of this chapter.

A NON-DETERMINIST ALTERNATIVE

I believe that the determinist view as described above is a pious and sincere effort to come to grips with the facts of special providence as presented in the Bible and to reconcile the concepts of divine sovereignty and human freedom. I do not believe, however, that this is the correct dogmatic framework for understanding these data and these concepts, nor do I believe that this framework is required by them. I do not believe that the Bible teaches that the causation or determination or foreordination of all things is the *sine qua non* of divine sovereignty. I do not believe that the concept of human freedom needs a radical redefinition in order to make it compatible with biblical teaching. But I do believe that if anyone does not agree with the determinist view, then he ought to be able to present a viable alternative. That is what I will attempt to do in this section. It is my conviction that the doctrine of special providence as it relates to sovereignty and free will is best understood on a non-determinist model, and that this is the model that is more true to the biblical teaching.

Divine Self-Limitation

A key to the proper understanding of biblical providence is the concept of divine self-limitation.[92] When God decided to create anything, his

92. The concept of divine self-limitation has already been discussed to some extent in Jack Cottrell, *What the Bible Says About God the Creator* (Joplin, Mo.: College Press, 1983), pp. 243ff., 285ff., 296ff.

sovereign choice to create was a choice to limit himself. The very *existence* of other being alongside God's being is a limiting factor. God can no longer claim to be the only being in existence. Of course he is the only self-existent, uncaused being; thus his uniqueness is not threatened. But in the very act of granting existence to other beings, he gives up his exclusive claim to being. As Brunner says, "The two ideas, Creation and self-limitation, are correlative. Anyone who has taken the first idea seriously has already conceived the second. . . . The idea of the divine self-limitation is included in that of the creation of a world which is not God."[93]

Once one has recognized the inherent self-limitation of creation as such, it is not difficult to accept the fact that God has limited himself with respect to his providential government also. This is not true of necessity, as in the case of creation, for God could have chosen some other method of ruling the world. He could have chosen the determinist model if he had so willed. But he did not. Instead he chose a self-limiting form of government in which his creatures have been endowed with a measure of self-determination. He has elected not to be the direct cause or determiner of everything that comes to pass. In Brunner's words, "omni-causality has been given up."[94] Thus he "limits Himself, in order to create room for the creature."[95]

We have already seen how this is true with regard to natural processes and natural law. By virtue of God's gift of relative independence natural causes are true causes and do not just "second the motion" initiated by God *unless* for purposes relating to his special providence God decides to intervene. Now, what is true of nature is also true of the free will acts of God's rational creatures, including mankind. In choosing to create such beings with minds and wills, God sovereignly limits himself by allowing them to use these gifts as a means of self-determination.[96] Thus God respects the integrity of the freedom with which he has endowed human beings, and does not intervene in their decisions

---

93. Emil Brunner, *The Christian Doctrine of Creation and Redemption: Dogmatics, Volume II*, tr. Olive Wyon (Philadelphia: Westminster Press, 1952), pp. 172-173.

94. Ibid., p. 173.

95. Ibid., p. 172.

96. Wilbur Tillett says, "When God created moral free agents he placed limitations upon his own will within the realm of human free agency" (*Providence, Prayer and Power*; Nashville: Cokesbury Press, 1926; p. 71). E. Y. Mullins says, "God has limited himself in his methods with free beings." "He is limited by human freedom" (*The Christian Religion in Its Doctrinal Expression;* Philadelphia: Judson Press, 1917; pp. 268, 348).

unless his special providential purposes call for it. Thus in the creation of free will beings God makes a commitment or a covenant with man to let him be what he was made to be, even if this means that at times man's decisions will go against what God himself would have decided if he had been determining everything. The following words by Paul M. van Buren are not directed specifically to the point of free will but they are relevant nonetheless:

> . . . Creation is presented in Scripture as an irreversible commitment on God's part, sealed with the rainbow.
>
> Once begun, creation is a condition on God. God cannot withdraw from this commitment, from the genuine and independent reality of the world, and therefore from his having become the God who has given his world this independence. From the time of Creation, God must, by his own decision, live with the world he has created. . . .[97]

Of course there are many who find it difficult to accept the fact of the divine self-limitation because they think that it is inconsistent with the sovereignty of God. But this is not the case for two reasons. First, God maintains his sovereignty because he reserves the *right* and the *power* to intervene in the decision-making process if his purposes demand it. It is true that God does not usually do this, and that he allows man to go his own way in most cases. But he can and does intervene if necessary; he is in complete control of the life of every individual. He is not like the lonely old woman in the fairy tale who made a gingerbread boy who came to life and escaped from her control. Free will is truly a limiting condition for God, as Baelz notes, but it is not ultimate.[98] God still has the ultimate word in everything. He is still sovereign. Contrary to Brunner's suggestion, he has not limited his absoluteness.[99] In fact he has it in his power to simply cancel the whole creation and send it back to nothingness. The "irreversible commitment" of which van Buren speaks is not irreversible because of some gap in God's power or sovereignty. It is such because of God's *faithfulness*. God is faithful to his purposes and to his creation; thus he maintains it in existence, and his control over it is still sovereign.

The second reason why self-limitation does not negate divine sovereignty is that it is *self*-limitation. The limitations with respect to

97. Paul M. van Buren, "Speaking of God," *Is God GOD?*, ed. Axel D. Steuer and James W. McClendon, Jr. (Nashville: Abingdon Press, 1981), p. 68.

98. Peter R. Baelz, *Prayer and Providence: A Background Study* (New York: Seabury Press, 1968), p. 132.

99. Emil Brunner, *The Christian Doctrine of Creation and Redemption*, p. 172.

natural processes and free will are not imposed upon God by powers existing independently outside him.[100] They are God's own choice; "the conditions themselves derive from the divine will."[101] Thus self-limitation in no way violates the divine sovereignty but is an expression of it. Pohle says,

> . . . That the First Cause should accommodate and conditionally subordinate itself to the nature and properties of the individual free creature, is not derogatory to the infinite dignity and sovereignty of God. . . . Having bound Himself by a solemn promise. . . , God cannot violate their free-will, but owes it to His own wisdom, sanctity, and justice to preserve it, to foster it, and to give it full sway. This is not derogatory to His dignity, nor does it imply self-abasement; it is simply a mystery of the divine omnipotence.[102]

Fisk agrees that "it is a noble view of God to see Him in His supremacy voluntarily allowing man a certain limited sphere of free action. . . . To allow man such a measure of self-determination is something which only a great and omnipotent God would do." Fisk continues,

> It should be borne in mind that if allowing man a measure of freedom were imposed upon God from without, or if it were forced upon Him by some strange necessity, objection to it might be made. But when it is that which He alone initiates—of His own voluntary doing—out of pure love and for high and lofty ends which His unmitigated omnipotence assures, it is only to the praise of His glory that it is so.[103]

We should note that the concept of self-limitation does not apply to the *being* of God, but only to his actions. God cannot limit or change what he is, nor can he limit himself by deciding not to do something necessitated by his nature. He can only limit himself by deciding not to do something which is not required by his nature in the first place. Since God's nature does not necessitate his direct causation of every natural event or his determination of every human decision, he is free to limit himself with respect to these.

---

100. See Georgia Harkness' discussion of the distinction between a *self-limited* God and a *finite* God (*The Providence of God;* Nashville: Abingdon Press, 1960; p. 105).

101. Peter Baelz, *Prayer and Providence*, p. 133.

102. Joseph Pohle, *God*, pp. 76-77.

103. Samuel Fisk, *Divine Sovereignty and Human Freedom* (Neptune, N.J.: Loizeaux Brothers, 1973), pp. 51-52.

Man's Relative Independence

I have chosen to use the term relative independence to describe the kind of freedom God has granted to his world via his self-limitation. This term is also used by Brunner and by Baelz.[104] As it applies to man it means that God has created human beings as persons with an innate power to initiate actions. That is, man is free to act without his acts having been predetermined by God and without the simultaneous coaction of God. As in the case of natural processes, the doctrine of concurrence is to be rejected as incompatible with human freedom and as unnecessary for divine sovereignty. In theory it is supposed to provide a way of regarding the human will as a genuine cause of action, though a secondary cause. In practice the secondary cause is usually absorbed into the ultimate causation of God. Thus concurrence is an unsatisfactory concept because it is too monergistic.[105] Acts 17:28 says that in God "we live and move and exist." This passage is usually quoted as a proof of concurrence, as in this statement by Pieper: "Acts 17:28 clearly teaches the thief or the murderer cannot perform his acts without God's concurrence; it states that all men, including the thieves and murderers, live in God, move in God, have their being in God."[106] This verse certainly shows why our independence is only relative, since it shows that we depend upon God for the constant preservation of our being and our lives. But the idea that we "move" in God does not mean that he concurs in or cooperates in every single thought or deed which springs from our hearts. It means rather that he preserves our status as rational beings who are free to act, while all the time maintaining his sovereign control over us.

Relative independence thus means that man is allowed to exercise his power of free choice without interference, coercion, or foreordination by God in the regular course of things, i.e., under God's general providence. At the same time, as noted above, the independence is *relative* because God maintains the right to intervene in order to influence and direct human decisions and behavior when his purposes call for it. And this is precisely what he does in the exercise of his special providence.

---

104. Emil Brunner, *The Christian Doctrine of God: Dogmatics, Volume I,* tr. Olive Wyon (Philadelphia: Westminster Press, 1950), p. 251; Peter Baelz, *Prayer and Providence,* pp. 133, 139.

105. Contrary to D. A. Carson, who is uneasy with the *term* "concurrence" because of its "synergistic overtones" (*Divine Sovereignty and Human Responsibility,* p. 210).

106. Francis Pieper, *Christian Dogmatics,* I:490.

How shall we define the freedom of the will under this concept of relative independence? We should note first of all, as the term indicates, that we are not talking about a total autonomy, though non-determinism often is accused of holding to such a view. The following scenario by Pink is an example of this:

> . . . For the sake of argument we will suppose that every man enters this world endowed with a will that is absolutely free, and that it is *impossible* to control him without *destroying* his freedom. If this were so, we have no guarantee against the entire human race committing moral suicide. Let all Divine restraints be removed and man be left absolutely free to do as *he* pleases, then all ethical distinctions would soon disappear, the spirit of barbarism would prevail universally, and pandemonium would reign supreme. Why not? . . .[107]

This is of course a caricature (in fact, a rather mild one) and does not represent the only alternative to determinism. True freedom is quite limited, not only by God's sovereignty but also by our own finiteness and by our self-inflicted sinfulness. We can agree with Fisk "that man's will is circumscribed in its exercise, that it operates within very definite limits, that it is bounded by the overall controlling plan and purpose of God, that the divine sovereignty is supreme in the larger outreach of all things."[108]

In the second place, it seems to me that some ability to choose between opposites must be maintained in the concept of free will. Sometimes this is called the power of contrary choice or the power of opposite choice. To be considered free with respect to any particular situation, a person must have alternative choices and the ability to actualize more than one choice. It may be that the alternatives will be only yes or no, or the ability to do something or not to do it. To say, for example, that a man locked in a room is free as long as he *wants* to stay in that room is little short of ridiculous. As long as there is no alternative to his staying in the room, an alternative that he can exercise, then he is not free with respect to that situation. For another example, when a sinner is confronted with the gospel and must decide whether to accept Christ as Savior or to reject him, that sinner is not free unless it is possible for him to do either one. To say that his total depravity leaves him with only one choice—to reject Christ, but that he is still free because that is the choice he prefers anyway, not only redefines freedom but simply defines it away.

107. A. W. Pink, *The Sovereignty of God*, p. 32.
108. Samuel Fisk, *Divine Sovereignty and Human Freedom*, p. 25.

We must insist, though, that such power of opposite choice not be equated with what is called the "liberty of indifference," as if the chooser had equal power and equal reason for selecting any one of the available alternatives. I think Hasker is deliberately exaggerating in the following description:

> . . . A great many reasons have been given why the experience of free choice cannot really be what it seems to be. Isn't it absurd to say that when we make choices, there is *no reason whatever* why we choose one way rather than another? But if there is such a reason, then doesn't this negate the idea that in making choices we, as it were, create our future out of nothing? . . .[109]

But this truly is a caricature of free will, even of the power of opposite choice, as is the following more serious statement by Carl Henry:

> Nearly all scholars who oppose predestination by emphasizing responsibility offer no theory of human responsibility. The fact is, that man does not have nor has he ever had, the freedom to decide and act in a manner that contradicts all his indicated decisions and deeds. What defines human nature is not the power of arbitrary decision and unpredictable action, but rather man's ability to act in view of reason and motive and hence in accord with character. To define human freedom as the power to act arbitrarily would equate freedom with unrestrained, capricious and random action. Humanity defined in terms of the Pelagian "liberty of indifference," that is of man's ability in each action to totally reverse his course and to be today the living contradiction of all that he was yesterday, reflects an abnormal and subrational rather than normative human experience. That sort of "free will" would make responsibility impossible. Responsible free agency consists in rational self-determination. To be morally responsible man needs only the capacity for choice, not the freedom of contrary choice. . . .[110]

It is really too bad that Henry leaves the impression that the freedom of contrary choice is necessarily defined as arbitrary, unpredictable, unrestrained, capricious, and random. Perhaps some have so defined it, but these characteristics are not of the essence of the concept. One does not have to be indifferent in order to be *able* to choose between opposites. The choices may not at all be equally appealing to him, and he may have a much stronger inclination to choose one over the other. Desires, motives, influences, and circumstances are all important factors in the distribution of preferences. One does not choose in a vacuum.

---

109. William Hasker, *Metaphysics*, p. 30.

110. Carl F. H. Henry, *God, Revelation and Authority*, VI:84-85.

But this does not mean that we are helpless in the face of circumstances and slaves to our own desires and motives. Sometimes a person chooses the more difficult course; sometimes he goes against his deepest desires and opts for duty; sometimes after much persuasion he may reverse his decision. As long as there is this possibility, there is freedom.

Finally, a third and most important consideration for the definition of free will is that it involves the ability to choose without that choice's being fixed or determined (either ahead of time or at the time) by some power outside the person himself. On the one hand this means the absence of force, coercion, constraint, or hindrance. On the other hand it means the absence of any condition or manipulating force that has limited a person's actual choices to just one, whether the person realizes it or not. Examples of such conditions or outside forces would be a brain abnormality, hypnotic suggestion, and an absolutely foreordaining decree. Hasker says that free will is sometimes defined as "the view that some human actions are chosen and performed by the agent without there being any sufficient condition or cause of the action prior to the action itself."[111] It seems to me that if the word *necessary* were substituted for *sufficient*, this would be closer to the truth. A free act is one performed without there being any *necessary* condition or cause. This of course means that the view that "a man acts freely if he does what he wants even if what he wants is predetermined"[112] is false. It will be remembered that this is the view favored by most determinists or compatibilists.

Thus we can say that free will is the ability to choose between opposites without that choice's being fixed or determined by some power outside the person's own will. We must remember that inner attitudes and outward circumstances do play an important role in influencing a person toward one choice or another. The relative independence of both nature and man himself means that the complex of circumstances in which most choices are made is the accumulated result of natural processes, the free acts of other people, and our own past choices. This is the basic context within which free will operates.

---

111. William Hasker, *Metaphysics*, p. 32. Italics omitted.

112. This view has been around at least since David Hume, according to Richard Swinburne (*The Coherence of Theism*, p. 143). See Hume's *An Enquiry Concerning Human Understanding*, section 8, "Of Liberty and Necessity." This work is included in *Hume: Theory of Knowledge*, ed. D. C. Yalden-Thomson (New York: Thomas Nelson and Sons, 1951).

But there is one other factor that enters into the context of our free choices, and that is the sovereign will of God. How does God's special providence relate to human decisions? That is the main point of this chapter, and it will now be specifically discussed.

God's Sovereign Control

If man has free will as described above, how does God maintain his sovereignty? How can he govern the world according to his purposes and toward his chosen ends? The answer lies in the difference between general providence and special providence. In the case of nature, as discussed above, God in his general providence allows the natural processes to operate without his direct interference. At the same time God keeps a constant watch over the whole of nature and stands ready and able to intervene, that is, to modify or even override the natural processes when necessary for his purposes. The same thing is basically true in reference to human free will. In his general providence God permits human beings to make their own decisions and forge their own ways in the historical process. But here is the whole point of special providence: when his special purposes require it, God does intervene in order to influence and direct and govern human decisions. And he is able to do this in such a way that his purposes are accomplished.

Our purpose now is to set forth the various ways in which God directs and uses human decisions and actions. It seems best to divide them into two categories, direct and indirect.

Direct Control

There are times when God has indisputably exercised direct control over human actions, times when he has caused people to do things they did not intend to do. There is the celebrated case of Balaam, the prophet-for-hire who intended to utter a curse upon Israel but under the Spirit of God pronounced a blessing instead (Num. 24:1ff.). Another example is King Saul, who along with others was trying to take David into custody. In the process, by the power of God's Spirit, he and the others were overcome by an ecstatic prophesying. "And he also stripped off his clothes, and he too prophesied before Samuel and lay down naked all that day and all that night" (I Sam. 19:24). A third example is the experience of speaking in tongues shared by the Apostles on the day of Pentecost (Acts 2:4ff.). In none of these cases did the participants choose to do what was done. God just took over and caused the actions to be performed.

One might point out, however, that all these examples seem to involve a miraculous intervention on the part of God, not a providential one. It seems that God was controlling the bodies of these people more than their minds and wills. But it does show that God is ready and able to enter the stream of history when he chooses and to control men's actions in a direct way according to his purposes.

Now the question is, is it possible that God at times might exercise some kind of direct control over the will itself, if his purpose should require it? Some would declare that this is impossible because it would violate the essence of man's freedom. But I am not sure that we can say it is *impossible* that God would ever do this. For comparison, we may consider the fact that a miracle is in a sense a violation of the natural processes. Ordinarily God respects the course of nature as he designed it, and even his special providence works within it and not outside it. But when necessary, on relatively rare occasions, God sets nature aside and works a miracle. I think we must leave open the possibility that he may do the same kind of thing with free will. Ordinarily he respects it as he designed it. But there may be rare occasions when God deems it necessary directly to cause someone's will to come to a particular decision. We must remember that both nature and man have a *relative* independence, not an absolute one.

As possible examples of such direct control we may consider the various occasions in the Old Testament when God is said to produce an effect on the hearts or attitudes of people. I am thinking particularly of the hardening of Pharaoh's heart, as well as the hearts of the Egyptian army, King Sihon, and Canaanite kings. I am also thinking of how the Lord gave the Israelites favor in the eyes of the Egyptians at the time of the Exodus, and I am thinking of how he put fear in the hearts of Israel's enemies. Other possible examples are the occasions when God moved the hearts of national leaders to make political and military decisions that led to the accomplishment of his purposes, such as the judicial destruction of nations such as Babylon, Assyria, and even Israel herself. We might also include the stirring up of King Cyrus to send the Israelites back to their homeland and the turning of the hearts of those kings who encouraged and helped in the rebuilding of the temple.

Even if we grant that cases such as these are examples of God's directly controlling the hearts and wills of individuals, we do not have any warrant for generalizing from these cases and assuming that this is the way God works with every decision of every will. For example, the statement in Proverbs 16:1, that "the plans of the heart belong to man, but the answer of the tongue is from the Lord," is perfectly illustrated in the case of Balaam. Certainly God can cause the tongue to say something different from what the person intended to say, if he wants to. If his purposes require such an overriding of the will, God will do it. But we have no reason to think that he does this as a general rule. If he simply allows us most of the time to go ahead and say what we planned to say, then the answer of the tongue is still "from the Lord" in the sense that he permitted us to say it. The same is true of Proverbs 21:1, the determinist proof-text which says that "the king's heart is . . . in the hand of the Lord; He turns it wherever He wishes." Let us grant that God can do this whenever he likes, but let us also refrain from assuming that this is supposed to be a general rule for all people at all times. We cannot even assume that *every* decision of *every* king is directly controlled by God. This verse is telling us what God *can* do if his purposes require it, and it may be that he has done it in the cases cited in the previous paragraph. It is a serious error to generalize from this or other such statements, as Clark does in the following statement:

> . . . Consider Proverbs 21:1, which says, "The king's heart is in the hand of the Lord: he turneth it whithersoever he will." It is amazing that anyone who calls himself a Christian and has read even a little part of the Bible can deny that God controls the mental operations of his creatures. The heart of man is in the hand of the Lord and the Lord turns man's heart in any direction the Lord pleases. The idea that man's will is free . . . is totally unbiblical and unchristian. As a clear denial of omnipotence, it dethrones God and takes man out of God's control.[113]

We must remember that the controlling factor in all of God's special providence is his special purposes. It is extremely important to remember that God's special purpose for Old Testament Israel was unique, and that the working out of this purpose required God to intervene in the course of history in ways unparalleled in any other time. This is why it is so perilous to take most of the Old Testament examples as paradigms or models for God's universal mode of controlling men's wills. It is also extremely important to note that in most of these cases, and even some in the New Testament, God's purpose in intervening was not to determine the eternal destiny of the individuals involved but to make Israel

113. Gordon H. Clark, *Biblical Predestination*, p. 125.

a fit receptacle for the coming of Christ. It was a question of service, not salvation. God may have enlisted individuals to serve his purpose for Israel without its affecting their eternal destiny one way or the other. The following comments by Sherlock are very perceptive on this point:

> . . . No man doubts, but that God can, when he pleases, by an irresistible power, turn men's hearts, and chain up their passions, and alter their counsels. . . . God may, by a secret and irresistible influence upon men's minds, even force them to do that good which they have no inclination to do, and restrain them from doing that evil which otherwise they would have done, which does not make them good men, but makes them the instruments of Providence in doing good to men; and God, who is the sovereign Lord of all creatures, may, when he sees fit, press those men, if I may so speak, to his service, who would not do good upon choice. This shows the difference between the government of grace, and Providence: the first has relation to virtue and vice, to make men good, to change their natures and sinful inclinations into habits of virtue, and therefore admits of no greater force than what is consistent with the freedom of choice, and the nature of virtue and vice; but the government of Providence respects the external happiness or misery, rewards or punishments of men or nations; and to this purpose God may use what instruments he pleases, and exercise such authority over nature or over men as is necessary to accomplish his own wise counsels of mercy or judgment. And it was necessary to premise the distinction, because the confounding these two has occasioned great difficulties and mistakes both in the doctrine of grace and providence.[114]

Sherlock is absolutely correct in saying that God's purposes will allow him to do things with men's wills via providence that they do not allow him to do in reference to their personal salvation. More specifically, we may say that in the strict sense of the word God does not *purpose* to save all men, otherwise he would effect a universal salvation because his purposes cannot be thwarted. He does *desire* that all should be saved, of course (Matt. 18:14; I Tim. 2:4; II Peter 3:9). But where salvation is concerned, his *purpose* is that those who freely accept his grace and lordship will be saved (Matt. 23:37; Rom. 10:9-13; Rev. 22:17). Thus, while it would be contrary to God's purpose to move the will directly to save a man, it is not impossible that he would do so to serve his subordinate purposes.

I stress the point that it is not *impossible* for God to do this, and I grant that he may have done it on some occasions. But I am not at

114. William Sherlock, *A Discourse Concerning the Divine Providence* (Pittsburgh: J. L. Read, 1848), p. 50.

all sure that we need to go this far in order to explain the biblical data about special providence. *Indirect* control, as discussed in the next section, may be sufficient to explain it all. We may consider, for example, the many occasions where God seemed to go to extraordinary lengths to influence or bring about a change of heart in people, usually repentance. He bombarded them with locusts, plagues, droughts, famines, and conquering foes. Sometimes it worked, but sometimes it did not. Amos 4:6-11 rehearses God's entire arsenal of special providences against Israel, interlaced with the refrain, "Yet you have not returned to Me." It occurs to me that if God were in the business, on a universal scope, of changing hearts directly, then he went to a lot of unnecessary (and at times, futile) trouble by using these indirect means. But perhaps that is the way he worked *all* the time, i.e., indirectly, and we are just not told the details.

It is no doubt the case that God's purposes do not always require the same kind of providential control of human acts and decisions. Berkouwer uses an illustration quite consistent with determinism when he says, "Man's activity falls, as the smaller of two concentric circles, completely within the greater circle of God's purpose."[115] But if man's acts and decisions are like circles, we should consider that they are not all related in the same way to the larger circle of God's purpose. Most of them simply just exist within the larger circle: some of them perhaps touch it tangentially here or there. There may be some that are concentric to the circle of God's purpose, bearing on it in a more direct way, but these are probably few. Most often God's control is indirect. How this is so will now be discussed.

Indirect Control

The key word for God's special providence and for his sovereignty as such is *control.* We would agree with Thiessen for instance, that God "exercises sovereign control" over his creation.[116] Control should not be equated with causation or determination, however. One does not have to cause every detail of a situation to be in control of it or to direct it toward the end that he desires. Thus it is with God and his world. God exercises control over all things pertaining to human beings and their actions through his ability to influence their decisions, usually

115. G. C. Berkouwer, *The Providence of God*, p. 92.

116. Henry C. Thiessen, *Introductory Lectures in Systematic Theology* (Grand Rapids: Eerdmans, 1949), p. 177.

by indirect means. As Mullins says, "God has limited himself in his methods with free beings" so that "his control is through means which have respect for their freedom."[117]

What is meant by "indirect" means of control? As I am using the term it means any influence that God can bring to bear upon the will that lies outside the will itself. Some of these means are listed by Thiessen. He includes the laws of nature, God's word in Scripture, appeals to reason, persuasion in preaching, inner checks and restraints, outward circumstances, closed doors, and open doors.[118] These are no doubt just a very small number of the ways known to the omniscient God.

> . . . Humanly speaking, we may say that God knows a thousand ways and means within the limits of given laws and ordinances unknown to us and knows the many channels of approach to individuals. . . . This divine influence, this intervention of the Divine Spirit within the realm of the free activities of the human spirit, may be a reality in the deepest sense, without resulting in setting aside the law or crushing the finite will of the individual. It is Divine power working within and through the law; it is the Divine will working upon . . . the human will, but not destroying its freedom. . . .[119]

I believe there are two main categories of indirect control, the first of which is outward circumstances. I am thinking, for instance, of God's use of natural forces in order to influence decisions. Many examples of this have already been given. But I am also thinking of the way God uses Scripture and exhortation and teaching, in the hands of his many servants. I am thinking not of miracles themselves but of the reports of miracles and of the mighty power of God that lies behind them. I am thinking of the family circumstances and the friends and the educational opportunities that God may arrange to shape a person in his formative years.

We may speculate as to how God may have used such means to accomplish many of the things reported in Scripture.[120] We are told, for example that the Lord "puts down one, and exalts another" (Ps. 75:7). Scripture often speaks of God's "raising up" a particular individual

---

117. E. Y. Mullins, *The Christian Religion in Its Doctrinal Expression*, p. 268.

118. Henry C. Thiessen, *Introductory Lectures*, pp. 185ff.

119. Wilbur Fisk Tillett, *Providence, Prayer and Power*, p. 74.

120. We must keep in mind that most of this *is* speculation, since Scripture usually does not go into detail as to the means God uses to do the things he does. It is no less appropriate to speculate as to the means, however, than to speculate that he uses no means but simply touches men's wills directly.

to serve his purposes: kings such as Pharaoh and Saul and David, priests such as Samuel, prophets such as Moses and Jeremiah. We know, for instance, how God prepared Moses by arranging the circumstances of his life for eighty years, including years of training in Egyptian culture and years of spiritual discipline as a shepherd. So when the Bible says of God that "He sent Moses His servant" (Ps. 105:26), we realize that he had been providentially preparing Moses for this for eighty years. Likewise when it says that God raised up Pharaoh (Rom. 9:17), we can justly conclude that God had been working through the circumstances of his life also, fitting him for his crucial role in God's plan. But in neither case is it necessary to think that such providential preparation violated the free will of Moses or Pharaoh. The same is true of the many others whom God "raised up" to serve his purposes.

Another possible example of control through circumstances is the way God may have put fear in the hearts of Israel's enemies (Exod. 23:27; Deut. 2:25). We have already granted the possibility that this may have been done directly; but we should now consider that the same thing may have been accomplished via indirect means, namely, through the widespread dissemination of the reports of God's mighty acts connected with the exodus and the trek through the wilderness. We have a clue to this from Rahab, who confides in the spies she harbored as follows:

> I know that the Lord has given you the land, and that the terror of you has fallen on us, and that all the inhabitants of the land have melted away before you. For we have heard how the Lord dried up the water of the Red Sea before you when you came out of Egypt, and what you did to the two kings of the Amorites who were beyond the Jordan, to Sihon and Og, whom you utterly destroyed. And when we heard it, our hearts melted and no courage remained in any man any longer because of you; for the Lord your God, He is God in heaven above and on earth beneath (Josh. 2:9-11).

Making sure that such reports continued to circulate would be a small task for God's providence.

Another example is the means by which God may have stirred up Cyrus to send the Israelites home from Babylon. How did God "stir up" his spirit? We should remember that Isaiah 44:28 and 45:1 had already named Cyrus as God's shepherd to lead his sheep home, some 150 years before the fact. It is difficult to imagine that none of the pious Jews in Babylon would have thought to call this prophecy to

Cyrus' attention. We can easily picture Daniel, a high-ranking official in the new administration, walking into Cyrus' presence with a scroll of the book of Isaiah under arm, opening it to the appropriate place, and showing Cyrus what had already been said about him—by name. That would probably "stir up" anyone's spirit!

One other possible example of indirect control has to do with the references to God's giving his people a new heart toward him after their return from Babylon.[121] Just as the reports of the exodus events struck fear into the hearts of Israel's enemies, so may the great deliverance of the restoration have melted the hearts of God's people to fear and serve him.

The other category of indirect control is mental states (external to the will itself) such as thoughts and memories. No one fully understands the workings of the mind, e.g., how we can call up at will (sometimes!) certain thoughts and experiences and miscellaneous data, bringing them from unconsciousness to consciousness. Often we are not at all sure of how or why we happen to be thinking about a certain subject, but we suddenly become aware that it is there. We are usually willing to grant that Satan has the power to "put certain thoughts into our minds" as a means of temptation. If this is possible for Satan, it is surely possible for God. I do not think it is at all unlikely that God may at times, for his special purposes, insert a particular line of thinking into our mind or raise the memory of a particular experience to our consciousness. I am not thinking of things such as revelation (new data) or inspiration (infallible memory), but just the manipulation, if you will, of the normal processes of thinking. Once the thoughts or memories are present in the mind, they become occasions for making decisions of one kind or another. These decisions are ours to make, but they may be influenced by the thoughts. Sherlock speaks of God's government of men's minds thus,

> . . . for these are the great springs of action, and as free a principle as the mind of man is, it is not ungovernable; it may be governed, and that without an omnipotent power, against its own bias, and without changing its inclinations; and what may be done, certainly God can do; and when it is necessary to the ends of Providence, we may conclude he will do it. Let a man be never so much bent upon any project, yet hope or fear, some present great advantage or great inconvenience, the powerful

121. Jeremiah 24:7; 32:39-40; Ezekiel 11:19-20; 36:26-27. These passages very likely contain a prophetic reference to the New Testament people of God, too.

> intercession of friends, a sudden change of circumstances, the improbability of success, the irreparable mischief of a defeat, and a thousand other considerations, will divert him from it; and how easy it is for God to imprint such thoughts upon men's minds with an irresistible vigour and brightness, that it shall be no more in their power to do what they had a mind to, than to resist all the charms of riches and honours, than to leap into the fire, and to choose misery and ruin.[122]

He says that God may accomplish his purposes through us "by strong and lively impressions upon our minds—by suggesting and fixing such thoughts in us, as excite or calm our passions, as encourage us to bold and great attempts, or check us in our career by frightful imaginations and unaccountable fears and terrors."[123]

As possible examples of this in Scripture we may think of Joseph's brothers, when they were planning to kill Joseph. Perhaps at this time God caused Reuben to think about his father's love for Joseph and how much this would hurt the old man; perhaps such thoughts as these influenced him to say, "Let us not take his life" (Gen. 37:21). Perhaps it was God who put into Judah's mind the idea of selling Joseph to the traders who just "happened" to come along at that time (Gen. 37:26-27).

The hardening of Pharaoh's heart may possibly be considered in this light. How did God harden his heart? Perhaps by flooding his mind with just such thoughts as mentioned by Sherlock in the quotation above, i.e., what a great loss of free labor it would be to lose these Israelites, or what a laughing-stock we will be when other nations hear how a bunch of slaves had their way with us. Such thoughts would have great validity to the mind of Pharaoh, and God could have made sure that he happened to think them at just the appropriate time, i.e., when he was weakening and about to let the people go.

Similar God-instilled thoughts of advantage or disadvantage may have contributed to the decisions of Jeroboam (I Kings 12:15), the king of Assyria (Ezra 6:22), and Artaxerxes (Ezra 7:27). It is also possible that God opened Lydia's heart by similar means, influencing her to respond to Paul's preaching of her own free choice (Acts 16:14).

If God uses such indirect means as outward circumstances and mental states, and I believe that he does, then he uses them in ways consistent with his special purposes—all of them, including his purpose

122. William Sherlock, *A Discourse Concerning the Divine Providence*, p. 51.
123. Ibid., p. 53.

for saving men. We must remember, though, that this purpose involves saving only those who freely choose to serve him; thus it is important to stress that these are *indirect* influences, leaving the actual decision to the individual. We should remember also that, although special providences may be employed as he sees fit, the principal influence which God uses in bringing men to salvation is his word (Rom. 10:17). This will help us to understand some of the proof-texts which supposedly teach determinism. For instance, when Acts 18:27 says that the disciples "had believed through grace," this probably refers to the preaching of "the word of His grace" (Acts 14:3; see 20:24). In Matthew 15:13 Jesus says, "Every plant which My heavenly Father did not plant shall be rooted up." But how does God plant his plants? Through the seed of the word, according to Luke 8:11-15. In John 6:44 Jesus says, "No one can come to Me, unless the Father who sent Me draws him." But a little later Jesus said, "And I, if I be lifted up from the earth, will draw all men to Myself" (John 12:32). The gospel of the grace of God in the cross of Christ is the drawing power that brings people to Jesus (Rom. 1:16). No one can come unless he is drawn, that is true; but the word of grace is the principal means of the drawing.

At this point we need to return to an important distinction made earlier, i.e., the distinction between God's purpose with respect to salvation and his purpose for Israel as a nation. Since the nature of these purposes is quite different, the methods of special providence will not be the same for each. Thus it is very important to discern when Scripture is referring to God's providential use of an individual to serve the purpose of preparation and when it is referring to God's influencing a person positively or negatively with regard to his salvation. Failure to make this distinction can lead to unwarranted deterministic conclusions.

The passage of Scripture that seems to cause the most confusion of this kind is Romans 9-11. Determinists commonly interpret chapter 9 especially as teaching that God sovereignly and unconditionally decides who will be saved and who will be lost: "So then He has mercy on whom He desires, and He hardens whom He desires" (9:18). He chose Isaac but not Ishmael (9:7-9), Jacob but not Esau (9:10-13). He hardened Pharaoh (9:17). Like a potter God makes some vessels for honor and some for destruction (9:20-22). "So then it does not depend on the man who wills or the man who runs, but on God who has mercy" (9:16).[124] The question is, however, whether Paul is talking about God's choosing for salvation or for service. Many understand him in the latter sense, and this makes a tremendous difference.[125]

The main question with which Paul is dealing in this passage is God's right to reject the Jews as his chosen people. In Romans 1-8 he affirms that justification is by faith. This means that the true Jew is the heart-believer, regardless of physical heritage and circumcision (2:25-29). Anyone who has faith in Jesus is a true son of Abraham (4:9-16). But where does this leave the Jews by birth? Didn't God choose them as his special people? Didn't he make a binding covenant with them, that they would be his people and he would be their God? Does this mean now that God is actually going back on his word? By abandoning Jewish exclusiveness, is God breaking his promise?

In answering these questions Paul has at least four main points. His first point is that God is sovereign and can choose whomever he wants to serve him and to help him work out his purpose of making grace available through Jesus Christ. He can also sovereignly reject whomever he pleases. There is a measure of arbitrariness in this choice. This is the point Paul is stressing in 9:7ff. God chose Isaac over Ishmael, not as a matter of salvation and damnation but as a matter of fathering the race that would prepare for Christ. The same applies to Jacob and Esau,[126] and even to Moses and Pharaoh. God's statement that "I will have mercy on whom I have mercy" (9:15) is taken from Exodus 33:19, where God grants Moses' request to be shown God's glory. Thus the "having mercy" does not refer to *saving* mercy. We should also note how often in the New Testament Paul refers to his selection as an

---

124. A detailed discussion of these verses by a determinist is John Piper, *The Justification of God* (Grand Rapids: Baker Book House, 1983).

125. For examples of this approach see Roger T. Forster and V. Paul Marston, *God's Strategy in Human History* (Wheaton: Tyndale House, 1974); Samuel Fisk, *Divine Sovereignty and Human Freedom*, pp. 118-132; James D. Strauss, "God's Promise and Universal History," *Grace Unlimited*, ed. Clark H. Pinnock (Minneapolis: Bethany Fellowship, 1975), pp. 190-208. See also Frederick Godet's *Commentary on the Epistle to the Romans*, tr. A. Cusin (Grand Rapids: Zondervan, 1956 reprint of 1883 edition).

126. With regard to verse 13, "Jacob I loved, but Esau I hated," two comments are appropriate. (1) The statement is taken from Malachi 1:2-3, where it refers not to individuals as such but to the nations that sprang from each. (2) The word *hate* in biblical usage does not always carry the strongly negative connotation we often put into it. See Genesis 29:30; Deuteronomy 21:15; Luke 14:26. For a complete discussion of this, see William G. Williams, *An Exposition of the Epistle of Paul to the Romans* (Cincinnati: Jennings and Pye, 1902), pp. 297-307.

apostle (a role of service) as an act of grace and mercy on God's part.[127] So in the crucial verses where God seems to be saying that he distributes mercy arbitrarily (9:15-18), it is not at all necessary to assume that this means saving mercy. It more likely refers to the mercy of choosing certain ones for privileges of service. This is the case with the Jews as a nation. If God had mercy on them and so chose them, that is his sovereign prerogative. Likewise if he chooses to harden and reject them in respect to this purpose, that is his prerogative, too.

Paul's second point is the very fact that Israel as a nation was chosen only for the service of preparation, not as the sole recipients of salvation. In fact, being a part of this chosen nation did not guarantee anything as far as salvation is concerned. So if God is rejecting the nation, it is not as if he were thereby excluding them from salvation. He is simply setting them aside as far as their purpose of preparing for the coming of Christ is concerned. The fact is that they actually had accomplished their purpose and were due to be set aside anyway (9:5; see Eph. 1-2). They had prepared the way for bringing the gospel to the Gentiles, also (9:23ff.). It is in this connection that Paul refers to God as a potter who is free to make vessels for whatever purposes he chooses. He chose to make the nation of Israel a vessel of honor, to be used for a glorious purpose (9:21). Over the centuries this chosen vessel soiled itself through idolatry and unbelief, and thus God determined to destroy it and not just set it aside honorably; but God delayed his wrath until its purpose was accomplished. This seems to be what Paul is saying in 9:22, "What if God, although willing to demonstrate His wrath and to make His power known, endured with much patience vessels of wrath prepared for destruction?" He endured their sin and idolatry long enough to make way for the new vessels of mercy, namely, the church as composed of believing Jews and Gentiles (9:23ff.). Thus the temporal dissolution of the Jews as God's exclusive people was both planned and deserved.

Paul's third point is that the *whole* nation was not being rejected, only those who refused to believe in Christ. There is a remnant that still

---

127. See Romans 15:15-16, "But I have written very boldly to you on some points, so as to remind you again, because of the grace that was given me from God, to be a minister of Christ Jesus to the Gentiles." See I Corinthians 7:25, "Now concerning virgins I have no command of the Lord, but I give an opinion as one who by the mercy of the Lord is trustworthy." (He is speaking of his apostolic authority.) See Ephesians 3:7-8, "I was made a minister, according to the gift of God's grace which was given to me . . . . To me, the very least of all saints, this grace was given, to preach to the Gentiles the unfathomable riches of Christ." See also I Corinthians 3:10; 15:10; II Corinthians 4:1; Galatians 2:9.

belongs to God. In fact, even when Israel enjoyed her status as the chosen people, not all Israelites were true people of God (9:6; 11:2-4). So it is today that there is still a faithful remnant (9:24; 27; 11:4-5).

The fourth point is perhaps the most crucial, namely, that any individual Jews who are rejected as far as salvation is concerned are rejected because of their unbelief, not because of an arbitrary decision on God's part. The fact is that most Jews were lost, and this is what grieved Paul (9:3). But he is very clear that unbelief is the cause (9:32; 11:20). At the same time he stresses that any individual Jew could be saved at any time by accepting Jesus as the Messiah (10:13-17; 11:23-24). In fact God is pictured as constantly pleading with Israel to come to him, but they were disobedient and obstinate (10:21). Their hardening as a nation (11:7) is thus a judicial confirmation of their own stubbornness, and does not preclude any individual Jew from being saved.

In this discussion of Romans 9-11 the point has been to try to separate the question of God's choosing and using people for service, and the question of how he decides to save and to damn. The conclusion is that God's rejection of the Jews as a nation with regard to their role of service was a matter of God's sovereign choice, while his rejection of individual Jews with regard to their salvation was conditioned on their unbelief. This is a model that applies to all of God's providential works.

As we conclude our discussion of the various indirect means of God's providential control, it is necessary to insist on two important qualifications. One is that this method of divine government is the exception, not the rule. It is *special* providence, not general. Again there is the danger that we might be tempted to generalize from the kinds of examples cited above and assume that God is doing this in every person's life all the time. But there is no reason to assume this. Such control is reserved for God's special purposes. We may recall the determinists' explanation of God's permissive decree as described above,[128] namely, to quote Dabney again, that God can "arrange and group events and objects around free agents by his manifold wisdom and power, as to place each soul, at every step, in the presence of those circumstances, which, He knows, will be sufficient objective inducement to it to do, of its own native, free activity." My main quarrel with this idea is the determinists' assumption that God determines every act of every man in this way. Such generalization is unwarranted.

128. See above, pp. 181-182.

The second qualification regarding God's indirect means of control is that they should not be considered as irresistible. I am not willing to go quite as far as Sherlock does when he says that it is impossible to resist once God imprints a thought on the mind. Dabney's "sufficient objective inducement" may be acceptable as long as *sufficient* is not confused with *necessary.* I do not believe these indirect influences shut an individual up into a set of circumstances that will infallibly produce one and only one decision. There is still a freedom to resist, though it may take extra effort. We must remember the times when God's chastisements did not produce the desired effect, as in Amos 4:6-11 and Haggai 1:2ff.

This leads us to ask the question, if God's providential influences can be resisted, how is he able to maintain control? Does this not jeopardize his sovereignty? How can he be sure that he will work out his purposes if his free-will creatures do not *always* yield to his special providential working? The answer lies in the foreknowledge of God.

The Foreknowledge of God

God's foreknowledge of the future free acts of men is a key element in his providential control. In the volume on God the Creator I have already discussed the doctrine of foreknowledge in some detail.[129] I have affirmed and defended the view that God has true foreknowledge of human actions. I have denied that this foreknowledge is based on the divine decree, and I have denied that foreknowledge in itself "fixes" human acts or renders them certain.

How is God's foreknowledge of free acts crucial for providence? Because it is by this means that God can allow man to be truly free in his choices, even free to resist his own special influences, and at the same time work out his own purposes infallibly. For if God foreknows all the choices that every person will make, he can make his own plans accordingly, fitting his purposes around these foreknown decisions and actions. Baelz says,

> . . . It may also be argued that the proposition that God already knows what choices we shall make does not entail the proposition that God predetermines our choices; that consequently it is logically possible for man to make his choices freely, but for God so to have determined the order

129. Jack Cottrell, *What the Bible Says About God the Creator*, pp. 279ff.

> of the world that the outcome of these choices will fit in with his own over-riding purposes. . . .[130]

Someone has written a poem called "The Weaver," which says that "life is but a weaving between my Lord and Me." The poem pictures both God and man as contributing to the pattern, with man working from the underside where the pattern is not clear and God working from above where he can put the pattern into place. Since God foreknows every bit of thread we will insert into the picture, he has already planned how the whole thing will turn out without his having to determine every move. We might say that God can thread his purposes into the tapestry of human decisions and make it come out in the pattern of his choice. But he can do this only by means of foreknowledge.

Acts 2:23 is a perfect illustration of the way God works through his foreknowledge. It says that Jesus was "delivered up by the predetermined plan and foreknowledge of God." We have already mentioned Gordon Clark's suggestion that we "note that *foreknowledge* is dependent on determinate counsel" in this passage.[131] Obviously the verse says nothing about a relationship of cause or dependence one way or the other. It refers simply to predetermination *and* foreknowledge. That is, the death of Jesus came about the way it did because of both of these factors. On the one hand, God had predetermined that Jesus would die as a propitiation for the sins of the world; this was his own unconditional plan for saving the world. On the other hand, the details of *how* this would be accomplished were planned in relation to God's foreknowledge of the historical situation and of the character and choices of men such as Judas. So at least in part we may say just the opposite of what Clark asserts, namely, that the predetermined counsel is dependent on the foreknowledge.

Special Providence and Sin

The role of foreknowledge in providence helps in part to explain the place of sinful acts in the purposes of God. This is no easy question whether one is a determinist or non-determinist. The former seems to be at a greater disadvantage, however, since he has to account for *all* sins in relation to the all-determining, sovereign decree. As far as my

130. Peter Baelz, *Prayer and Providence*, p. 123. See Mark Pontifex, *Freedom and Providence* (New York: Hawthorn Books, 1960), p. 80.

131. Gordon H. Clark, "The Sovereignty of God," p. 4.

own approach is concerned, God's *general* providence is the umbrella under which most sins occur, and this allows man to make his choices unhindered by God. Here the concept of permission is sufficient, and there is no sense in which God can be called the *cause* of sin.[132] "If, then, God permits sin, this must mean that he permits a cause to operate which he does not cause himself, since it opposes his plan. To permit sin means to refrain from stopping it, and hence it implies that there is a cause operating which is not caused by God."[133]

The only problem is that this explanation does not seem to suffice for *special* providence, because it seems at times that God is not just permitting sin but actually using it as a *part* of his plan. Perhaps this would not be so serious a problem if it were not for such biblical teaching as James 1:13, which says that "God cannot be tempted by evil, and He Himself does not tempt any one." So how do we account for the place of sinful acts within God's special providence?

I will suggest four possible ways to approach this question, all of which when taken together may provide a somewhat satisfactory answer. None of these ways involves direct causation of evil by God.

The first possibility is that God providentially sets up circumstances which constitute a strong influence toward evil, or which lead to evil-doing on the part of someone. It may be that the hardening of Pharaoh's heart would come under this heading. We have already suggested that God may have worked indirectly to influence Pharaoh by inserting certain thoughts into his mind. Whether the resultant hardening of his heart was a sinful act has been disputed,[134] but it is difficult to see it in any other light. One might include Psalm 105:25 here also, "He turned their heart to hate His people." I confess that I am very uneasy with this suggestion in reference to these particular acts, since it seems to violate James 1:13. On the other hand, a passage like Jeremiah 19:9 seems to fit easily here: "And I shall make them eat the flesh of their sons and the flesh of their daughters, and they will eat one another's flesh in the siege and in the distress." God "makes" them engage in cannibalism only because he has brought about the conditions under which this takes place, and his purpose in bringing about those conditions was not to cause the cannibalism but to bring judgment on a wicked people.

---

132. Someone might say that this goes too far, since God might be called the cause of sin in the indirect sense that he has created free-will creatures who have the potential to sin.

133. Mark Pontifex, *Freedom and Providence*, p. 78.

134. Forster and Marston, *God's Strategy in Human History*, pp. 155-177.

A second possibility is that God brings sinful acts into his overall plans by allowing Satan to tempt and deceive in certain specific ways. This in a sense would fall under the general heading of permission, but it is not quite the same as the ordinary permission of sin that occurs under general providence. It is more like a *directed* permission. We know that Satan does tempt, and we know that he can use many different means in the process. We also know that he sometimes does this with the express permission of God. The account of Job confirms all this. The various evils that befell Job included the theft of his livestock and murder of his servants by the Sabeans, the loss of more livestock and servants to lightning ("fire of God . . . from heaven"), more such losses through a raid by the Chaldeans, the death of his children from a windstorm, and only then his plague of boils (Job 1:12-19; 2:7). It is clearly indicated that Satan caused these things by God's express permission (Job 1:12; 2:6-7). All this was done to tempt Job to sin (Job 1:8-11; 2:3). What is most striking is that even though he was involved only in the sense that he permitted Satan to do these things, nevertheless God is said to have done them! Job 42:11 speaks of "all the evil that the Lord had brought on him." God said to Satan that "you incited Me against him" (Job 2:3). When confronted with all his losses, Job acknowledged that "the Lord has taken away" (Job 1:21). Since Satan was the actual agent in these things, we cannot say that God actually caused them; but since they were done with his permission they were under his sovereign control.

This model undoubtedly explains a number of the troublesome incidents of special providence presented earlier. The sending of the deceiving spirit to entice Ahab into battle is almost an exact parallel to the case of Job (see I Kings 22:19ff.). II Thessalonians 2:11 can be explained in the same way, namely, the statement that "God will send upon them a deluding influence so that they might believe what is false." Verse 7 indicates that God sends this influence only in the sense that he withdraws his restraint upon the forces of evil. II Corinthians 4:4 says that it is the god of this world who blinds the minds of the unbelieving but he undoubtedly does so only by God's permission. We may suggest also that II Samuel 24:1 is to be explained by God's permitting Satan to tempt David. It says that God's anger incited David to begin the census. But I Chronicles 21:1 says that Satan moved David to do this. Again this was probably Satan doing it with God's permission. The evil spirit sent upon King Saul probably is to be explained in the same way.

A third possibility is that God simply foreknows men's evil inclinations and choices, and is able to "deflect" these choices or to work his own purposes in around them without the slightest taint of responsibility for them. Forster and Marston say that God "maneuvers" men's sins;[135] we could also use the word *manipulate* with some justification. Sherlock says, "There is no colour nor reasonable pretence of an objection against God's making the sins of men serve wise and good ends, if he can do this without having any hand in men's sins."[136] It is not difficult to see how this can explain the role of Joseph's brothers in God's plan for his life, and the role of Judas in the Great Plan. It also explains how God could use the lust of Samson (Judg. 14:1ff.) and of Absalom (II Sam. 12:11ff.; 16:22) in his plans. It also adequately explains God's weaving of wicked kings and nations into his purpose for Israel. This is no doubt the most important factor in the working out of God's special providence in relation to sinful acts.

A final point is that some of the evil connected with God's providential working is not moral evil but natural or physical evil and does not lead to any particular problems. For instance, the King James Version of Isaiah 31:2 says that God will "bring evil," and in Isaiah 45:7 it says, "I make peace, and create evil: I the Lord do all these things." It is usually understood that these passages refer to evils in the sense of punishments and sufferings for sin. The NASB uses the words *disaster* and *calamity*. This is also how we should understand God's role in bringing about the death of individuals; death per se is not a moral evil but a natural one. Nebuchadnezzar's madness may be similarly explained, and perhaps even the "evil spirit" that plagued Saul could possibly be understood as a spirit of derangement.

Thus we see how it is possible for God to work men's sinful decisions into his purposes while respecting their freedom either to sin or not to sin. The only loose end here is whether or not one or two of these explanations can be satisfactorily harmonized with James 1:13.

True Freedom, True Sovereignty

In this section I have attempted to present a non-determinist understanding of God's special providence, one that does justice both to human freedom and to divine sovereignty. Few would doubt that the

135. Ibid., p. 92.

136. William Sherlock, *A Discourse Concerning the Divine Providence*, p. 57.

kind of freedom which I have defended here is a genuine freedom. There is some tendency, however, for it to suffer the discourtesy of caricature at the hands of its enemies or to be carried to an extreme by its friends. To hear some determinists describe it, the power of contrary choice results in a sinister metaphysical dualism that makes man as ultimate as God. At best it puts him in the position of being able to thwart God's plans and purposes. Gruenler declares that the phrase "genuinely free," at least as some use it, "means nothing unless God's plans can be thwarted by contrary human choices."[137] The problem with this complaint is its all-or-nothing implications. It implies that "genuine freedom" would enable man to negate *all* of God's plans. But it does not have to be carried this far. Can we not say that man is genuinely free if he can do *anything at all* contrary to God's will and desire for him? And obviously this *is* possible. Every sin is in a real sense a defiance of God's will. Forster and Marston show how the Bible indicates over and over that God's plan is rejected and his will defied by sinful man.[138] And certainly the fact that some people reject God's salvation and are eternally lost is contrary to his stated will (I Tim. 2:4; II Peter 3:9). Tillett puts it very strongly, "The dignity and nobility of man's nature as a rational and moral free agent carries necessarily along with it the possibility and peril of defying and defeating the will of his Creator."[139] But of course this ability to defeat and to thwart God's plans has its limits. It is true only with regard to God's will and desire for each person as an individual; it is *not* true with regard to God's plans for his creation as such and for the purposes of redemption that he is working out in history. Genuine freedom does not require this, and it is in fact not the case.

The kind of freedom that we have described here is most consistent with the biblical teaching concerning conditionality and responsibility. It does justice to the many, many passages in Scripture which present God's blessing and punishment as conditioned upon human choices, and it does so without mystery or contradiction. This is typified in Deuteronomy 11:26-28:

> See, I am setting before you today a blessing and a curse: the blessing, if you listen to the commandments of the Lord your God, which I am

---

137. Royce Gruenler, *The Inexhaustible God: Biblical Faith and the Challenge of Process Theism* (Grand Rapids: Baker Book House, 1983), p. 44.

138. Forster and Marston, *God's Strategy in Human History*, pp. 27ff.

139. Wilbur Fisk Tillett, *Providence, Prayer and Power*, p. 71.

> commanding you today; and the curse, if you do not listen to the commandments of the Lord your God, but turn aside from the way which I am commanding you today, by following other gods . . . .[140]

Only when man is truly free to actualize both of these options can he be responsible for his choice and therefore justly blessed or condemned.

In addition to true freedom I have attempted in this section to present a view of true sovereignty. I am aware of the extreme difficulty that some see in doing justice to both of these at the same time. The secular philosopher J. L. Mackie says, "There is a fundamental difficulty in the notion of an omnipotent God creating men with free will, for if men's wills are really free this must mean that even God cannot control them, that is, that God is no longer omnipotent."[141] Many determinist theologians apparently accept this view. D. A. Carson says that "to accept . . . a metaphysical definition of free will which binds it to power to contrary is to sacrifice the certainty of divine sovereignty for the contingency of human decision."[142] As Gruenler puts it, "Whenever theology focuses on a defense of human freedom, God's sovereignty will be subtracted from and modified to accommodate the rights of the creature, but never will a satisfactory ratio be arrived at."[143] The concept of a future that is open and indefinite for God, he says, is "logically incompatible with the doctrine of a sovereign God."[144]

This alleged logical incompatibility between real freedom and real sovereignty is itself a fallacy, however, because it is simply erroneous to say that freedom entails loss of control or an open future for God. Such a view ignores or denies the reality of God's foreknowledge of future free events. It is *foreknowledge* that enables God to maintain complete control of his world despite the freedom of his creatures. God *knows* the future; it is not open or indefinite for him. This gives God the genuine option of either permitting or preventing men's planned choices, and prevention is the ultimate in control. James 4:13-15 chastises the man who blithely says, "Today or tomorrow, we shall go to such and such a city, and spend a year there and engage in business and make a profit." But wait a minute, says James. You are

---

140. See also Deuteronomy 28:2-9, 15-20; 30:15ff.; I Kings 11:38; Isaiah 1:19-20; Jeremiah 22:4ff.; Mark 16:16; John 7:17; Romans 11:22-23.

141. J. L. Mackie, "Evil and Omnipotence," *God and Evil: Readings in the Theological Problem of Evil*, ed. Nelson Pike (Englewood Cliffs, N.J.: Prentice-Hall, 1964), p. 57.

142. D. A. Carson, *Divine Sovereignty and Human Responsibility*, p. 207.

143. Royce Gruenler, *The Inexhaustible God*, pp. 43-44.

144. Ibid., p. 39.

not taking account of God's sovereignty. "Instead, you ought to say, 'If the Lord wills, we shall live and also do this or that.'" In other words, it is not wrong to have plans, but we should always acknowledge God's power to veto them. (See Luke 12:19-20 for an example of just this.) This is the significance of Proverbs 19:21, "Many are the plans in a man's heart, but the counsel of the Lord, it will stand" (see also Prov. 16:9). In addition to permitting and preventing, God's foreknowledge also enables him to plan his own responses to and uses of man's choices even before they are made, even in eternity. Thus he is not to be equated with William James' master chessman, which James felt was a good analogy of God:

> An analogy will make the meaning of this clear. Suppose two men before a chessboard,—the one a novice, the other an expert player of the game. The expert intends to beat. But he cannot foresee exactly what any one actual move of his adversary may be. He knows, however, all the *possible* moves of the latter; and he knows in advance how to meet each of them by a move of his own which leads in the direction of victory. And the victory infallibly arrives, after no matter how devious a course, in the one predestined form of checkmate to the novice's king.
>
> Let now the novice stand for us finite free agents, and the expert for the infinite mind in which the universe lies. Suppose the latter to be thinking out his universe before he actually creates it. Suppose him to say, I will lead things to a certain end, but I will not *now* decide on all the steps thereto. At various points, ambiguous possibilities shall be left open, *either* of which, at a given instant, may become actual. But whichever brand of these bifurcations become real, I know what I shall do at the next bifurcation to keep things from drifting away from the final result I intend.
>
> The creator's plan of the universe would thus be left blank as to many of its actual details, but all possibilities would be marked down. The realization of some of these would be left absolutely to chance; that is, would only be determined when the moment of realization came. Other possibilities would be *contingently* determined; that is, their decision would have to wait till it was seen how the matters of absolute chance fell out. But the rest of the plan, including its final upshot, would be rigorously determined once for all. So the creator himself would not need to know *all* the details of the actuality until they came; and at any time his own view of the world would be a view partly of facts and partly of possibilities, exactly as ours is now. Of one thing, however, he might be certain; and that is that his world was safe, and that no matter how much it might zigzag he could surely bring it home at last.[145]

---

145. William James, "The Dilemma of Determinism," *The Will To Believe and Other Essays in Popular Philosophy* (New York: Longmans, Green, and Co., 1896), pp. 151-152.

In my frank opinion this analogy is not as devastating to the concept of divine sovereignty as many evangelicals think it is,[146] but it must be rejected because it is not true to the reality of God's foreknowledge. God not only knows how to counter all possible moves of his "opponents," but he also foreknows all their actual moves.

It is difficult to see how anyone can complain about this view of sovereignty unless he is predisposed to equate sovereignty with causation in some real sense. I believe that it is perfectly compatible with Elisha Coles' definition of sovereignty—"That the great God, blessed forever, hath an absolute power and right of dominion over his creatures, to dispose and determine them as seemeth him good"[147]—as long as the *determining* is seen as an option to be applied when necessary and not as the universal rule. It is even compatible with Carson's own summary statement: "The crucial point is that his activity is so sovereign and detailed that nothing can take place in the world of men without at least his permission; and conversely, if he sets himself against some course, then that course cannot develop."[148] The problem is that Carson himself will not let this statement stand as it is, for he does not really accept the concept of *permission*. He says,

> . . . Distinctions between permissive will and decretive will appear desperately artificial when applied to an omniscient and omnipotent being; for if this God 'permits' sin, it cannot be unknowingly and unwillingly, and therefore his 'permission' must be granted knowingly and willingly. Wherein then does this permission differ from decree?[149]

The inability to see a real distinction here, I would suggest, is due to the fact that true permission *does* require foreknowledge (it must be granted "knowingly"), and to the determinist foreknowledge is equivalent to predetermination.

My main point is that true sovereignty consists in absolute control, but absolute control does not require causation, predetermination, or foreordination of all things. True control entails these when necessary, but it also means allowing free creatures to go their own way unless there is a reason to intervene. As Mullins says, "God's sovereignty

---

146. See Royce Gruenler, *The Inexhaustible God,* p. 44; D. A. Carson, *Divine Sovereignty and Human Responsibility,* p. 220.

147. Elisha Coles, *God's Sovereignty* (Grand Rapids: Baker Book House, 1979 reprint of 1831 edition), p. 11.

148. D. A. Carson, *Divine Sovereignty and Human Responsibility,* p. 28.

149. Ibid., pp. 213-214. See also p. 220.

means, then, that he keeps the reins of government in his own hands. He guides the universe to his own glorious end."[150] The point is that a truly sovereign God does not *need* to predetermine or foreordain all things in order to maintain complete control over his creation. His sovereignty is *greater* than that! After affirming that God has created innumerable men and angels with the power of free (opposite) choice, Raymond perceptively states, "We assume that God is competent to govern an infinite number of morally responsible beings, persons who have power within limits of determining what they will do; and we insist upon it that this concept of a divine government is incomparably superior to that of our opponents."[151]

In the final analysis what is at stake here is not just man's freedom but *God's* freedom also. A sovereign God is a God who is free to limit himself with regard to his works, a God who is free to decide *not* to determine if he so chooses, a God who is free to bestow the gift of relative independence upon his creatures. Such freedom does not diminish God's sovereignty; it magnifies it.

THE DETERMINIST STUMBLING BLOCK

Before closing this chapter we need to return briefly to the determinist interpretation of providence in order to identify its most central and basic difficulty. The main stumbling block for determinists seems to be *conditionality.* They cannot bring themselves to admit that anything God does can be conditioned by man or can be a reaction to something in the creation. This sort of thing is regarded as a contradiction of sovereignty. As sovereign, God must always *act* and never *react.* James Daane cites two examples of this, one of which is Francis Turretin. For Turretin, says Daane, "God himself is not free . . . to respond to and accommodate his actions to what is external to him. God's grace, for example, cannot be regarded as God's free response to human sin."[152] The other example is Herman Hoeksema.

> . . . Hoeksema emphasized that God is sovereign, and he took divine sovereignty to mean that nothing God does is a *response* to what man has done. God is never conditioned by man. Man's actions cannot

150. E. Y. Mullins, *The Christian Religion in Its Doctrinal Expression,* p. 267.

151. Miner Raymond, *Systematic Theology* (Cincinnati: Walden and Stowe, 1877), I:505-506.

152. James Daane, *The Freedom of God: A Study of Election and Pulpit* (Grand Rapids: Eerdmans, 1973), p. 159.

> become conditions for God's responses. God's judgments and his acts of reprobation are not a response to man's sin. God as sovereign determines and accomplishes whatever comes to pass. . . .[153]

We may cite Lewis Chafer as a third example. In discussing the relation between free will and divine foreknowledge, Chafer notes that non-determinists "claim to recognize that certain things—notably the free acts of men—are not at all derived from God, but rather from the creature." Any view such as this, he says, "places God in the unworthy position of being dependent upon His creatures."[154]

In my judgment this is the watershed between determinists and non-determinists. Does divine sovereignty prevent God's reacting to anything done by his creature? The basic assumption of determinism is that it does; and whether it is acknowledged or not, this leads consistently to a concept of total causation. Gordon Clark's statement is the voice of consistent determinism: if God does not cause all events, then he has ceased to be God.[155]

I will now show how this concept of unconditionality is central in the concepts of the sovereign decree, sovereign foreknowledge, and sovereign grace; and I will point out some problems and inconsistencies for those who hold this view.

The Unconditional Decree

As we have seen, for the determinist the sovereign decree is unconditional or absolute. This means that everything in the decree is dependent upon God alone, and nothing in it is there as a response to any creature.[156] At the same time it is held that the unconditional decree includes such things as God's permission of sin, second causes that are real causes, and genuine free will. But it is my conviction that these three concepts in particular—permission, second causes, and free will—are incompatible with unconditionality, and the attempt to hold to them results in serious ambiguities. As these concepts are used they tend to tilt precariously back and forth between their true meanings and the uncertain meanings imposed upon them by the unyielding adherence to unconditionality.

---

153. Ibid., p. 25.
154. Lewis S. Chafer, *Systematic Theology*, I:230.
155. Gordon H. Clark, "The Sovereignty of God," p. 4.
156. Lewis Berkhof, *Systematic Theology*, p. 105.

Permission

The concept of permission as involved in the "permissive decree" presents a real problem for conditionality. We will remember that the determinist introduces permission only to explain God's relation to sinful acts; it refers to sin and to nothing else. The reason why this is a problem is that the very notion of permission sounds so *conditional*; it sounds like a reactive response. Of course one person might give another person under his authority the general permission to act as he pleases; in this case the permission is active and the consequent behavior is dependent upon it. But with respect to specific acts of behavior, the person in authority can allow it to take place only if he knows in advance that that specific act is planned. In other words, the permission is a response to a plan or an intention known in advance. Now, for the determinist God's permission is not general but specific; it has to be if it applies selectively to sins and not to good acts. Thus it seems that God's permission of sin is very much like a reaction. But if it is, it is inconsistent with the decree. How then can any part of God's decree be unconditional and permissive at the same time?

It is no wonder that many determinists feel uneasy about the concept of permission, as we have seen. And it is no wonder that it is usually given a connotation that sounds much more like determination than true permission. A. A. Hodge says that "God's permissive decree does truly determine the certain futurition of the act."[157] Berkouwer notes Calvin's displeasure with the term, and acknowledges that "Reformed theology . . . dismissed the 'bare permission' idea as too simple a solution." Instead, he says, "the idea of permission is always qualified as being active in nature, and as forming no limitation to God's purposeful activity. Divine permission is, in fact, meant by Reformed theology as a work of Divine majesty."[158] Some even speak of an "efficacious permission."[159]

The problem is only compounded when the permissive part of the decree is limited to sin and is not applied to good acts. This means that good acts must be accounted for in some way other than permission. But there seem to be only two alternatives to permission: prevention

---

157. A. A. Hodge, *Outlines of Theology*, p. 170.

158. G. C. Berkouwer, *The Providence of God*, pp. 137-138.

159. Dr. Edwin Palmer used this term when he was teaching a course in "theology proper" at Westminster Theological Seminary, in response to a query by one of his students.

and causation. Certainly good acts are not prevented; therefore this leaves causation as the only viable explanation for them. This makes it difficult for determinists, because most of them do not like to use this word even for good acts, since it has unwanted implications with regard to free will.

The problem might be solved if the concept of permission were applied to both kinds of acts, the good and the sinful. The determinist is reluctant to do this, however. If he uses the same term for both, and allows the connotation to tilt too much toward the side of determination, this gives the appearance of making God responsible for sin. But if he uses the same term for both, and allows the connotation to slide more toward true permission, then this would mean that man is able to perform good acts of his own volition—which is not acceptable.[160] How can man perform good acts of his own volition if the sovereign decree is efficacious and unconditional? But let us stop and think about this. If sovereignty is what is at stake here, are we not faced with an inconsistency? For if God can *permit sin* without sacrificing his sovereignty, why can he not *permit good acts* in the same way without doing so? Shedd says that the permissive decree is quite adequate with respect to sin, for it maintains the divine sovereignty.[161] Then why wouldn't the divine sovereignty be maintained if good acts were simply permitted in the same way?

I believe that if it were not for the "God never reacts" stumbling block, there would be more willingness on the part of determinists to apply the concept of permission to good acts as well as bad, and to use it in a sense truer to its ordinary meaning. And this is as it should be, for the question of whether God *causes* or whether he *permits* is an issue that relates to the question of man's free acts as such, not just to man's sinful acts. Barth has the right idea when he speaks of permission as relating to "creaturely freedom" and not just to the freedom to sin.[162]

But the stumbling block presents a dilemma. One can either be consistent and make the whole decree unconditional—and thereby make

---

160. A. H. Strong, *Systematic Theology*, p. 354: "This permissive decree is the only decree of God with respect to sin. Man of himself is capable of producing sin. Of himself he is not capable of producing holiness."

161. W. G. T. Shedd, *Dogmatic Theology*, I:407.

162. Karl Barth, *Church Dogmatics, Volume III: The Doctrine of Creation, Part 3*, tr. G. W. Bromiley and R. J. Ehrlich (Edinburgh: T. & T. Clark, 1961), p. 166.

God the cause of sin; or he can introduce the concept of permission with regard to sin. But if it is real permission, then the unconditionality of the decree is compromised. But if it is not, then we are back to the first horn of the dilemma.

It is quite likely that the whole idea of a permissive decree would never have been tacked on to the concept of the decree as such, if it did not provide a way of exonerating God from the responsibility for sin.[163] But I do not think that it succeeds in doing this anyway, since the term is redefined so far in the direction of determinism. But it is inevitable that this should happen, because real permission is incompatible with unconditionality; and the determinist seems to be unalterably committed to the latter.

Second Cause

Another ambiguity of the unconditional decree is the concept of second cause. It is introduced into the system mainly to provide some plausibility to the idea of free will. But in an unconditional, non-reactive decree, there are no true second causes. To be sure, the determinist affirms that both God and man are genuine causes of every act of the latter. As Berkhof says, "Each deed is in its entirety both a deed of God and a deed of the creature."[164] "In a very real sense the operation is the product of both causes."[165] But I would suggest that the term *cause* is meaningful when applied to persons only when the second cause operates *alongside* the first cause, not when it is an *instrument* of the first cause. As an analogy, we may think of a man who is attempting to lift a large rock. He can almost do it, but not quite. He asks another man standing nearby to help him. Thus both of them lifting together cause the rock to be lifted. Each is a genuine cause. But if the first man uses a lever instead of his friend to help him lift the rock, the lever is not a true second cause but is only an instrument of the real cause of the movement. Despite protestations to the contrary, in an unconditional decree only the latter model can apply. Man is not a second cause but an instrument used by God. When Berkhof says

---

163. See G. C. Berkouwer, *The Providence of God*, p. 138: "That the word permission is not totally repudiated by Reformed theology can be accounted for by its strong distaste—on Biblical grounds—for determinism and by a desire to express the thought that good and evil do not originate in the same way, as 'effects' of one general Divine causality."

164. Lewis Berkhof, *Systematic Theology*, p. 172.

the decree is unconditional, he does not exclude the use of means or conditions on the part of God in order to accomplish his purposes. "But then," he says, "these means or conditions have also been determined in the decree."[166] This is exactly the status that man himself occupies in the decree. God may indeed use second causes, including man; but the causes themselves are caused by God. They do not operate alongside of God even in a secondary role; but rather they operate in sequence, logical if not chronological. The first cause causes the second cause to cause X, as a man causes a lever to lift a rock.

An example of this is Thomistic theology (which Pohle says was not really founded by Thomas Aquinas but by "the learned Dominican theologian Banez [1528-1604]").[167] "The very foundation on which the Thomistic system rests," says Pohle, is the principle that "no secondary cause can act unless it be efficaciously determined by the First Cause by an application of the latter to the former as of potency to act."[168] Reformed theologians agree with this principle if not the terminology. Berkhof himself says, "In every instance the impulse to action and movement proceeds from God. . . . So God also enables and prompts His rational creatures, as second causes, to function, and that not merely by endowing them with energy in a general way, but by energizing them to certain specific acts."[169] Berkouwer sums up Bavinck's view as the idea that "God enters with His omnipotence into every second cause, is present with His essence in the beginning, continuing, and end of every second cause, and, thus, causes both its willing and working according to His good pleasure."[170]

My contention is that the concept of cause does not have any real significance when used in this sense for human beings. Man contributes nothing that has not already been predetermined and "fed into him" by the First Cause. Berkouwer speaks of the "interweaving" and "interlacing" of divine and human acts,[171] but this is not a meaningful analogy with an unconditional decree. None of the threads in the pattern really come from man—not even the sinful ones; they all come from the unconditional decree, some of them being placed into the pattern directly

165. Ibid., p. 173.
166. Ibid., p. 105.
167. Joseph Pohle, *Grace*, p. 232.
168. Ibid., p. 239.
169. Lewis Berkhof, *Systematic Theology*, p. 173.
170. G. C. Berkouwer, *The Providence of God*, p. 130.
171. Ibid., pp. 93, 95.

and some indirectly through man as means. The result is, as Raymond notes, "that the divine will is the sole agent in the universe—all that is not God acts only as acted upon."[172]

Free Will

The third term that loses its integrity within the confines of unconditionality is *free will.* The most common understanding of free will among determinists is that the will is free as long as it is able to choose voluntarily as influenced by a person's own desires and motives. As long as a person can choose to do what he wants to do, his will is free. So it is said.

In my judgment this is a false concept, because the ability to act in accord with one's desires is not in itself a sufficient criterion of freedom. This can easily be demonstrated even in a non-theistic context. For instance, a person may be acting under the influence of hypnotic suggesion (and therefore not freely), but in his own consciousness he is doing what he wants to do. Hasker points out that secular determinists can plausibly account for an individual's present desires through a sequence of prior sufficient causes which in effect nullify any real freedom.[173]

This is even more clearly the case within the context of the unconditional decree. As we have already seen, the determinist theologians who say that man is free to act according to his desires also say that God is the one who determines the desires (or motives, or circumstances). As John Dick says, liberty is "the power of acting according to the prevailing inclination, or the motive which appears strongest to the mind." And it does not matter what produced the state of mind (motives, desires) that produces the volition. "If God fore-ordained certain actions, and placed men in such circumstances that the actions would certainly take place agreeable to the laws of the mind, men are nevertheless moral agents, because they act voluntarily, and are responsible for the actions which consent has made their own."[174] Nash calls this view the "liberty of spontaneity": as long as the acts of men and women are the expression of what they want, they "remain free even if their

---

172. Miner Raymond, *Systematic Theology,* I:496.

173. William Hasker, *Metaphysics,* pp. 34-37.

174. John Dick, *Lectures on Theology,* 2 vols. in 1 (New York: R. Carter and Brothers, 1878), p. 186; cited in Lewis S. Chafer, *Systematic Theology,* I:243.

decisions and their wants were determined in some sense. God would simply see to it that His creatures want to do what He has determined them to do."[175]

In my judgment this is a farcical use of the term *freedom*; it is robbed of its real meaning. Dick says, "If this definition of liberty be admitted, you will perceive that it is possible to reconcile the freedom of the will with absolute decrees; but we have not got rid of every difficulty."[176] This is obviously the case, and the difficulty stems from the unnatural connotation in the word *freedom*. Dick's continuing comments make this clear:

> . . . By this theory, human actions appear to be as necessary as the motions of matter according to the laws of gravitation and attraction; and man seems to be a machine, conscious of his movements, and consenting to them, but impelled by something different from himself.
>
> Upon a subject, no man should be ashamed to acknowledge his ignorance. . . .[177]

In the face of this sort of conceptual confusion it is no wonder that we encounter such ambiguities as "decreed self-determination"[178] and (concerning the decree) "It determines the free act through the free will of the free agent."[179]

The cause of this ambiguity again is the idea of unconditionality. Determinists are properly concerned to maintain free will, but at the same time they will not allow God to react to anything in man. But these two goals are simply incompatible. If man's action is truly free, then God does not cause it but responds to it. If he cannot respond to it, then he must cause it. This latter is the only alternative consistent with an unconditional decree.

Unconditional Foreknowledge

The concept of unconditionality surfaces most explicitly for the determinist in relation to God's foreknowledge. It is strongly affirmed that God's foreknowledge can in no way be derived from or conditioned

---

175. Ronald Nash, *The Concept of God*, p. 54.

176. John Dick, *Lectures on Theology*, p. 186; cited in Lewis S. Chafer, *Systematic Theology*, I:243.

177. Ibid.

178. W. G. T. Shedd, *Dogmatic Theology*, I:404.

179. A. A. Hodge, *Outlines of Theology*, p. 169.

by the creature; God does not "look into the future" and find out what man is going to do. This is the precise point Chafer is making when he remarks that conditioned knowledge "places God in the unworthy position of being dependent upon His creatures."[180] As another writer says, "If God's knowledge is conditioned by and dependent upon events that occur in this world, then he cannot have a provident governance of this world."[181] If divine knowledge is dependent on man's choices, says Berkhof, then this "virtually annuls the certainty of the knowledge of future events, and thus implicitly denies the omniscience of God."[182] If God's foreknowledge is not based on human acts themselves, then upon what *is* it based? "His foreknowledge of future things and also of contingent events rests on His decree."[183] God knows what he himself determines to do.

Being thus related to the decree, foreknowledge itself becomes an active and causative force. As we have seen, most determinists consider foreknowledge in and of itself as sufficient to render all future events certain. It is practically equated with foreordination. "The terms 'foreordain' and 'foreknow" are used synonymously in the Bible; God's foreknowledge is a divine foreordination," says Henry.[184] Why does this have to be the case? Because if it is not active, then it must be reactive or passive; and this is seen as impossible for the sovereign, omniscient God. We should point out, however, that such active, unconditional knowledge is not true foreknowledge. That is, it is not foreknowledge of what creatures will do; it is rather knowledge of what God himself plans to do.

I must agree that divine foreknowledge means that future events are in some sense certain. Raymond says, "All that foreknowledge does is to *prove* the certainty of future events, and that must be admitted without proof; all things will be as they will be, whether known or not, whether decreed or not; the future history of the universe will be in one single way and not two."[185] But if this is true, then how *is* foreknowledge different from foreordination? It differs with respect to that which *makes* man's future acts certain. What makes them certain? The

180. Lewis S. Chafer, *Systematic Theology*, I:230.

181. Roland H. Teske, "Omniscience, Omnipotence, and Divine Transcendence," *The New Scholasticism* (1979), 53:282-283; cited in Ronald Nash, *The Concept of God*, p. 61.

182. Lewis Berkhof, *Systematic Theology*, p. 68.

183. Ibid., pp. 67-68.

184. Carl F. H. Henry, *God, Revelation and Authority*, VI:85.

185. Miner Raymond, *Systematic Theology*: I:502.

foreknowledge itself? No, it does not *make* them certain; it only means that they *are* certain. The decree, then, as Berkhof says? No, not in any determinative or unconditional sense. Then what makes them certain? *The acts themselves,* as viewed by God from his perspective of eternity. All would agree that past events are certain. What makes them so? The simple fact that they have already happened the way they happened. The acts themselves have made them so. Now, even though future events have not occurred yet, the transcendent God who is not limited by time sees them as if they had already happened. Thus he has an infallible foreknowledge of them, though he does not cause them.[156] We freely admit that this means that God's knowledge is to this extent conditioned by his creatures, but this in no way impinges upon his omniscience or his sovereignty. That conditionality contradicts sovereignty is a presupposition without basis in fact or Scripture.

Unconditional Grace

Even in the area of grace the idea that sovereignty requires unconditionality results in distortion. If God is to be sovereign in the bestowal of grace, it is said, then everything related to the sinner's salvation must be the work of God. Every volition and every deed must come from him (Phil. 2:13). Faith is a gift; repentance is a gift; the ability to do good works is a gift. Nothing about salvation can be conditional. This is seen most explicitly in the very choice of who will be saved and who will not. God alone makes this choice, and his choice is not conditioned on anything in the sinner, such as foreseen faith. This is the doctrine of unconditional election. If it were otherwise, then God's decisions would then be dependent upon man; and this can never be. Daane points out that Hoeksema does not even consider the preaching of the gospel as an *offer* of salvation. This would imply that God's gift of salvation is contingent upon whether or not man accepts the offer. But this can never be. "God makes no offers to man, presents no conditions for human acceptance and fulfillment." The gospel does not *offer*; it *actualizes.*[187]

---

186. This has been discussed already in Jack Cottrell, *What the Bible Says About God the Creator*, pp. 287-288. This does not entail the notion that God *per se* is "timeless," that he does not experience succession of moments or interact with his creation in its own time. It simply means that his *knowledge* is not limited by time. See ibid., pp. 259-263.

187. James Daane, *The Freedom of God*, pp. 24-25.

We should note here that the necessity for grace to be unconditional is not just the result of the doctrine of total depravity, but is an essential aspect of the presupposition that sovereignty *per se* cannot brook conditions.

Berkouwer calls the doctrine of sovereign grace a "*skandalon*" (i.e., a stumbling block).[188] Indeed it is, but it is a man-made *skandalon*, created when the grace of God is fused and confused with sovereignty. Even when it is not distorted, sovereignty is an unnatural qualifier of grace. Sovereignty speaks of power, the power of sheer might and strength, the power to create and to command and to destroy. But grace is the expression of a totally different kind of power, the drawing power of love and compassion and self-sacrifice (see John 12:32). In the unnatural hybrid of sovereign grace, sovereignty dominates and overwhelms grace, so that grace is not allowed to be grace.[189] And this problem is compounded all the more when sovereignty is identified with unconditionality—the true *skandalon* for determinists.

The doctrine of unconditional grace results in a serious distortion of the whole concept of salvation, for in relation to the basic biblical distinction between salvation by law and salvation by grace, law is not contrasted with grace as such but with *sovereign* grace. "Salvation by grace" thus becomes unconditional salvation; "salvation by law" becomes salvation involving any conditions whatsoever. Then *nothing* that man does—faith, repentance, baptism—is allowed as a condition for salvation by grace. If there is faith, it is because God has worked it in the heart of the sinner. If there is repentance, God has bestowed it as a gift. Even the baptism which Scripture connects with salvation is limited to *spiritual* baptism, which God can sovereignly bestow. None of these is a condition which man can meet where grace is sovereign and monergistic. But without the distorting lenses of unconditionality, the relation between law and grace appears quite different. They differ according to the *kind* of conditions required for salvation, not as to whether there are conditions or not. The fact is that a person could *theoretically* be saved (made right with God) by the conditions of law itself, i.e., perfect obedience. Such would not be contrary to sovereignty; it just is not true to fact (Rom. 3:23).

---

188. G. C. Berkouwer, *Divine Election*, tr. Hugo Bekker (Grand Rapids: Eerdmans, 1960), p. 8.

189. Jack Cottrell, "Conditional Election," *Grace Unlimited*, ed. Clark H. Pinnock (Minneapolis: Bethany Fellowship, 1975), p. 66.

Removing the Stumbling Block

The determinist model of providence is not the biblical model, and I believe that this would be recognized more readily if the stumbling block of unconditionality were removed. It is essential to see that the idea that God cannot react to creatures and be sovereign at the same time is an unwarranted presupposition.[190] The fact is that God is constantly responding to and reacting to his creatures, especially man, without the slightest threat to his sovereignty. This is the way the Bible pictures it. Virtually every major action of God recorded in the Bible after Genesis 3:1 is a response to human sin. The Abrahamic covenant, the establishment of Israel, the incarnation of Jesus Christ, the death and resurrection of Christ, the establishment of the church, the Bible itself—all are part of the divine reaction to man's sin.

Such an arrangement, i.e., where God reacts to man's choices, would be a violation of sovereignty *only* if God were forced into it, only if it were a necessity imposed upon God from without. But this is not the case. It was God's sovereign choice to bring into existence a universe inhabited by free-will creatures whose decisions would to some extent determine the total picture. When these creatures then do just what God designed them to do, how can this destroy his sovereignty? Is it not rather an expression of it?

Do we have to choose between sovereignty and freedom? Not unless one or the other of them is misinterpreted in an extreme sense. God's sovereignty minus arbitrary unconditionality, and man's freedom minus absolute autonomy, combine into a view of special providence that is in perfect harmony with itself and with the Bible.

---

190. See ibid., pp. 63-65; Jack Cottrell, *What the Bible Says About God the Creator*, pp. 285-287.

Chapter Six

MIRACLES

God's involvement in the on-going world is not limited to general and special providence. There is also the category of miracle. Though much of our concern with the subject of miracles is related to apologetics, we shall not enter into that aspect of the problem here. In this chapter we are assuming their reality as taught in the Bible. What we shall discuss here are the nature and purpose of miracles, especially as related to providence and the natural world.

TERMINOLOGY

The three main terms for miracles in the Bible are *power, wonder,* and *sign*. These three terms occur together at least four times, in Acts 2:22, where Jesus is said to have performed "miracles and wonders and signs"; II Corinthians 12:12, where Paul says he performed "signs and wonders and miracles"; II Thessalonians 2:9, which refers to Satanic "power and signs and false wonders"; and Hebrews 2:4, which refers to God's confirmation of his word "by signs and wonders and by various miracles."

In the New Testament the Greek word for "power" is *dynamis*. It is the word commonly translated "miracle" in our English versions. It refers to the *source* of miracles, namely, the mighty power of God. A symbol for divine power, particularly in the Old Testament, is the hand of God, whence come miracles. "So I will stretch out My hand, and strike Egypt with all My miracles" (Exod. 3:20). "And when Israel saw the great power which the Lord had used against the Egyptians, the people feared the Lord, and they believed" (Exod. 14:31). This was something they were never to forget, "for with a powerful hand the Lord brought us out of Egypt" (Exod. 13:16; see Deut. 6:21; 26:8). Moses praised God thus: "O Lord God, Thou hast begun to show Thy servant Thy greatness and Thy strong hand; for what god is there in heaven or on earth who can do such works and mighty acts as Thine?" (Deut. 3:24). "Thou who hast done great things; O God, who is like Thee?" (Ps. 71:19).[1]

The second word is *wonder* (Greek, *teras*). In the Old Testament it occurs often in combination with the word *sign*: "But I will harden

1. A word similar to this but not as strong is *work* (*ergon*). It is used often in reference to the miracles of Jesus, especially in John's gospel (5:20, 36; 7:3, 21; 9:3-4; 10:25, 32, 37-38; 14:11; 15:24).

Pharaoh's heart that I may multiply My signs and My wonders in the land of Egypt" (Exod. 7:3); "He sent signs and wonders into your midst, O Egypt" (Ps. 135:9). God "hast set signs and wonders in the land of Egypt, and even to this day both in Israel and among mankind" (Jer. 32:20).[2] In the New Testament the word is used only in combination with *sign* and always in the plural.[3] It refers mainly to the *result* the miracles had on the minds of those who observed them, namely, wonder, awe, and amazement at the power of God. "Who is like Thee among the gods, O Lord? Who is like Thee, majestic in holiness, awesome in praises, working wonders?" (Exod. 15:11). "Say to God, 'How awesome are Thy works!'" (Ps. 66:3). Following the wonders of Pentecost, "everyone kept feeling a sense of awe; and many wonders and signs were taking place through the apostles" (Acts 2:43). When Peter and John healed the lame man, the people "were filled with wonder and amazement at what had happened to him" (Acts 3:10). This is as it should be. "The miraculous is that which arouses in us the feeling of wonder, of awe, and even of humility in its presence."[4]

The third word, *sign* (Greek, *sēmeion*), is used often for miracles. The sun's retreating ten steps was a sign to Hezekiah that God's promises to him would come true (Isa. 38:7-8). Jesus' raising Lazarus was a sign (John 12:18). Though the word sometimes carries the weaker meaning of symbol or token, in reference to miracles it means "proof" or "confirmation." This stronger meaning is seen at times even in non-miraculous contexts, such as Luke 2:12, "And this will be a sign for you." Here the idea of proof or confirmation is evident, says Rengstorf.[5] He adds, "The word simply denotes something which may be perceived and from which those who observe it may draw assured conclusions."[6] With regard to miracles this word is used to express their *purpose*. A miracle is performed for the purpose of providing a sign. (This will be discussed more fully in the next section.)

We should note here that no one of these words in itself is sufficient to express the full significance of a miracle. A miracle is a *power*, but

2. See also Deuteronomy 4:34; 6:22, 26:8; Daniel 6:27.

3. See Matthew 24:24; John 4:48; Acts 2:19, 43; 4:30; 5:12; 6:8; 7:36; 14:3; 15:12; Romans 15:19.

4. Alan Richardson, *Christian Apologetics* (London: SCM Press, 1947), p. 155.

5. Karl H. Rengstorf, "σημεῖον, etc.," *Theological Dictionary of the New Testament*, ed. Gerhard Friedrich, tr. Geoffrey Bromiley (Grand Rapids: Eerdmans, 1971), VII:231.

6. Ibid., p. 232. See also p. 259, where Rengstorf suggests "proof of authenticity" for the meaning of the word in II Thessalonians 3:17.

tokens of God's power are everywhere within the scope of providence. Miracles are specialized works of power. Also, a miracle is a *wonder*, but wonders abound even in the natural world. Thus miracles must be very special or extraordinary wonders.[7] And a miracle is a *sign*, but so may a thousand things be designated. Thus it takes a very powerful and wonderful sign to be called a miracle. In this light we can see how appropriate it is for these terms to be used in combination, and particularly for all three to be used together.

THE PURPOSE OF MIRACLES

We have seen that the term *sign* expresses the purpose of miracles. This point now must be discussed more fully, since some very serious errors arise when the purpose of miracles is not clearly discerned. For instance, critics have noticed that naive people often simply apply the term *miracle* to any natural phenomenon which they cannot understand. This allows them to declare the concept of miracle outdated now that we have a better scientific understanding of such things. As Berkouwer puts it, "As nature becomes more transparent the possibility of the Biblical miracles fades."[8] Thus it is important to see that the purpose of miracles is not just to provide an explanatory device for the mysterious.

For another example, a common misunderstanding among believers is that God works miracles simply out of compassion or out of a desire to meet the needs of his people. We grant that God seems to have done this at times. For instance, he kept Moses alive on the mountain for forty days without food or drink (Exod. 34:28; Deut. 9:9). He kept the clothes and shoes of the Israelites from wearing out during their forty years in the wilderness (Deut. 8:4; 29:5). He miraculously provided food for Elijah as the latter fled from Jezebel (I Kings 19:6-8). Elisha caused the iron head of a borrowed axe to float so that it could be recovered and returned to its owner (II Kings 6:6). Also, it is often assumed that Jesus healed the sick purely out of compassion for them in their state of suffering. But can we really say that, as a general principle, the reason why God worked miracles was to meet the needs of

---

7. Edward John Carnell, *An Introduction to Christian Apologetics: A Philosophic Defense of the Trinitarian-Theistic Faith* (Grand Rapids: Eerdmans, 1948), p. 252: "But a miracle . . . is an *extraordinary* wonder of God's working in nature."

8. G. C. Berkouwer, *The Providence of God*, tr. Lewis B. Smedes (Grand Rapids: Eerdmans, 1952), p. 194.

his people? I do not think so. The few cases cited above are clearly exceptions to the general rule. And even where compassion is involved in the healing miracles, it is secondary. As Richardson says, "The motive of compassion is not prominent and certainly is not primary" in any of the gospels.[9] Thus Werner Schaaffs, in seeking to establish that miracles are not outside of natural law, argues from a false premise when he says that it is wrong to think that "God can help his congregations in need only by rescinding his natural laws."[10] How God can help his people is irrelevant to the question, since this is not the purpose of miracles in the first place.

Miracles Are Signs

An examination of the biblical data leads overwhelmingly to the conclusion that the principal function of miracles is to be a *sign* (evidence, proof, confirmation) of the truth of the revelation which they accompany. Because of their character and dominant superiority, the miracles of Scripture are seen as evidence of the presence and endorsement of God. Even Pharaoh's demonically-empowered magicians, after reaching the limits of their black arts, were forced to capitulate and confess concerning Moses' power: "This is the finger of God" (Exod. 8:19). When Nicodemus came to Jesus he acknowledged, "Rabbi, we know that You have come from God as a teacher; for no one can do these signs that You do unless God is with him" (John 3:2).

We have already pointed out that one of the main biblical words for miracles is *sign*. But even when this word is not used, the evidential purpose of miracles is very clear. Their fundamental intent is to show that the miracle-worker himself is a messenger of God. Moses was given certain signs so that the Israelites themselves "may believe that the Lord . . . has appeared to you" (Exod. 4:5). Following the miracle of the exodus, when Moses stretched out his hand over the Red Sea, the people "believed in the Lord and in His servant Moses" (Exod. 14:31). Gideon asked the Angel of the Lord for a sign to verify his identity, and the Angel complied (Judg. 6:17-22). After Elijah raised her son from the dead, the widow of Zarephath exclaimed, "Now I know that you are a man of God" (I Kings 17:24). In his contest with

9. Alan Richardson, *The Miracle-Stories of the Gospels* (New York: Harper and Brothers, n.d.), p. 31.

10. Werner Schaaffs, *Theology, Physics, and Miracles,* tr. Richard L. Renfield (Washington, D.C.: Canon Press, 1974), p. 28.

the prophets of Baal, Elijah prayed for God to let it be known not only that he was Israel's God, but also "that I am Thy servant" (I Kings 18:36). The fire from heaven provided ample proof. The miracles of Jesus himself must be seen in this light. They verified his claims to be the Messiah, the divine Son of God. When John the Baptist sent the question to Jesus, "Are You the One who is coming, or do we look for someone else?" Jesus sent back the answer, "Go and report to John what you have seen and heard: the blind receive sight, the lame walk, the lepers are cleansed, and the deaf hear, the dead are raised up" (Luke 7:20-22). "The works that I do in My Father's name, these bear witness of Me," he said (John 10:25). As Peter commented on Pentecost, Jesus was "attested to you by God with miracles and wonders and signs which God performed through Him" (Acts 2:22). The resurrection was the supreme attestation: Jesus "was declared with power to be the Son of God by the resurrection from the dead" (Rom. 1:4). The apostles established their own credentials via their miracles, as Paul indicates: "The signs of a true apostle were performed among you with all perseverance, by signs and wonders and miracles" (II Cor. 12:12).

The purpose of authenticating a messenger, of course, is to authenticate the truth of his message. His word is thus believed as a revelation from God. The widow's testimony concerning Elijah says it all: "Now I know that you are a man of God, and that the word of the Lord in your mouth is truth" (I Kings 17:24). Jesus said that his claims should be believed because of his works (John 10:37-38; 14:11). When the apostles went forth preaching, God "confirmed the word by the signs that followed" (Mark 16:20). The Samaritans paid attention to what Philip said because they "saw the signs which he was performing" (Acts 8:6). After the gospel was first spoken, "it was confirmed to us by those who heard, God also bearing witness with them, both by signs and wonders and by various miracles" (Heb. 2:3-4).

Perhaps the most specific indicator of the evidential function of miracles is the many times a statement of purpose is given in connection with a miracle. Such a statement usually reads, "So that they may believe," or "So that you may know." Moses was told to perform the miracle with his staff "that they may believe that the Lord . . . has appeared to you" (Exod. 4:5). When he inflicted the first plague on Egypt, Moses said, "Thus says the Lord, 'By this you shall know that I am the Lord'" (Exod. 7:17). The plague of insects would affect every place but Goshen, "in order that you may know that I, the Lord, am in the midst of the land" (Exod. 8:22). The plague of hail ceased at Moses' command, "that you may know that the earth is the Lord's" (Exod. 9:29). God instructed the Israelites to tell their offspring about these signs, "that you may know that I am the Lord" (Exod. 10:2). God delivered them from Egypt by signs and wonders "that you might know that the Lord, He is God; there is no other besides Him" (Deut. 4:34-35). When God announced that he would halt the raging Jordan to allow his people to cross into Canaan, he said, "By this you shall know that the living God is among you" (Josh. 3:10). This was not just for their sake, but so "that all the peoples of the earth may know that the hand of the Lord is mighty, so that you may fear the Lord your God forever" (Josh. 4:24). Elijah prayed for a miracle so that God could "let it be known that Thou art God in Israel" (I Kings 18:36). Jesus prefaced his healing of the paralytic with these words concerning his own divine authority: "In order that you may know that the Son of Man has authority on earth to forgive sins" (Mark 2:10). The miracles that John recorded in his gospel, he said, "have been written that you may believe that Jesus is the Christ, the Son of God" (John 20:30-31). In all of these cases it is clearly stated that the miracle was being performed (or reported) in order to provide grounds for belief.

Scripture connects the working of miracles with faith in many other ways. Moses' response to his commission from God was, "What if they will not believe me, or listen to what I say?" (Exod. 4:1). Then God gave him a miracle to elicit their belief. Then he gave him another, so "that if they will not believe you or heed the witness of the first sign, they may believe the witness of the last sign" (Exod. 4:8). Then he gave him still a third sign. When Moses then confronted his people, he "performed the signs in the sight of the people. So the people believed" (Exod. 4:30-31). When Israel saw God's power over Egypt, they feared and believed (Exod. 14:31). In view of the signs they had seen, the unbelief of the people was inexcusable: "How long will they not believe in Me, despite all the signs which I have performed in their midst?" (Num. 14:11). The same was true of many who saw Jesus work miracles: "But though He had performed so many signs before them, yet they were not believing in Him" (John 12:37). Though he chastised them for needing signs before they would believe (John 4:48), still he performed them; and "many believed in His name, beholding His signs which He was doing" (John 2:23; see 2:11; 4:53-54). Even the *reports* of miracles should be a sufficient basis for faith; see Exodus 10:2; Joshua 4:23-24; Psalm 106:7, 21-22; John 20:30-31.

Thus it would seem to be incontrovertible that the principal purpose of miracles is to provide evidence of the divine origin and truth of the message brought by the miracle worker. In fact, no other major purpose surfaces in the biblical teaching itself. Thus we are not surprised at the widespread agreement among Bible students as to this fact. "It has been argued from the earliest days of the Church that miracles authenticate the message of the messenger," says Ramm, "and this is not to be refuted simply because trite or traditional."[11] The fact is, says Ramm, that the tremendous claims of Christ make miracles a necessity.[12] As Ketcherside says, "Divine testimony must be established by supernatural means." Also, "What is needed is something that no human power can do, and that will attest to the fact that God is working in, through, and by the subject, directly and unequivocally."[13] So miracles are "intended to confirm the divine mission of those who perform them, and to add to the weight of their testimony," says Christlieb.[14] Alan Richardson attempts to soften the concept of *sign* as it applies to miracles. He rejects the idea that the chief significance of the miracles lay in their "evidential value."[15] He interprets them more in the sense of "symbolic actions" that point to Jesus as the Messiah.[16] The distinction does not seem to be as crucial as Richardson suggests, however, since he freely acknowledges that "the miracles are evidence . . . as to Who Jesus is,"[17] and "evidences of the drawing nigh of the Kingdom of God."[18] A sign, he says, is an occurrence which authenticates a message, and Jesus' miracles "authenticate His message."[19] Geisler sums it up nicely: "In short, miracles are God's way of accrediting His spokesmen. There is a miracle to confirm the message as true, a sign to substantiate the sermon, an act of God to verify the Word of God."[20]

---

11. Bernard Ramm, *Protestant Christian Evidences* (Chicago: Moody Press, 1959), p. 134.

12. Ibid., p. 136.

13. W. Carl Ketcherside, "No Credibility Gap," *Christian Standard* (August 28, 1983), 118:10.

14. Theodore Christlieb, *Modern Doubt and Christian Belief*, tr. G. H. Venables and H. U. Weitbrecht (New York: Charles Scribner's Sons, 1903), p. 317.

15. Alan Richardson, *The Miracle-Stories of the Gospels*, pp. 20-22.

16. Ibid., pp. 50-57.

17. Ibid., p. 31.

18. Ibid., p. 38.

19. Ibid., p. 57.

20. Norman Geisler, *Miracles and Modern Thought* (Grand Rapids: Zondervan, 1982), p. 115.

We should note that miracles do not have a unique relation to Jesus; any spokesman sent by God may be empowered to perform signs to authenticate his own message (e.g., Moses, Elijah, Paul). The miracles which Jesus himself performed were not necessarily qualitatively superior to those of other messengers from God; even Elijah raised someone from the dead (I Kings 17:22). What makes Jesus' miracles more significant is the superiority of the *claims* that were being substantiated thereby.

It is possible to go to extremes in our consideration of miracles as signs. Colin Brown warns us that miracles are not "irrefragable objective proofs" or "demonstrative proofs."[21] Many have assumed that a sign is the same as a proof, but Brown denies that this is so. "A sign is not the same as a proof. It is never completely free from ambiguity. It is a pointer, an indication. As such, it falls short of conclusive demonstration."[22] Certainly he is correct if all he means is that miracles can never be considered as *absolute* proof or as a deductive demonstration yielding one hundred percent certainty. This much is always true of any proof from an historical event, whether observed or received by testimony. On the other hand, it is possible to be too cautious and to compromise the clear biblical teaching that miracles are intended as proof or evidence. The sign-function of a miracle may not be the same as demonstrative proof, but it does involve proof of an objective kind. I do not think that Brown makes this clear enough. Alan Richardson definitely obscures this point. Though he says Jesus' miracles "authenticate His message," nevertheless "they are signs which are readable only by those who possess the gift of faith."[23] Berkouwer has certainly gone too far in saying, "Miracles are not proofs addressed to the intellect that thereby man should be convinced. They do not make faith superfluous."[24] Biblical miracles *are* meant to convince, and faith is in part the state of having been convinced by sufficient evidence that a statement reported to us by someone else is true. When miracles have accomplished their purpose, the result *is* faith with regard to the testimony which they accompany.

Miracles and Revelation

Some have assumed that there is a miracle on every page of the Bible, but this is not so. And it is a good thing that it is not so, for as

21. Colin Brown, *Miracles and the Critical Mind* (Grand Rapids: Eerdmans, 1984), p. 205.

22. Ibid., p. 286.

23. Alan Richardson, *The Miracle-Stories of the Gospels*, p. 57.

24. G. C. Berkouwer, *The Providence of God*, p. 215.

Brown correctly remarks, "If miracles were as commonplace in antiquity as we popularly assume, they would hardly have counted as miracles at all and would have been indistinguishable from the normal course of events."[25] As Birks long ago pointed out, "Miracles, to fulfill their great object of attesting and confirming messages from God, must retain an unusual and exceptional character. When they become habitual with any regular law of recurrence, they cease to be miraculous, and only add one more element to the immense number of natural laws."[26] But in the pages of Scripture, as Birks notes, there is a "wise parsimony" with regard to their occurrence. In fact, "miracles were a rare exception and not the ordinary rule of Divine Providence."[27]

Since this is the case we may appropriately inquire into the specific occasion for their appearance. Remembering that they function as signs or credentials for God's messengers, we would expect them to appear mainly in those eras when God is giving new revelation.[28] And this is indeed the case. Miracles have not occurred at random or arbitrarily but for the most part have been grouped in what Hoover calls "revelatory clusters."[29] Two main clusters are usually identified, namely, the inauguration of the nation of Israel beginning with the exodus, and the inauguration of the new covenant age beginning with the incarnation of Christ. Lesser clusters occur at the time of Elijah and Elisha and at the time of Daniel, when true religion was making a stand against idolatry.

This leads to the question of whether revelation is part of the very purpose of miracles. This was the view of A. B. Bruce, who said that miracles "enter into the very substance of revelation, and are not merely signs confirmatory of its truth." They are "an essential part of revelation" and "are as important as the revelation itself."[30] Christlieb agreed that at least in part, "their purpose in the scheme of redemption is likewise an *educational* one."[31] We must acknowledge that it is inevitable that God's miracles should reveal something about him, such as

---

25. Colin Brown, *Miracles and the Critical Mind,* p. 281.

26. T. R. Birks, *The Bible and Modern Thought* (Cincinnati: Curts and Jennings, 1861), p. 156.

27. Ibid., pp. 159-160.

28. Ibid., p. 163.

29. Arlie J. Hoover, *Dear Agnos: A Defense of Christianity* (Grand Rapids: Baker Book House, 1976), p. 147.

30. Alexander Balmain Bruce, *The Miraculous Element in the Gospels,* 2 ed. (London: Hodder and Stoughton, 1890), p. 285.

31. Theodore Christlieb, *Modern Doubt and Christian Belief,* p. 317.

his power, his compassion, and his justice. As the Lord said to Pharaoh, "For this cause I have allowed you to remain, in order to show you My power, and in order to proclaim My name through all the earth" (Exod. 9:16). But even though this element often enters in, and sometimes perhaps as even a secondary purpose, we must insist that the main purpose for miracles is evidence and not revelation. Indeed, miracles themselves give no information, but can be understood only in connection with the revelation they accompany. The miracle worker speaks a message or makes a claim, and then he works a miracle in order to verify his message or his claim. The revelational content always comes from the accompanying message, not from the miracle *per se.*

The connection of miracles with revelation, in their role as signs, is of utmost importance. The fact of this connection should always be stressed, as it was by Christlieb: "The entire series of miracles perceptible to the senses, from the time of Abraham and Moses down to that of Christ, has accompanied every step of *the divine relevation, in order either to confirm it or to prepare the way for it.*"[32] This connection is also noted by Carnell: "We need special revelation to complete our view of God and man, but how shall we recognize this revelation when it comes along?" Also, "Without special revelation we cannot find a philosophic solution to reality's riddle; but without miracles we cannot be assured that he who bears a revelation actually is from God."[33] To B. B. Warfield, "the inseparable connection of miracles with revelation, as its mark and credential," was an important point. "They belong to revelation periods, and appear only when God is speaking to His people through accredited messengers, declaring His gracious purposes."[34]

Why is this important? For two reasons. First, it shows that miracles are not an arbitrary phenomenon which one might just as reasonably expect to occur at one time or another, or in one place as another. They occur in accord with a specific purpose. Second, it helps us to answer the question of whether miracles are still occurring today. If they are inseparably connected with revelation, then to say miracles are still occurring today one would have to affirm that revelation is also being given today. In relation to this issue it is important to see still another connection, namely, that between revelation and redemption. As Vos points out, "Revelation does not stand alone by itself, but is . . .

32. Ibid., p. 318.

33. E. J. Carnell, *An Introduction to Christian Apologetics*, pp. 268-269.

34. Benjamin B. Warfield, *Miracles: Yesterday and Today, True and False* (Grand Rapids: Eerdmans, 1965 reprint of 1918 edition entitled *Counterfeit Miracles*), pp. 25-26.

inseparably attached to another activity of God, which we call *Redemption*. . . . Revelation is the interpretation of redemption; it must, therefore, unfold itself in installments as redemption does." He explains that he is referring only to those objective, central redeeming acts of God such as the atonement, and not subjective events such as regeneration.[35] Thus when this grand work of redemption was completed and initially explained, revelation ceased. Robert Reymond puts these two points together into a convincing argument against the continuation of genuine miracles after the apostolic era. "Non-repeatable historical events of redemption, special revelation, and miracles of power stand related to each other in a chain-like pattern," he says.

> . . . Special revelation (after the Fall) serves the non-repeatable historical events of redemption as the latter's explanation (Vos); miracles of power in turn serve special revelation as the latter's authentication (Warfield). It is the non-repeatable historical events of redemption which call forth special revelatory explanation; it is special revelation in turn which calls forth miraculous authentication. Where the first is absent, there is no necessity for the second; where the second is absent, there is no necessity for the third. When the first has been sufficiently and permanently interpreted (in inscripturated form) by the second, and the second sufficiently authenticated by the third, there is no further need for the continuation of either the second or the third, and in fact the revelatory process and the authenticating miracles do not continue. Once the second and third have occurred, however, the first takes its place in the world as an explicated, authenticated incontrovertible fact of history.[36]

These connections are evident in Hebrews 2:3-4,

> . . . How shall we escape if we neglect so great a salvation? After it was at the first spoken through the Lord, it was confirmed to us by those who heard, God also bearing witness with them, both by signs and wonders and by various miracles and by gifts of the Holy Spirit according to His own will. . . .

Here the redemption ("so great a salvation") is first explained via revelation ("spoken through the Lord"), which is then authenticated by miracles ("confirmed to us by those who heard").

35. Geerhardus Vos, *Biblical Theology: Old and New Testaments* (Grand Rapids: Eerdmans, 1948), p. 14.

36. Robert L. Reymond, "*What About Continuing Revelations and Miracles in the Presbyterian Church Today?*" (Phillipsburg, N.J.: Presbyterian and Reformed, 1977), pp. 55-56.

Though this is not the only consideration relevant to the question of whether miracles are continuing today,[37] it is an extremely important one and (I think) points us toward the proper answer to the question.

Miracles as Remedy

An old objection against miracles, sometimes from skeptics and sometimes from Deists, is that a competent workman would not have made a world of such poor quality that it would be necessary for him to intervene in order to remedy some defect by means of a miracle.[38] A statement attributed to Renan sums up this point: "Miracles are special interpositions like those of a watchmaker, who, though he has made a very fine watch, yet is compelled to regulate it from time to time, in order to compensate for the insufficiency of the mechanism."[39] A contemporary skeptic puts it this way:

> A miracle is an arbitrary interruption, by a deity, of the ordinary sequences of natural law, a temporary suspension of normal processes. As Voltaire long ago pointed out, to hope for a miracle is implicitly to argue the nonexistence of God's omniscience and omnipotence, implicity to argue that God was unable to create a world in which He does not have to intervene miraculously in order to make things go as He wishes. A proper God would never *need* a miracle.[40]

Such a criticism is off target simply because it misconstrues the purpose of a miracle in God's world. It has nothing to do with God's reaching in to patch up or remedy some mistake he made in the first place. This is a false understanding of miracles.

A variation on the idea of miracles as remedy is quite common among Bible believers, however. It is pointed out that the defects in the world that make miracles necessary are present not because of

37. Other relevant considerations are (1) the apparent necessity for the laying on of an apostle's hands in order to convey miracle-working power, as in Acts 8:14-18 (see B. B. Warfield, *Miracles: Yesterday and Today*, pp. 22-24); and (2) the interpretation of the *teleion* in I Corinthians 13:10 as the completed New Testament (see Jack Cottrell, *What the Bible Says About God the Creator*; Joplin, Mo.: College Press, 1983; pp. 317-319; Knofel Staton, *Spiritual Gifts for Christians Today*; Joplin, Mo.: College Press, 1973; Chapters 3 & 4).

38. See this objection stated in T. R. Birks, *The Bible and Modern Thought*, p. 75; and C. S. Lewis, *Miracles: A Preliminary Study*, 2 ed. (New York: Macmillan, 1960), p. 95.

39. Ernest Renan, cited in Revere Franklin Weidner, *Theologia, or the Doctrine of God* (New York: Fleming H. Revell Company, 1902), p. 104.

40. Randel Helms, "On Miracles," *Free Inquiry* (Spring 1984), 4:44.

God's poor workmanship in the creation, but because of the corrupting influences of human sin.[41] Thus it is agreed that miracles function as a *remedy*, but a remedy whose object is "to heal and restore God's order of the world which has been destroyed through sin and death."[42]

The context in which this idea is most often stressed today is in the discussion of the relation between miracles and natural law (which will be discussed more fully in the next section). It is part of the fairly common denial that miracles are some kind of violation of natural law. Miracles are not against nature, it is said; rather, they are against sin. In fact, the purpose of miracles is to *restore* nature. This view has been stated eloquently by Christlieb. It is man's sins, and not miracles, he says, that have made a "rent" in the world and introduced unnatural elements into it. But "the unnatural is removed by means of the miraculous, and the original laws of nature are re-established." Miracles "aim at the restoration, salvation, *and consummation of the world*. . . . They are isolated manifestations of a new creative activity of the divine will, infusions of a reorganizing power into the life of nature, whereby it is agitated and excited." Miracles "are the first strokes of God's hammer, which is to break the great prison of nature and of the human world, and to loose the chains of corruption and death." Christlieb affirms, "This holy purpose lies, without exception, at the foundation of all true miracles."[43]

This sentiment is echoed widely today. Berkhof says concerning miracles, "They do not aim at a violation, but rather at a restoration of God's creative work."[44] Speaking specifically of miracles of resurrection, Geisler says that "the reversal of death and decay is not against nature; it is in fact *for* nature's rejuvenation."[45] Johann Diemer says, "Through the signs and wonders the disintegrating power of sin is broken and its results overcome. . . . Nothing happens against nature but only against sin and its results." The miracles restore nature's original state. This is true even of pagan miracles.[46] Berkouwer describes miracles as "a redeeming reinstatement of the normality of world and life through the new dominion of God." They are themselves a part of God's saving

41. Theodore Christlieb, *Modern Doubt and Christian Belief*, pp. 311-313.

42. R. F. Weidner, *Theologia*, p. 104.

43. Theodore Christlieb, *Modern Doubt and Christian Belief*, pp. 314-316.

44. Louis Berkhof, *Systematic Theology* (London: Banner of Truth Trust, 1939), p. 177.

45. Norman Geisler, *Miracles and Modern Thought*, p. 132.

46. Johann H. Diemer, *Nature and Miracle*, tr. Wilma Bouma (Toronto: Wedge Publishing Foundation, 1977), pp. 25-26, 29.

work.[47] What C. S. Lewis calls the "Miracles of the New Creation" (Miracles of Reversal, Miracles of Perfecting) would also be described in this way.[48]

This view of miracles can be characterized as a romanticized distortion. The only miracle to which this way of thinking truly applies is the resurrection of Jesus Christ, and that not because it is a miracle *per se* but because it is an integral part of Christ's redemptive work. The resurrection is a true saving act, a true reversal of sin's effects upon the old creation, a truly restorative work. As such, however, it is not to be regarded simply as the largest and brightest jewel in a whole cluster of jewels composed of the other miracles. As a saving work it exists still alone in a category that awaits even its second member, for it is a work of the end time appearing in time ahead of time, a work later to be joined by the resurrection of the bodies of the redeemed and the bursting forth of the new heavens and new earth.[49]

It is true enough that some of Jesus' miracles are of the same general form as his resurrection in that they counteract sin's effects for a time. This applies especially to his healing miracles and the occasions when he raised the dead. But while there is a relationship, it is only symbolic. These miracles of healing and resurrection produced results that were only temporary and individual. There were no lasting, saving results, no true reversal of sin's imprint on nature.

Because they provide a kind of symbolic foretaste of the real reversal begun in Christ's resurrection and completed at the end, these particular miracles are especially fitting and congruous with the focal point of Christ's mission and message. It is appropriate that the one who came to defeat sin and death and Satan should authenticate himself through miracles that showed his complete authority over these enemies. It is supremely appropriate that the crowning act of salvation should also function as the ultimate miracle of confirmation for the Redeemer. This guarantees that the resurrection as miracle will have an existential impact upon those who open their minds to it, for it "speaks to universal human need," as Montgomery says.[50] Stephen Wykstra is wrong to

---

47. G. C. Berkouwer, *The Providence of God*, pp. 208, 211.

48. C. S. Lewis, *Miracles*, p. 142.

49. See Wolfhart Pannenberg, "Dogmatische Thesen zur Lehre von der Offenbarung," *Offenbarung als Geschichte*, ed. Wolfhart Pannenberg, 3 ed. (Göttingen: Vandenhoeck and Ruprecht, 1965), pp. 104ff.

50. John W. Montgomery, "Science, Theology and the Miraculous," *Journal of the American Scientific Affiliation* (December 1978), 30:149.

dismiss so lightly the significance of the existential relevance of the miracle of resurrection.[51]

At best, then, *some* of Christ's miracles can be said to participate *symbolically* in the restoration of sin-stricken nature. But this includes only part of the whole category of events in Scripture known as signs, wonders, and powers. There are many miracles which do not have this relation to the restoration. Though the exodus itself was surely a saving act, the ten plagues that preceded it were hardly a reversal of the corruption of nature. Rather, they magnified it. Paul's striking a man blind (Acts 13:11) hardly qualifies as a "redeeming reinstatement of normality." Floating axe heads and water-walking do not reverse any consequence of sin on nature, as far as I can see. It is easy to forget such miracles as these and to focus only on the great miracles of the gospels when we are formulating our doctrine of miracles in general, but this is an inexcusable mistake.

The approach to miracles that considers them as remedies to sin's corruption of nature is inadequate. At best this applies only to some, and even then in a symbolic way only. This approach obscures the true purpose for miracles that is broadcast throughout Scripture, namely, to confirm the revelation which they accompany. In a related way it distorts the relation between miracles and natural law, as we shall see in the next section.

There is one point in this approach that is correct, however, and that is the emphasis on the fact that miracles are necessary because sin has come into the world. Failing to recognize this leads the Deist and the skeptic astray, as we saw at the beginning of this section. But even those who recognize it must be careful to understand it aright. Some think that sin now makes miracles necessary as a more striking mode of revelation. I.e., before sin entered, God's general revelation in nature was sufficient; but now God must speak to sinful man in a louder voice.[52] Others think that miracles are now necessary as a way of remedying sin. But neither of these approaches is correct. The *remedy* for sin lies in the mighty works of redemption accomplished by Jesus; the preparatory and explanatory *revelation* has come principally through verbal messages given to God's spokesmen. Miracles are necessary in

---

51. Stephen J. Wykstra, "The Problem of Miracle in the Apologetic from History," *Journal of the American Scientific Affiliation* (December 1978), 30:157-159.

52. See T. R. Birks, *The Bible and Modern Thought*, pp. 86-87; Walter J. Chantry, *Signs of the Apostles: Observations on Pentecostalism Old and New*, 2 ed. (Carlisle, Pa.: Banner of Truth Trust, 1976), p. 7.

this scheme not as the remedy and not as the revelation, but as God's means of *confirming* the revelation.

MIRACLES AND NATURAL LAW

Exactly how miracles are related to natural law has been the focus of considerable controversy. Popular piety has always assumed that miracles by definition must in some way fall outside the boundaries of the natural. With the rise of scientism and the concept of natural laws as absolute, prescriptive causes, attacks on miracles as impossible violations of such laws became common. Believers have never been comfortable with the idea of natural laws as inflexible and unalterable causes;[53] but in the twentieth century, under the influence of Einstein's theories, there is general agreement even among unbelievers that such laws can no longer be considered absolute. As Montgomery says, "No one (believer or unbeliever) who lives in today's Einsteinian universe can benefit from the luxury of an absolute natural law."[54] Definitions today tend to be descriptive rather than prescriptive, i.e., the laws are generalized descriptions of what has thus far been observed to occur in nature.[55] As Carnell says, "As nature is but the totality of the moving universe, so natural laws are but approximate descriptions of the pattern that this moving universe follows."[56] Also, "Laws of nature are a description of what *happens*, not a handbook of rules to tell us what *cannot happen*."[57]

This relativizing of natural law has been greeted with enthusiasm by many Christian theologians and apologists, since they feel that it removes the old stigma of miracles as "violations" of an inviolable natural law. A place has been made now for the possibility of miracles.[58] As Montgomery says, "For us, unlike people of the Newtonian epoch,

53. See the statement made in 1861 by T. R. Birks, *The Bible and Modern Thought*, p. 81: "These laws of nature, which before were nothing else than a summation of observed facts, are transformed into real causes, inflexible and unalterable as the fates of the old heathens, which admit neither God, nor angel, nor man, to interfere with their absolute and supreme dominion."

54. John W. Montgomery, "Science, Theology and the Miraculous," p. 146.

55. See David Basinger and Randall Basinger, "Science and the Concept of Miracle," *Journal of the American Scientific Affiliation* (December 1978), 30:164-165. Compare Birks' 1861 definition: "summation of observed facts" (see footnote 53 above).

56. E. J. Carnell, *An Introduction to Christian Apologetics*, p. 250.

57. Ibid., p. 258.

58. See G. C. Berkouwer, *The Providence of God*, pp. 201-202.

the universe is no longer a tight, safe, predictable playing-field in which we know all the rules. Since Einstein no modern has had the right to rule out the possibility of events because of prior knowledge of 'natural law.'"[59] Thus even the resurrection of Jesus must be accepted as within the bounds of the possible.[60] But is the situation as positive as this? Does the revised concept of natural law mean that miracles are no longer a stumbling block to modern man? Unfortunately, no. It may be that the problem has been eased in one direction, but at the same time it has been intensified in another. For if natural law is now considered to be open-ended, then it becomes exceedingly difficult to *define* a miracle and to *distinguish* it from the natural. And if it cannot be clearly identified and distinguished, then how can it function as a wonder-evoking, confirming sign from God? As Wykstra sums it up,

> The correct epistemological moral to draw from the Einsteinian revolution is thus not: "Aha, now we see that miracles are possible after all!"; rather it is: "If we can no longer claim to *know* what natural processes in themselves are capable of producing, how then can we know whether any anomaly is a 'miracle'?" The crucial question is thus underscored: If miracles do occur, by what criteria can we distinguish them, *qua miracles*, from those natural events that are startling only because our theories of nature (and the expectations these theories give us) are defective?[61]

Thus we see how important it is that we give some attention to the relation between miracles and natural law. That is the purpose of this section. First, we will consider the idea that miracles are *within* the scope of natural law, then we will examine the view that they are somehow *outside* its scope.

Are Miracles Within Natural Law?

In an effort to formulate a response to the critics of supernaturalism who reject miracles as violations of natural law, many Christian theologians have denied that miracles should be defined in this way. Not only do miracles not violate natural law; they are, in fact, wholly within its boundaries. For example, Pollard says that a miracle is not something unnatural, outside of nature; it is really just a clear and striking instance

59. John W. Montgomery, *History and Christianity* (Downers Grove, Ill.: InterVarsity Press, 1965), p. 75.

60. Ibid.

61. Stephen Wykstra, "The Problem of Miracle," p. 156.

of providence. "A miracle is not a special kind of event possessing a quality which common happenings do not share."[62] Speaking specifically of the miracles of Jesus, T. F. Torrance says they are

> . . . within the limits, conditions, and objectivities of our world, not as involving in any way the suspension of the space-time structures which we call 'natural law', far less implying the abrogation of the God-given order in nature they express, but rather as the re-creating and deepening of that order in the face of all that threatens to break it down through sin, disease, violence, death, or evil of any kind.[63]

Werner Schaaffs says, "God *never* rescinds his own natural laws, which constitute and maintain his creation." Since he has pronounced everything "very good," this means that "all the miracles of the Old and New Testaments, including the Resurrection, are consistent with the natural laws of creation." Matthew 5:18 includes the meaning that God "does not set aside so much as a tittle of natural law, but rather carries it out fully."[64] Carnell likewise includes miracles within the limits of nature. God works them, he says, through the same kind of secondary means he uses to order any phenomenon. "This sets our definition squarely in the realm of science, and relieves the scientist of his false notion that miracles are inexplicable, mysterious, and beyond rational explanation." This means that miracles "are theoretically discernible by a patient application of the scientific method." They are part of the data for drawing up the laws of nature. "If Christ walked on the water and was raised from the dead, these, like any other phenomena of history, make up the actual limits of laws."[65]

One way of explaining this view is to say that the unusual or unnatural element in a miracle is not its content but its *timing*. The event itself may not be impossible in terms of natural law, but that it should have happened at just that time and place—that constitutes the miracle. Schaaffs says, "The really miraculous element in the biblical miracles is the time of their occurrence." The event itself is always a scientific possibility, but the time "is determined by things that cannot be conceived or influenced physically."[66] He gives three examples: the star of the Wise Men, the crossing of the Red Sea by the Israelites, and Moses' burning bush. Concerning the last of these, for example, he

62. William G. Pollard, *Chance and Providence: God's Action in a World Governed by Scientific Law* (New York: Charles Scribner's Sons, 1958), pp. 112-118.

63. Thomas F. Torrance, *Divine and Contingent Order* (New York: Oxford University Press, 1981), p. 24.

64. Werner Schaaffs, *Theology, Physics, and Miracles*, pp. 27-28.

65. E. J. Carnell, *An Introduction to Christian Apologetics*, pp. 249, 252.

66. Werner Schaaffs, *Theology, Physics, and Miracles*, p. 56.

says that when several factors coincide in just the right combination, the ether of the diptam or Dictamnus albus bush will indeed burn with a reddish flame. That this rare phenomenon should have happened at just the time when Moses came into its vicinity was the miraculous part.[67] This is also Pollard's view. "The majority of the Biblical miracles," he says, "are . . . the result of an extraordinary and extremely improbable combination of chance and accident." Miracles of healing, for example, can be explained by the "extremely improbable circumstance" that all the necessary physico-chemical, physiological, and psychological changes occurred together. Individually none of these changes would be unusual; that they all conjoined at once is the miracle.[68] Birks in 1861 had already allowed for this as one type of miracle, which he called "improper miracle." These are those "which result from rare and unusual combinations of second causes. In these foresight, and not power, is the really-supernatural element."[69] This is also what is today often called the *contingency* or *coincidence* concept of miracles.[70] Over eighty years ago Warfield criticized this view as an "understatement" of the nature of a miracle. "By such definitions," he said, "miracles are reduced to the category of the natural. For the forces of nature, under whatever guidance, can produce nothing but natural effects. They are thus confused with what we know as 'special providences.'"[71]

An even more common way of expressing the view that miracles are within the limits of nature is the idea that miracles are not beyond natural law as such but only beyond our *knowledge* of natural law. Augustine is usually cited as holding this view, since he said, "A portent, therefore, happens not contrary to nature, but contrary to what we know as nature."[72] A modern example is Alan Richardson, who

67. Ibid., pp. 49-51.

68. William Pollard, *Chance and Providence*, p. 115.

69. T. R. Birks, *The Bible and Modern Thought*, p. 85.

70. See Colin Brown, *Miracles and the Critical Mind*, pp. 174-175.

71. Benjamin B. Warfield, "The Question of Miracles," *Selected Shorter Writings of Benjamin B. Warfield*, ed. John E. Meeter (Nutley, N.J.: Presbyterian and Reformed, 1973), II:168-169.

72. Augustine, "The City of God," XXI:8, tr. Marcus Dods, *Basic Writings of Saint Augustine*, ed. Whitney J. Oates (New York: Random House, 1948), II:575. Though this statement is often cited (e.g., G. C. Berkouwer, *The Providence of God*, p. 198), it is hardly parallel to the idea as held in modern times. Augustine is making the point that the Creator is free to do *whatever he wishes* with his creation; therefore the *nature* of a thing is *whatever God wills* it to be. We can never know in advance what God may will with regard to a particular item. Thus our ignorance is not of nature *per se* in the modern sense, but of *God's intent* with regard to any item in nature. Augustine's purpose is not to enclose miracles within the compass of the natural, but to assert God's freedom to raise any natural circumstance to the level of a miracle.

declares that "miracle is merely that which occurs according to the operation of those laws of nature which are as yet unknown to us."[73] Berkouwer's idea of miracles as the new and the novel may fall into this category.[74] This view is a natural outgrowth of the Einsteinian approach to the universe. If natural law is open-ended, then, as Montogmery suggests, "all events, however strange, can be considered as falling within natural boundaries."[75] What we call "miracle" would just be those things for which our present knowledge of nature cannot account. Some day, however, even the most anomalous events (such as the resurrection) may be scientifically explainable. "If we knew everything about the total system of nature, as God does, then a miracle wouldn't appear as a break to us."[76]

A. B. Bruce long ago criticized this view as for all practical purposes eliminating the category of miracle. It simply "declares the belief that every miraculous event happens in accordance with some physical law, though from the nature of the case we are in ignorance what it is." Such a view, he says, "saves miracles as events by the sacrifice of their miraculous significance." He regards it as just an apologetic device to make miracles less offensive to scientific minds.[77] The point is, if we say that a miracle is not contrary to nature but just to our understanding of nature, what right do we have to assert that it is a miracle at all? Who are we to say that it has a supernatural cause, when all we can really say is that its cause is not understood at the present?[78] Brown points out that modern advances in scientific knowledge are indeed making certain biblical miracles more easily accepted by skeptics. For instance, certain of the healing miracles appear to be more reasonable in light of what we now know of psychosomatic factors and the phenomenon of remission. But this is no real gain, says Brown. "In such cases the skeptic simply changes his categories. He grants the possible facticity of the report, but at the price of denying its miraculous character. If no explanation is at hand, the event is relegated to the twilight domain of anomalies awaiting elucidation by the onward march of science."[79] But Montgomery suggests that science will have to march a long, long way in order to be able to accommodate such miracles as the instant

73. Alan Richardson, *Christian Apologetics*, p. 155.
74. G. C. Berkouwer, *The Providence of God*, pp. 204ff.
75. John W. Montgomery, "Science, Theology and the Miraculous," p. 150.
76. Arlie Hoover, *Dear Agnos*, p. 143.
77. A. B. Bruce, *The Miraculous Element in the Gospels*, pp. 48-51.
78. See Norman Geisler, *Miracles and Modern Thought*, pp. 48, 64.
79. Colin Brown, *Miracles and the Critical Mind*, p. 282.

regrowth of fingers lost to leprosy or the resurrection of a man dead four days. I.e., there is a point where it becomes more reasonable simply to grant that a miracle (unique, non-analogous event) has occurred than to harbor a blind faith that some day a natural law will come to light that will explain it all.[80]

The view that miracles occur wholly within nature can be defended only by ignoring the biblical teaching concerning the purpose for miracles. If one adopts a false view of purpose, then he can perhaps consistently defend this view. Thus Schaaffs' belittling the idea that "God can help his congregations in need only by rescinding his natural laws"[81] reflects his combining of this view with the *remedy* purpose of miracles. Indeed, the concept of miracles as remedy goes hand in hand with miracles as the essence of the natural, and even encourages this view. But as we have seen, this is not the biblical purpose for miracles. In Scripture they are not meant to restore nature as such, but ultimately to *point to* the Restorer. That is, they are confirming signs, evidences given to confirm the divine origin of the message they accompany. And the question is, *how can they function in this way unless they are in some way outside the natural?* A. B. Bruce deplored what was even in his day a tendency to "naturalize the miraculous."[82] Opening up the order of nature indefinitely means that "anything may happen, a centaur may turn up, or a dead man come to life. But what then? Why should we be surprised? Why think that a miracle, something very wonderful has taken place?" When it is no longer necessary to posit a supernatural cause for the occurrence, it ceases to function as a miracle. "Miracles can have no evidential force unless they be supernatural."[83] As C. S. Lewis expresses it, if the biblical miracles "were not known to be contrary to the laws of nature how could they suggest the presence of the supernatural? How could they be surprising unless they were seen to be exceptions to the rules?"[84] In Hoover's words, "If the event didn't run counter to natural law it wouldn't be considered a miracle at all, for a wonder must have a background of uniform activity to stand out as unique."[85]

---

80. John W. Montgomery, "Science, Theology and the Miraculous," p. 151.
81. Werner Schaaffs, *Theology, Physics, and Miracles*, p. 28.
82. A. B. Bruce, *The Miraculous Element in the Gospels*, pp. 43-44.
83. Ibid., pp. 46-47.
84. C. S. Lewis, *Miracles*, p. 47.
85. Arlie Hoover, *Dear Agnos*, p. 139.

Thus despite the difficulties involved in such an affirmation, we must say that miracles are in some sense *outside* of natural law if they are to function as Scripture says they do.

Miracles Are Outside Natural Laws

If miracles cannot be included within the scope of natural law, in what sense can they be said to be outside it? Only skeptics such as David Hume[86] seem comfortable in declaring that miracles are a *violation* of the laws of nature or are *contrary* to nature. Evangelicals stand in line to disavow such a concept, for various reasons. The examples are too numerous to list; one will suffice: "Therefore, miracles and laws are different, but it is wrong to define a miracle with words like 'violate,' 'transgress,' or 'contradict.'"[87] Occasionally one encounters such language as "Miracles contradict all known laws of nature" or "Miracles are all in conflict with well-known natural laws,"[88] but these are rare exceptions. Thinking mainly of Hume and other skeptics, Ramm says, "Any such definitions that emphasize the words *violation* or *contradictory* or *in opposition to* prejudice the case immediately against miracles."[89]

How, then, shall we describe the relationship? Here we encounter a plethora of terms. Miracles are a suspension of natural law. They supersede it; they counteract, transcend, overrule, supplement, modify, and bypass it. They set it aside. They interfere with it. They are exceptions to natural law; they interrupt it; they are interventions into it. Miracles are above, beyond, and outside natural law. They are extra-natural, not anti-natural.

What those terms are meant to express is that something happens in a miracle that cannot be explained by natural law alone. This is usually explained as follows. A miracle is the intervention of a non-natural, supernatural *cause* in order to bring about an *effect* that is consistent with nature. It is a supernatural means to a natural end. The cause comes from outside of nature; the effect is encompassed within it. As Brunner says, God is not tied to the laws of nature. They

86. David Hume, "An Enquiry Concerning Human Understanding," X:1, *Hume: Theory of Knowledge*, ed. D. C. Yalden-Thomson (New York: Thomas Nelson and Sons, 1951), p. 118. He says, "A miracle is a violation of the laws of nature."

87. Arlie Hoover, *Dear Agnos*, p. 139.

88. These examples are cited by Johann Diemer, *Nature and Miracle*, p. 18.

89. Bernard Ramm, *Protestant Christian Evidences*, p. 125.

are relative; he alone is absolute. Thus he is free to work outside the sphere of natural causality if he desires. The result is a miracle.[90] Another way of putting it is that when God works miraculously "He works immediately or without the mediation of second causes."[91] Miracles are "unexplainable in terms of the physical secondary agents."[92] They are "inexplicable in terms of ordinary natural forces."[93] I.e., the cause lies outside of nature.

Some have pointed out that the ordinary course of nature is constantly being acted upon by a power that lies in a sense outside it, namely, the human will. Under ordinary circumstances the forces of nature will keep a rock lying on the surface of the ground. But a human being may intervene and lift the rock and even throw it into the air with a force that counters gravity. By analogy, and in a much higher sense, the divine will may also intervene and produce effects in the natural world that would not have come about otherwise.[94] As C. S. Lewis explains it, a natural law simply tells us what we can expect to happen in nature, *provided nothing interferes.* But it precludes neither human interference nor divine.[95]

Since it is fed into nature from outside it, a miracle is something like an act of creation.[96] As Christlieb says, miracles

> . . . are creative acts of God, *i.e,* supernatural exertions of power upon certain points of Nature's domain, through which, by virtue of His own might already working in the course of nature, God, for the furtherance of His kingdom, brings forth some new thing which natural substances or causalities could not have produced by themselves . . . .[97]

Thus a miracle is distinguished by its *cause*—a cause which is non-natural, supernatural and immediate.

At this point, it is said, the mechanics of the miracle change somewhat. Though the cause is supernatural, the effect produced is not something strange and weird and contrary to nature. As soon as the

90. Emil Brunner, *The Christian Doctrine of Creation and Redemption: Dogmatics, Volume II,* tr. Olive Wyon (Philadelphia: Westminster Press, 1952), pp. 160-161.

91. Louis Berkhof, *Systematic Theology,* p. 176.

92. Walter Chantry, *Signs of the Apostles,* p. 7.

93. James Oliver Buswell, Jr., *A Systematic Theology of the Christian Religion* (Grand Rapids: Zondervan, 1962), I:176.

94. A. B. Bruce, *The Miraculous Element in the Gospels,* pp. 63ff.

95. C. S. Lewis, *Miracles,* pp. 57ff.

96. Bernard Ramm, *Protestant Christian Evidences,* p. 128.

97. Theodore Christlieb, *Modern Doubt and Christian Belief,* p. 291.

effects have taken place, they "range themselves in the natural course of things, without any disturbance arising on their account."[98] This is why nature itself is not violated by a miracle. As soon as its effect enters the world, "it becomes subject to the laws of nature, and obeys them in its further existence. Apart from its origin, it ceases with its entrance into the world to be a miracle, and becomes part of the natural and the actual."[99] This is the same point that C. S. Lewis states so eloquently in his chapter on "Miracles and the Laws of Nature":

> It is therefore inaccurate to define a miracle as something that breaks the laws of Nature. It doesn't. If I knock out my pipe I alter the position of a great many atoms: in the long run, and to an infinitesimal degree, of all the atoms there are. Nature digests or assimilates this event with perfect ease and harmonises it in a twinkling with all other events. It is one more bit of raw material for the laws to apply to, and they apply. I have simply thrown one event into the general cataract of events and it finds itself at home there and conforms to all other events. If God annihilates or creates or deflects a unit of matter He has created a new situation at that point. Immediately all Nature domiciles this new situation, makes it at home in her realm, adapts all other events to it. It finds itself conforming to all the laws. If God creates a miraculous spermatozoon in the body of a virgin, it does not proceed to break any laws. The laws at once take it over. Nature is ready. Pregnancy follows, according to all the normal laws, and nine months later a child is born. We see every day that physical nature is not in the least incommoded by the daily inrush of events from biological nature or from psychological nature. If events ever come from beyond Nature altogether, she will be no more incommoded by them. Be sure she will rush to the point where she is invaded, as the defensive forces rush to a cut in our finger, and there hasten to accommodate the newcomer. The moment it enters her realm it obeys all her laws. Miraculous wine will intoxicate, miraculous conception will lead to pregnancy, inspired books will suffer all the ordinary processes of textual corruption, miraculous bread will be digested. The divine art of miracle is not an art of suspending the pattern to which events conform but of feeding new events into that pattern. It does not violate the law's proviso, "If A, then B": it says, "But this time instead of A, A_2," and Nature, speaking through all her laws, replies, "Then B_2" and naturalises the immigrant, as she well knows how. She is an accomplished hostess.
>
> A miracle is emphatically not an event without cause or without results. Its cause is the activity of God: its results follow according to

98. Ibid.
99. Ibid., p. 308.

> Natural law. In the forward direction (i.e. during the time which follows its occurrence) it is interlocked with all Nature just like any other event. Its peculiarity is that it is not in that way interlocked backwards, interlocked with the previous history of Nature. . . .[100]

What has been presented here is probably the most widely accepted explanation of how miracles can be outside of natural law without violating it. I personally agree with this explanation of the nature of a miracle, but it seems to me that there is an unnecessary quibbling over terminology. If an effect is introduced into the course of nature by a cause that lies outside the natural chain of causes and effects, *some* natural law has been violated, whether the effect is natural or not. When a man dead four days is miraculously brought back to life and wholeness, the very natural processes of decay and decomposition are violated. When a man walks on water, the very natural law of gravity is violated. We may say that it is suspended, transcended, overruled, or bypassed; but these are just euphemisms for *violated.* When the sun stops for one day; when it retreats ten steps; when iron floats; when a person is kept alive for forty days without water—natural laws are surely being violated. And it should be pointed out that sometimes even the *effects* are not natural: walking on water, which must certainly be regarded as the effect in this particular miracle, is *contrary* to natural law. Thus the fact that a miracle has a supernatural, non-natural cause is a violation of natural law; and at least on some occasions the effect constituted by the miracle violates natural law.

I see no reason to shrink from this terminology, and that for several reasons. (1) It is in no way contrary to God's nature that he should violate the natural laws that he himself established. It is neither physically impossible nor morally objectionable that he should do so. (2) Contrary to Ramm, it does not prejudice the case against miracles to speak in this way. The critic's argument against miracles involves two premises: miracles are a violation of natural law, and natural law is inviolable. It is the *second* premise that is false, not the first. We do not have to reject both premises in order to refute his argument. (3) Though a miracle violates natural law, what it does *not* violate—and this is the crucial point—is the principle of cause and effect. As Geisler says, "If a miracle occurs, it would not be a violation or contradiction of the ordinary laws of cause and effect, but a *new effect* produced by the introduction of a supernatural cause."[101] Finally, (4) though miracles

100. C. S. Lewis, *Miracles*, pp. 59-60.
101. Norman Geisler, *Miracles and Modern Thought*, p. 13.

may violate natural *laws*, they do not violate *nature* as such. I think this is a valid distinction. It agrees with the point made by Christlieb and Lewis above, that nature assimilates the products of a miracle (at least, *most* of them) and makes them her own. It agrees with the point made by those who argue that miracles are restorative or remedial, i.e., that miracles are not against nature but against sin and its effect upon nature.

We must now consider several objections to this point, whether it is expressed in terms of "violation of natural law" or "outside of natural law." The first is the idea that if miracles are in any sense outside of natural law, then science would be impossible. Barrows Dunham complains that it "would turn the world from a system into a chaos" and "would place it at the whim of some supernatural being."[102] With miracles popping up arbitrarily here, there, and everywhere, the whole scientific enterprise—which depends upon the predictability of natural law—would be completely undermined. Now, this objection may certainly be appreciated, but it is without foundation. In the first place, as we have seen, miracles do *not* arbitrarily pop up in scientific laboratories at random; rather they are found in very specific contexts functioning according to a very specific purpose. Outside those contexts one may proceed with scientific business as usual. In the second place, even when miracles are thought of as violating natural laws, they do not abolish those laws as if they will never be trustworthy again. Even when there is an interference, as Lewis says, the natural laws themselves remain quite intact.[103] The fact is that when miracles are seen as operating *within* natural law, it is *then* that miracles make the laws obsolete and require them to be revised.

The second objection is that when miracles are placed outside of natural law, this constitutes some kind of put-down of the natural and the ordinary. If God should rescind his natural laws, says Schaaffs, that would be the same as treating them as inadequate.[104] This view of miracles "devaluates the 'ordinary' work of God," says Berkouwer.[105] In response we may simply say that such an objection does not take full account of the stated purpose for miracles. They are never performed

102. Barrows Dunham, *Man Against Myth* (Boston: Little, Brown, 1948), p. 28; cited in E. J. Carnell, *An Introduction to Christian Apologetics*, p. 243.

103. C. S. Lewis, *Miracles*, p. 57. See Norman Geisler, *Miracles and Modern Thought*, p. 53; Theodore Christlieb, *Modern Doubt and Christian Belief*, p. 307.

104. Werner Schaaffs, *Theology, Physics, and Miracles*, pp. 27, 29.

105. G. C. Berkouwer, *The Providence of God*, p. 215.

as some kind of judgment upon nature, but as signs connected with God's revelation.

A third objection is similar to the second. It is the strange idea that if God is involved in works that bypass or surpass the laws of nature, then that somehow implies that he is not involved in the natural. Brown suggests that when miracles are understood according to the *violation* model, this creates the danger

> . . . of identifying divine activity only with those instances where nature appears to be set aside and no explanation at all is possible. There is a double danger with such a view. It banishes God from the normal, and it suffers from the same weakness as the old God-of-the-gaps apologetics. If God is to be found only in the gaps of our natural knowledge, he progressively dies the death of a thousand explanations, as science gradually fills those gaps.[106]

Baelz has alleged the same point:

> . . . If we wish to point to miraculous events in order to identify the activity of God, we are implying that he is active in the extraordinary events, *p, q, r,* but *not* in the ordinary events, *x, y, z.* We have thereby identified God at the expense of robbing him of his ultimacy and universality, and we have landed ourselves with a finite god of the gaps. . . .[107]

This is a classic case of *non sequitur* reasoning: it does not follow. Just because God works extraordinarily via miracles gives no grounds at all for excluding him from the ordinary work of providence. In fact, as we have seen in the last three chapters, the Bible makes it *very* clear that God is at work everywhere and in every event in his providence.

The final and most serious objection is the one touched on at the beginning of this section, namely, that miracles cannot be considered as being outside the limits of natural law because natural law is no longer considered as having any limits. This does indeed pose a problem, for it does seem that this understanding of miracle depends upon a concept of natural law which not only is limited but whose limits can be discerned. As Lewis asks, "How can anything be seen to be an exception till the rules are known?"[108] But this is precisely the problem: "Can we be sure that

---

106. Colin Brown, *Miracles and the Critical Mind,* p. 291.

107. Peter R. Baelz, *Prayer and Providence: A Background Study* (New York: Seabury Press, 1968), pp. 62-63.

108. C. S. Lewis, *Miracles,* p. 47. Werner Schaaffs says that to prove that the biblical miracles clash with nature, "one would need a *total* knowledge of all the laws of nature." Since such is impossible, miracles cannot be defined thus (*Theology, Physics, and Miracles,* p. 28).

we know the limits of the natural world and of the realm in which secondary causes operate?"[109]

The common answer today is no, we *cannot* be sure. Apart from the purely epistemological problem of the impossibility of total inductive knowledge, there is a consensus today that natural law is relative and open-ended. That is, it is not just that we cannot know its limits; rather, there are no limits to be known. The shift from the Newtonian to the Einsteinian world view has had something to do with this. Mary Hesse has observed, "There is no doubt that abandonment of the deterministic world-view in physics has made it more difficult to regard the existing state of science as finally legislative of what is and what is not possible in nature."[110] Wykstra points out, however, that this shift is not really the decisive point. The pivotal issue, he says, is "whether one chooses to believe that the natural order is 'closed' or 'open.'"[111] As Warfield notes, Thomas Huxley was already advocating an open-ended order before the Einsteinian physics was in place. Even the most extraordinary event, claimed Huxley, is not beyond the powers of nature. "Every wise man will admit that the possibilities of nature are infinite," he said. "In truth, if a dead man did come to life, the fact would be evidence, not that any law of nature had been violated, but that these laws, even when they express the results of a very long and uniform experience, are necessarily based on incomplete knowledge, and are to be held only as grounds of more or less justifiable expectation." What appears impossible today "may appear in the order of nature tomorrow." If a so-called "miracle" occurs, then one should simply "enlarge his experience and modify his hitherto unduly narrow conception of the laws of nature." We simply "frame new laws to cover our extended experience."[112]

Here, then, is the problem. If natural law is flexible enough to accommodate *any* occurrence, then in principle *nothing* that happens can be considered as "outside natural law." There is no such thing as a "violation" of natural law. Thus there is no room in the universe for a

---

109. Peter Baelz, *Prayer and Providence*, p. 62. See also T. R. Birks, *The Bible and Modern Thought*, p. 84.

110. Mary Hesse, "Miracles and the Laws of Nature," *Miracles: Cambridge Studies in Their Philosophy and History*, ed. C. F. D. Moule (New York: Morehouse-Barlow, 1965), p. 38; cited in Colin Brown, *Miracles and the Critical Mind*, p. 179.

111. Stephen Wykstra, "The Problem of Miracle in the Apologetic from History," p. 156.

112. T. H. Huxley, *Hume* (London: 1879), pp. 129-133, cited in B. B. Warfield, "The Question of Miracles," p. 195.

miracle as thus defined. "Even if an event occurs which can be proven to be a valid counterinstance to a present descriptive law, what *necessarily* follows is only that we presently possess no descriptive generalization (working hypothesis) to 'explain' the occurrence."[113] What, then, counts as a miracle? This is the main question with which Wykstra deals in his article: "By what criteria, if any, can we defensibly determine whether an event is a 'miracle'?" The definition of miracle as a violation or transgression of the laws of nature, he says, is claiming in effect that a miraculous event is one which rationally compels a man to admit, "Only God could do this thing; nature alone could not!"[114] (Compare Warfield's statement, "A miracle then is specifically an effect in the external world, produced by the immediate efficiency of God."[115]) But in a open-ended universe nature can in principle do anything; thus the definition of a miracle as something "beyond nature" no longer works; there is nothing in this category.

The only solution, according to Montgomery, is to redefine what we mean by miracle. "A miracle can no longer be understood as a 'violation of natural law,' for we are unable to assert that physical laws, being but the generalized product of our observations, are indeed 'natural'—i.e., absolute and unalterable."[116] But if a miracle can no longer be defined as being outside natural law, then it must be understood as somehow being *within* natural law; and that brings us back to all the problems mentioned in the previous section. Miracles lose their supernatural quality and become just a part of the natural order. Thus follows the most serious consequence of all: miracles are no longer able to function as evidence or signs, which according to Scripture is their God-intended purpose.

As far as I know, a good solution to this problem has not been worked out. Personally I believe that the concept of miracle as outside of (or a violation of) natural law must be maintained, in view of the biblical teaching concerning their evidential purpose. If it were possible to frame a definition of miracle *within* the scope of natural law in such a way that they remain clearly distinguishable from non-miraculous natural events and thus retain their value as signs, this would be acceptable. But at the present I do not see any way to do this.

---

113. David Basinger and Randall Basinger, "Science and the Concept of Miracle," p. 165.

114. Stephen Wykstra, "The Problem of Miracle in the Apologetic from History," p. 155.

115. B. B. Warfield, "The Question of Miracles," p. 170.

116. John W. Montgomery, "Science, Theology and the Miraculous," p. 147.

Some have attempted to define miracles without reference to any variance from natural law, but the results usually mark little gain; the problem of *how* to distinguish them from the non-miraculous still remains. An example of this is the idea of miracle as "a unique, non-analogous occurrence," as discussed by Montgomery.[117] In an open-ended universe *whether* an event is unique would be difficult to tell, and the question of *why* it is unique would still have to be answered. I.e., an event could be unique without necessarily being miraculous. The same applies to the concept of miracle as "either singular or extraordinarily improbable."[118]

Others have apparently agreed to "bite the bullet" and redefine miracle as a purely religious concept. "In its broadest terms a miracle is an event which is apprehended by a worshipping community as a clear instance of the divine activity in the shaping of history," says Pollard.[119] The Basinger brothers assert, "The most viable alternative, it seems, is to define 'miracle' as a religious concept (an act of God) which derives it uniqueness not from its explicability status, but from the fact that it is part of an unusual event sequence."[120] The only problem is that such a view sacrifices the apologetical value of a miracle as a sign—which Scripture will not permit.

Others have suggested that we simply think of miracles as "permanently inexplicable events."[121] The idea here is that a miracle is *so* radically different from known scientific laws that there will never be a revision of those laws that can accommodate it. But this view seems to suffer from the same problems as the concept of miracle as an event contrary to *known* laws. Who are we to say that there will *never* be a revision that can accommodate the 'miraculous,' even if we do not know of one now?

As said earlier, I do not think that we can surrender the concept of miracle as outside natural law. Here I will offer a tentative approach to the problem which retains this concept and which at the same time attempts to do justice to the problems raised above. My approach benefits from the way this whole issue was handled by two older writers, and first I will cite some relevant passages from them. One of these is

---

117. Ibid.

118. William Pollard, *Chance and Providence*, p. 107.

119. Ibid., p. 106.

120. David Basinger and Randall Basinger, "Science and the Concept of Miracle," p. 168.

121. See ibid., pp. 165ff., for a discussion of this.

T. R. Birks, whose book, *The Bible and Modern Thought,* was written in 1861 as an answer to the notorious critical volume, *Essays and Reviews.* In his discussion of miracles Birks notes the difficulty of defining them as "a direct act of God, in contrast to all agency of second causes." On such a view, he says, "it must be impossible to know when a miracle has been wrought, unless we could know all the possible results of second causes." But no one has such knowledge. Hence we must make some other approach to miracles. Birks decides that they may be of three different types: (1) immediate miracles, which *are* accomplished without second causes; (2) mediate miracles, such as those worked through power bestowed upon God's messengers; (3) improper miracles, which "result from rare and unusual combinations of second causes."[122] In this last type the miraculous element would be the timing. Birks then draws this conclusion:

> These three kinds of miracles, however distinct in their definition, it may be impossible in many cases to distinguish from each other. Their value, as evidence, can not then depend upon such a discrimination having been previously made. We need a practical definition which shall include them all, and bring into relief that common feature on which their strength as evidence for a Divine revelation depends.
>
> Miracles, then, viewed as evidences for revelation, are "unusual events not within the ordinary power of man, nor capable of being foreseen by man's actual knowledge of second causes, and wrought or announced by professed messengers of God, to confirm the reality of their message." The definition has a negative and a positive element. There must be no second causes, or at least none within human knowledge, that will account for the event; and there must be an apparent connection with some plain moral object or some professed message from God. Whenever these two conditions meet, we have a case of miraculous evidence. Some of these, by the progress of science in later times, might come within the range of man's actual power over nature, or his insight into natural changes, and would then cease to be miraculous; while others may surpass not only human, but superhuman power, and imply a direct exercise of the Divine Omnipotence.[123]

The second writer is B. B. Warfield, who makes the following comments in response to the position of Huxley (which is remarkably similar to that of many today):

---

122. T. R. Birks, *The Bible in Modern Thought,* pp. 84-85.

123. Ibid., pp. 85-86.

> A third important fact now claims our attention. This is that we have no right to apply our abstract categories to the Biblical miracles in a mechanical manner. The question is not, in the case of each of them, whether such an effect as that produced can possibly be produced by natural forces; but rather whether it was on the occasion recorded probably produced by natural forces. The conditions and circumstances must be taken into account; and it is whether the effect recorded can be believed to have been produced by the natural forces present and active at the place and time of its production that we need to investigate, and not the merely academic question whether a similar effect is capable of being produced by natural forces in other times and circumstances than those that then obtained. Telegraphs, telephones, wireless telegraphy did not exist in Biblical times and cannot be utilized to explain the Biblical marvels: nor can any other appliances not then existent and in use. Men seem often to proceed in their reasoning on the assumption that, if any possible way can be imagined in which natural forces can be made to simulate the effects of miraculous action recorded in Scripture, it is fair to assume that these effects were produced by means of these natural forces operating in this way. Nothing could be more hopelessly academic than such an abstract manner of dealing with concrete facts. At this rate, the tricks of the magicians of Egypt would be made to confound the miracles of Moses. We have no right to call in for the explanation of these marvels any other natural forces than those that can be shown to have been present and operative at the time and place of the performance of the marvel. We have no right to assume that Jesus made use of wireless telegraphy to ascertain that Lazarus was dead: that the secrets of chemistry were utilized by him in the making of the wine at Cana: that a hidden magnet was employed to make the axe-head rise in the water; and the like. The point never is, whether natural forces may not be made to simulate these effects. The question is, what were the actual forces really employed for their production. It is remarkable how many of the so-called natural explanations of the miracles of Scripture become absurd when they are confronted with the conditions of time and place.[124]

With these comments as background, I will offer the following suggestion as a way of identifying miracles even though they are outside of natural law, thus permitting us to justify their apologetic value as signs. I suggest that a miracle is an event which occurs outside the knowledge and control of natural law *as available to the miracle worker*, and which occurs purposefully within a context where it is intended to

124. B. B. Warfield, "The Question of Miracles," pp. 202-203.

function as a sign. As thus defined, it does not matter whether natural law is open-ended or not. Also, we do not have to have a complete knowledge of natural law for this definition to function. All we have to know is whether the event was within the capabilities of the miracle worker in his particular context, given the knowledge which we can reasonably assume was available to him at the time. If we judge that the necessary knowledge and control were not available to him, then we can conclude that the event was indeed outside natural law and was a miracle. Thus the event can function as a true sign.

This is not the same as saying that a miracle is an event that is beyond our knowledge of natural law. Indeed, as Birks says, it does not matter whether now or some day in the future we may possess enough knowledge to duplicate certain things that were truly miracles when performed as such. The important point is that such an event was beyond the knowledge of natural law *at the time*. And even this point is not left to stand as the final characterization of the miracle. Rather, this point—that the event was beyond the knowledge of natural law at the time—becomes the criterion for judging that the event was outside natural law as such. In other words, that the event was outside natural law relative to its time is the criterion for its being outside natural law in an absolute sense.

In this sense a miracle *is* a "permanently inexplicable event" (i.e., permanently inexplicable in terms of natural law, not as miracle). It may be, of course, that some day science will discover another way to do the same thing, e.g., an anti-gravity device that allows water-walking. But that possibility does not affect the fact that such technology was *not* available to Jesus or Peter. It is "permanently inexplicable" that *they* could have done it *at that time* and *under those circumstances*. It is not just whether such an event can possibly be produced naturally, but whether it could possibly have been so produced at the time. If not, then its miraculous character is vindicated and its evidential value preserved.

MIRACLES AND PROVIDENCE

This final section deals briefly with the relation between miracles and providence. We have seen that the doctrine of providence deals with the modes of God's relation to the on-going world. We have seen that general providence involves God's permissive control over nature and history, as he allows his creatures to function in relative independence according to the gifts of natural law and free will. We have seen that special providence involves God's intervention within nature and history to accomplish his special purposes by redirecting the natural means already present in the world. Now, how do miracles relate to this? They are a step beyond special providence as follows. Although special providence is the supernatural intervention of God into the world, the desired effects are produced through natural processes and means which are influenced or manipulated. A miracle, however, is an act of God by which his supernatural power produces the desired effect directly, apart from natural means. No natural cause is involved.

It is important that Christians clearly distinguish between special providence and miracle. These can easily be confused, especially since the term *miracle* is used popularly and uncritically to refer to things that are merely awe-inspiring or unexplainable. It is a fairly common practice for Christians and non-Christians alike to apply this term to events or effects that should actually be attributed to special providence. Generally speaking, answers to prayer (unless one is a prophet like Elijah) are matters of special providence. God definitely intervenes, but usually through natural means. As Buswell points out, "In the experience of Christians . . . there are numberless events, constantly recurring, in which those who know the Lord can see the hand of God at work, but in which there is not the demonstrative 'sign' element."[125] In such cases the term *miracle* does not apply and should not be used. A miracle is something recognizably extraordinary, an effect not possible via natural means.

This applies especially to God's healing of sickness in answer to prayer. Ketcherside correctly observes, "Many healings are called miraculous in which there is no element of a miracle present."[126] James exhorts those who are sick to call for the elders, who should then pray and anoint the sick with oil in the name of the Lord; "and the prayer offered in faith will restore the one who is sick" (James 5:14-15). Healing is thus promised as an answer to prayer, but not necessarily *miraculous* healing. Ensign and Howe say, "We believe that the teaching of James 5:14-16 is now the primary basis for the

125. J. O. Buswell, Jr., *A Systematic Theology*, I:176-177.

126. W. Carl Ketcherside, "The Hand of God," *Christian Standard* (August 7, 1983), 118:10.

providential healing of those who are sick."[127] The key word here is *providential*. These writers also say,

> On the one hand, we reject as inadequate and erroneous the view that God does not answer the prayers of Christians today in a remarkable and extraordinary manner which results in the restoration to health of those for whom we pray. But we also reject as erroneous and contrary to both Scripture and experience that *miracles* of healing like those in the Bible are being done by God in the world today. . . .[128]

As Warfield says, "All Christians believe in healing in answer to prayer. Those who assert that this healing is wrought in a specifically miraculous manner, need better evidence for their peculiar view than such as fits in equally well with the general Christian faith."[129]

There are a number of other works of God in the world which are definitely supernatural, but which do not fall into the category of special providence because they are direct and immediate acts, and which do not qualify as miracles in the strict sense because they are not open and observable and thus evidential. These include revelation, inspiration, the incarnation, the atonement, regeneration, the work of the indwelling Spirit, and the operation of ordinary spiritual gifts. There is no one term or category which neatly fits all of these marvelous divine works. Those that occur in the soul of the Christian are sometimes called "spiritual miracles"[130] or "miracles of grace" (as opposed to "sign miracles").[131] It seems best, however, to reserve the term *miracles* for those external signs reported to us in the pages of Scripture.

---

127. Grayson H. Ensign and Edward Howe, *Bothered? Bewildered? Bewitched? Your Guide to Practical Supernatural Healing* (Cincinnati: Recovery Publications, 1984), p. 98.
128. Ibid., p. 94.
129. B. B. Warfield, *Miracles: Yesterday and Today*, p. 187.
130. Theodore Christlieb, *Modern Doubt and Christian Belief*, pp. 293-294.
131. J. O. Buswell, Jr., *A Systematic Theology*, I:181.

Chapter Seven

THE SOVEREIGN

As explained in the volume on God the Creator, my methodology in this study of the doctrine of God is to focus primarily upon the *works* of God, and then to explain the nature or attributes of God as they are exhibited in those works.[1] In this volume we are concentrating on the doctrine of providence, or the work of God in his relations with the on-going world. Now that the main aspects of providence have been set forth, we must turn our attention to the nature of the God who works so marvelously in general providence, special providence, and miracles.

Who is this God who holds the entire universe in the palm of his hand, and preserves it from oblivion by the mere force of his will? Who is this One whose power and presence penetrate and envelop every particle of the cosmos? What kind of God holds the reins of nature so that clouds turn, snow falls, thunder roars, and stars explode at his command? What kind of God knows every star and sparrow by name, and cares about them? What kind of God is this who can endow the crown of his creation with free will and still maintain constant control over the events and flow of history? How shall we describe the God who turns kings' hearts wherever he wills; who metes out life and death, blessing and calamity; whose power bursts forth in signs and wonders in the heavens and on earth?

Only one title seems to do justice to the God of providence and miracle: THE SOVEREIGN. He is the sovereign one, and his relation to the on-going world is one of complete sovereignty. It is understandable that this theme has already surfaced on a number of occasions in previous chapters; but we have not given it our systematic attention, as we now intend to do in this chapter. First we shall examine the concept of the sovereignty of God as reflected in the teachings of Scripture, then we shall explore the various attributes of God that are the hallmarks of sovereignty. Finally we shall discuss briefly the concept of God's immanence.

THE NATURE OF SOVEREIGNTY

We may safely say that the doctrine of the sovereignty of God is not eagerly embraced by the world today, nor even by many professing

1. Jack Cottrell, *What the Bible Says About God the Creator* (Joplin, Mo.: College Press, 1983), pp. 43-45.

Christians. Some of this may be an over-reaction to determinist extremes; but much of it has to do with the spirit of our age, which may be characterized by such terms as autonomy, rebellion, and liberation. The typical cry of our times is the same as that expressed in Psalm 2:2-3, "The kings of the earth take their stand, and the rulers take counsel together against the Lord and against His Anointed: 'Let us tear their fetters apart, and cast away their cords from us!'" As Boice says, "The basic reason why women and men do not like the doctrine of God's sovereignty is that they do not want a sovereign God. They wish to be autonomous."[2]

Nevertheless it is a reality that must be reckoned with either now or later, for it is a doctrine taught throughout the pages of the Bible: God is the Sovereign Ruler of the universe. We not only need to acknowledge this fact, but we also need to understand what it means. What exactly is the nature of sovereignty? What does it mean to say that God is sovereign? In a sense we may say that sovereignty is an attribute of God, similar to his power and his greatness and his majesty. But on more careful analysis it may appear to be more like a *right* that God possesses because of who he is. Charles Hodge expresses it well: "Sovereignty is not a property of the divine nature, but a prerogative arising out of the perfections of the Supreme Being."[3] In this section we want to see what is involved in this right or prerogative.

The Essence of Sovereignty

The sovereignty of God may be concisely summed up as *absolute Lordship*. It is the same as the concept of kingdom or kingship or dominion. This concept may be applied in a relative way to earthly rulers, but only God has *absolute* dominion over all things. As Lightner says, "Divine sovereignty means that God is the absolute and sole Ruler in the universe."[4]

Lordship

Sovereignty is lordship, lordship is ownership, and ownership is control. This seems to be the essence of the whole matter. Basically

2. James Montgomery Boice, *Foundations of the Christian Faith, Volume I: The Sovereign God* (Downers Grove, Ill.: InterVarsity Press, 1978), p. 153.

3. Charles Hodge, *Systematic Theology,* (Grand Rapids: Eerdmans reprint, n.d.), I:440.

4. Robert P. Lightner, *The First Fundamental: GOD* (Nashville: Thomas Nelson, 1973), p. 77.

the term *lord* signifies the owner of something, a meaning preserved in our common term *landlord*. To say that God is sovereign means that he is Lord in the sense of the owner of all things. Melchizedek and Abraham refer to him as "possessor of heaven and earth" (Gen. 14:19, 22). Moses says, "Behold, to the Lord your God belong heaven and the highest heavens, the earth and all that is in it" (Deut. 10:14). Psalm 24:1 echoes this: "The earth is the Lord's, and all it contains, the world, and those who dwell in it" (see I Cor. 10:26). "All the earth is Mine," says the Lord (Exod. 19:5). "Whatever is under the whole heaven is Mine" (Job 41:11).

The biblical concept that most specifically embodies the idea of God's sovereignty is that of the *kingdom* of God (Hebrew, *malkuth*; Greek, *basileia*). As noted already at the beginning of chapter four above,[5] this term basically means "rule, royal power, dominion, kingship, lordship." God himself is described as the King who reigns and rules over all. Those who approach the Bible from the standpoint of philosophical theology or modern liberal theology often object to this characterization of sovereignty.[6] H. M. Hughes, for example, says that God's sovereignty is best understood in terms of his fatherhood: "The Sovereign purposes of God are those of fatherhood. . . . God's ways of ruling men are fatherly ways. The Sovereign on the throne is in His inmost nature Father."[7] "The Fatherhood of God is to be interpreted in the light of His Sovereignty. . . . So too the sovereignty must be interpreted in the light of fatherhood."[8] It is true, of course, that God is Father, but this concept would seem to be more appropriately understood in connection with God's role as Redeemer, rather than his role as Sovereign Ruler of the universe. A kind of fatherly care may indeed be one aspect of God's rule, but only one among many. God's sovereignty is a broader concept than this, and it is more naturally and properly understood in terms of kingship. "The Lord reigns!" is a common means of expressing praise in the Old Testament (I Chron. 16:31; Pss. 93:1-2; 96:10; 97:1; 99:1; Isa. 52:7). "For the kingdom is the Lord's, and He rules over the nations" (Ps. 22:28). "The Lord has established His throne in the heavens; and His sovereignty rules over all" (Ps. 103:19).

---

5. See p. 118 above.

6. See Nels F. S. Ferre, *The Christian Understanding of God* (New York: Harper & Brothers, 1951), pp. 98ff.; H. Maldwyn Hughes, *The Christian Idea of God* (London: Duckworth, 1936), pp. 113ff.

7. H. Maldwyn Hughes, *The Christian Idea of God*, p. 113.

8. Ibid., p. 118.

God is given the title of King (Isa. 6:5; 33:17, 22; 43:15; I Tim. 1:17). He is called the Great King (Ps. 47:2; Malachi 1:14; Matt. 5:35), the King of Glory (Ps. 24:7-10),[9] King of the nations (Jer. 10:7; Rev. 15:3), and "my King" (Pss. 5:2; 44:4; 84:3).

Absolute Lordship

The essence of sovereignty is lordship, but in reference to divine sovereignty it is *absolute* Lordship. Earthly kings have relative sovereignty, but God alone is Lord over all: King of kings, Lord of lords, God of gods. "For the Lord your God is the God of gods and the Lord of lords, the great, the mighty, and the awesome God" (Deut. 10:17). King Nebuchadnezzar's confession to Daniel is true: "Surely your God is a God of gods and a Lord of kings" (Dan. 2:47). Paul testifies that God is "King of kings and Lord of lords," followed by an appropriate doxology: "To Him be honor and eternal dominion! Amen" (I Tim. 6:15-16). This same title will be worn by Jesus—God the Son—at his triumphant return: "And on His robe and on His thigh He has a name written, 'KING OF KINGS, AND LORD OF LORDS'" (Rev. 19:16). See Psalm 136:2-3; Daniel 11:36.

God's Lordship is absolute in the sense that it is eternal. He is "the everlasting King" (Jer. 10:10), "the King eternal" (I Tim. 1:17). "The Lord is King forever and ever" (Ps. 10:16); "the Lord sits as King forever" (Ps. 29:10); "the Lord will reign forever" (Ps. 146:10). As the psalmist praises God, "Thy kingdom is an everlasting Kingdom, and Thy dominion endures throughout all generations" (Ps. 145:13; see Dan. 4:34; Lam. 5:19).

God's Lordship is absolute because it is universal. Nothing is outside the scope of his sovereign rule. He is "God of all the earth" (Isa. 54:5), "Lord of all the earth" (Josh. 3:11; Mic. 4:13), "the Lord Most High over all the earth" (Ps. 97:9; see 83:18; 97:5), the "great King over all the earth" (Ps. 47:2; see 47:7), "Lord of heaven and earth" (Matt. 11:25; Acts 17:24). Of Jesus Christ—God the Son—it is specifically said that "He is Lord of all" (Acts 10:36) and that he is "over all" (Rom. 9:5). He is also described as "far above all rule and authority and power and dominion, and every name that is named, not only in this age, but also in the one to come"; all things are "in subjection under His feet" (Eph. 1:21-22).

9. Compare I Corinthians 2:8, where Jesus is called the "Lord of glory."

Special emphasis is given to God's universal Lordship over all the peoples and nations of the earth. He is "the God of all flesh" (Jer. 32:27), the "ruler over the realm of mankind" (Dan. 4:25, 32). "He rules over the nations" (Ps. 22:28). "God reigns over the nations, God sits on His holy throne. The princes of the people have assembled themselves as the people of the God of Abraham; for the shields of the earth belong to God; He is highly exalted" (Ps. 47:8-9). Jehoshaphat praises God thus: "Art Thou not God in the heavens? And art Thou not ruler over all the kingdoms of the nations?" (II Chron. 20:6). And Isaiah likewise: "O Lord of hosts, the God of Israel, who art enthroned above the cherubim, Thou art the God, Thou alone, of all the kingdoms of the earth" (Isa. 37:16).

One title for God that occurs frequently in the Old Testament is most expressive of his sovereignty, namely, *'elyōn,* which is usually translated "Most High." Often it is found simply by itself, as in Psalm 9:2, "I will sing praise to Thy name, O Most High."[10] Sometimes it is used with other names for God, namely, *Yahweh 'elyōn,* "the Lord Most High" (Pss. 7:17; 47:2; 97:9); and *'ēl* or *'elohīm 'elyōn,* "God Most High" (Gen. 14:20; Pss. 57:2; 78:35, 56). In Genesis 14:22 Abraham speaks of "the Lord God Most High, possessor of heaven and earth." This title in all its forms affirms that no one is above or alongside God; he is the Sovereign Lord over all.

The reality and the wonder of God's absolute Lordship are the focus of David's praise in I Chronicles 29:11-13:

> . . . Thine, O Lord, is the greatness and the power and the glory and the victory and the majesty, indeed everything that is in the heavens and the earth; Thine is the dominion, O Lord, and Thou dost exalt Thyself as head over all. Both riches and honor come from Thee, and Thou dost rule over all, and in Thy hand is power and might; and it lies in Thy hand to make great, and to strengthen everyone. Now therefore, our God, we thank Thee, and praise Thy glorious name.

The Ground of Sovereignty

Sovereignty is lordship, lordship is ownership, and ownership is control. If God is absolute Lord, then he has absolute ownership and absolute control over the universe. This is, to say the least, a rather extravagant claim. What ground or basis does God have for his claim

10. See also Psalms 18:13; 21:7; 78:17; 82:6; 83:18; 87:5; 91:1; 92:1; Daniel 4:25, 32, 34.

to sovereignty? The answer is the fact that he has created all things from nothing. The fact of creation is the ground of divine sovereignty. We may refer again to the volume on God the Creator, where this has already been discussed to some extent.[11] The fact of creation means, of course, that God is the source of all things. "All things originate from God," says Paul (I Cor. 11:12). "The earth is the Lord's, and all it contains, the world, and those who dwell in it. For He has founded it upon the seas, and established it upon the rivers" (Ps. 24:1-2). "The heavens are Thine, the earth also is Thine; the world and all it contains, Thou hast founded them" (Ps. 89:11). "The sea is His, for it was He who made it; and His hands formed the dry land" (Ps. 95:5). His claim to be the only true God is rooted in creation (Neh. 9:6; Isa. 37:16).

Authority

The fact of creation provides the ground for two elements essential to real sovereignty, namely, authority and freedom. Regarding the first of these, it is important to see that true sovereignty rests not just upon sheer power, but also on the *right* to rule. "Might makes right" is not a valid principle even when applied to God. In other words, he must have not only the power to rule, but also the *authority* to rule. And God's authority, his legitimate and deserved right to absolute Lordship, is his by virtue of creation. God has the right to do with his creation whatever he wishes because he owns it; and he owns it because he created it. As Charnock observes, "Much more hath God a rightful claim of dominion over his creatures, whose entire being, both in matter and form, and every particle of their excellency, was breathed out by the word of his mouth."[12]

In this connection, we may note that if there is no Creator-God, then there is no authority at all, for there is no other basis whereby one person may claim the *right* to tell another person what to do, or to do with another person what he thinks best. In an uncreated universe one personal being or group of personal beings may have the *power* to do these things, but not the right. Thus in such a universe absolute individual autonomy would be the only consistent viewpoint. But in a created universe, the Creator—and the Creator alone—has both the power and the right to rule in whatever way he desires. All authority

11. Jack Cottrell, *What the Bible Says About God the Creator*, pp. 161-162, 401-404.
12. Stephen Charnock, *The Existence and Attributes of God* (Grand Rapids: Kregel reprint, 1958), p. 670.

resides ultimately in him. He may delegate a measure of authority to some of his creatures if he chooses, as he has done to parents in the home, elders in the church, and civil rulers in the state. But such authority is not absolute; it is relative and derived. "For there is no authority except from God, and those which exist are established by God" (Rom. 13:1). Thus we see how crucial is the divine sovereignty, which includes the authority to rule as grounded in the fact of creation. Without this there remain only the chaos and anarchy spawned by a blind commitment to "might makes right." These are the only consistent choices.

Freedom

The second element of sovereignty grounded in the creation is the divine freedom. All created being is contingent and dependent upon the Creator; it is limited and conditioned by that which lies outside itself. It is capable only of the potentiality bestowed upon it by the Creator. But none of these limitations apply to the Creator himself. Being eternal and uncreated, he is dependent upon nothing outside himself; he is totally unconditioned in his being.[13] This is crucial for his absolute Lordship. As Barth says, the mode of his Lordship "is characterised by the fact that it is absolutely God's own, in no sense dictated to Him from outside and conditioned by no higher necessity than that of His own choosing and deciding, willing and doing."[14] Herein lies the divine freedom, which is the very essence of sovereignty. God's freedom is his Lordship. Barth also remarks, "With the idea of freedom we simply affirm what we would be affirming if we were to characterise God as the Lord . . . . There are other sovereignties, but freedom is the prerogative of divine sovereignty."[15] He continues,

> . . . Freedom in its positive and proper qualities means to be grounded in one's own being, to be determined and moved by oneself. This is the freedom of the divine life and love. In this positive freedom of His, God is also unlimited, unrestricted and unconditioned from without. . . .[16]

Scripture affirms that the sovereign Creator owes no one anything; he does not have to ask anyone's permission to do something; there

---

13. This is the attribute of self-existence or aseity. See Jack Cottrell, *What the Bible Says About God the Creator,* pp. 245ff.

14. Karl Barth, *Church Dogmatics, Vol. II: The Doctrine of God, Part I,* ed. G. W. Bromiley and T. F. Torrance, tr. T. H. L. Parker et al. (Edinburgh: T. & T. Clark, 1957), p. 301.

15. Ibid.

16. Ibid.

are no hindrances to the carrying out of his purposes. "Who has given to Me that I should repay him?" says God. "Whatever is under the whole heaven is Mine" (Job 41:11). God's messenger Elihu silences any complaints against God with these words: "Who gave Him authority over the earth? And who has laid on Him the whole world?" (Job 34:13). Also, "Who has appointed Him His way?" (Job 36:23). The point is that *no one* has done these things. God does not receive his authority from someone else; it is his by inherent right. Therefore, he is free to do as he pleases. He does not have to take orders from anyone or ask advice of anyone. It seems that Job learned this lesson well when he replied to the Lord, "I know that Thou canst do all things, and that no purpose of Thine can be thwarted" (Job 42:2).

God's sovereign freedom means that he is able to do whatever he pleases. "He does according to His will in the host of heaven and among the inhabitants of earth" (Dan. 4:35). "Our God is in the heavens; He does whatever He pleases" (Ps. 115:3). "Whatever the Lord pleases, He does" (Ps. 135:6). When God determines to do something, it is certain to be done. He needs only to utter the order, and it is sure to be accomplished.

> . . . For as the rain and the snow come down from heaven, and do not return there without watering the earth, and making it bear and sprout, and furnishing seed to the sower and bread to the eater; so shall My word be which goes forth from My mouth; it shall not return to Me empty, without accomplishing what I desire, and without succeeding in the matter for which I sent it. . . . (Isa. 55:10-11)

As Sherlock says, "He who has power to do whatever he will, can do whatever he will; and that is the definition of a sovereign and absolute will."[17]

To say that God is free to do whatever he wants to do allows for the limitations (if it is proper to call them that) upon God that are due to his own holy and rational nature. He is limited by nothing *outside himself*, but his own nature prevents him from lying or doing what is self-contradictory.[18] God cannot go against himself. This should hardly be thought of as a limitation, however. It is rather a strength that enhances and increases his freedom.

---

17. William Sherlock, *A Discourse Concerning the Divine Providence* (Pittsburgh: J. L. Read, 1848), p. 70.

18. See Jack Cottrell, *What the Bible Says About God the Creator*, pp. 300-301.

While the fact of creation guarantees the freedom of God, at the same time it represents what is perhaps the most sovereign expression of that freedom, namely, God's freedom to limit himself. The act of creation was itself a free act,[19] a decision freely entered into by God and not necessitated in any way. But as we have already pointed out,[20] the very fact that God has brought something into existence besides himself places certain limitations upon him. God can not be totally unlimited or unconditioned in reference to the world. Barth has missed this point in his statements that "God is free to be and operate in the created world either as unconditioned or as conditioned"; "God is free to be entirely unlimited over against the world."[21] Contrary to this, once the world is in existence, there are conditions and limitations for God. But this does not diminish his sovereign freedom, for God *freely chose* to place these limitations upon himself. He freely chose to bind himself in relationships with his creatures. He freely chose to make beings in his own image and to give them free will. He freely chose to bind himself in covenant faithfulness to these beings. Freely-chosen self-limitation is not a threat to sovereignty.

Many find it difficult to accept this idea. Christian determinists, for example, fear that God's sovereignty would be compromised by created free will and therefore reject true freedom in order to preserve his sovereignty. This has already been discussed in chapter five above. At the other extreme are those who likewise think that absolute sovereignty and true freedom are incompatible, but who therefore surrender genuine sovereignty. Nels Ferre, for example, attacks the whole idea of a sovereign God's limiting himself. "A self-limited God has been the refuge for many a torn thinker on this subject," he says. "But a self-limited God is not sovereign while He is thus limited. He is limited." This is especially true if he has given man the power of free will. "He has in such a case given a power for eternity which is not His and therefore He is not sovereign. If power be ultimate and if man be genuinely free, there can be no solution of the problem of sovereignty."[22] If God has shared his power or surrendered his power to created freedom, he no longer has sovereign power.[23] Ferre's solution is to accept the

19. Ibid., pp. 117ff.
20. See pp. 187-188 above.
21. Karl Barth, *Church Dogmatics*, II/1, pp. 314-315.
22. Nels F. S. Ferre, *The Christian Understanding of God*, pp. 99-100.
23. Ibid., pp. 99-101.

concept of a finite God who is not omnipotent in the first place and whose true sovereignty is the power of love.[24]

Such a view as Ferre's misrepresents the concept of self-limitation. By creating a world, and even by creating free-will beings, God is not *sharing his power* with them or surrendering his power to them. The implications of this would be that the creatures themselves can now limit God, that they themselves are the source of the limitation. But this is not the case. In creating even free-will creatures and entering into relationships with them, God is not limited by them but by *himself,* and specifically by his own *word*. For every word that God utters in reference to the creation is in a real sense a limitation upon himself. The word of creation, the word of command, the word of threat, the word of promise, the word of prophecy—all of these bind God to *do* something at some point following their utterance. God is thus limited by his own word, and by his faithfulness to his word. There is no surrender of sovereignty in this. As we have said, it is perhaps the highest expression of sovereignty. God is not only free; he is free *not to be free* if he so chooses. As Barth perceptively says,

> . . . He enters into and faithfully maintains communion with this reality other than Himself in His activity as Creator, Reconciler and Redeemer. According to the biblical testimony, God has the prerogative to be free without being limited by His freedom from external conditioning, free also with regard to His freedom, free not to surrender Himself to it, but to use it to give Himself to this communion and to practice this faithfulness in it, in this way being really free, free in Himself. God must not only be unconditioned but, in the absoluteness in which He sets up this fellowship, He can and will also be conditioned. He who can and does do this is the God of Holy Scripture, the triune God known to us in His revelation. This ability, proved and manifested to us in His action, constitutes His freedom.[25]

Thus we conclude that God's sovereignty or absolute Lordship over the universe, including his authority and freedom to rule as he pleases, is grounded in his work of creation.

The Expression of Sovereignty

Whether considered as an attribute of God or as a prerogative which he possesses, sovereignty itself is something intangible within the nature

24. Ibid., pp. 98-109. See his entire chapter, "The Sovereignty of God," pp. 98-123.
25. Karl Barth, *Church Dogmatics,* II/1, p. 303.

of God and is asserted or expressed only in certain specific ways. The general over-all way in which sovereignty is exercised is through control. One who is sovereign over something maintains control over it. God as absolute Lord thus maintains complete control over his entire creation at all times. He is, as it were, "in charge" in every sense of the word. But in addition to this general concept of control, there are a number of specific ways in which God shows sovereignty and brings it to expression in the creation.

Decision

The first way that God expresses his sovereignty is by making the decisions that establish the purpose and direction and goal of creation. This is somewhat equivalent to what some prefer to call the decree. The point is that God as Sovereign is the one who makes these and lesser decisions. He decided to create. He decided to provide redemption for the fallen creation. He chose Israel to be the nation that would bring the Redeemer into the world. He chose the various individuals who would serve his purposes: Abraham, Moses, Pharaoh, David, Jeremiah, the Twelve, Paul—to name a few. God sovereignly selects the ends he wants to pursue through his creatures, and he determines the means by which he will accomplish those ends. He decides when he will enter into covenant relationships with his people, and he sets up the conditions for those relationships. He lays down the conditions that sinners must meet to receive salvation. He chooses the positive laws that he wants men to obey in particular ages. That is, he is free to establish the law of circumcision for the Old Covenant, and free to revoke it when that covenant comes to an end. It is his free decision to require the Lord's Supper, for instance, under the New Covenant.

In the making of these and countless other decisions, God is exercising his sovereign prerogative as absolute Lord of the universe.

Causation

The second way in which God expresses his sovereignty is through causation, i.e., the direct or indirect application of his power in order to bring about a specific result. This applies particularly in the areas of special providence and miracle. If God wants a cloud to follow a specific path, he causes it to do so. If he wants rain to fall in a certain place, he causes it to happen. If he wants to punish an Israel or a Babylon or an Assyria, he causes the circumstances that will bring it about. If he wants the lot to fall on Jonah, he causes it. If he wants the Red Sea to part, he causes it. If he wants to raise a dead person to life, he causes it. "The One forming light and creating darkness, causing well-being and creating calamity; I am the Lord who does all these," declares the Sovereign (Isa. 45:7).

We have noted that some have the opinion that God is not sovereign unless he is "the cause of all things."[26] But there is a fallacy here. It is true that God is "the cause of all things" in the sense that he is the *Creator* of all things. But this does not mean, nor does sovereignty require, that he be the direct cause of every event that occurs subsequent to the creation. In other words, absolute causation applies to creation but not to providence. Bloesch says that it is an error to equate omnipotence with omnicausality. "God's omnipotence does not mean that he is the direct or sole cause of all that happens; rather he is Lord over all that happens."[27] Causation is *one* expression of sovereignty, but not the *only* one. We should remember that control and not causation is the essential and all-embracing expression of God's Lordship over nature and history.

Command

If God had not determined to create beings with free will, decision and causation would almost suffice as the modes under which God's sovereignty could be expressed. The making of free creatures, however, means that his Lordship will be expressed in ways that would not apply otherwise. One of these ways is through laws or commands. Here is an example of the divine self-limitation. It is God's will that the beings made in his image should be holy (morally pure) as he is holy. But since they are free beings, he cannot accomplish this through causation. Hence he works through commands. In a figurative sense God is said to command the impersonal elements of nature (Ps. 147:15). Strictly speaking however, a command is something addressed to one person by another person.

The right to issue commandments which others have the duty to obey is a function of sovereignty. In fact, in Charnock's opinion, making

26. Louis Berkhof, *Systematic Theology* (London: Banner of Truth Trust, 1939), p. 76.

27. Donald G. Bloesch, *Essentials of Evangelical Theology, Volume One: God, Authority, and Salvation* (San Francisco: Harper & Row, 1978), p. 28.

laws is "the first act of sovereignty," or "the first and clearest manifestation of sovereignty." Charnock correctly observes that "his sovereignty doth not appear so much in his promises as in his precepts. . . . What laws God makes, man is bound by virtue of his creation to observe; that respects the sovereignty of God."[28] Kingship and lawgiving go hand in hand: "The Lord is our lawgiver, the Lord is our king" (Isa. 33:22). The one who is King over all is the one who has the authority to command. "There is only one Lawgiver," says James 4:12, and he is "the One who is able to save and to destroy." God the Sovereign issues the commands, and "we must obey God" (Acts 5:29).

Permission

A further expression of sovereignty is God's allowing or permitting things to happen in accordance with their created abilities without his interfering with them. This applies mainly to general providence, which includes the ordinary functioning of natural laws and the unhindered free acts of men. In keeping with the integrity of free will God often permits men to do things which his commands expressly forbid. This applies to all sins, and to the general course of sinful lives and sinful nations. Paul remarks that in the Old Testament era God "permitted all the nations to go their own ways" (Acts 14:16). Concerning the pagans who rejected his general revelation, "God gave them over" to follow the evil desires of their hearts (Rom. 1:24, 26, 28).

We should note that God permits such things to happen not because he is weak and unable to stop it, but because it is his free and sovereign choice to do so. Permission does not represent a lack of control; it rather is an expression of it.

We should also note that such permission is not a moral permission but a physical permission. God does not "give his permission" when men engage in sin; he permits it only in the sense that he does not prevent it.

Prevention

This leads to the fifth expression of sovereignty, namely, prevention. This is a correlative of permission. In the exercising of control over his free creatures, God may either permit them to go their intended

28. Stephen Charnock, *The Existence and Attributes of God*, p. 685.

ways, or he may intervene and prevent what would come about if their plans were carried to fruition. He prevented Pharaoh's letting the Israelites go too soon by hardening his heart. He prevented Paul's carrying out his plan to go to Rome (Rom. 1:13). He prevented Jonah's escaping his assigned task. He prevented Balaam from cursing Israel. He prevented the Assyrians from attacking Jerusalem by slaying 185,000 of their soldiers. Death is the ultimate control, and God applies it if he chooses.

Judgment

The final way that sovereignty expresses itself is in judgment. The Bible is emphatic in ascribing to God the prerogative of judgment. He is called "the Judge of all the earth" (Gen. 18:25; see Ps. 94:2). "Say among the nations, 'The Lord reigns; . . . He will judge the peoples with equity'" (Ps. 96:10). He is "the judge of all" (Heb. 12:23); he is "ready to judge the living and the dead" (I Peter 4:5).

That he should judge others is indeed a mark of sovereignty, for the Bible clearly affirms that it does not work the other way around. That is, no one has the right to sit in judgment upon God. He is, as Sherlock says, "absolute and unaccountable."[29] Elihu upbraids Job for questioning God's decisions: "Why do you complain against Him, that He does not give an account of all His doings?" (Job 33:13). The point is that the Sovereign does not have to do so. "Behold, God is exalted in His power; who is a teacher like Him? Who has appointed Him His way, and who has said, 'Thou hast done wrong'?" (Job 36:22-23). "Who then is he that can stand before Me?" asks God (Job 41:10). "For who is like Me, and who will summon Me into court?" (Jer. 50:44). The apostle Paul silences those who try to question God's decisions: "Who are you, O man, who answers back to God? The thing molded will not say to the molder, 'Why did you make me like this,' will it?" (Rom. 9:20). God is sovereign; he is Judge, not judged.

To say that God is Judge means that he has the right to determine who deserves praise and who deserves blame. He has the right to determine whom he will bless and whom he will condemn. Thus judgment can be either positive or negative. On the positive side, God's judgment is a vindication of his people: "For the Lord will judge His people, and will have compassion on His servants" (Ps. 135:14). "For

---

29. William Sherlock, *A Discourse Concerning the Divine Providence*, p. 70.

the Lord is our judge . . . ; He will save us" (Isa. 33:22). But on the negative side, God's judgment means condemnation upon those who have ignored his commands, vengeance upon those who have defied his sovereignty. "Vengeance is Mine, and retribution," says God (Deut. 32:35; see Rom. 12:19). Those who keep on sinning must realize that they have "a certain terrifying expectation of judgment, and the fury of a fire which will consume the adversaries" (Heb. 10:27). God's condemning judgment is often temporal, meted out through providence in this world. We have seen many examples of this from the Old Testament especially. Sometimes his temporal judgments are nothing short of miraculous, as in the cases of Sodom and Gomorrah and of Ananias and Sapphira. But those who escape temporal judgment will still receive their deserved punishment at the Great White Throne in the last day. For God is sovereign, and no one will escape.

The exercise of judgment is what makes command and permission to be viable expressions of sovereignty. Without the certainty of judgment, God's law would be more like whispered requests than thundered commands, and his permission would be weakness rather than strength. Rather than an exercise of sovereignty, they would be an exercise in futility. But with judgment as the final and ultimate manifestation of his sovereignty, God's Lordship is absolute indeed.

This concludes our discussion of the nature of sovereignty. We have seen that its nature is that of absolute Lordship; its ground is the fact of creation, which guarantees God's authority and freedom; and its main mode of expression is control, which is maintained through decision, causation, command, permission, prevention, and judgment. This is what we mean when we say that our God is sovereign. What it means to the Christian in his personal life is well summed up by Curtis Dickinson thus:

> The Sovereignty of Almighty God is ground for these applications:
>
> (1) The worldwide upheaval of evil powers now in process is not outside God's dominion; it is all part of the unfolding of the plan by which God brings to consummation His eternal purpose: the elect to be saved and glorified and the rest to be destroyed in Judgment. The present chaos only appears to be such from our temporal earthly point of view. From God's point of view it may indicate the final step in the working of His overall purpose.
>
> (2) The work of God through His church must be something quite different from what is generally portrayed as church work. The average concept of a church program holds that the work that God would do is

> subject to the cleverness of His servants; hence, the frenzied activity of ministers and their associates to find new methods, new gimmicks, tantalizing bait and activities which are "relevant" to the pagan world. The attitude prevails that unless we find better methods and skill ourselves in worldly techniques by which to hold the church together and build it up, God will fail. The work becomes man's work with God depending upon man. But the church is Christ's and Christ is God's. Christ will build His church; it is man's task to proclaim God's word and to be faithful to Him, that the church may yield fully to His sovereign will.
>
> (3) The believer may have perfect peace and perpetual assurance in spite of the distressing circumstances that surround him. Whatever happens, however tragic as viewed in the world, it cannot be otherwise than profitable in the overall plan. The Christian is totally under the Sovereign Power of God. "The very hairs of your head are numbered." (Matt. 10:30).
>
> "All things are of God." (II Cor. 5:18).[30]

And a final quote from Charles Hodge:

> . . . This sovereignty of God is the ground of peace and confidence to all his people. They rejoice that the Lord God omnipotent reigneth; that neither necessity, nor chance, nor the folly of man, nor the malice of Satan controls the sequence of events and all their issues. Infinite wisdom, love, and power, belong to Him, our great God and Saviour, into whose hands all power in heaven and earth has been committed.[31]

THE ATTRIBUTES OF SOVEREIGNTY

Having explored the nature of sovereignty as such, we now turn to the nature of the Sovereign. What is the nature of the God who rules over the whole of creation with a Lordship that is absolute? What are the attributes that make such sovereign rule possible? What are the attributes that determine the character of his rule? Four will be emphasized here: knowledge, power, wisdom, and goodness.

Knowledge

The two main attributes of sovereignty are knowledge and power. Without these God's sovereign rule would be impossible. But because of his unlimited awareness and unlimited power, he is able to keep the

30. Curtis Dickinson, "The Sovereign," *The Witness* (May 1969), 9:2.
31. Charles Hodge, *Systematic Theology*, I:441.

universe under his control and to control the final outcome of it all. "He rules by His might forever; His eyes keep watch on the nations" (Ps. 66:7).

God's omniscience or unlimited knowledge has already been discussed in detail in the volume on God the Creator.[32] In addition to a presentation of the biblical data on omniscience the point there was to show that God's knowledge is unlimited just *because* he is the Creator. Only the one who stands in this relationship to the world can be unlimited by time and space and thus have full and simultaneous knowledge of every detail of the visible and invisible creation from its beginning to its end.

Such knowledge is essential to sovereignty; it is essential for God's providential control over nature and history. If anything is outside of God's awareness even for a limited time, then it is potentially out from under his control. Of course, knowledge alone does not guarantee control, but it is a necessary condition for it. How could God meet the needs of his people if he did not know those needs? How could he answer prayer if he did not know what prayers are being offered up to him? How could he stay in control of free beings making free choices if he did not know every choice of every person?

But he does know these things, just as he knows everything. This is clearly taught in Scripture, as the following selected verses will show. "And there is no creature hidden from His sight, but all things are open and laid bare to the eyes of Him with whom we have to do" (Heb. 4:13). "His eyes are upon the ways of a man, and He sees all his steps" (Job 34:21). "God is greater than our heart, and knows all things" (I John 3:20). He knows the number of the stars (Ps. 147:4) and the number of hairs on every head (Matt. 10:30). Thus we may say that God has an intimate knowledge of every detail in the entire universe, large and small. He keeps a constant surveillance, as it were, of every passing event in nature and history. He monitors the cosmos. Some have suggested that God does not clutter up his mind with unnecessary details. The following statement is attributed to Jerome:

> As for the rest, it is an absurd detraction of the majesty of God to say that God knows every moment how many gnats are born and how many die; how many bedbugs, fleas, and flies there are on earth, what number of fishes live in the water. We are not such fatuous sycophants of God that while we make His power concern itself with most insignificant

32. Jack Cottrell, *What the Bible Says About God the Creator,* pp. 273-292.

> creatures, we are unfair to ourselves by assuming a like providence extending over rational and irrational creatures.[33]

This is a rather weak understanding of divine omniscience. Jerome seems to think that it requires some kind of effort on God's part to add such extra bits of knowledge to his consciousness. Such is not the case. He does not have to concentrate harder to know such things; it is his *nature* to know. His eye is on the sparrow—and the gnats and the fleas and the fish. These do not compete with man for God's attention; he knows us all with equal thoroughness. He knows our every thought, word, and deed. His omniscience probes the very depths and secret places of our hearts and minds. Nothing is hidden from him.

In reference to his sovereign providence, perhaps the most important part of God's knowledge is his foreknowledge. God's knowledge of future contingencies is what enables him to bestow a relative independence upon his creation. It enables him to create beings with free will without surrendering his sovereignty in the least. Through his foreknowledge of man's free choices God maintains control. He is not taken by surprise. He is able to work out his purposes in spite of and by means of these foreknown choices. His absolute Lordship remains intact without his having to resort to omnicausality.

Here we may recall the determinist contention that foreknowledge of free acts that are not actually caused by God destroys God's sovereignty. If God simply foreknows what men will freely choose, this suggests that God's knowledge and even God himself are to some degree conditioned by and dependent upon man. "Hence God becomes dependent upon the world; he derives from the world a knowledge which he could not have derived from his own being, and consequently, as far as his knowledge is concerned, God is no longer simple and independent; in other words, he ceases to be God."[34] So says Herman Bavinck. But this is just another version of the false notion that only unconditionality is consistent with sovereignty, a view discussed in chapter five above. Here we will make two other comments. First, the determinist argument is often based on exaggeration and misrepresentation, as is the case with the comment by Bavinck above. The fact that God's knowledge of

33. Jerome, *Commentary on Habakkuk* 1:13; cited in Francis Pieper, *Christian Dogmatics*, tr. Theodore Engelder et al. (St. Louis: Concordia Publishing House, 1950), I:485.

34. Herman Bavinck, *The Doctrine of God*, ed. and tr. William Hendriksen (Grand Rapids: Eerdmans, 1951), p. 193. He is commenting specifically on the concept of middle knowledge or mediate knowledge.

free acts is derived from those acts themselves via foreknowledge does *not* make God "dependent upon the world." This way of speaking is quite misleading; it suggests that somehow man is instructing God, telling him something that he did not know. It also suggests that if God does not have that knowledge, he will somehow lose his deity; and it suggests that man somehow holds God's own fate in his hands in that he has the power either to reveal this knowledge or to withhold it from God. This is of course quite silly, and Bavinck would probably reject it outright. But I would contend that his statement and others like it from the determinist viewpoint are quite consistent with this scenario. We may note that Bavinck goes on to say (concerning mediate knowledge specifically) that in such a case "the entire history of the world is withdrawn from the controlling and directing power of God, and is made subject to the will of man. . . . Mediate knowledge does indeed make God the slave of man."[35] Even though I do not subscribe to the specific view called "mediate knowledge," I deplore Bavinck's exaggerated rhetoric as completely untrue with regard to that view and certainly with regard to the view presented here.

My second comment is that God's foreknowledge of truly free acts, rather than destroying his sovereignty, as a matter of fact enhances it and demonstrates its magnificence. The very fact that God is *able* to foreknow free choices can only magnify his glory. He and he alone can do this, simply because he is the transcendent, sovereign God. It is inconceivable that anyone could think that this detracts from his sovereignty. As a very rough analogy, we may compare it with the knowledge man has accumulated via the electron microscope. Would anyone dare to call this inferior knowledge, or to say that man is somehow demeaned, because this knowledge is derived only through an instrument? Of course not! The fact is that we applaud such an accomplishment as this and consider man's scientific status to be greatly enhanced by it. The same thing applies in an infinite sense to God. How can we possibly think that God's real foreknowledge of truly free acts demeans God and diminishes his sovereignty? It is in fact a marvelous ability and accomplishment, one that shows just how great the sovereignty of God is. Only if God could *not* foreknow such acts would we have reason to question his sovereignty.

The conclusion is that omniscience, including foreknowledge, is one of the primary attributes of sovereignty.

35. Ibid.

Power

Knowledge and power combine to make sovereignty possible. Though knowledge is essential for effective power and is in a certain sense a form of power, unless knowledge—even omniscience—is accompanied by the power to act upon what is known, it is of limited value. In the same way power—even omnipotence—will not be able to function sovereignly without an accompanying knowledge. But both attributes are found in the nature of God our Sovereign. He is not only omniscient; he is also omnipotent.

Omnipotence is an attribute manifested first and foremost in God's work of creation *ex nihilo*. Thus it has already been discussed in detail in the volume on God the Creator.[36] But here we must say that God's unlimited power is also exhibited in his work of providence. This is seen, for example, in his preserving all things in existence. Hebrews 1:3 says that our Lord "upholds all things by the word of His power." Indeed, it is almost impossible to imagine the kind of power that must be involved in the preservation of the atomic structure of all the matter of nearly 100 billion galaxies, or the kind of power that is required for maintaining the existence of the countless spiritual creatures—angels, demons, human souls—in God's creation. It is God's unimaginable power that keeps it all—us all—from slipping back into nothingness.

In addition to this constant exertion of preserving power, we must consider the individual expenditures of energy manifested in the innumerable acts of special providence and miracle. He is able to harness the wrath of nations as well as to calm the fearful heart of a child. He is able to carry out his purposes over the scope of millennia and within the compass of heaven and earth. He who rides the clouds like a chariot (Ps. 104:3) can make the sun stand still in relation to the earth, i.e., halt the rotation of the earth in an instant, and then start it up again, without disturbing the relative calm of the earth's surface. His power can send a shower that saves a crop or a flood that destroys the world. He is indeed *God Almighty*.

Such unlimited power makes God's providential control possible and guarantees his absolute Lordship over all of creation. As Bloesch says, "God is omnicompetent, capable of dealing with all circumstances," so that "nothing can ultimately defeat or thwart his plan for his people."[37] He is *free* to do whatever he pleases because he is *able* to do whatever

36. Jack Cottrell, *What the Bible Says About God the Creator*, pp. 292-305.

37. Donald Bloesch, *Essentials of Evangelical Theology*, I:28.

he pleases. He can establish his purposes and infallibly carry them out, because he has the power to do so. Indeed, Charnock defines the power of God as "the strength . . . whereby he is able to effect all his purposes."[38] Thus it is a primary attribute of sovereignty.

Wisdom

The next two attributes, wisdom and goodness, may be called secondary attributes of sovereignty because they do not make his absolute Lordship possible but rather determine its character. Sovereignty is inconceivable without knowledge and power, but one might conceive of an omniscient, omnipotent God who did not possess wisdom and goodness. In such a case his governance of the world would certainly be inferior to that of a deity who did possess these attributes. Only a providence characterized by wisdom and goodness would be welcomed by those creatures who have to live under it. And so it is with our God and his providence: he is wise and good, and his providential rule is worthy of our praise and thanksgiving.

It is generally agreed that wisdom is the ability to choose the best possible end, and to choose the best possible means of achieving that end.[39] It is not the same as knowledge, but is rather the ability to put one's knowledge to practical use. As Packer says,

> . . . Wisdom is a moral as well as an intellectual quality, more than mere intelligence or knowledge, just as it is more than mere cleverness or cunning. To be truly wise, in the Bible sense, one's intelligence and cleverness must be harnessed to a right end. Wisdom is the power to see, and the inclination to choose, the best and highest goal, together with the surest means of attaining it.[40]

Or as Charnock says, "Knowledge is an understanding of general rules, and wisdom is a drawing conclusions from those rules in order to particular cases."[41] To say it another way, wisdom is the ability to make the right decisions when judging between two different courses of action. When one rules with wisdom, his decisions will be fair and just and right. This is what King Solomon desired from God more than

38. Stephen Charnock, *The Existence and Attributes of God*, p. 665.

39. See, for instance, Louis Berkhof, *Systematic Theology*, p. 69: God's wisdom "points to the fact that He always strives for the best possible ends, and chooses the best means for the realization of His purposes."

40. J. I. Packer, *Knowing God* (Downers Grove, Ill.: InterVarsity Press, 1973), p. 80.

41. Stephen Charnock, *The Existence and Attributes of God*, p. 270.

anything else, namely, a wise and discerning heart to be able to rule well over Israel (I Kings 3:5-12). When God gave it to him and when he exercised it, the people respected him, "for they saw that the wisdom of God was in him to administer justice" (I Kings 3:28).

Scripture testifies to the wisdom of God. Daniel declares, "Let the name of God be blessed forever and ever, for wisdom and power belong to Him" (Dan. 2:20). And Paul exults, "Oh, the depth of the riches both of the wisdom and knowledge of God! How unsearchable are His judgments and unfathomable His ways!" (Rom. 11:33). He is "the only wise God" (Rom. 16:27). "He is mighty in strength of understanding" (Job 36:5); "His understanding is inscrutable" (Isa. 40:28). He does not seek counsel or advice from anyone: "With whom did He consult and who gave Him understanding? And who taught Him in the path of justice and taught Him knowledge, and informed Him of the way of understanding?" (Isa. 40:14). "For who has known the mind of the Lord, or who became His counselor?" (Rom. 11:34). The answer, of course, is no one. God himself is the original fountain of wisdom.

God's wisdom is exhibited both in his work of creation (Ps. 104:24; Prov. 3:19; 8:22ff.; Jer. 10:12) and in his work of redemption (I Cor. 1:18-25; 2:7; Eph. 3:10). But it is particularly manifested in his work of providence, as God formulated his plan and purpose for the whole of creation from the very beginning. "God is wise," says Barth, "in so far as His whole activity, as willed by Him, is also thought out by Him, and thought out by Him from the very outset with correctness and completeness."[42] This includes the "eternal purpose which He carried out in Christ Jesus our Lord," a purpose characterized by wisdom, says Paul (Eph. 3:10-11). It includes also all the means by which God is carrying out his purpose from one end of history to the other.

We will remember that "God's wisdom is His intelligence as manifested in the adaptation of means to ends."[43] And this is really what stands out in the whole course of providence: the wisdom of God's own acts, and the wisdom of his use of men's acts, as he adapts them all toward the fulfillment of his purpose. This is seen, for example, in the kinds of laws which God gives to govern man. Moses exhorted the Israelites to keep the commandments which God gave them, "for that is your wisdom and your understanding in the sight of the peoples who will

42. Karl Barth, *Church Dogmatics*, II/1, p. 425.
43. Louis Berkhof, *Systematic Theology*, p. 69.

hear all these statutes and say, 'Surely this great nation is a wise and understanding people.' For . . . what great nation is there that has statutes and judgments as righteous as this whole law which I am setting before you today?" (Deut. 4:6-8). David adds this judgment: "The law of the Lord is perfect, restoring the soul; the testimony of the Lord is sure, making wise the simple. The precepts of the Lord are right, rejoicing the heart; the commandment of the Lord is pure, enlightening the eyes" (Ps. 19:7-8). Because of this God is said to be "great in counsel" (Jer. 32:19); he "has made His counsel wonderful and His wisdom great" (Isa. 28:29; see Isa. 9:6). "I will bless the Lord who has counseled me," says David (Ps. 16:7). God's commands are indeed of such a nature that if they were followed, his purpose would certainly be realized.

But God's wisdom in adapting means to ends is seen also in the way he uses men's decisions, even when they do *not* obey his commands. Through his foreknowledge of all free acts, good and evil, God is able to adapt whichever ones are appropriate to the carrying out of his plan. Those that do not affect his purpose one way or another are simply permitted to proceed unhindered, and those that would have a negative impact are prevented. The wisdom of God knows which to use, and which simply to permit or prevent. His wisdom is particularly seen in the way he can use even the sinful acts of men to accomplish good purposes. "He uses the sins of evil instruments for the glory of his justice," Charnock reminds us. "Thus he served himself of the ambition and covetousness of the Assyrians, Chaldeans, and Romans, for the correction of his people and punishment of his rebels." This shows a wisdom peculiar to the Creator of nature: "to make things serviceable, contrary to their own nature."[44]

This is why Paul can affirm with conviction, "And we know that God causes all things to work together for good to those who love God, to those who are called according to His purpose" (Rom. 8:28). This shows a complete confidence in the wisdom of God. It indicates that God is not frustrated or thwarted by any contingency, either from sin-corrupted nature or from the evil hearts and hands of men themselves. Even pain and suffering may be harnessed for good results by the all-wise Ruler. Emil Brunner offers these perceptive remarks as to God's ability to weave all things together to effect his own purpose for and through history:

44. Stephen Charnock, *The Existence and Attributes of God*, p. 293.

> In the New Testament . . . the idea of the Divine Wisdom is found more frequently in connexion with God's governance in History than in connexion with the Creation. This implies that the Wisdom of God is the fundamental category of a Christian philosophy of History. It is the absolute mastery of the Architect who builds the City of God, the absolute planning of God, above all that is accidental and frustrating in the course of this world. In all the apparent meaningless [sic] of this process of history, in all theories of teleology *and* dysteleology, in good and in evil, in the beautiful and in the ugly, in that which leads to death, and in that which leads to life, in that which is significant, and in that which has no meaning, God controls and rules all by His Wisdom, and He weaves all these various threads—so different in kind and in origin—into His tapestry; He uses all these strange materials as stones for His building for the final establishment of His Kingdom—as yet still hidden and secret, but one day to be revealed to all men.[45]

If we truly believe that God is all-wise as well as all-knowing and all-powerful, then we will not attempt to criticize or to judge what God brings to pass or even allows to happen in this world. We will not challenge God's decisions and works. Even if God's wisdom brings disaster, we will acknowledge that God makes no mistakes and take comfort in Romans 8:28. "Yet He also is wise and will bring disaster, and does not retract His words" (Isa. 31:2). Why should God call back his words? "Shall not the Judge of all the earth deal justly?" (Gen. 18:25). So then, "Why do you complain against Him?" (Job 33:13). Only someone who is wiser than God (let him step forward and identify himself!) has a right to sit in judgment upon God's providence. This is in a sense what Job was presuming to do, and God let him know in no uncertain terms that his wisdom was pea-sized and puny in comparison with that of the omnipotent Creator. The force of the argument, says Sherlock, is "that so weak and ignorant a creature as man is, ought not to censure the divine Providence, how mysterious and unaccountable soever it be."[46] We must remember what Paul says in Romans 11:33, "Oh, the depth of the riches both of the wisdom and knowledge of God! How unsearchable are His judgments and unfathomable His ways!" If we *really* believe that God's wisdom is unsearchable, says Sherlock, "this would put an end to all the disputes about Providence." We would just *expect* there to be things we cannot understand.

---

45. Emil Brunner, *The Christian Doctrine of God: Dogmatics, Vol. I,* tr. Olive Wyon (Philadelphia: Westminster Press, 1950), pp. 283-284.

46. William Sherlock, *A Discourse Concerning the Divine Providence,* p. 80.

> . . . If the wisdom of God be unsearchable, why should we not allow his wisdom in governing the world, to be as unsearchable as his wisdom in making it? For an incomprehensible wisdom will do incomprehensible things, whatever it employs itself about; and when we know, that if the world be governed at all, it is governed by an infinite and incomprehensible wisdom, there is no reason to wonder that there are many events of providence which we cannot fathom, and much less reason to deny a providence, because we cannot comprehend the reasons of all events.[47]

"It is great pride and as contemptible folly," he adds, "to think that if there be a God who is infinitely wise, he should not be able to do things above our understanding."[48] Pieper concurs: "We dare never criticize God's wisdom, but must stand before it in adoration and praise."[49]

The only response to an all-wise providence is complete trust in the God who makes all things work together for good. "The more perfect and excellent the wisdom is, the less we can understand it, but the more safe we are under its conduct."[50] Only a wise sovereignty engenders such trust. If God were merely omnipotent, we would have more reason to be afraid of him than to put our confidence in him. But God is wise as well as powerful: "Wisdom and power belong to Him" (Dan. 2:20). Charnock says, "His infinite wisdom stood not silent while mere dominion acted. Whatsoever God doth, he doth wisely as well as sovereignly." "When those two, wisdom and power, are linked together, there ariseth from both a fitness for government."[51] As Packer puts it, "Wisdom without power would be pathetic, a broken reed; power without wisdom would be merely frightening; but in God boundless wisdom and endless power are united, and this makes him utterly worthy of our fullest trust."[52]

Goodness

Another attribute of God that establishes the character of his sovereign rule is his goodness. Scripture gives abundant testimony to this aspect

---

47. Ibid., p. 81.
48. Ibid., p. 83.
49. Francis Pieper, *Christian Dogmatics*, I:453.
50. William Sherlock, *A Discourse Concerning the Divine Providence*, p. 83.
51. Stephen Charnock, *The Existence and Attributes of God*, pp. 274, 277.
52. J. I. Packer, *Knowing God*, p. 81.

of his nature. "Good and upright is the Lord" (Ps. 25:8); "the Lord is good" (Nah. 1:7). "O taste and see that the Lord is good; how blessed is the man who takes refuge in Him!" (Ps. 34:8). The psalmists continually exhort us to praise God for his goodness: "Give thanks to Him; bless His name. For the Lord is good; His lovingkindness is everlasting, and His faithfulness to all generations" (Ps. 100:4-5). See Psalms 106:1; 107:1; 118:1; 136:1; Jeremiah 33:11. When a man addressed Jesus as "Good Teacher," our Lord replied, "Why do you call Me good? No one is good except God alone" (Mark 10:18). Hebrews 11:6 says that faith is first of all believing that God exists, and then believing "that He is a rewarder of those who seek Him." That is, we must believe that God's character is basically good.

What does it mean to say that God is *good*? One connotation for this word is that of excellence. We say, for example, that a product is good if it meets the standards of excellence for that product. It is good rather than poor. Some would say that this is the basic meaning of the word when applied to God. That is, his goodness is his absolute perfection in every way. Pieper says that "goodness is that quality in God whereby He is the absolute Good, the unconditioned and essential Perfection."[53] "His goodness is one with his absolute perfection," says Bavinck.[54] Berkhof sums it up this way: "The fundamental idea is that He is in every way all that He as God should be, and therefore answers perfectly to the ideal expressed in the word 'God.'"[55] This is probably the sense in which, as Jesus says, God alone is good; for only God has all the perfections of deity.

Another connotation of the word is *morally* good, such as we mean when we say to our children, "Be good!" Certainly God is good in this sense, but this does not seem to be the main emphasis in the biblical use of the term.

The third connotation of goodness, and the principal one as the Bible applies the term to God, is that of *benevolence*. That God is good means that he is good *to others;* he has a benevolent spirit, a spirit of giving and sharing and blessing. Hodge calls it "the disposition to promote happiness."[56] Packer calls it the quality of generosity: "Generosity means a disposition to give to others in a way which has

53. Francis Pieper, *Christian Dogmatics*, I:460.
54. Herman Bavinck, *The Doctrine of God,* p. 204.
55. Louis Berkhof, *Systematic Theology,* p. 70.
56. Charles Hodge, *Systematic Theology.* I:427.

no mercenary motive and is not limited by what the recipients deserve, but consistently goes beyond it. Generosity expresses the simple wish that others should have what they need to make them happy."[57] As James 1:5 says, God "gives to all men generously and without reproach." Charnock describes this as the *bounty* of God, as "his inclination to deal well and bountifully with his creatures."[58] Since it is a spirit of affection and good will, a caring for the welfare of his creatures, God's goodness is very close to the concept of love in the sense of *agapē*. The main difference is that the former is the broader term, applying to all creatures, while *agapē* is directed toward persons. Another related word is *kindness*. All in all, then, goodness is an attitude of God toward his creatures, the desire to do good to them and for them. As the psalmist says, "Thou art good and doest good" (Ps. 119:68). We use the term this way when we sing, "God is so good; he's so good to me," and when we pray the children's prayer, "God is great, God is good; let us thank him for our food."

Another possible connotation of the term *good* as applied to God is that he is *desirable*, the object of desire. Bavinck comments, "He is the one unto whom all creatures strive to attain, whether consciously or unconsciously; he is the object of every one's desire."[59] As Psalm 73:25 says, "Whom have I in heaven but Thee? And besides Thee, I desire nothing on earth." This idea is of course relative to the previous one; God is desirable because he is so good toward us. Charnock observes concerning goodness,

> This is the most pleasant perfection of the divine nature. His creating power amazes us, his conducting wisdom astonisheth us, his goodness, as furnishing us with all conveniencies, delights us, and renders both his amazing power and astonishing wisdom delightful to us.[60]

Perhaps this is what some of the Protestant creeds and confessions meant when they said that man's chief end is not only to glorify God but also to "enjoy him forever."

That God is good means that his providential rule over his creatures is characterized by goodness, particularly in the third sense above. His attitudes and actions toward his creatures *as creatures* are marked by good will and kindness. If God is good, then all that he does is good.

57. J. I. Packer, *Knowing God*, p. 146.
58. Stephen Charnock, *The Existence and Attributes of God*, pp. 541-542.
59. Herman Bavinck, *The Doctrine of God*, p. 205.
60. Stephen Charnock, *The Existence and Attributes of God*, p. 542.

His creation itself is good: "For everything created by God is good" (I Tim. 4:4; see Gen. 1:31). He maintains a benevolent concern for all his creatures, even the non-rational ones. He supplies rain just "for His world" (Job 37:13; 38:25-27). "He gives to the beast its food, and to the young ravens which cry" (Ps. 147:9; see Ps. 104:27; Matt. 6:26). One reason God did not want to destroy Nineveh was because of the many animals there (Jonah 4:11). Indeed, "the Lord is good to all, and His mercies are over all His works. . . . The eyes of all look to Thee, and Thou dost give them their food in due time. Thou dost open Thy hand, and dost satisfy the desire of every living thing" (Ps. 145:9, 15-16). Charnock says,

> . . . All things are not only before his eyes, but in his bosom; he is the nurse of all creatures, supplying their wants, and sustaining them from that nothing they tend to. . . . The whole world swims in the rich bounty of the Creator, as the fish do in the largeness of the sea, and birds in the spaciousness of the air. The goodness of God is the river that waters the whole earth. . . . And as the sun illuminates all things which are capable of partaking of its light, and diffuseth its beams to all things which are capable of receiving them, so doth God spread his wings over the whole creation, and neglects nothing wherein he sees a mark of his first creating goodness.[61]

Though the whole universe basks in the goodness of God, the bulk of his providential care is reserved for mankind. God's general providence makes no distinctions among men; he blesses man simply as man, as the crowing glory of his earthly creatures. "He causes His sun to rise on the evil and the good, and sends rain on the righteous and the unrighteous" (Matt. 5:45). Throughout past generations "He did good and gave you rains from heaven and fruitful seasons, satisfying your hearts with food and gladness" (Acts 14:17). He "richly supplies us with all things to enjoy" (I Tim. 6:17). "Every good thing bestowed and every perfect gift is from above, coming down from the Father" (James 1:17). Packer comments, "Since God controls all that happens in His world, every meal, every pleasure, every possession, every bit of sun, every night's sleep, every moment of health and safety, everything else that sustains and enriches life, is a divine gift."[62] And this applies even to the wicked, "for He Himself is kind to ungrateful and evil men" (Luke 6:35). Charnock comments on how the whole earth is full of messengers of his goodness:

---

61. Ibid., p. 607.
62. J. I. Packer, *Knowing God,* p. 147.

> . . . Food communicates the goodness of its nourishing virtue to our bodies, flowers the goodness of their odours to our smell, every creature a goodness of comeliness to our sight, plants the goodness of healing qualities for our cure, and all derive from themselves a goodness of knowledge objectively to our understandings. The sun by one sort of goodness warms us, metals enrich us, living creatures sustain us, and delight us by another; all those have distinct kinds of goodness, which are eminently summed up in God, and are all but parts of his immense goodness. It is he that enlightens us by his sun, nourisheth us by bread . . . . It is all but his own supreme goodness, conveyed to us through those varieties of conduit pipes. . . .[63]

Even God's special providence, where he does make distinctions among men, is characterized by goodness. When the wicked are punished by providential means, they are not being treated unfairly. They receive no more than what is due to them. "Why should any living mortal, or any man, offer complaint in view of his sins?" (Lam. 3:39). In this sense even the justice of God falls within the scope of his goodness. On the other hand, to those who turn to him in repentance and submission, his goodness is multiplied beyond measure. "The Lord is good to those who wait for Him, to the person who seeks Him" (Lam. 3:25). "For He has satisfied the thirsty soul, and the hungry soul He has filled with what is good" (Ps. 107:9). "How great is Thy goodness, which Thou has stored up for those who fear Thee" (Ps. 31:19). "For the Lord God is a sun and shield; the Lord gives grace and glory; no good thing does He withhold from those who walk uprightly" (Ps. 84:11). As Packer says, "God is good to all in some ways and to some in all ways."[64] Even when God's providence brings trials and suffering, we trust that this is his goodness disciplining us and making us strong. For we remember Romans 8:28, that "God causes all things to work together for good to those who love God." As James exhorts us, "Consider it all joy, my brethren, when you encounter various trials, knowing that the testing of your faith produces endurance" (James 1:2-3).

Without this confidence in the goodness of God, it would be very difficult to love him and trust him. If God were not good, his attitudes and actions toward us would be characterized either by cruelty or

63. Stephen Charnock, *The Existence and Attributes of God*, p. 545. See also pp. 568-569.

64. J. I. Packer, *Knowing God*, p. 147.

indifference. Such a sovereign, omnipotent ruler would be unendurable. We hear Charnock again:

> . . . Greatness without sweetness is an unruly and affrighting monster in the world, like a vast turbulent sea casting out mire and dirt. Goodness is the brightness and loveliness of our majestical Creator. To fancy a God without it, is to fancy a miserable, scanty, narrowhearted, savage God, and so an unlively and horrible being. . . . Infinite goodness is more necessary to, and more straitly joined with, an infinite Deity, than infinite power, and infinite wisdom; we cannot conceive him God, unless we conceive him the highest good. . . .[65]
>
> . . . Power without goodness would deface, instead of preserving. Ruin is the fruit of rigour without kindness; but God, because of his infinite and immutable goodness, cannot do anything unworthy of himself, and uncomely in itself, or destructive to any moral goodness in the creature. It is impossible he should do anything that is base, or act anything but for the best, because he is essentially and naturally, and therefore necessarily, good. . . .[66]

Because he is good, we can trust him: "Goodness is the first motive of trust."[67] Because he is good, we can love him: "This attribute of goodness renders him more lovely than any other attribute."[68]

> . . . His power to do good is admirable, but his will to do good is amiable. This puts a gloss upon all his other attributes. Though he had knowledge to understand the depth of our necessities, and power to prevent them or rescue us from them, yet his knowledge would be fruitless and his power useless, if he were of a rigid nature, and not touched with any sentiments of kindness.[69]

The goodness of God takes many specific forms, depending on the particular needs of its object. The attributes of mercy, love, grace, patience, and long-suffering are in a real sense just aspects of the basic attribute of goodness. Pieper says that these terms "bring God's goodness into full view, just as the various facets refract and reflect the brilliance of the diamond."[70] When Moses asked to see the glory of God, God replied, "I Myself will make all My goodness pass before you" (Exod. 33:19). The actual event was then accompanied by

---

65. Stephen Charnock, *The Existence and Attributes of God*, p. 541.
66. Ibid., p. 634.
67. Ibid., p. 641.
68. Ibid., p. 638.
69. Ibid.
70. Francis Pieper, *Christian Dogmatics*, I:461.

God's pronouncement, "The Lord, the Lord God, compassionate and gracious, slow to anger, and abounding in lovingkindness and truth; who keeps lovingkindness for thousands, who forgives iniquity, transgression and sin" (Exod. 34:6-7). This suggests that goodness includes these other qualities in God's nature. Charnock comments, "What is this but the train of all his lovely perfections springing from his goodness? The whole catalogue of mercy, grace, long-suffering, abundance of truth" are "summed up in this one word. All are streams from this one fountain; he could be none of this were he not first good."[71] These more specific attributes are most clearly revealed in relation to sin and salvation, and will be discussed in more detail in the volume on God the Redeemer.

There is another side of God's nature revealed in providence. We behold therein not only his kindness but also his severity (Rom. 11:22). We have noted how judgment and wrath have been executed upon individuals and nations, especially in relation to God's purpose for Old Testament Israel. These attributes will also be discussed in more detail in the next volume.

The main attributes of providence, however, are those that have been discussed here, namely, God's knowledge, power, wisdom, and goodness. The former two make his Lordship truly sovereign, and the latter two make it praiseworthy.

THE INTIMACY OF SOVEREIGNTY

One other point calls for brief attention, namely, what I will call the intimacy of God's sovereign rule. Sometimes this is known as God's *immanence*. Just as the work of creation magnifies the transcendence of God,[72] so does his work of providence magnify his immanence. To say that God is transcendent does not mean that he is outside of the universe or spatially separated from it; it means that he is qualitatively different from it. His transcendence in no way excludes his immanence in the world; we do not have to choose between these two aspects of the nature of God.

To say that God is immanent means that he is present within the world, or present to every part of his creation. It is similar to his

71. Stephen Charnock, *The Existence and Attributes of God*, p. 542.

72. Jack Cottrell, *What the Bible Says About God the Creator*, Chapter 5.

omnipresence;[73] they differ only in emphasis. Whereas omnipresence lays stress on the *omni-*, or on the universality of God's presence, immanence emphasizes the presence itself. Omnipresence means that God is present everywhere as opposed to just some places; immanence means that God is present in and to his creation as opposed to being outside it or absent from it. This does not mean that God is wholly contained within the world as if he were finite, nor does it mean that he is to be identified with the world as in pantheistic views. It simply means that God is present, that he is close to his creatures, that they are in his presence at all times. God is near, and not far off.

To say that the Sovereign Ruler, God Most High, maintains such an intimate relationship with his subjects is contrary to the tendency that prevails in human relationships. In reference to the latter, the higher one is in business or government, usually the further removed he is from everyday events and from contact with the general populace. Such details are taken care of by underlings. How different it is with God! Though he is the King of the universe, yet he is *with us,* in our midst, working among us, by our side, giving his personal, intimate attention to every detail of his creation and of our lives.

Scripture testifies to the intimate nearness of the Sovereign. It is not futile to seek God, says Acts 17:27-28, for "He is not far from each one of us; for in Him we live and move and exist." Here is the basic affirmation of immanence. A similar testimony is found in Jeremiah 23:23-24, "'Am I a God who is near,' declares the Lord, 'And not a God far off? Can a man hide himself in hiding places, so I do not see him?' declares the Lord. 'Do I not fill the heavens and the earth?' declares the Lord." The omnipresence of God means that he is near to all.

The intimate relationship between God and his creation is alluded to in many, many ways in the Bible. "I know every bird of the mountains," he says (Ps. 50:11). He leads the stars through their paths in the heavens (Job 38:32). Thunder declares God's presence (Job 36:33). He observes the birth of baby mountain goats and baby deer (Job 39:1). He monitors the growth of the baby in the womb (Ps. 139:13-16). He is as close to his people as a shepherd is to his sheep: "But He led forth His own people like sheep, and guided them in the wilderness like a flock" (Ps. 78:52). "We are the people of His pasture, and the sheep of His hand" (Ps. 95:7). "As a shepherd cares for his herd in the day when he is among his scattered sheep, so I will care for My sheep,"

73. Ibid., pp. 264-273.

says the Lord. "I will feed My flock and I will lead them to rest" (Ezek. 34:12, 15). The intimacy of God's presence as Shepherd is seen nowhere better than in the twenty-third Psalm:

> The Lord is my shepherd, I shall not want. He makes me lie down in green pastures; He leads me beside quiet waters. He restores my soul; He guides me in the paths of righteousness for His name's sake. Even though I walk through the valley of the shadow of death, I fear no evil; for Thou art with me; Thy rod and Thy staff, they comfort me. Thou dost prepare a table before me in the presence of my enemies; Thou hast anointed my head with oil; my cup overflows. Surely goodness and lovingkindness will follow me all the days of my life, and I will dwell in the house of the Lord forever.

Another image that conveys the intimacy of God's sovereign care is that of the shelter of his wings: "Be gracious to me, O God, be gracious to me, for my soul takes refuge in Thee; and in the shadow of Thy wings I will take refuge" (Ps. 57:1). "Thou hast been my help, and in the shadow of Thy wings I sing for joy" (Ps. 63:7; see Ps. 61:4).

We should note that God does not *have* to be present in order to perform the mighty works of providence and miracle. He *could* do it by "remote control," as it were, from a distance, just as Jesus healed the centurion's servant without his being present (Matt. 8:5ff.). An intimate nearness is not essential to his providential government; he could just exert his power or issue a command. But he does not choose to do it this way. He chooses to be present with his creatures, which is what we would expect in view of the goodness of God, in view of his benevolent concern and care for his own. If one truly cares for something or someone, he wants to be near the object of his affection; and surely this is true of God. Thus he is personally and purposefully present with his creatures. He is present in his general providence in his preserving and overseeing of all that he has made. He is present in his special providence, stretching forth his hand to curse or to bless. He is present in his miracles, showing forth his mighty power.

God is near. The challenge to us is to cultivate an awareness of his presence, to do as David resolved to do: "I have set the Lord continually before me; because He is at my right hand, I will not be shaken" (Ps. 16:8). We should "delight in the nearness of God" (Isa. 58:2). Over three hundred years ago a Roman Catholic monk known as Brother Lawrence urged upon us all the "practice of the presence of God." It is possible, he said, to be aware of God's presence at all times, even in the midst of ordinary and menial activities such as kitchen work (which was his own job in the monastery). Here are some selected words of advice from Brother Lawrence:

> Were I a preacher, I should, above all other things, preach the practice of *the presence of God;* and were I a director, I should advise all the world to do it, so necessary do I think it, and so easy, too.[74]
>
> . . . He requires no great matters of us: a little remembrance of Him from time to time; a little adoration; sometimes to pray for His grace, sometimes to offer Him your sufferings, and sometimes to return Him thanks for the favors He has given you, and still gives you, in the midst of your troubles, and to console yourself with Him the oftenest when you are in company; the least little remembrance will always be acceptable to Him. You need not cry very loud; He is nearer to us than we are aware of.[75]

Frank Laubach has written a small booklet called *The Game with Minutes,* in which he offers suggestions on how to follow Brother Lawrence's advice. The goal, he says, is "to have God in mind each minute you are awake."[76] This is not impossible for those who will discipline themselves, he says, since reminders of God are everywhere. "Every tree, every cloud, every bird, every orchestra, every child, every city, every soap bubble is alive with God to those who know his language."[77]

God is sovereign, but God is near. That both of these should be true is a marvel beyond comprehension. That the absolute Lord of the universe is by my side, that I am in the immediate presence of the King of kings and Lord of lords—could there be any greater cause for wonder or praise?

---

74. Brother Lawrence, *The God-Illuminated Cook: A New Edition of the Practice of the Presence of God,* ed. Robin Dawes et al. (Callicoon, N.Y.: Lifesavers Library, 1975), p. 89.

75. Ibid., pp. 95-96.

76. Frank C. Laubach, *The Game with Minutes* (Syracuse, N.Y.: New Readers Press, 1960), p. 7.

77. Ibid., p. 27.

Chapter Eight

THE WILL OF GOD

It is probably true that nothing has perplexed Christians more than questions about the will of God. If God is the Sovereign Ruler of the universe, should we not be able to say that "whatever happens is the will of God"? But how does this apply to specific events, especially those that bring tragedy and suffering? A young baby dies of cancer. Is this truly "God's will"? A young mother or father is seriously injured in an accident. We pray earnestly for her or his recovery; but we piously add, "Thy will be done." If recovery is denied and death ensues, has "God's will" been done? A college student is convinced that God has a particular, ideal plan for each individual's life. Thus he agonizes over the question, "What is God's will for *my* life?" Trying to find a sure formula for "how to know the will of God" is the preoccupation of many Christians.

These and other questions concerning the will of God are part of the larger subject of providence; thus we shall attempt to deal with them at this point. We may begin by listing the main New Testament words which express the concept of "the will of God." The first is *prothesis* (verb, *protithēmi*), which is usually translated "purpose" (e.g., Rom. 8:28; 9:11; II Tim. 1:9). The second is *boulē* (verb, *boulomai*), which means "purpose, will, counsel" (e.g., Acts 2:23; 4:28; Eph. 1:11). A third term is *eudokia*, meaning "good pleasure, desire," as in Ephesians 1:5, 9; Philippians 2:13. The fourth term is *thelēma* (verb, *thelō*), which means "will, desire" (e.g., Matt. 7:21; 18:14; Rev. 4:11). The final term is *epitrepō*, a verb meaning "to permit" (see I Cor. 16:7; Heb. 6:3). Though these words reflect some distinct connotations, few conclusions can be drawn from a word study alone, since the words tend to overlap in meaning to a great extent. Thus our theological distinctions and conclusions will depend to a large degree on how the words are used in context and how they are related to the larger subject of sovereignty and free will.

As we proceed through this chapter, we shall see first of all that the concept of the will of God has three main connotations, roughly corresponding to the ideas of purpose, desire, and permission. Then we shall see how this relates to the notion that God has an individual will for each person's life. Finally we shall give some attention to the question of interpreting providence, i.e., whether we can discern if a particular event occurs as the result of God's purpose, God's desire, or God's permission.

IS EVERYTHING THAT HAPPENS "THE WILL OF GOD"?

Since God is the Sovereign Ruler of the universe, he is in complete control of everything. He has the final word with regard to anything that happens. Nothing escapes his sovereignty. Then is it correct to say, "Whatever happens is the will of God"? The answer is yes. *Whatever happens is the will of God.*

But this must be carefully qualified. Unless certain important distinctions are made, this idea can be theologically misleading and personally devastating. It is true that whatever happens is God's will, but not always in the same sense. This is extremely important. In fact there seem to be three different senses in which this term, "the will of God," is used. Whatever happens is God's will in one or the other of these senses, but it makes a world of difference as to which of these senses applies in certain cases.

Our goal in this section is to explain the three aspects or connotations of the will of God. As already indicated, these are not delineated neatly by three specific biblical words. Nor are there three sharp and crisp English words which capture these three connotations precisely, though a number of suggestions have been offered. Some suggest that God's will is either purposive, preceptive, or permissive. Others prefer the terms purposive, provisional, and permissive. Sam Stone suggests that we speak about what God performs, what he prefers, and what he permits.[1] Above I have spoken of God's purpose, God's desire, and God's permission. Each of these suggestions has some validity, and each could apply with some degree of appropriateness to the three categories presented below. I do not have an exclusive preference for any one of them, although Stone's terminology seems to apply very well.

I am posing the question here in terms of what actually happens, not in terms of what may happen or could happen ideally. Everything that actually happens falls within the will of God in one of three senses. It may happen 1) according to God's desire and God's decision. Or it may happen 2) according to God's desire and man's decision. Finally, it may happen 3) according to man's decision and God's permission. Every event falls into *one* of these categories, but *only* one. There is no overlapping.

---

1. Sam Stone, "Knowing God's Will, Part Three: Man Should Choose God's Will," *The Lookout* (April 13, 1980), 92:3.

God's Desire and God's Decision

Some events occur because God wants them to occur *and* because he himself takes whatever steps are necessary to see that they do occur. God wills them to happen in the sense that he deliberately chooses to *cause* them to happen. This is sometimes called God's sovereign will because he will sovereignly see that it is carried out; it is not dependent upon or conditioned upon any contingency whatsoever. It is sometimes called his determined will, because it refers to what God determines to accomplish (as over against what he commands others to do, for instance). Sometimes it is called his purposive will since it is what God purposes to do by his own power and might. It is also called his decretive will in that it refers to what he determines to bring to pass in his eternal decree. It could be called his predetermined or foreordained or predestined will, since the determination to accomplish its objectives was made before anything was even created. No matter what term one chooses, the main point is that God not only desires these things to happen; he also determines that they will happen or causes them to happen. "God wills it" means in effect "God causes it."

The Determinist View

This aspect or understanding of the will of God is very important in the determinist system of theology, since it is for all practical purposes equivalent to the eternal, comprehensive decree. God's decretive or determining will is thus seen as universal and all-inclusive. *Everything* is the will of God in the same sense, i.e., in the sense that he determines it. J. G. Howard calls this the "determined will of God" and includes everything in it. He declares,

> Scripture teaches us that God has a predetermined plan for every life. It is that which *will happen*. It is inevitable, unconditional, immutable, irresistible, comprehensive, and purposeful. It is also, for the most part, unpredictable. It includes everything—even sin and suffering. It involves everything—even human responsibility and human decisions.

God "does it all on His own," Howard continues. "He does not react to situations; He creates them. . . . Everything that happens, happens within the determined will of God."[2] "Your career, marriage partner, home location, grades in school, friends, sicknesses, accidents, honors,

---

2. J. Grant Howard, Jr., *Knowing God's Will—And Doing It!* (Grand Rapids: Zondervan, 1976), p. 12.

travels, income, retirement, etc., are all part of God's determined will but are not revealed to you ahead of time."[3]

In a popular book called *Decision Making & the Will of God,* Garry Friesen makes the same point about what he calls the sovereign will of God, which "can be defined as God's predetermined plan for everything that happens in the universe."[4] "He is the Ultimate Determiner of everything that happens. He does have a sovereign will." Friesen says it is "exhaustive."[5]

Berkhof agrees, saying that "Christian theology has always recognized the will of God as the ultimate cause of all things."[6] This "decretive will" is that "by which He purposes or decrees whatever shall come to pass."[7] This language is similar to that of Bavinck: "God's decree is his eternal purpose whereby he has foreordained whatsoever comes to pass. Scripture everywhere affirms that whatsoever is and comes to pass is the realization of God's thought and will, and has its origin and idea in God's eternal counsel or decree."[8] Thus "the final answer to the question why a thing is and why it is as it is must ever remain: 'God willed it,' according to his absolute sovereignty."[9] Besides the various passages cited in our discussion of special providence in earlier chapters, the favorite proof text for this view is Ephesians 1:11, which says that God "works all things after the counsel of His will." There are no exceptions; everything is included, such as sins, sickness, child abuse, torture, accidents, unbelief, and the consignment of unbelievers to hell.

But obviously this cannot be the whole picture for the determinist, since the Bible says that some things that happen are not willed by God. For instance, II Peter 3:9 says God does not will that any should perish, but some do perish nevertheless. How is this explained? The determinist's answer is that God has two wills. In addition to the all-inclusive decretive will which is infallibly accomplished, there is the

---

3. Ibid., p. 15.

4. Garry Friesen with J. Robin Maxson, *Decision Making & the Will of God: A Biblical Alternative to the Traditional View* (Portland, Ore.: Multnomah Press, 1980), p. 32. See p. 82.

5. Ibid., p. 202.

6. Louis Berkhof, *Systematic Theology* (London: Banner of Truth Trust, 1939), p. 76.

7. Ibid., p. 77.

8. Herman Bavinck, *The Doctrine of God,* ed. and tr. William Hendriksen (Grand Rapids: Eerdmans, 1951), p. 369.

9. Ibid., p. 371.

preceptive or moral will, which consists of the laws and duties which men are commanded to live by. Whether or not this will is accomplished depends upon human choices, since man can disobey God's commands.[10] Passages such as II Peter 3:9 and I Timothy 2:4 are said to be speaking of God's moral will.[11]

It is important to see that for the determinist these are not two different aspects of God's will in the sense that some things fall into the first category and some fall into the second. This can hardly be the case, since the decretive will is all-inclusive. They are rather like two levels of his will. The *decretive* will is the higher (or deeper) level; it is secret, hidden, and inaccessible. God has determined what he intends to do so that the course of history is absolutely fixed; but he has not told us very much of this, except in predictive prophecies. Once a thing happens, of course, then it is no longer hidden. The *preceptive* will is the revealed will of God; God has seen fit to make this level of his will known to us. This distinction between the secret and revealed will of God, which is quite common in determinist theology,[12] is said to be reflected in Deuteronomy 29:29, "The secret things belong to the Lord our God, but the things revealed belong to us and to our sons forever, that we may observe all the words of this law."

What this means is that sometimes on the level of his revealed will God expresses a *desire* for something to happen which he *decrees not* to happen on the level of his secret will. For instance, I Timothy 2:4 says that God "desires" (a form of *thelō*) that all men be saved and come to the knowledge of the truth. This expresses God's desired or preceptive will. But obviously all men do *not* come to the knowledge of the truth and are *not* saved, which means that God's sovereign, decretive will, his secret will, has determined that this shall not happen. Also, II Peter 3:9 says that God is "not wishing" (a form of *boulomai*) for any to perish but for all to come to repentance. But this is only God's moral will; since some *do* perish, it must be his sovereign, secret will that they not repent and that they perish. Nevertheless, at least in the mind of the determinist, "the decretive and preceptive will of God can never be in conflict."[13]

---

10. Garry Friesen, *Decision Making & the Will of God*, p. 151; Louis Berkhof, *Systematic Theology*, p. 77.

11. Garry Friesen, *Decision Making & the Will of God*, pp. 232-233.

12. See Louis Berkhof, *Systematic Theology*, pp. 77-78; Herman Bavinck, ***The Doctrine of God***, pp. 237-238; Charles Hodge, *Systematic Theology* (Grand Rapids: Eerdmans reprint, n.d.), I:403-404.

13. Charles Hodge, *Systematic Theology*, I:404.

The Biblical View

There *is* such a category as the decretive or purposive will of God, i.e., that which God purposes to accomplish himself. I have referred to it as the things which happen by God's desire and God's decision. The concept of God's purpose is definitely taught in Scripture. This differs from the determinist view, however, in that the Scriptural concept of God's decretive will does *not* include *everything* that happens. This is in accord with the reality of relative independence as God has granted it to both natural processes and his free moral creatures. God does not cause everything, but he does cause or determine *some* things. He wills that some things shall definitely occur. As Proverbs 19:21 says, "Many are the plans in a man's heart, but the counsel of the Lord, it will stand." "The counsel of the Lord stands forever, the plans of His heart from generation to generation" (Ps. 33:11). Isaiah 14:27 says, "For the Lord of hosts has planned, and who can frustrate it? And as for His stretched-out hand, who can turn it back?"

What are the things that Scripture says are included within the decretive will of God, those things which God desires to occur and decides to accomplish? The first is the creation itself. Revelation 4:11 says that everything that exists was created because of God's will (*thelēma*). The next significant event after the creation was the Fall of man, the sin of Adam and Eve. But there is absolutely nothing in the Bible to suggest that God decreed or determined that this should happen. Once it did happen, or rather, once God foreknew that it would happen, he purposed to accomplish the work of redemption through the incarnate Son of God, Jesus Christ. This then becomes the central element of God's purposive will. According to Acts 2:23, Jesus was "delivered up by the predetermined plan and foreknowledge of God." It was God's will or plan (boulē) from the beginning that the Savior would be delivered up unto death; his foreknowledge of Judas' character and inclinations enabled him to use the betrayer's free choices to bring this about. Acts 4:28 says that when Jesus' enemies put him to death, they were only doing "whatever Thy hand and Thy purpose [*boulē*] predestined to occur." The redemptive act was purposed by God. That is, it was purposed that it would occur; it was predestined to happen. This does not mean that God caused Judas to betray Jesus or the Romans to nail him to the cross; again, he used what he foreknew about their free choices as a means of working out his infallible plan.

Very often in Scripture the redemptive mission of Jesus is referred to as "the will of God." Jesus declared, "My food is to do the will of

Him who sent Me, and to accomplish His work" (John 4:34). "I do not seek My own will, but the will of Him who sent Me," he said (John 5:30). The words of Psalm 40:6-8 are put into the mouth of Jesus by the inspired writer of Hebrews: "Behold, I have come . . . to do Thy will, O God" (Heb. 10:7). When Jesus "gave Himself for our sins" to deliver us from this present age, he did so "according to the will of our God and Father," says Paul (Gal. 1:4). In the extremity of Gethsemane Jesus prayed for the cup of suffering to be removed from him, but he yielded himself to the Father with these words: "yet not My will, but Thine be done" (Luke 22:42). The will of the Father—the purposive, decretive will—was that Jesus should drink the cup of redemptive suffering for every one (Heb. 2:9).

With the saving death of Jesus as the central focus of God's purposive will, most of the other things that are included therein either lead to it or flow from it. This includes especially God's sovereign choice of Israel as the unique instrument of preparation, along with all the acts of special providence related to her history. God first established this unchangeable purpose (*boulē*) with Abraham (Heb. 6:17), then with other specific individuals in the line of Abraham. For instance, it was God's purpose (*prothesis*) to choose Jacob rather than Esau as the son of Isaac through whom the preparation for redemption would be continued (Rom. 9:11). David was also selected to serve God's purpose (*boulē*), according to Acts 13:36. If God purposed for someone or some nation to participate in this great historical drama, there was no resisting his will (Rom. 9:18-19). We have already seen how this was so in our study of special providence. Time after time God's purposive will included his determination to use or punish a particular nation in the process of refining Israel for her task. The prophets continually praised God for these specific elements of his plan, including "what the Lord of hosts has purposed against Egypt" (Isa. 19:12); "the plan of the Lord which He has planned against Edom, and His purposes which He has purposed against the inhabitants of Teman" (Jer. 49:20); and "the purposes of the Lord against Babylon" (Jer. 51:29). Regarding his plan to use Sennacherib king of Assyria the Lord says, "Have you not heard? Long ago I did it, from ancient times I planned it. Now I have brought it to pass" (Isa. 37:26). Regarding his own people God's purposive will determined her conquest and captivity: "The anger of the Lord will not turn back until He has performed and carried out the purposes of His heart" (Jer. 23:20). But he also planned to deliver them from captivity: "'For I know the plans that I have for you,' declares the Lord, 'plans for welfare and not for calamity to give you a future and a hope'" (Jer. 29:11). Regarding all these and other aspects of God's special providence Isaiah says, "O Lord, Thou art my God; I will exalt Thee, I will give thanks to Thy name; for Thou hast worked wonders, plans formed long ago, with perfect faithfulness" (Isa. 25:1). As God declares, his purposes are sure: "My purpose will be established, and I will accomplish all My good pleasure . . . . Truly I have spoken; truly I will bring it to pass. I have planned it, surely I will do it" (Isa. 46:10-11).

Just as it was God's purpose to use Israel to bring the Redeemer into the world, so it was his purpose to nullify this arrangement once Christ had come. As we saw earlier in our discussion of Romans 9-11, this was partly a judicial punishment deserved by Israel because of her unbelief, and it was partly God's intention whether Israel had accepted the Messiah or not. The latter is true because the necessity for Israel's role as God's *exclusive* people ceased with the coming of Christ. Therefore God had purposed all along to merge all believing Israelites and all believing Gentiles into one new body called *the church.* This is the main point of the book of Ephesians, and it is the key to understanding the often-misused passage in Ephesians 1:1-11.

It is quite obvious that Ephesians 1 puts considerable emphasis on God's purposive will, or on what God desires and decides to do. Verse 5 says, "He predestined us to adoption as sons through Jesus Christ to Himself, according to the kind intention [*eudokia*] of His will [*thelēma*]." Verse 9 says, "He made known to us the mystery of His will [*thelēma*], according to His kind intention [*eudokia*] which He purposed [*protithēmi*] in Him." Then in verse 11 we read that "we have . . . been predestined according to His purpose who works all things after the counsel of His will." Here we find three words—*prothesis, boulē,* and *thelēma*—practically piled on top of one another in an effort to stress the concept of eternal purpose. The verse also says that God works "all things" after the counsel of his will. This is why determinists speak of an eternal decree that is all-inclusive and universal: does not Paul say *all things?*[14] But those who take this in an absolute sense have ignored the immediate context and the main theme of Ephesians as a whole. The

14. See J. Grant Howard, *Knowing God's Will,* pp. 53-54: "God is involved in all the circumstances of our lives. Ephesians 1:11 states that He 'works all things after the counsel of His will.' The context deals with the fact that salvation in all of its grandeur is ours because of what God has done for us in Christ. What has happened to the believer has happened because God is at work. As a matter of fact, says Paul, He is working all things (salvation and everything else) according to the counsel of his will."

term "all things" (*panta*) is not necessarily absolute and must be understood within the limitations imposed by the context. This is seen quite clearly in I Corinthians 12:6, which says that God is the one "who works all things [*panta*] in all persons." The language is exactly parallel to that of Ephesians 1:11; even the verb is the same (*energeō*). Yet the context of I Corinthians 12 clearly limits the reference to "all things" to spiritual gifts from the Holy Spirit, and verse 11 says so specifically: "But one and the same Spirit works all these things, distributing to each one individually just as He wills." In a similar way, the context of Ephesians 1:11 does not allow us to think of the "all things" in an absolute sense, but shows us the specific focus of God's purpose which is in view here.

What is this focus? The key to a proper understanding of this lies in Paul's reference to "the mystery of His will" in verse 9. What is the *mystery* of which Paul speaks here? He refers to it again in chapter 3, where he marvels that he in particular was given the privilege of knowing this mystery. He says that "by revelation there was made known to me the mystery, as I wrote before in brief. And by referring to this, when you read you can understand my insight into the mystery of Christ" (3:3-4). "To me," he exults, "the very least of all saints, this grace was given, to preach to the Gentiles the unfathomable riches of Christ, and to bring to light what is the administration of the mystery which for ages has been hidden in God" (3:8-9). We must be careful not to make the mystery too general, as if it were simply the fact of Christ or the fact of salvation. No, it is much more specific than this. Paul states it most specifically in 3:6, namely, "that the Gentiles are fellow-heirs and fellow-members of the body, and fellow-partakers of the promise in Christ Jesus through the gospel." This is the great mystery "which in other generations was not made known to the sons of men, as it has now been revealed to His holy apostles and prophets in the Spirit" (3:5). And the Apostle Paul, who was appointed to be the Apostle to the Gentiles, was simply overwhelmed at this fact. No one was more committed to Jewish exclusiveness than Saul of Tarsus; thus no one was more amazed at the fact that God was now, in Christ, abandoning that exclusiveness and uniting the Gentiles (the *Gentiles!*) with the Jews into a new kind of body called the church (3:10). In chapter two he comments on the fact that Jesus broke down the barrier that divided Jews and Gentiles and thus made the two groups into one new man, reconciling them both in one body to God through the cross (2:11-16). Even his reference to marriage—"the two shall become one flesh"—reminds him again of this great mystery, that the two groups

(Jews and Gentiles) have become one body in Christ and his church (5:31-32).

This is the same mystery that he is writing about in chapter one of Ephesians. Yes, God works *all things* after the counsel of his will, but what specific counsel or plan is in view here? The plan to unite the Jews and Gentiles in one body to the praise of his glory. This specific purpose is seen in the immediately-following verses, 1:12-14:

> . . . to the end that we who were the first to hope in Christ should be to the praise of His glory. In Him, you also, after listening to the message of truth, the gospel of your salvation—having also believed, you were sealed in Him with the Holy Spirit of promise, who is given as a pledge of our inheritance, with a view to the redemption of God's own possession, to the praise of His glory.

In these verses (as in 1:4-11) the "we" and the "you" refer to Jews and Gentiles. In this case Paul identifies himself with the Jews, whom he calls "the first to hope in Christ." In the previous verses he dwells on God's purpose for the Jews as a nation: how God chose them ("us") before the foundation of the world, how he predestined them to adoption as sons, how he offered them the gospel of grace first.[15] It should be noted that the references to predestination in Ephesians 1 are strictly speaking of the predestination of the *nation* of Israel, not of individual believers. His main emphasis up through verse twelve is on God's purpose for the Jews ("us"). But then in the next verses he begins speaking in the second person, "you," i.e., you Gentiles. In verse twelve he says that "we who were the first to hope in Christ" were used to the praise of his glory, but now "*you also*" have been brought into the sphere of salvation "to the praise of His glory." This is the theme he continues to develop, then, in chapters two and three especially.

Thus we see that the "all things" in Ephesians 1:11 does not have a universal reference; God's purposive or decretive will does not include all things that happen in the whole scope of nature and history. It does include the establishment of the church, however, as the body which unites Jews and Gentiles under the one head, Jesus Christ. This is probably the main reference in Ananias' commission to Saul of Tarsus

15. See Romans 1:16, "to the Jew first and also to the Greek." See also Romans 2:9-10.

in Acts 22:14, "The God of our fathers has appointed you to know His will."[16] See also Colossians 1:27.

Another aspect of God's purposive will is the manner in which this new unified body in Christ is constituted. Prior to Christ God purposed to enter into a covenant relationship with all who were descended by natural birth from Abraham through Isaac and Jacob. But in the Christian age it is God's purpose to call his children only those who are born in a different way, namely, those who are born again, of water and Spirit, through the word. As John 1:12-13 says, "But as many as received Him, to them He gave the right to become children of God, even to those who believe in His name, who were born not of blood, nor of the will of the flesh, nor of the will of man, but of God." The birth that brings one into God's family or kingdom is not one that a man can accomplish by an act of his own will. A sinner can receive Jesus and believe in his name, but the work of the new birth or regeneration is something that only God can perform. Jesus says, "Unless one is born of water and the Spirit, he cannot enter into the kingdom of God" (John 3:5). A sinner can meet the Lord in the baptismal water and trust that God is there giving him the promised Spirit (Acts 2:38-39), but he will not be able to see the Spirit and the Spirit's work any more than he can see the wind (John 3:8). It is a spiritual act. James 1:18 says, "In the exercise of His will He brought us forth by the word of truth, so that we might be, as it were, the first fruits among His creatures." We are brought forth or born by believing and following the promises and instructions in the word of God, but it is an exercise of God's will that causes the birth to take place. Thus when God calls us "according to His purpose" (Rom. 8:28), this is how he does it: he calls us through the word to receive the Spirit in Christian baptism in an act of spiritual rebirth. Such is God's purpose for the gathering of his family in the New Testament era. See II Timothy 1:9.

Finally we may note that God's purpose will culminate in the work of "bringing many sons to glory" (Heb. 2:10). It has been God's plan from the beginning to glorify all those whom he is now calling according to the terms which he has purposed. That is, he has determined to raise them from the dead and give them an immortal body like that of the risen Christ. "For this is the will of My Father," says Jesus, "that

16. Paul quite rightly understood his very appointment as an apostle to the Gentiles as a part of this purposive will of God. He refers to himself regularly as "an apostle of Jesus Christ by the will of God" (I Cor. 1:1). See II Corinthians 1:1; Ephesians 1:1; Colossians 1:1; II Timothy 1:1.

every one who beholds the Son, and believes in Him, may have eternal life; and I Myself will raise him up on the last day" (John 6:40). Through his foreknowledge God knew who these would be even before the creation; thus he could predestine them to glory even then. "For whom He foreknew, He also predestined to become conformed to the image of His Son, that He might be the first-born among many brethren" (Rom. 8:29).

We have seen that the things which happen according to God's desire and God's decision have to do mainly with the working out of the plan of redemption. They do not include "whatever happens." There is no biblical basis whatsoever for a *secret, all-inclusive,* determining will of God. God does have a determining or purposive will, but he has revealed his purposes to us. Paul told the Ephesian elders that he had proclaimed "the whole purpose [*boulē*] of God" among them (Acts 20:27). God has hidden nothing from us; we know the main points of his intentions for us and for the world. And we know that if God has purposed it, it will surely come to pass.

God's Desire and Man's Decision

Some of the things that God desires he has decided to accomplish himself. But there are many things which God desires that may or may not be accomplished, because he has left it up to man to decide whether they shall be done or not. In the exercise of his sovereign freedom God created mankind with free will and relative independence. Subsequently he has expressed his will to man in the sense of what he desires of us. God honors the integrity of the freedom with which he endowed us and permits us to make the decision as to whether his desires shall be fulfilled. Sometimes, to our shame and destruction, they are not. But very often we who have been given this responsibility do carry out the desired will of our Creator. Many things thus occur according to God's desire and man's decision.

Sometimes this aspect of God's will is called his desired or his preferred will. This is accurate, but it is not precise enough. God also desires the things which he himself purposes to accomplish. The distinctive factor about this particular aspect of God's will is not his desire, but the fact that man's decision will determine whether it occurs or not. Another term commonly used here is the preceptive or moral will of God, but this is too limited. It refers to only one part of the things which God desires and man decides. Some of the things that fall into this category are not exactly precepts or commandments, but are best thought of as things that God just desires or wants.

God's Precepts

The concept of God's preceptive will is valid and constitutes a major part of this general category. The Bible often speaks of God's will in the sense of his commandments or laws which we are expected to obey. On the one hand, much emphasis is placed on the necessity of *knowing* God's will. It has been revealed to us in Scripture, to be sure, but we still have the responsibility of studying it and meditating on it in order to see how we should apply it to our everyday decisions. "So then do not be foolish, but understand what the will of the Lord is," says Ephesians 5:17. In Colossians 1:9 Paul says he has "not ceased to pray for you and to ask that you may be filled with the knowledge of His will in all spiritual wisdom and understanding." In Romans 2:18 Paul speaks of hypocrites who "know His will" and even teach it, but do not obey it themselves.

This leads to the other emphasis found in Scripture, namely, that we should be diligent to *do* or *obey* God's prescriptive will. We should be "willing to do His will" (John 7:17); we should be "doing the will of God from the heart" (Eph. 6:6). God can equip us "in every good thing to do His will" (Heb. 13:21). Jesus says, "For whoever shall do the will of My Father who is in heaven, he is My brother and sister and mother" (Matt. 12:50; see Mark 3:35). "Not every one who says to Me, 'Lord, Lord,' will enter the kingdom of heaven," he says, "but he who does the will of my Father who is in heaven" (Matt. 7:21). Thus we should be diligent to "prove what the will of God is" (Rom. 12:2), i.e., to put it to the test in our own lives, for "the one who does the will of God abides forever" (I John 2:17). Thus "you have need of endurance, so that when you have done the will of God, you may receive what was promised" (Heb. 10:36).

This is how God guides us, namely, through his revealed preceptive will. "With Thy counsel Thou wilt guide me, and afterward receive me to glory" (Ps. 73:24). "For such is God, our God forever and ever; He will guide us until death" (Ps. 48:14). "And the Lord will continually guide you," says Isaiah 58:11. Thus we are exhorted to "stand perfect and fully assured in all the will of God" (Col. 4:12) and to live "for the will of God" (I Peter 4:2).

God's Desires

It is clear from the above passages that the term "will of God" occurs quite often with the connotation of God's preceptive will. It is also clear that this will, being left to man's decision for its fulfillment, is thwarted and not carried out on countless occasions. Every sin frustrates God's will in this sense of the word. But there are other instances where God's will is spoken of in the more general sense of his desire for us, where the idea of precept does not seem to be prominent but where it is still possible for man's decisions to frustrate God's desires. The clearest of such passages refer to God's desire for all men to be saved. The Lord "is patient toward you," says II Peter 3:9, "not wishing [*boulomai*] for any to perish but for all to come to repentance." God does *not* desire for any to perish, but in their stubborn rebellion many will perish anyway, thus going against what God desires. God also wants everyone to come to repentance, but not everyone does. Paul tells us that God "desires all men to be saved and to come to the knowledge of the truth" (I Tim. 2:4), but all do not. Likewise Jesus says that "it is not the will of your Father who is in heaven that one of these little ones perish" (Matt. 18:14).

There are other occasions where God expresses his desires and indicates that their fulfillment is contingent upon human decisions. "I desire compassion, and not sacrifice," he says (Matt. 9:13; 12:7; see Hosea 6:6; Hebrews 10:5, 8). The scribes and Pharisees "rejected God's purpose [*boulē*] for themselves, not having been baptized by John" (Luke 7:30). Peter says that "such is the will of God that by doing right you may silence the ignorance of foolish men" (I Peter 2:15). I.e., this is God's desire. Paul's statement in I Thessalonians 4:3 also seems to fit here: "For this is the will of God, your sanctification." God has given us precepts to obey, and he desires that we obey them and attain sanctification. With regard to Jesus' desires, Mark 7:24 tells us that once Jesus entered a house for a rest and "wanted no one to know of it; yet He could not escape notice."

Perhaps the most pointed reference to this aspect of God's will is found in Matthew 23:37, when Jesus lamented, "O Jerusalem, Jerusalem, who kills the prophets and stones those who are sent to her! How often I wanted to gather your children together, the way a hen gathers her chicks under her wings, and you were unwilling." Here we see very clearly that God's desires are sometimes thwarted by man's decisions. Some think that this destroys the sovereignty of God; that is why they have invented the concept of a sovereign, secret will whereby God actually decides everything that happens. But in view of this and other passages, that would put us in the awkward position of saying that God sometimes does things (according to his secret will) contrary to his own desires (as known from his revealed will). We would be saying that God *desires* that all should repent and be saved, just as Jesus desired to gather Jerusalem under his saving power, but that he has *determined* that some shall *not* repent and be saved. There is no way for a determinist to explain away the conflict that is evident here.

The problem is resolved, though, when we see that these two aspects of God's will (his determined will and his desired will, to use Howard's terms[17]) are not overlapping but are distinct and refer to completely different events. God's determined will is *not* all-inclusive, as we saw in the last section; there are many things which lie outside its scope. The things which God desires but which man must decide are of such a nature. They are not among the things which God has purposed one way or the other. They are a completely separate aspect of God's will. Thus there is no conflict or contradiction when a human decision goes against a desire of God or a precept of God, for such decisions are not the result of God's purposive will.

Man's Decision and God's Permission

The third and final aspect of the will of God includes those things which God neither purposes nor desires, but which he allows man in his freedom to bring to pass. Sometimes this is called God's *permissive will,* although the way this term is usually used is not exactly equivalent to this third category. In the most precise use of the term, God's permissive will embraces *all* the free acts of men including the ones in the second category above, namely, those which God desires of us but permits us to do of our own free choice. Thus, although at times, for the sake of convenience I may use the term *permissive will* for this third aspect of God's will, strictly speaking it is applicable to the previous category, too.

What makes this third category of events distinct is not the presence of God's permission, but the absence of a stated desire on God's part that they should happen. Though God does not purpose them nor expressly desire them, nevertheless he permits them to occur. This includes those things which are *contrary* to his stated desires, such as man's sins. These are within the will of God *only* in the sense that he permits them to happen. But this category also includes that whole host of things concerning which God has expressed no desire or preference, things which we sometimes call "matters of opinion" or "matters

17. J. Grant Howard, *Knowing God's Will,* p. 19.

of indifference." These are the decisions that we make, foreseen by God, the implementation of which he has no reason to prevent. Thus he permits or allows them to occur as we have planned.

This is an aspect of God's will not truly recognized by determinist theologians. As we have seen, they do speak of God's permission; but it is actually a part of God's *decretive* will or determining will. As Berkhof says, God's decretive will "is that will of God by which He purposes or decrees whatever shall come to pass, whether He wills to accomplish it effectively (causatively), or to permit it to occur through the unrestrained agency of His rational creatures." This is also the same as his secret will, which "pertains to all things which He wills either to effect or to permit, and which are therefore absolutely fixed."[18] But this must be qualified in two ways. As we have seen, in the determinist system the only things which fall within the range of God's permission are man's *sins*; no good works and no indifferent decisions are included here. These are all things which God *effects*. Also, as we have seen,[19] within the determinist system there is no true permission; the term is employed euphemistically as a device for relieving God of the responsibility for sin. Even the "permission" is efficacious. Thus even the things that are permitted are part of the decretive will of God.

But in Scripture this is not so. There are things which God does not determine and which he does not necessarily desire, things which God truly permits to be effected by man's decisions. For instance, Acts 14:16 refers to God's non-interference with the ways of heathen nations prior to Christ: "And in the generations gone by He permitted all the nations to go their own ways." This would include especially his allowing them to follow the way of idolatry and degradation, i.e., his permission of their sinful acts. Another example has to do with a desire of Paul that falls more or less into the area of opinion. He expresses his plan to spend a considerable amount of time with the Corinthian church: "For I do not wish to see you now just in passing; for I hope to remain with you for some time, if the Lord permits" (I Cor. 16:7). Paul recognized that he would be able to carry out his plan *only* if God permitted him to do so, because he knew that in his sovereign providence God could *prevent* such a visit if he so chose. Hebrews 6:3 speaks in a similar fashion. After stating in 6:1-2 the need for going deeper into the study of Christian doctrine, the writer says, "And this

18. Louis Berkhof, *Systematic Theology*, pp. 77-78.
19. See above, pp. 219ff.

we shall do, if God permits." The verb used in these last two passages is *epitrepō*, which is the ordinary verb meaning "to allow, to permit." A passage illustrating God's providential power to hinder man's decisions is Acts 16:7, which says that "when they had come to Mysia, they were trying to go into Bithynia, and the Spirit of Jesus did not permit them." The verb here (as in Acts 14:16) is *eaō*, which also means "to permit." In all of these passages we see either God exercising his permissive will or the biblical writers recognizing the sovereign control of his permissive will.

Several passages in the New Testament make the same point, but use the verb *thelō*, which means "to desire, to will." In these passages the concept of permissive will is quite specific. One is Acts 18:21, where Paul says, "I will return to you again if God wills." Another is I Corinthians 4:19: "But I will come to you soon, if the Lord wills." The thought in these verses (and even the word structure in the latter) is identical with that of the verses that read "if God permits." There is no reason to think that Paul is talking about either God's determination or God's desire. It is not "if God causes it" nor "if God desires it," but "if God permits it."

One other passage that clearly teaches the concept of God's permissive will is James 4:13-15. James reprimands those who make plans without taking account of God's providential control over all things: "Come now, you who say, 'Today or tomorrow, we shall go to such and such a city, and spend a year there and engage in business and make a profit.' Yet you do not know what your life will be like tomorrow." Then James tells us the proper way to state our plans: "Instead, you ought to say, 'If the Lord wills, we shall live and also do this or that.'" Here "if the Lord wills" is identical in form and meaning to "if the Lord permits." We will note that James says first of all that we will be *living* tomorrow only if the Lord permits. "In Him we live" (Acts 17:28); if he should decide at any moment to withdraw our life, he could do so. But in most cases, he permits us to continue to live. The same is true of any plans we may have for tomorrow or any time in the future. God may permit us to attempt to carry them out without interfering; but if for any reason he thinks it would be best, he could prevent it in a thousand different ways.

Several other New Testament passages are probably best understood in terms of God's permissive will. Paul prays concerning his desire to visit Rome that "perhaps now at last by the will of God I may succeed in coming to you" (Rom. 1:10). He asks the Roman Christians to pray "so that I may come to you in joy by the will of God" (Rom. 15:32). The prayer is that God would permit him to carry out his plan. When Agabus the prophet warned Paul against going to Jerusalem, Paul declared that he would go even if it meant that he would be killed for Christ (Acts 21:10-13). When Paul's companions saw that he could not be dissuaded, they simply said, "The will of the Lord be done!" (Acts 21:14). That is, whatever the Lord allows to happen, we will accept. This is probably the idea in I Peter 3:17 too: "For it is better, if God should will it so, that you suffer for doing what is right rather than for doing what is wrong." And I Peter 4:19: "Therefore, let those who suffer according to the will of God entrust their souls to a faithful Creator in doing what is right." Is Peter saying that God causes Christians to suffer or that he desires that they suffer? Probably not. Most likely he is saying that if God *permits* us to suffer, then we should accept it in the indicated manner.

It is very important to see that the idea of God's permissive will is a concept of sovereignty. Some think that anything less than causation or determination is a denial of God's sovereign Lordship, but this is simply not the case. The key to sovereignty is control, not necessarily causation. Through his absolute foreknowledge of every plan of men's hearts, and through his absolute prerogative and ability to either permit the fruition of each particular plan or to prevent it, God maintains a complete and sovereign control over the entire universe. Nothing can happen unless he permits it to happen; if he decides that it should not happen, he prevents it. The power to prevent means that God has the final word in everything. Psalm 2:1-4 presents a graphic picture of this kind of sovereignty. Here we see a group of rebellious world leaders plotting against the Lord: "Let us tear their fetters apart, and cast away their cords from us!" What is God's response? Does he pull their strings as if they were puppets? No, he simply lets them rage on, because he knows he is in control: "He who sits in the heavens laughs, the Lord scoffs at them." They forgot to say, "If the Lord permits"!

We should remember, too, that the idea of permission in this context is that of physical permission, not moral permission.

It is true, then, that "whatever happens is God's will." Everything that happens falls within the sovereign will of God in one sense or another. But it is crucial to see that there are three different senses in which this may be true, and that it is true in only one sense with regard to any given event or aspect thereof. Sometimes an occurrence is the will of God in the sense that he desires it and he decides it. It happens because God makes it happen. But as we have seen, this purposive will of God is limited in Scripture mostly to the working out of the plan of redemption. But sometimes an occurrence is the will of God in the sense that he desires it and then man decides to do what God desires. This applies mostly to God's commandments and to his desire for our salvation. Then finally, an occurrence sometimes is the will of God in the sense that a person or group of persons decide to bring it about, and God permits it to happen. These distinctions are crucial especially when we are confronted with tragedies and sufferings brought about by the sinful or careless acts of others, such as a murder or a fatal accident caused by a drunken driver. Unless we have very good reason to think otherwise, we should not say of such an event that it was "the Lord's will" in any purposive or causative sense. We can and must say that the Lord permitted it to happen, but this is true of most things that occur in the free-will universe that God created. Even a tragedy that occurs through the processes of nature must be regarded in the same way, since God has established a relative independence even in the natural realm. It is true that in his sovereign special providence God could prevent any event from occurring, including any disaster or tragedy. But we must also allow God to respect the integrity of the freedom that he has granted to his world, and we must trust his wisdom in knowing what good can be drawn from those tragic episodes that he permits to take place.

DOES GOD HAVE AN INDIVIDUAL WILL FOR EACH PERSON'S LIFE?

"What is God's will for my life?" Usually when this question is asked, the presumption is that God does have an individual, specific will for every person, that he has an ideal and detailed blueprint already drawn up for each individual's life. For every decision we face, there is a particular choice that God truly wants us to make. This applies to the kind of car he wants us to buy, the school he wants us to attend, the vocation he wants us to choose, the specific person he wants us to marry, and a countless host of lesser decisions. The only difficulty is that he has not spelled out his will on these matters in the pages of Scripture; he has left it up to us to figure it out in the best possible way. He has even left it up to us to figure out what is the best possible way to figure it out.

In his book *Decision Making & the Will of God,* Garry Friesen gives a good summary of this view:

> "God's *individual* will is that ideal, detailed life-plan which God has uniquely designed for each believer. This life-plan encompasses every decision we make and is the basis of God's daily guidance. This guidance is given through the indwelling Holy Spirit who progressively reveals God's life-plan to the heart of the individual believer. . . ."[20]
>
> "God wants to reveal His will to you more than you want to know it. God's ability to communicate His will is perfect. He never stutters. On the basis of God's desire to communicate and His ability to communicate, I can say to you that you can know God's will for your life with complete certainty."[21]

This is not Friesen's personal view, but rather his understanding of it as held by its advocates.

In pondering the perennial search for the will of God, Philip Yancey says that he made an important discovery, namely, that the Bible itself contains very little specific advice on the techniques of guidance. Even sections of Scripture that he previously thought were filled with specific advice, such as the Psalms, he discovered to be of a different nature altogether. Thus he concludes, "I cannot help thinking this whole issue of divine guidance, which draws throngs of seekers to seminars and sells thousands of books, is powerfully overrated. It deserves about as much attention as the Bible devotes to the topic."[22]

Garry Friesen has concluded that the usual approach to the question, as described above, is quite mistaken; and his book on *Decision Making* is a thorough refutation of it. "The idea of an *individual will* of God for every detail of a person's life is *not found in Scripture,*" he says. "It simply will not do to *assume* that God has a unique plan for each life that must be discovered as the basis for making decisions."[23] He shows that the rational and experiential arguments for this view are fallacious, and that the arguments from Scripture are guilty of faulty exegesis.[24]

Some of Friesen's points regarding the supposed Scriptural basis for the "traditional view" (as he calls it) are worth noting here. It is

---

20. Garry Friesen, *Decision Making & the Will of God,* p. 35.

21. Ibid., p. 30.

22. Philip Yancey, "Finding the Will of God: No Magic Formulas," *Christianity Today* (September 16, 1983), 27:27.

23. Garry Friesen, *Decision Making & the Will of God,* pp. 82-83.

24. Ibid., pp. 83ff.

argued, for instance, that the Bible is filled with examples of individuals for whom God had a specific plan, such as Moses, David, John the Baptist, and Paul. But Friesen rightly argues that these cannot be considered as normative for the average Christian's life. Each was highly unusual and had a unique relationship to the working out of God's redemptive plan. And perhaps most important of all, in the examples of the biblical individuals for whom God had a specific plan, that plan was communicated to them by special revelation, which is usually excluded as a means of knowing God's will today. Friesen concludes that the Bible contains "no normative examples of ordinary believers making decisions in the manner outlined by the traditional view."[25] I agree.

Another good point made by Friesen is that the biblical passages usually cited in support of an individual will actually refer to the moral or preceptive will of God instead. The passages he discusses are Proverbs 3:5-6; Psalm 32:8; Isaiah 30:20-21; Colossians 1:9; 4:12; Romans 12:1-2; Ephesians 2:10; and Ephesians 5:15-17. When these passages are studied in their contexts, as Friesen shows, "a stronger case can be made for understanding them in terms of the moral will of God" instead of an individual will.[26]

A final point to be noted from Friesen's book is his discussion of the widespread view that the indwelling Holy Spirit is a main source of guidance as to God's individual will. He rightly disputes the interpretation of Romans 8:14 and Galatians 5:18, which speak of being "led by the Spirit," as referring to inward guidance concerning personal decisions. As he says, the context of these passages has to do with the moral or preceptive will of God; the point is that the indwelling Spirit empowers us to obey God's commandments as revealed in Scripture.[27] Friesen also lays bare a very common hermeneutical blunder, i.e., the interpretation of John 16:12-14 as applying to individual Christians. In this passage Jesus speaks of the Holy Spirit thus:

> I have many more things to say to you, but you cannot bear them now. But when He, the Spirit of truth, comes, He will guide you into all the truth; for He will not speak on His own initiative, but whatever He hears, He will speak; and He will disclose to you what is to come. He shall glorify Me; for He shall take of Mine, and shall disclose it to you.

25. Ibid., pp. 89-92.
26. Ibid., p. 97. See all of chapter 6, pp. 97-115.
27. Ibid., pp. 137-139.

Friesen points out what should be an obvious fact to anyone who pays attention to such basic hermeneutical rules as the necessity for interpretating a passage in its context: these words are part of a private conversation and instructional session between Jesus and his apostles on the night before his death. This promise regarding the Holy Spirit was given specifically to the apostles, not to Christians in general.[28] It refers to revelation and inspiration and the writing of the Bible, not to inner guidance for individual Christians.

In basic agreement with Friesen, Charles Smith points out that following the so-called "rules" for *knowing* God's will as advocated by the "traditional view" may ironically cause one to *miss* God's will. For instance, one may miss God's will if he delays any service for the Lord while waiting for God to deal with him in the same way that he dealt with the apostles or other special servants in the Bible. Or, one may miss God's will if he delays any service while waiting to be "led by the Spirit."[29]

I agree with Friesen's main point, that God does not have an individual will for each person's life. Where does that leave us, then? Is the will of God irrelevant for our daily decisions? Should we never ask, "What is God's will for me in this situation?" No, this would be going to the opposite extreme. The will of God *is* relevant to our daily lives, particularly his moral or preceptive will as revealed in Scripture. This is the reference point for all decision making. The most sophisticated technique for "finding the will of God" is no substitute for a thorough knowledge of the commandments and general principles in the Bible. In what follows in this section I will suggest how this preceptive will of God is the key to our knowledge of the will of God for our personal lives.

First of all, it is obvious that some things are *required* by God's preceptive will. These are the things that God wants us to do and expects us to do. Whatever God commands us to do is his will for our lives. Where do we find God's preceptive will? Only in the pages of the Bible. Thus, in answer to the question, "How can I know God's will for my life?" we can say: look in the Bible! You can know the will of God for your life by reading and studying and meditating upon its moral teaching. If God *wants* you to do it, it's in the Book.

28. Ibid., pp. 139-140. An example of the incorrect understanding of this passage is found in J. Grant Howard, *Knowing God's Will*, p. 32: "This is the thrust of the teaching ministry of the Holy Spirit in the life of every believer. Predicted in John 14:26, 'He will teach you all things,' and John 16:13, 'He will guide you into all truth,' it is now that potential available to every believer."

29. Charles R. Smith, "How To Miss God's Will," *Spire* (Winter 1982), 10:3.

Secondly, not only are some things required by God's preceptive will; some things are *forbidden* by it. These are the things he does *not* want us to do. Sometimes we do them anyway (i.e., we commit sin), and God allows it according to his permissive will. But they are not God's will for us in the sense of what he *wants* us to do.

Before going on to the third point, we may note several characteristics of God's preceptive will as it relates to what he requires and forbids. For one thing, it is *objective* rather than subjective. Guidance concerning God's will does not come from within us, through inward, subjective impressions which are always subject to misinterpretation regarding origin and meaning. It comes rather from outside ourselves, from an objective source available in the same way to all. For another thing, God's preceptive will is *universal;* it is the same for all of us. This does not apply to those practices which God ordained for certain limited purposes and limited times, such as circumcision, animal sacrifices, and miraculous gifts. We are speaking rather of the eternal moral law of God which applies equally to all people in all ages. We may also note that God's preceptive will is usually *general* in nature. It is composed mostly of general moral principles that we must diligently and conscientiously apply to the specific issues which confront us. Even the most clearcut and straightforward commandments, such as "You shall not murder," are relevant to quite a broad spectrum of problems and require us to go from the general to the particular in making applications. Some comments on how to do this will be given shortly.

Now we come to the third point, which is quite crucial with regard to this whole issue of how to know God's will. We have seen that some things are specifically required by God's preceptive will and some things are forbidden by it. But this actuallly applies to only a relatively small number of acts and decisions. The fact is that most possibilities that confront us in decision-making situations are neither required nor forbidden by God's preceptive will; they are matters of indifference or matters of opinion. We may say that these are things that are *within* God's will, though they are not specifically required by it. In this category of things that are *within* the will of God, we have the freedom to make our own choices without worrying whether we have selected the only one that God really wanted.

We may illustrate this with a consideration of I Timothy 5:8, "But if any one does not provide for his own, and especially for those of his household, he has denied the faith, and is worse than an unbeliever."

This statement of God's moral will requires, among other things, that a parent provide nourishing food for his children. As long as this general requirement is met, the specific decision of whether to have hamburgers and green beans *or* macaroni and cheese and peas for supper *does not really matter to God.* He does not care whether we eat in the kitchen or the dining room. He does not care whether the beans are fresh or frozen. He does not care whether we have the hamburgers for supper or for breakfast.

The point is that as long as we are taking account of general requirements such as neighbor-love and good stewardship and honesty, God does not really care which specific choices we make on most decisions. There may be a whole range of choices, each of which is acceptable to God. Knofel Staton compares God's general moral will with an umbrella. "As long as we stay under that umbrella," he says, "we can choose from many alternatives in making our daily decisions. God allows us flexibility as long as we do not violate His revealed will."[30] Friesen calls these our "nonmoral decisions" and says they are to be guided by "the principle of freedom of choice within revealed limits."[31]

Understanding this point can be a really liberating experience for those who have been under the impression that God wants us to choose a specific way in every decision. In a chapter dealing with this point Friesen remarks,

> It may interest the reader to know that the most common response to the teaching of this chapter has been one of relief. As the truth of the principle of freedom within the moral will of God has sunk in, many have experienced a sense of release, as though they were being set free from some kind of burden. . . .[32]

The key to this relief is seeing the difference between "This *is* God's will" and "This is *within* God's will."

From a practical standpoint we should note that it is sometimes still difficult to make specific decisions even when we know the preceptive will of God and know that a whole range of choices are acceptable to him within its limits. We still find ourselves faced with two kinds of problems. First, there are those cases where the general moral will

30. Knofel Staton, *How to Know the Will of God,* revised edition (Cincinnati: Standard Publishing, 1979), p. 8.

31. Garry Friesen, *Decision Making & the Will of God,* pp. 151, 167.

32. Ibid., p. 171.

may be clear, but we are having difficulty applying it to a specific ethical issue. For example, we know it is wrong to murder, but is abortion murder? And if abortion is wrong, is *in vitro* fertilization also wrong, since it almost always involves the discarding of a number of fertilized ova as waste? Second, when making non-moral decisions, sometimes we cannot help but think that among all the *good* choices which fall under the umbrella, one of them must be the *best* choice; and surely we should look for that one.

Thus it seems that we still need some kind of help in "knowing the will of God." Does God provide this help? Yes, he does. It is promised in James 1:5; it is known as *wisdom*: "If any of you lacks wisdom, let him ask of God, who gives to all men generously and without reproach, and it will be given to him." Wisdom is not a magic formula, nor is it "instant omniscience," as Friesen notes.[33] Nor is it received passively; it must be actively sought and cultivated: "Acquire wisdom!" says Proverbs 4:5. For those who desire wisdom and pray for it and seek to cultivate it with God's help, here are some suggestions.

(1) Know as much about God as possible. "The fear of the Lord is the beginning of wisdom," says Psalm 111:10. The more we know about God, the more we will stand in reverence and awe before his holiness, and the more we will be sensitive to the things that are closest to his heart. This seems to be Yancey's point when he says that "the Bible contains very little specific advice on the techniques of guidance, but very much on the proper way to maintain a love relationship with God." What God wants, says Yancey, is "a conscious and willing acceptance of his presence whenever I make a decision. The spotlight of guidance shifts from technique to relationship."[34] Included here is not just knowledge *about*, but a knowledge *of* God. Yancey comments on the value of the Psalms as a model for this needed intimacy between man the decision-maker and his God. He notes that David is called "a man after God's own heart."

> . . . I now understand why. In his life, David always took God seriously. He intentionally involved God in every minor and major triumph and every minor and major failure. He railed at God, exalted him, doubted him, praised him, feared him, loved him. But regardless of what happened, God was never far from David's thoughts. David practiced the presence of God in daily details, and then took the time to keep a revealing poetic record of the intimacy between them. . . .[35]

33. Ibid., p. 195.
34. Philip Yancey, "Finding the Will of God," p. 27.
35. Ibid.

Such is the beginning of wisdom. If we never think of God except to pray for wisdom, we may as well not waste time praying.

(2) Know as much about God's word as possible. We may recall that wisdom has to do with how we use the knowledge we have. Knowledge is a prerequisite for it. Thus we should pray for wisdom, but not consider this to be a substitute for Bible knowledge. As Friesen says, James 1:5 is not "suggesting that wisdom is divinely injected 'intravenously' apart from a regular diet of God's revealed wisdom, the Bible."[36] Packer notes that "wisdom is divinely wrought in those, and those only, who apply themselves to God's revelation." We get wisdom "by soaking ourselves in the Scriptures, which, as Paul told Timothy . . . , 'are able to make thee *wise* unto salvation' through faith in Christ, and to perfect the man of God for 'all good works' (II Tim. 3:15-17)."[37]

(3) Know as much about life as possible. This is a tall order, and one that can be filled to a great extent only by experience. It involves the accumulation of facts, for without the proper facts some decisions cannot be responsibly made. If a person did not know, for instance, that *in vitro* fertilization usually involves the destruction of fertilized ova, it would be difficult to make a responsible decision. But knowing about life is more than the accumulation of facts; it is also a reflection upon them and an observing of how they affect life. It is the accumulation of what is often called "common sense." The fact that such comes only through experience is what makes the advice of our elders very important. Thus the seeking of wisdom will often involve consultation with those who have seen more of life than we have.

(4) The final suggestion is that we know as much about wisdom itself as possible. As Friesen says, it is not instant omniscience; it is not specific bits of knowledge fed into our minds like words imprinted on a computer screen. We do not wait until a specific decision is facing us, then pray for wisdom and expect God to flash the proper answer on the screen. Many have misunderstood wisdom in this way. Every time a situation arises calling for a decision, they say a prayer for wisdom. Then no matter what they decide, they assume that that particular decision was supplied to them by God. But wisdom does not work this way. It is not specific answers to specific questions, but rather a quality of the heart and mind, an ability to discern the best from the better and to apply the general to the specific. It is a *skill,* not a bit of information. As a skill it grows and increases with study and exercise and

36. Garry Friesen, *Decision Making & the Will of God*, p. 195.

37. J. I. Packer, *Knowing God* (Downers Grove, Ill.: InterVarsity Press, 1973), p. 91.

experience, and with God's help. By applying it we become more and more confident that our decisions are good ones, but we should not expect it to guarantee infallibility. Even a skilled basketball player sometimes misses a shot, and a skilled typist sometimes hits the wrong key. And even a wise person sometimes makes a bad decision. But we continue to develop and sharpen the skill of wisdom, trusting that God is helping us to become better at the craft of decision making.

IS IT POSSIBLE TO INTERPRET PROVIDENCE?

Is it possible to discern the will of God in or through the circumstances of life and history? Can we read or interpret the providential activity of God so as to know his will? When we observe a particular event or go through a personal experience, can we tell from that event or experience exactly what God is doing in it? Can we tell in what sense God's will is being done?

This is the question of whether or not it is possible to interpret or read providence. Many assume that this is the case. For example, those who hold the view of a secret, sovereign, universal, determinative will of God will say that everything that happens is God's purposive will. We cannot know ahead of time what God's will may be with regard to a particular situation; but once it has occurred, we can say with certainty, "That's what God wanted to happen. That was his purposive will. That is what he decreed."

Others have thought that it is possible to discern God's preceptive will from a right interpretation of providence. This was a very popular theme when the secularization fad went through Christendom in the 1960's, and it continues today to a large extent in liberation theology. The assumption here is that God does not work in the world merely through the church or through the gospel or by means of evangelism. Rather, God is working in the world in any situation where social justice and liberation are being fought for. The task of the church is to look around the world, see where such action is taking place, and join in. The church thus learns what God wants it to do by interpreting providence. For example, the *Plan of Union* prepared for the Consultation on Church Union states that the church must "recognize what it is that God is doing in the world and join him in his action."[38] "As Jesus Christ came to and is at work in the world, the church is called to pursue

38. *A Plan of Union for the Church of Christ Uniting*, II:16 (Princeton: Consultation on Church Union, 1970), p. 11.

his mission in the world. . . . This missional activity always addresses such specific social issues as peace, justice, hunger."[39] Another writer says, "The primary obedience of the Church is to find out where 'the action' is, to be sensitive to the points at which God is working in history on the frontiers of social change, and there to serve him in it."[40] Harvey Cox cites a dubious analogy. He says the church

> . . . is a people whose institutions should enable them to participate in God's action in the world—the liberation of man to freedom and responsibility. Archie Hargraves puts it graphically. He compares the work of God in the world, where Jesus Christ is present, to a "floating crap game" and the church to a confirmed gambler whose "major compulsion upon arising each day is to know where the action is" so he can run there and "dig it."[41]

For one final example of this way of thinking, at the 1967 Disciples of Christ convention Ian McCrae said in a speech to teenagers, "The young Christian not in politics in 1967 isn't working with God. . . . Decide where God is working in the political scene, then join in 'Making Whoopee' for God."[42] In all of these examples, a particular aspect of providence assumes the role of a commandment from God, ordering the church and the Christian to action.

There are many other ways in which Christians attempt to interpret providence. Those who believe in an individual will for each Christian try to discern partly from circumstances what that will is for a particular decision. Others read unusual events as signs from God, e.g., a minor heart attack may be interpreted as a warning from God to slow down. Others may consider disasters to be a punishment from God. And then, every Christian at one time or another reads certain providential activity as God answering their prayers.

What shall we say about this? Is it possible to interpret providence? Can we accurately interpret God's will in the events that occur around

---

39. Ibid., III:5, p. 16.

40. Richard P. McBrien, *The Church in the Thought of Bishop John Robinson* (Philadelphia: Westminster Press, 1966), p. ix; cited in Colin W. Williams, *New Directions in Theology Today, Volume IV: The Church* (Philadelphia: Westminster Press, 1968), p. 24.

41. Harvey Cox, *The Secular City*, revised edition (New York: Macmillan, 1966), p. 108. He is citing Archie Hargraves, "Go Where the Action Is," *Social Action* (February 1964), p. 17.

42. Russell Chandler, "Disciples Debate Community and Unity," *Christianity Today* (November 10, 1967), 12:56.

us? Generally speaking, the answer to such questions is no, with a qualification to be mentioned shortly. The problem lies in our inability to distinguish between God's purposive will and his permissive will without special revelation. We must remember that God's sovereign, purposive will is *not* universal in scope; it does not include "whatsoever comes to pass." Thus the determinist view, i.e., that once a thing has happened you know that it was God's purposive will, is false. It does not even take account of the fact that there *is* a separate, *permissive* will of God, in which God does not purpose or determine the things that occur but sovereignly allows them to happen through man's free choices. Now, whenever anything occurs as the result of a human action, it is really impossible for us to tell whether God is working out some purpose via special providence, or whether he is just permitting it to take place. That is, it is impossible to tell this without special revelation from God. This should be evident from Scripture. There we see that one of the main tasks of the prophets was to do this very thing, i.e., interpret God's providential activities to his people. Only God can give a sure interpretation of his own acts.

From another perspective it is impossible to interpret providence without special revelation because we are not able to discern whether a particular event is the result of God's general providence or whether it may be ascribed to his special providence. The former basically corresponds to God's permissive will, as both natural processes and human free will are allowed to operate via their relative independence. Only in the latter, in special providence, do we find God's special purposes being worked out. We must remember, too, that natural processes have been corrupted to some degree by the presence of sin in the world. Thus how can we know for sure whether a flood or a tornado or an earthquake is a purely natural event, an excess caused by the corruption of nature, or an act of special providence? Only God can give us the sure word on this.

Once we take it upon ourselves to interpret a particular event, we are almost sure to come into conflict with someone else's interpretation or with our own second thoughts. Or we find ourselves offering an exactly opposite interpretation to an exactly parallel event at another time. Tillett reflects on the problems we confront in such cases:

> Some people are much given to interpreting providence. Certain ills or misfortunes come to a bad man; they are quick to assert that it is a divine judgment sent upon him in view of his sin. Certain blessings come to a good man; they are sure the blessings are heaven-sent in view of

> his extraordinary piety. A den of vice perchance burns down: it is, say they, a divine judgment, in view of the owner's corrupt character and ill-gotten gains. But presently the property of an unquestionably pious and consecrated Christian man is swept away by the flames! A church building is struck by lightning and destroyed! What now is the "providence"? The "oracles" fail to explain; and so they do in innumerable other cases, as, for example, when two men, a saint and sinner, are prostrated on beds of sickness. The former, in spite of prayer and piety, continues to grow worse, and perhaps dies; while the other, without piety or prayer, is restored to health.[43]

Friesen makes a similar point when he suggests what various church members might say if the church steeple is struck by lightning. "God is telling us to relocate in the suburbs," one says. Another replies, "Oh no, I think it's quite obvious He's saying 'no' to our expansion plans." "Maybe the Lord is telling us that there is sin holding back the work in our church," says another.[44] Friesen's comment is short and to the point: "An event cannot communicate a message apart from divine revelation."[45]

An erroneous approach to providence that confuses God's purposive will with his permissive will is the idea that success is a sign of God's blessing. We might call this the Gamaliel fallacy, after the false principle offered by Gamaliel in Acts 5:38-39, "If this plan or action should be of men, it will be overthrown; but if it is of God, you will not be able to overthrow them." In this connection Berkouwer stresses the fact "that prosperity and success can never be confused with God's blessing."[46] There are many implications of this. The fact that a particular doctrine or church practice endures for centuries is no sign that it is from God or approved by God. The fact that it is accepted by the greater part of Christendom does not mean that it is true. The fact that a particular congregation or church denomination is growing by leaps and bounds does not mean that it has God's approval. The fact that a particular book is a best seller does not mean that its doctrine is sound. All of these things could fall within God's permissive will and be contrary to both his purpose and his desire.

---

43. Wilbur Fisk Tillett, *Providence, Prayer and Power* (Nashville: Cokesbury Press, 1926), p. 126.

44. Garry Friesen, *Decision Making & the Will of God*, p. 213.

45. Ibid., p. 215.

46. G. C. Berkouwer, *The Providence of God*, tr. Lewis B. Smedes (Grand Rapids: Eerdmans, 1952), p. 172.

Another erroneous approach that does not take account of God's permissive will is the one mentioned above in connection with secularization and liberation theology. In this case, God's permissive will is confused with his preceptive will. The corrective measure is the same, however: a sure knowledge of God's preceptive will, as in the case of his purposive will, is found only in the pages of Scripture.

The point is that we must curb our tendencies to offer quick and glib interpretations of events in terms of God's will. For example, in the fictional case of the church steeple's being struck by lightning as mentioned above, perhaps it was just the result of natural processes operating under God's general providence according to his permissive will, with no special purpose in it at all.

But now for the qualification mentioned above. While recognizing that we cannot give a sure interpretation of providence without a prophetic message from God, I believe that it is appropriate for a Christian to entertain his own private pious speculations as to what God *may* be doing in a particular event or situation. He may at times even have a strong conviction as to the meaning of an event. If he knows from Scripture what it is possible for God to do through his special providence, and if he knows the various aspects of the will of God, and if he maintains a close relationship with God, then he may suggest (at least to his own mind) that certain particular events seem to bear the stamp of God's special activity. Indeed, it is almost impossible for him *not* to meditate upon providence and upon the possibilities related to it. This is especially true with regard to answered prayer. How can a Christian who has prayed for a specific favor with perseverance and intensity avoid the conclusion that God has answered his prayers, if that particular favor becomes his? Such a conviction is proper, at least within the bounds of his own personal piety, even if a pagan neighbor received a similar favor without the benefit of prayer.

Above all the Christian will remember the words of Romans 8:28, that "God causes all things to work together for good to those who love God." Thus he does not *have* to burden his mind with the problem of whether a particular event in his own experience is God's purposive will or just God's permissive will. Whether it is one or the other, he knows for sure that whatever happens always has either a good *purpose* or a good *result*. More than this he can await heaven to find out.

Chapter Nine

PREDESTINATION*

One aspect of the purposive will of God that requires more detailed attention is the subject of predestination. This topic is closely related to the doctrine of salvation; and if that were its only theological point of reference, it would be more appropriate to deal with it in the next volume on God as Redeemer. But the general concept of predestination is broader than this. It actually includes everything that falls within the purposive will of God, everything that God desires and decides. The term *predestination* applies here since God's decisions to carry out all that he has purposed to do were made in eternity past, prior to the creation of the world. Everything that God purposed was predestined to occur.

There are two main aspects of predestination, and this chapter will deal with them in turn. The first has to do with predestination to *service*, or God's choice of individuals and groups to serve as instruments in the accomplishment of his purposes. The second has to do with predestination to *salvation* (or at least a certain aspect thereof), or his designation of certain individuals to share the glories of heaven for eternity.

Before turning to these main points we may briefly mention the relevant terminology. The New Testament terms that are especially relevant are the words *proöridzo,* meaning "to predestine, to predetermine, to decide beforehand"; and *eklegomai*, meaning "to elect, to choose, to select." Related terms are the adjective *eklektos*, meaning "elect" or "chosen"; and the noun *eklogē*, meaning "the election."

In the context of the doctrine of election there is no significant theological distinction between the words *predestine* and *elect.*[1] The word

---

* This is a revised version of an earlier essay entitled "Conditional Election." Any of the original material used here is reprinted by permission from *Grace Unlimited*, ed. Clark Pinnock, published and copyrighted 1975 by Bethany House Publishers, Minneapolis, Minnesota 55438.

1. Robert Shank attempts to distinguish them thus: "Both election and predestination are acts of determination, but the election is God's choice of men *per se*, whereas the predestination looks beyond the fact of election itself to the *purpose and objectives* comprehended in election." Also, he says, "election is the act whereby God chose men for Himself, whereas predestination is His act determining the *destination* of the elect whom He has chosen" (*Elect in the Son*; Springfield, Mo.: Westcott Publishers, 1970; p. 156). This distinction, however, is neither inherent in the terms nor warranted by the various contexts. The word *proöridzo* as such does not contain the idea of destination; nor is the use of the middle voice for *eklegomai* theologically conclusive (as Shank claims), since this is the common form of the word whenever used. That both terms are used with reference to the purposes, objectives, and circumstances of election is evident from a comparison of Romans 8:29-30 and I Peter 1:2. (See also II Thessalonians 2:13, where *haireomai*, a synonym for *eklegomai*, is used.)

predestine does include a time element by means of its prefix; and it may be a more general term in that it can refer to events as well as to persons, while *elect* is limited to persons. But no doctrinal point is at stake in these distinctions.

PREDESTINATION TO SERVICE

It is very important to see that the biblical doctrine of predestination is much broader in scope than election to eternal glory. Its broadest context is the total redemptive purpose of God. In choosing the cast for the grand drama of redemption, the Sovereign Ruler selected certain people to fill certain roles and to accomplish specific limited tasks.

The Election of Jesus

The primary character in the drama is the Redeemer himself, the one who must do what is necessary in order to set humanity free from sin's guilt and bondage. The one chosen for this role is Jesus of Nazareth, son of a humble Jewish maiden. He alone is qualified to accomplish this task because he alone, by God's plan, is the incarnate Son of God.

This election of Jesus is the central and primary act of election. All other aspects of election are subordinate to it and dependent upon it. It is the very heart of the redemptive plan.

Through Isaiah the prophet the Lord speaks of Jesus as the elect one: "Behold, My Servant, whom I uphold; My chosen one in whom My soul delights" (Isa. 42:1). Matthew 12:18 quotes this passage and refers it to Jesus. At the transfiguration God spoke directly from heaven and announced the election of Jesus in these words: "This is My Son, My Chosen One; listen to Him!" (Luke 9:35). As Peter says, Jesus is the choice or chosen cornerstone (I Peter 2:4, 6).

The election of Jesus was part of the divine plan even in eternity, before the worlds were created. Foreknowing both the obedience of the Redeemer and the disobedience of his enemies, God predetermined the accomplishment of redemption through Jesus of Nazareth (Acts 2:23; I Peter 1:20). Jesus was predestined or foreordained to die for the sins of the world (Acts 4:28).

The Election of Israel

Although Jesus has the leading role in the drama of redemption, there is a large cast of supporting characters. These are necessary in order to prepare the way for Christ's appearance upon the stage of history.

The primary element of God's preparatory plan was the election of Israel as the people who would produce the Christ. Deuteronomy 7:6 says, "For you are a holy people to the Lord your God; the Lord your God has chosen you to be a people for His own possession out of all the peoples who are on the face of the earth" (see Deut. 14:2). The Israelites were God's "chosen ones" (I Chron. 16:13). Paul begins his sermon in the synagogue at Antioch by reminding his fellow Jews that "the God of this people Israel chose our fathers, and made the people great during their stay in the land of Egypt" (Acts 13:17).

Several significant points about the election of Israel must be noted. In the first place, it was an election to service and not to salvation. Being chosen as the people from whom the Christ would come carried with it some of the highest privileges known to man (Rom. 9:4-5), but salvation was not necessarily among them. Whether an Israelite was saved or not did not depend simply on his membership in the chosen people. The nation could serve its purpose of preparing for the Christ even if the majority of individuals belonging to it were lost.

This leads to a second point, namely, that the election of Israel was the election of a group or a corporate body, not the election of individuals. As Daane says, "Divine election in its basic Old Testament form is collective, corporate, national. It encompasses a community of which the individual Israelite is an integral part."[2] Berkouwer grants that even Romans 9 must refer to the nation of Israel and not to the eternal destiny of individuals.[3] In other words, God's purpose of preparing for the Messiah was served through the nation as such, not necessarily through every individual member of the nation.

Since Israel was chosen specifically to prepare the way for the Messiah's appearance, her purpose was accomplished and her destiny fulfilled in the incarnation, death, and resurrection of Jesus Christ (Acts 13:32-33).[4]

---

2. James Daane, *The Freedom of God: A Study of Election and Pulpit* (Grand Rapids: Eerdmans, 1973), p. 104.

3. G. C. Berkouwer, *Divine Election*, tr. Hugo Bekker (Grand Rapids: Eerdmans, 1960), pp. 210ff. His main concern is to avoid the conclusion of individual reprobation as a symmetrical counterpart of individual election.

4. According to James Daane, "God's election of Jesus does fulfill the purpose of Israel's election" (*The Freedom of God*, p. 107).

The Election of Individual Servants

In the third place it must be noted that at times certain individuals were chosen for special roles in order to facilitate the purposes of God. Some of these were chosen in connection with Israel's purpose. In order to create Israel God chose Abraham, Isaac, and Jacob (see Neh. 9:7; Rom. 9:7, 13). He chose Moses (Ps. 106:23) and David (Pss. 78:70; 139:16), among others. He even chose certain Gentile rulers to help carry out his purpose for Israel (e.g., Pharaoh, Rom. 9:17; and Cyrus, Isa. 45:1).

Just as God chose certain individuals for special service in relation to Israel, so did he select a group of individuals who would be his instruments in establishing the church. From among his disciples Jesus "chose twelve of them, whom He also named as apostles" (Luke 6:13). Later he asked them, "Did I Myself not choose you, the twelve?" (John 6:70). Christ is speaking to the apostles when he says, "You did not choose Me, but I chose you, and appointed you, that you should go and bear fruit" (John 15:16; see 13:18; 15:19). Likewise was the Apostle Paul chosen for special service (Gal. 1:15-16).

Included in this chosen group, of course, was Judas himself, for Judas played a key predestined role in God's purpose of redemption. When Jesus was betrayed or delivered up unto death, it was "by the predetermined plan and foreknowledge of God" (Acts 2:23). The predetermined plan was that Jesus would die for the sins of the world; the circumstances of this plan, including Judas' role, were worked into it by virtue of God's foreknowledge of the life and works of all the individuals associated with Jesus. What Judas would do was known to Jesus even before he chose him as an apostle; this is no doubt why he was chosen. "Did I Myself not choose you, the twelve," said Jesus, "and yet one of you is a devil?" John tells us specifically that "He meant Judas the son of Simon Iscariot, for he, one of the twelve, was going to betray Him" (John 6:70-71).

The reference to foreknowledge in Acts 2:23 is very important. It shows that Judas did not betray Jesus because he was chosen to do so; rather, he was chosen because he would betray Jesus. This is the way we would understand God's predestination of the many other individuals whom he chose to have a part in his plan, too.

A point to remember is that the election of these individuals for some specific service in the history of redemption does not mean that they were chosen for personal salvation (or personal condemnation, for that matter).

The Election of the Church

The drama of redemption is not complete, of course, when Israel has finished her role. Neither has it ended when Christ has accomplished his saving work in history. Christ was chosen in order to redeem sinners and to bring them back into fellowship with God. Thus the drama is not complete until his redemptive work has borne its fruit, until there is a body of redeemed persons. These, too, are included in the historical enactment of the drama.

God had already decided to create on this side of the cross a new nation, a new Israel. Her role differs from that of Old Testament Israel. Her purpose is not the preparation for the coming of Christ, but rather participation in his saving work and the proclamation of it.

This new elect body is the church.

As was the case with Old Testament Israel, the election of the church is a corporate or collective election. The church as a body is now God's elect people, chosen to complete God's purpose of redemption. This corporate election of the church is reflected in Peter's reference to the "chosen race" (I Peter 2:9) and in John's description of local congregations as the "chosen lady" and her "chosen sister" (II John 1, 13).

As with Old Testament Israel, the election of the church is in part an election to service. The church is God's vehicle for the proclamation of the good news of redemption in Christ. When Peter describes the church as a "chosen race," he adds this purpose for the choosing: "that you may proclaim the excellencies of Him who has called you out of darkness into His marvelous light" (I Peter 2:9).

In many ways, then, Old Testament Israel and the New Testament church are parallel with respect to God's electing purpose. The election of each is a corporate election; each is elected to service (Israel for preparation, the church for proclamation); and as pointed out in the previous section, certain individuals are chosen for special roles in connection with each.

PREDESTINATION TO SALVATION

Regarding predestination there is one other similarity of extreme importance, namely, in both Old and New Testament times, in both Israel and the church, God not only predestined some individuals for service, but he also predestined some to salvation. We affirm this for Old Testament times by inference rather than by direct statement, since the specific teaching about soteriological predestination is found mainly in the New Testament. Though it is reasonable to make this inference regarding Old Testament election, the rest of this section will focus on predestination to salvation as it is described for those living in the church age.

It is quite clear from New Testament teaching that the church is elected not only for the proclamation of, but also for participation in, the saving work of Christ. The church is the very object of Christ's love and redemptive sacrifice (Acts 20:28; Eph. 5:25). We are chosen unto salvation (II Thess. 2:13). This raises the most controversial question associated with the whole subject of predestination, namely, what is the relationship of *individuals* to the process of election to salvation? Are individuals elected or predestined to be saved? If so, in what way?

Such questions as these, of course, have long been the center of confusion and controversy. Since the Reformation era no Biblical doctrine has been more misrepresented and more maligned than the doctrine of predestination (or election). Many people do not consider the idea to be Biblical at all. This is because they have equated it in their minds with a particular interpretation of predestination, namely, the determinist view developed by Augustine and made popular through the influence of John Calvin. Recognizing Calvinist predestination to be alien to the Bible, they dismiss it or explain it away altogether.

This is extremely unfortunate, since the doctrine of predestination is definitely Scriptural; and when rightly understood it is one of the most significant and rewarding teachings of the Bible. It enhances the majesty, wisdom, love and faithfulness of God; and it strengthens the heart of the believer. The whole counsel of God is not proclaimed when this doctrine is ignored.

In this section our purpose is to give a brief summary of the determinist view of predestination, and then to offer a fuller discussion of this subject as understood from the non-determinist point of view. The latter is my understanding of the biblical view.

The Determinist View: *The Unconditional Election of Individuals*

Probably the best-known view of predestination is the determinist version of the doctrine, which can be traced back to Augustine but which is usually associated with Calvinistic theology. Calvinism teaches that certain individuals are unconditionally elected or predestined to become believers in Jesus Christ and thus be saved. From among the total mass of sinful humanity, even before it has been created, God chooses which individuals he wants to respond to the gospel call. When the call is issued, those who have been chosen are irresistibly enabled to answer it. These are saved, while the rest of mankind are condemned to hell forever.

On what basis does God choose the ones whom he saves? This is known only to God himself, and he has determined not to reveal it. God has his own reasons for the decisions which he makes, but they cannot be known by men.[5] Thus from the standpoint of human knowledge, the election is totally unconditional. There are no established conditions which one may meet in order to qualify for being chosen.

This view was taught by John Calvin. In the *Institutes* he says,

> As Scripture, then, clearly shows, we say that God once established by his eternal and unchangeable plan those whom he long before determined once for all to receive into salvation, and those whom, on the other hand, he would devote to destruction. We assert that, with respect to the elect, this plan was founded upon his freely given mercy, without regard to human worth; but by his just and irreprehensible but incomprehensible judgment he has barred the door of life to those whom he has given over to damnation. . . .[6]

Also to the point is Calvin's statement that "God was moved by no external cause—by no cause out of Himself—in the choice of us; but that He Himself, in Himself, was the cause and the author of choosing His people."[7]

The Westminster Confession of Faith (III:5) explains it thus:

> Those of mankind that are predestinated unto life, God, before the foundation of the world was laid, according to his eternal and immutable purpose, and the secret counsel and good pleasure of his will, hath chosen in Christ, unto everlasting glory, out of his mere free grace and love, without any foresight of faith or good works, or perseverance in either of them, or any other thing in the creature, as conditions, or causes moving him thereunto; and all to the praise of his glorious grace.[8]

---

5. G. C. Berkouwer, *Divine Election*, p. 60.

6. John Calvin, *Institutes of the Christian Religion*, III.xxi.7, ed. John T. McNeill, tr. Ford L. Battles (Philadelphia: Westminster Press, 1960), II:931.

7. John Calvin, "A Treatise on the Eternal Predestination of God," *Calvin's Calvinism*, tr. Henry Cole (Grand Rapids: Eerdmans, 1956), p. 46.

8. *The Creeds of Christendom*, 4 edition, ed. Philip Schaff (New York: Harper and Brothers, 1919), III:609.

According to Calvinism, then, specific individuals are the object of election; and they are chosen unconditionally.

A Non-Determinist View: The Conditional Election of Individuals

A major part of Christendom has never been able to accept the concept of the unconditional election of individuals as the biblical teaching concerning predestination. They declare that such an idea is not found in Scripture, and that it appears to be unjust and arbitrary on God's part while leading to pessimism and quietism on man's part. They would agree that the doctrine of soteriological predestination must be explained in non-determinist terms, which basically means that it is conditional rather than unconditional. That is to say, God's election is based on certain conditions which anyone may meet.

In the following presentation of the biblical doctrine of election, two major points will be stressed. One is that election is conditional, i.e., that God predestines those who meet the gracious conditions which he has set forth. The other is that election is individual, i.e., that God predestines specific individuals to salvation and not just a general class of men and women.[9]

Election Is Individual

Most non-determinists agree that predestination to salvation is conditional, but not all will agree that it has to do with specific individuals. Some feel very strongly that it refers only to a certain class or group without reference to any particular individuals which may be in that group. This view is held by many non-determinists (sometimes called Arminians) and is sometimes thought to be *the* Arminian view on the subject. Emphasizing the corporate character of election, H. Orton Wiley, the eminent Nazarene theologian, has stated, "I hold, of course, to *class* predestination."[10] He finds it objectionable to say "that God

---

9. See Jack Cottrell, "Conditional Election," *The Seminary Review* (Summer 1966), 12:57-63; also, Jack Cottrell, "The Predestination of Individuals," *Christian Standard* (October 4, 1970), 105:13-14.

10. H. Orton Wiley et al., "The Debate Over Divine Election," *Christianity Today* (October 12, 1959), 4:3.

has determined beforehand whether some should be saved or not, applied to individuals."[11]

Another Nazarene theologian, Mildred B. Wynkoop, states that theories about predestination are the watershed between Calvinism and Wesleyan Arminianism.[12] She traces the origin of the idea of personal, particular, individual predestination to Augustine.[13] Arminius' theory of predestination, she says, is just the opposite: "Individual persons are not chosen to salvation, but it is Christ who has been appointed as the only Saviour of men. *The way of salvation is predestined.*"[14]

Robert Shank, in his book *Elect in the Son*, presents a similar view. Election, he says, is primarily corporate and only secondarily particular.[15] Individuals become elect only when they identify with or associate themselves with the elect body.[16] He summarizes his view of election as "potentially universal, corporate rather than particular, and conditional rather than unconditional."[17]

Now, we recognize this view as an earnest attempt to present a biblical alternative to the determinist doctrine of unconditional, particular election. In an effort to avoid one extreme, however, it seems that the pendulum has swung too far in the other direction. The main problem with determinist or Calvinistic election is its unconditional nature, not its particularity. It is proper to reject the former, but doing away with the latter is an overreaction and a distortion of the Bible's own teaching. The popular idea that "God predestined the plan, not the man" is too limited an idea. The fact is that God predestines *both*. Predestination is individual or personal.

This is the way the Bible speaks. When it refers to predestination to salvation, it always refers to *persons* who are predestined and not just to some abstract, impersonal plan. This is so obvious that it hardly seems necessary to mention it. In Romans 8:29-30 Paul is speaking of persons. The same persons who are predestined are also called, justified, and glorified. In II Thessalonians 2:13 he says that "God has chosen you," the Christian people of Thessalonica, "for salvation."

11. Ibid., p. 5.

12. Mildred Bangs Wynkoop, *Foundations of Wesleyan-Arminian Theology* (Kansas City, Mo.: Beacon Hill Press, 1967), p. 14.

13. Ibid., pp. 30-31.

14. Ibid., p. 53.

15. Robert Shank, *Elect in the Son*, p. 45.

16. Ibid., pp. 50, 55.

17. Ibid., p. 122.

Ephesians 1:4-5, 11 speaks of God's predestination in relation to his plan, but it is specifically stated that God predestined *us* (persons) to adoption as sons *in accordance with* his purpose and plan. (As noted in the previous chapter, this section of Ephesians 1 is speaking of God's predestination of the Jews. The emphasis in this case is on predestination to salvation rather than service. Within the nation as such there was always a faithful and elect remnant. With the coming of Christ and the preaching of the gospel, the line between this group—the predestined—and the faithless Jews became very distinct.)

Election, then, is not limited to an impersonal plan but applies to persons as well. But does it apply to *particular* persons? Are specific individuals predestined to salvation? The answer is yes. No other view can do justice to Biblical teaching in several respects.

First it should be noted that the Bible often speaks of predestination in terms that specify particular individuals. Many passages do refer to the elect in general, but other references focus upon specific persons. In Romans 16:13 Rufus is identified as an elect person. In I Peter 1:1-2 the apostle greets the elect Christians in certain specific geographical locations. A very clear statement of the predestination of individuals to salvation is II Thessalonians 2:13. Here Paul says to the Thessalonian brethren that "God has chosen you from the beginning for salvation." This statement cannot be generalized and depersonalized.

Another point that should be noted is that Revelation 17:8 speaks of those "whose name has not been written in the book of life from the foundation of the world." This is a negative statement; but it would be meaningless to say that some persons' names have *not* been written in the book of life since the beginning unless there are others whose names *have* been written there from the beginning.

There is some question as to whether names can be blotted out of the book of life (see Exod. 32:32-33; Ps. 69:28; Rev. 3:5). If so, these would not be the names written there from the foundation of the world, but those having the status, perhaps, of the seeds which sprouted in rocky or weedy soil (Matt. 13:20-22). Those who overcome are specifically promised that their names will not be blotted out (Rev. 3:5), and these are in all probability the ones written from the foundation of the world.

In any case, there are certain individuals whose names have been in the book of life since the foundation of the world, and whose names will not be blotted out. Who can these be except those whom God has predestined individually to salvation? And the point here is that their very *names* have been known to God from the beginning. What can this be but individual predestination? "Rejoice that your names are recorded in heaven"! (Luke 10:20).

How is it possible that God could determine even before the creation which individuals will be saved, and could even write their names in the book of life? The answer is found in the fact and nature of God's foreknowledge. The Bible explicitly relates predestination to God's foreknowledge, and a correct understanding of this relationship is the key to the whole question of election to salvation.

Romans 8:29 says, "For whom He foreknew, He also predestined to become conformed to the image of His Son, that He might be the first-born among many brethren." Peter addresses his first epistle to those "who are chosen according to the foreknowledge of God the Father" (I Peter 1:1-2). In other words, God's foreknowledge is the means by which he has determined which individuals shall be conformed to the image of his Son (in his glorified resurrection body).

To say that God has foreknowledge means that he has real knowledge or cognition of something before it actually happens or exists in history. This is the irreducible core of the concept, which must be neither eliminated nor attenuated. Nothing else is consistent with the nature of God.[18]

One of the basic truths of Scripture is that God is eternal. This means two things. One, it means that when time is considered as a linear succession of moments with a *before* and a *now* and an *after*, God is infinite in both directions. He has existed before now into infinite past time (i.e., eternity) without ever having begun, and he will exist after now into infinite future time (again, eternity) without ever ending. "Even from everlasting to everlasting, Thou art God" (Ps. 90:2).

18. Most Calvinists try to avoid the clear implications of God's foreknowledge by changing the meaning of it from "foreknow" to "forelove" or something similar. The idea of cognition is made subordinate to some other concept. For instance, Roger Nicole says, "The passages dealing with foreknowledge are not at all difficult to integrate, inasmuch as the term foreknowledge in Scripture does not have merely the connotation of advance information (which the term commonly has in nontheological language), but indicates God's special choice coupled with affection" (H. O. Wiley et al., "The Debate Over Divine Election," p. 16). This is an arbitrary definition, however, and is not consistent with the use of the term in Acts 2:23, where it can mean no more than prescience. See Samuel Fisk, *Divine Sovereignty and Human Freedom* (Neptune, N.J. Loizeaux Brothers, 1974), pp. 73-75, 106-107. See also Roger T. Forster and V. Paul Marston, *God's Strategy in Human History* (Wheaton, Ill.: Tyndale House, 1974), pp. 178-208.

But to say that God is eternal means more than this. God's eternity is not just a quantitative distinction between him and his creation. Eternity is also qualitatively different from time. That God is eternal means that he is not bound by restrictions of time; he is above time. At any given moment, what is both past and future to a finite creature is present to God's knowledge. It is all *now* to God, in a kind of panorama of time; he is the great "I AM" (Exod. 3:14).

To get some idea of the majesty of the infinite and eternal Creator, as contrasted with the finiteness of all creatures, one must read the Lord's challenges to the false gods and idols in Isaiah 41-46. The very thing that distinguishes God as God is that he transcends time, and sees it from beginning to end at one and the same moment. God challenges the false gods to recite past history and to foretell the future. They cannot, but he can, because he is God; and his knowledge of past and future *proves* he is God. Here is what he says:

> "Present your case," the Lord says. "Bring forward your strong arguments," the King of Jacob says. Let them bring forth and declare to us what is going to take place; as for the former events, declare what they were, that we may consider them, and know their outcome; or announce to us what is coming. Declare the things that are going to come afterward, that we may know that you are gods . . . (Isa. 41:21-23).
>
> Who has declared this from the beginning, that we might know? Or from former times, that we may say, "He is right!"? Surely there was no one who declared, surely there was no one who proclaimed, surely there was no one who heard your words (Isa. 41:26).
>
> "Thus says the Lord, the King of Israel and his Redeemer, the Lord of hosts: 'I am the first and I am the last, and there is no God besides Me. And who is like Me? Let him proclaim and declare it; yes, let him recount it to Me in order, from the time that I established the ancient nation. And let them declare to them the things that are coming and the events that are going to take place. Do not tremble and do not be afraid; have I not long since announced it to you and declared it? And you are My witnesses. Is there any God besides Me, or is there any other Rock? I know of none'" (Isa. 44:6-8).
>
> "Remember the former things long past, for I am God, and there is no other; I am God, and there is no one like Me, declaring the end from the beginning and from ancient times things which have not been done, saying, 'My purpose will be established, and I will accomplish all My good pleasure'" (Isa. 46:9-10).

In light of the Biblical teaching concerning God's eternity and foreknowledge, and the relation between this foreknowledge and predestination, it should be evident that predestination must be of individuals. He cannot help but foreknow, just because he is God. He sees the entire scope of every individual's lifetime long before it flashes on the screen of history. Then by means of this foreknowledge he can and does determine every individual's destiny—even before the foundation of the world.[19]

Election Is Conditional

Many non-determinists affirm God's foreknowledge while at the same time denying individual predestination. They do not seem to notice the inconsistency involved in this.[20] The reason why they are so determined to reject individual election is because they believe it to be inseparable from the Calvinistic doctrine of election. This is not the case, however. Calvinism does teach individual predestination, but this is not what makes it Calvinism. The essence of the Calvinistic doctrine, as noted earlier, is that election is unconditional. The watershed is not between particular and general, but between conditional and unconditional election. The Calvinistic error is avoided by affirming *conditional* election.

The foreknowledge of God has been emphasized. God elects individuals according to his foreknowledge. But the question may well be

19. Calvin acknowledged that this was the view of the early church fathers, and even of Augustine for a time. But he suggests that we pay no attention to this and just "imagine that these fathers are silent" (*Institutes*, III.xxii.8 [II:941-942]). Berkouwer notes that "Bavinck goes so far as to call this solution 'general,' for it is accepted by the Greek Orthodox, Roman Catholic, Lutheran, Remonstrant, Anabaptist, and Methodist churches" (G. C. Berkouwer, *Divine Election,* p. 37).

20. For instance, Wiley objects to applying predestination to individuals, yet grants that God has foreknowledge of who will believe in Christ (H. O. Wiley et al., "The Debate Over Divine Election," pp. 5, 15). Shank's treatment of foreknowledge is puzzling: "Thus it is evident that the passages positing foreknowledge and predestination must be understood as having as a frame of reference *primarily* the corporate body of the Israel of God and *secondarily* individuals, not unconditionally, but only in association and identification with the elect body" (Robert Shank, *Elect in the Son,* p. 154). It is as if corporate election were the opposite of unconditional election. Further, Shank says that "whether God has actively foreknown each individual—both the elect and the reprobate—may remain a moot question. The Biblical doctrine of election does not require such efficient particular foreknowledge, for the election is primarily corporate and objective and only secondarily particular. The passages positing foreknowledge and predestination of the elect may be understood quite as well one way as the other" (ibid., p. 155).

asked, foreknowledge of what? The answer is that he foreknows whether an individual will meet the *conditions* for salvation which he has sovereignly imposed. What are these conditions? The basic and all-encompassing condition is whether a person is *in Christ*, namely, whether one has entered into a saving union with Christ by means of which he shares in all the benefits of Christ's redeeming work. Whom God foreknew to be in Christ ("until death"—Rev. 2:10), he predestined to be glorified like Jesus himself.

This is the import of Ephesians 1:4, which says that "He chose us in Him"—in Christ—"before the foundation of the world." The elect are chosen *in (en)* Christ, that is, because they are in Christ; they are not chosen *into (eis)* Christ, that is, in order that they may be in Christ. They are in Christ before the foundation of the world not in reality but in the foreknowledge of God.

That the basic condition for election is our being *in Christ* preserves the Christological character of predestination, which seems to be a major concern for many.[21] It must not be forgotten that Jesus Christ is *the* elect one, and that all other redemptive election is in him. Thus even though election is conditional, it all depends upon Christ and the gracious benefits of his saving work.

Of course, there are also conditions which one must meet in order to *be* in Christ, i.e., in order to enter into saving union with Him and to remain in this union. The basic condition is faith (Gal. 3:26; Eph. 3:17; Col. 2:12). Other related conditions are repentance and baptism (Acts 2:38; Gal. 3:27; Col. 2:12). These conditions are in no way to be interpreted as meritorious on man's part, since they are graciously and sovereignly imposed by God himself. Thus having set forth these conditions for being in Christ, God foreknows from the beginning who will and who will not meet them. Those whom he foresees as meeting them are predestined to salvation.

How, then, is Biblical predestination to be described? The determinist says, "God unconditionally selects *sinners* and predestines them to become *believers*." This is contrary to the teaching of Scripture, however, which instead says, in effect, that God selects all *believers* and predestines them to become his *children* in glory.[22]

---

21. See Robert Shank, *Elect in the Son*, pp. 27ff.; G. C. Berkouwer, *Divine Election*, pp. 132ff.

22. The Calvinistic mind sees election as bringing about the transition from unbelief to belief, hence making unbelievers the object of election. The Arminian says that this transition is made by a free act of will; election then is an act of God directed toward

(*Continued on page 345*)

In other words, it is important to see exactly what it is to which individuals are elected. They are predestined to salvation itself, not to the means of salvation. They are not predestined to become believers; they are not predestined to faith. Their choice of Jesus Christ is not predestined; the choice is foreknown, and the subsequent blessings of salvation are then predestined.[23]

The Bible is quite clear about this. Romans 8:29 says that those whom he foreknew were predestined by God "to become conformed to the image of His Son, that He might be the first-born among many brethren." The reference to Christ's being the "first-born" is a reference to his resurrection from the dead into a glorified state (Col. 1:18; Rev. 1:5). Our being conformed to his image here refers to our glorification (Rom. 8:30), when we will receive a resurrection body like his own (Phil. 3:21). Thus we are chosen to become God's glorified children, Christ being the first-born among many brethren. (Similar to this is Ephesians 1:5, which states that we are predestined unto adoption as children.)

Believers are predestined not just to receive future glory, but also to enjoy the present benefits of Christ's saving work. As II Thessalonians 2:13 says, "God has chosen you from the beginning for salvation." In I Peter 1:1-2 this salvation is seen to include a life of good works and justification by the blood of Christ ("chosen . . . that you may obey Jesus Christ and be sprinkled with His blood").

The Biblical doctrine of election, then, definitely includes the conditional election of individuals to salvation. Through his foreknowledge God sees who will believe on Christ Jesus as Savior and Lord, and become united with him in Christian baptism; then even before the creation of the world he predestines these believers to share the glory of the risen Christ.

---

the believer after the transition has been made. Ignoring this important distinction, James Daane criticizes the Arminian view of election as being unpreachable in that "it turns God's election into a human act." It makes election to be merely "a description of the possibilities of human freedom." Thus "Arminianism cannot preach election because it does not regard election as an act of God and, therefore, as an action of his Word; election is merely a possible response the sinner may make to the Word" (*The Freedom of God*, pp. 15-18). His criticism misses the mark, however, since election is not something directed toward unbelievers but toward believers. True, the transition from unbelief to belief is not an act of God, but it is not the result of election either. See Samuel Fisk, *Divine Sovereignty and Human Freedom*, pp. 37-40.

23. The supralapsarian-infralapsarian controversy is misplaced. It argues whether God's decree to elect is prior to or subsequent to his decree regarding the Fall. But the focal point of election is not man's decision to sin, but rather his decision with regard to God's offer of grace. The crucial question is whether God's decree to elect is prior to man's decision to accept Christ or whether it follows it. The latter is the Biblical view.

PREDESTINATION AND THE NATURE OF GOD

The strongest objection to the doctrine of predestination as outlined above is that it contradicts the very nature of God. I do not believe that this objection is valid. Rather, I am convinced that the biblical doctrine of conditional, individual election is most consistent with the nature of God, particularly with regard to the crucial attributes of sovereignty, grace, and justice.

The Sovereignty of God

It should be quite evident by now that we consider no doctrine more important than the sovereignty of God. M. B. Wynkoop has rightly said,

> . . . God's total sovereignty is the basis of the whole of Christian theology. No philosophical theory which permits the slightest break in that sovereignty can be permitted. Every Christian doctrine hangs on this doctrine. . . . A less than sovereign God cannot support Christian faith.[24]

One of the most common objections to conditional election is that it necessarily violates God's sovereignty. Berkouwer sums up the objection thus: "In such a notion God's decision is made dependent on man's decision."[25] It is clear, he says, that predestination according to foreknowledge "casts shadows on the sovereignty of God's election and is a flagrant contradiction of the nature of Christian faith."[26] This is why it was rejected by both John Calvin[27] and the Synod of Dort.[28] Calvin's rejection of foreseen faith, as summarized by Berkouwer, is as follows:

> . . . He sees in it an attack against God's greatness. It supposes a waiting God whose judgment and final act depend on and follow upon man's acceptance and decision, so that the final and principal decision falls with man; it teaches self-destination instead of divine destination (*Inst.* I, xviii, 1).[29]

This is basically the same objection voiced by Roger Nicole:

> I find it objectionable that in the Arminian position the ultimate issues seem to depend upon the choice of man rather than upon the choice

24. Mildred Bangs Wynkoop, *Foundations of Wesleyan-Arminian Theology*, pp. 87-88.
25. G. C. Berkouwer, *Divine Election*, p. 42.
26. Ibid., p. 35.
27. Ibid., p. 36.
28. Ibid., p. 26.
29. Ibid., p. 36.

of God. And it seems to me that both the Scriptures and a proper understanding of divine sovereignty demand that the choice be left with God rather than with man. . . .[30]

Another example of this objection comes from a book by Kenneth Johns called *Election: Love Before Time*. Here he says that those who hold to the view of conditional election

> . . . take away from His sovereignty. They make it subject to man's free-will. Man is exalted to a position where he is capable of choosing God. God is lowered to a position where He is only choosing those who choose Him. He is not the Initiator. He is only the Responder. He moves second. Man moves first.[31]

The one who holds this view, says Johns, "Makes God's choice dependent upon man's choice. He takes away from the sovereignty of God and adds to the sovereignty of man." God is not able to choose "without regard to human merit and initiative"—a thought which Johns abhors.[32]

The careful reader will recognize that this objection to conditional election is just a part of the larger and most basic problem in determinist theology, namely, the inability to acknowledge the validity of the concept of conditionality as such in reference to God's providence.[33] We freely admit that conditional election does mean that in some sense God reacts and responds to a decision made by man. But as we have already argued, conditionality is not a violation of sovereignty. This would be so *only* if God were forced into a situation where he had to react, only if it were a necessity imposed upon God from without. But this is not the case. It was God's sovereign choice to bring into existence a universe inhabited by free-will creatures whose decisions would to some extent determine the total picture. Besides all this, when God established the system of conditional election, it was God alone who sovereignly imposed the conditions. James Daane presents an irresponsible and totally false caricature of conditional election when he says, "Reformed theology rejects Arminianism because it makes God comply with *human* conditions. It rejects the notions that God is not free to operate except within conditions laid down by man and that God cannot save man unless man first decides to believe and choose God."

30. H. O. Wiley et al., "The Debate Over Divine Election," p. 5.

31. Kenneth D. Johns, *Election: Love Before Time* (Phillipsburg, N.J.: Presbyterian and Reformed, 1976), p. 1.

32. Ibid., pp. 2-3.

33. See above, pp. 217ff.

He then refers to "the Arminian's imposition of restrictions on God."[34] It is difficult to imagine a more exaggerated misrepresentation.

Well, not really. In fact, the alleged description of conditional election by Kenneth Johns above is also a vicious caricature. The rather typical implication that man is "the Initiator" leaves a totally false impression. Man moves first, says Johns. God moves second, forced to respond to human initiative. Surely Mr. Johns knows that such language would be appropriate only if someone were denying God's initiative in planning salvation from all eternity, his initiative in calling and cultivating Israel for nearly two millennia, his initiative in sending his only-begotten Son, his initiative in the cross and the resurrection, and his initiative in making the gospel available so that "whosoever will" may turn to the Lord and be saved. As long as one holds to these basic doctrines, as Evangelical non-determinists generally do, it takes a great deal of nerve for anyone to claim that the so-called "human initiative" of humbly accepting God's offer of salvation puts man in the driver's seat and detracts from the sovereignty of God.

That God reacts and responds to man's decision in conditional election is not unique. As we have already pointed out,[35] the Bible consistently represents God as reacting to man's acts and decisions from beginning to end. Salvation as such, in all its aspects, is a response to man's sin. As C. S. Lewis has pointed out, God would not forgive sins if man had committed none. "In that sense the Divine action is consequent upon, conditioned by, elicited by, our behavior."[36]

Likewise, God's judgment on unrepentant sinners is a reaction to human sin. It is very interesting that Berkouwer himself argues for this point,[37] even though in so doing he undermines his whole case against conditional election. His inconsistency here is the result of his inability to accept an unconditional reprobation that is symmetrical to unconditional election. Thus he says that "Scripture repeatedly speaks of God's rejection as a divine answer in history, as a reaction to man's sin and disobedience, not as its cause." God's rejection of sinners "is clearly His holy reaction against sin."[38] It is "a reactive deed, a holy, divine answer to the sin of man."[39]

34. James Daane, *The Freedom of God*, p. 127.

35. See above, p. 228.

36. C. S. Lewis, *Letters to Malcolm: Chiefly on Prayer* (London: Geoffrey Bles, 1964), p. 72.

37. G. C. Berkouwer, *Divine Election*, pp. 183ff.

38. Ibid., p. 183.

39. Ibid., p. 184.

In light of such affirmations as these, how can Berkouwer or any Calvinist continue to argue that conditional election is a violation of the sovereignty of God? If God can maintain his sovereignty while reacting to man's sin, he surely can do so while reacting to man's (foreseen) faith. To say that this makes God dependent on man or that man is thereby *causing* God to do something is an unfounded caricature. The whole idea that unconditional election is the *sine qua non* of the sovereignty of God is, as Shank rather crudely says, "theological humbug" and "one of the great fallacies of Calvinism."[40]

The Grace of God

Another equally strong objection to conditional election is that it violates the grace of God. That is, if God elects by means of his foreknowledge of faith, this would make man to some extent the cause or source of his own salvation. Where, then, is grace?[41]

Both Augustine and Calvin rejected conditional election as inconsistent with grace and as implying justification by works.[42] This was due in part to the fact that many people whom they opposed still taught some kind of salvation by merit, and therefore they taught predestination on the basis of foreseen *merit*. Ambrose, for instance, commenting on Romans 8:29, says that God "did not predestinate them before He knew them, but He did predestinate the reward of those whose merits He foreknew."[43]

One of Calvin's main opponents, Pighius, was, as Wendel says, "the inheritor of a long tradition which has endeavoured to make predestination dependent upon foreknowledge of merits."[44] This certainly prejudiced Calvin's formulation of the problem, as shown in the following statement:

---

40. Robert Shank, *Elect in the Son*, pp. 143-144.

41. James Daane says that "Arminians held that God decreed to elect all men and then, in response to the unbelief of many men, decreed to elect only those who believe. Reformed thought found this unacceptable, for it surrenders the truth of man's salvation by grace alone" (*The Freedom of God*, p. 54).

42. G. C. Berkouwer, *Divine Election*, p. 36. See Mildred Bangs Wynkoop, *Foundations of Wesleyan-Arminian Theology*, p. 56.

43. Ambrose, "Exposition of the Christian Faith," V:82, *A Select Library of Nicene and Post-Nicene Fathers of the Christian Church*, Second Series, ed. Philip Schaff and Henry Wace; Volume X, *St. Ambrose: Select Works and Letters*, tr. H. De Romestin et al. (Grand Rapids: Eerdmans reprint, 1979), p. 294.

44. Francois Wendel, *Calvin: The Origins and Development of His Religious Thought*, tr. Philip Mairet (New York: Harper and Row, 1963), p. 271.

> . . . But it is a piece of futile cunning to lay hold on the term foreknowledge, and so to use that as to pin the eternal *election* of God upon the *merits* of men, which election the apostle everywhere ascribes to the alone purpose of God. . . .[45]

It is quite proper to reject foreseen merit as incompatible with grace. But the Calvinist does not stop here. Even when one rejects all notions of merit and insists on foreseen *faith*, not works, the Calvinist still cries that grace is vitiated. This is because he cannot see the Biblical distinction between faith and works. Berkouwer asserts that "election does not find its basis in man's works and *therefore* not in his foreseen faith."[46] Whether it be merit or faith that is foreseen, "God's decision is made dependent on man's decision. The initiative and the majesty of God's grace is overshadowed."[47] Grace is thus "limited and obscured."[48]

This kind of objection to conditional election overlooks one of the most basic principles in the system of grace, namely, that faith and works are qualitatively different. Grace is consistent with *faith* as a condition, but not with *works* as a condition (Rom. 4:4-5, 16; 11:6). "For by grace you have been saved through faith," *but* "not as a result of works" (Eph. 2:8-9). In these passages Paul clearly shows that faith is not in the category of works. They are qualitatively distinct.

Thus we must agree that foreseen works, merit, or holiness as a condition for election would be contrary to grace. But must we say the same about foreseen faith? Of course not. Faith by its very nature is consistent with grace, whether foreseen or not. If God can give salvation on the condition of faith *post facto,* then he can predestine a believer to salvation as the result of his foreknowledge of that faith.[49] Thus to say that election is of grace does not mean that it is unconditional; it simply means that it is not conditioned on works.

We have already noted the problems that arise when the notion of sovereignty is unnaturally wed to the concept of grace.[50] The resulting hybrid of "sovereign grace" forces the tender shepherd to play the role

---

45. John Calvin, "A Treatise on the Eternal Predestination of God," p. 48; see p. 64. See also John Calvin, *Institutes,* III.xxii.3 (II:934-935), where Calvin speaks of the foresight of holiness and good works.

46. G. C. Berkouwer, *Divine Election*, p. 42; italics supplied.

47. Ibid.

48. Ibid., p. 43.

49. See Samuel Fisk, *Divine Sovereignty and Human Freedom*, pp. 77-78; and Robert Shank, *Elect in the Son*, pp. 125, 144-145.

50. See above, pp. 226-227.

of warrior. It is important just to let grace be grace, to let it come to us on its own terms. Grace does not want to force its way. Like Christ, it stands at the door and knocks (Rev. 3:20). The Bible teaches very plainly that the gifts of grace are appropriated by faith. If by works, then grace is no longer grace. On this all agree. But likewise, if it is by sovereign imposition, then grace is also no longer grace.

Conditional election, then, is quite consistent with grace; it opposes only the false hybrid of *sovereign* grace.

The Justice of God

Finally it should be noted that the conditional election of individuals is consistent with the justice of God. God's justice leads him to treat all persons alike, and to bestow no special favors with respect to salvation.

This is the point of the Bible's teaching that God is no respecter of persons. (See Acts 10:34; Rom. 2:11; Eph. 6:9; Col. 3:25; I Peter 1:17.) The Calvinist often quotes this Biblical teaching to prove unconditional election. This is done by taking it to mean that God does not take account of anything in the person himself (i.e., no certain conditions) when selecting him to receive the gift of faith and salvation. The principle is given in Scripture, however, to show exactly the opposite, namely, that God *does* reward and punish *only* on the basis of what he finds in the person himself. The contexts in which the principle is asserted establish this. It is meant to teach God's justice and fairness in judgment.

The very thing that would violate this principle of justice would be deciding on an individual's eternal destiny without taking account of anything in him. But this is exactly what the doctrine of unconditional election asserts. Only the doctrine of conditional election, where God elects to salvation those who comply with his graciously given and announced terms of pardon, can preserve the justice and the impartiality of God.[51]

---

51. See Samuel Fisk, *Divine Sovereignty and Human Freedom*, p. 47. H. O. Wiley makes an unfortunate statement when he says that "it impugns God's justice, for him to decide—regardless of whether a man believes or not—whether he can, whether he will be saved" ("The Debate Over Divine Election," p. 5). Wiley means this as a criticism of unconditional, individual predestination; but it does not accurately represent that position nor anyone else's.

CONCLUSION

In conclusion we shall note two ways in which a proper understanding of the biblical doctrine of conditional predestination should affect us. First, it should give us a keen sense of personal responsibility. It respects our God-given free will and our ability to come to our own decision regarding faith in Christ. It makes the blame rest solely upon us if we do not meet the gracious conditions for election to glory. It relieves God of the awful stigma of somehow being arbitrary and unjust for choosing some and leaving others (even though arbitrariness and injustice are not necessarily a part of the doctrine of unconditional election). It forces the unbeliever to face the problem of his own destiny squarely and without excuse. He cannot say, "What's the use? My fate is sealed anyway." Conditional election also warns the believer that he must give diligence to make his calling and election sure (II Peter 1:10, KJV).

Second, the doctrine of conditional predestination should give us a sense of personal relief. Usually it is the proponent of unconditional election that makes such a claim. To know that our salvation in no way depends on our own sinful and fickle selves, but wholly upon the sovereign grace of God, is supposed to give the believer great peace of mind. Ideally it should; and in fact it no doubt does comfort many. But it is also true that the idea of unconditional election has been the source of great anguish to many. "Since I can do nothing but wait," they say (even if the doctrine itself does not warrant it), "how can I really be sure God has chosen me?" If the conditions for choosing one person and not another lie wholly within the secret counsels of God, a person may *always* wonder whether those conditions apply to him or not. He may always wonder if his faith is a genuine gift of God or a temporary imitation conjured up by his own will (according to the determinist interpretation of Matthew 13:5-7, 20-22).

Conditional election, despite the possibility that a believer may forsake his faith (Rom. 11:20-22), is a source of great comfort. How can one be assured that he is among God's elect? Because God has shown us what the conditions are for being given this status, and every man can know whether he has met those conditions. There is no mystery. If a person has not met the conditions, then he must be warned that the doctrine of predestination is not intended to be a comfort for unbelievers. If he has met them (and is meeting them), then he can confidently sing, "Blessed assurance, Jesus is mine; O what a foretaste of glory divine!"

Chapter Ten

PRAYER

How God is related to the on-going world is the subject matter of the doctrine of providence. One aspect of this is the doctrine of prayer. Christianity is not unique in its belief that God hears us when we pray to him, and that he acts upon the world in response to our prayers. The question here is whether our belief that God relates to the world in this way is consistent with our total conception of God. The answer is yes.

Some who begin with a more philosophical than biblical concept of God argue that prayer is more properly considered as a response to God, rather than something to which God himself responds. The fact of the matter is that it is both of these. Prayer is not just one thing; it is multi-dimensional. In many of its dimensions it *is* a response to what God has done for us through his providence and otherwise. But in at least one of its dimensions it has the character of petition or request; we call upon God to hear and answer and respond to our supplications. Both of these aspects are proper and biblical, as the following discussion will show.

PRAYER AS A RESPONSE TO PROVIDENCE

Thus far in our study of providence we have seen that God has done many wonderful things and that he continues to perform his marvelous and praiseworthy works around us and for us every day. When we pause to meditate on the fact of God's presence and the multitude of his sovereign deeds that touch our lives, we cannot help but make some response. A failure to respond to providence is a warning sign of a dead soul.

This response may take different forms, but one form will surely be prayer. Prayer is speech directed to God. We may talk about God and say many wonderful things about him; we may tell others about his glory and his might and his works of wisdom and goodness. But prayer is not talking to others about God; it is rather talking to God himself. And part of what we do when we talk to God is to comment on his providential works. We do this in several different ways.

Thanksgiving

"Every good thing bestowed and every perfect gift is from above, coming down from the Father of lights" (James 1:17). When we really accept the truth of this statement, our prayers will be filled with expressions of thanksgiving. "The giving of thanks is the joyful acknowledgment that God has granted His grace or benefit," says Heiler.[1] The word *joyful* here is important. Thanksgiving is not just dutiful enumeration of our blessings and an acknowledgment that they have come from God. It involves a genuine feeling of gratitude, a real joy and happiness that have been kindled within us by God's blessings. Thus when we express our heartfelt gratitude to God, we are telling him how we feel about him and his gifts. We are in a sense describing ourselves to God, telling him of the joy that we have experienced—all as the result of his providential care.

The Bible contains many examples of prayer as thanksgiving. Some of them are general in nature. In I Chronicles 29:10-12 David extols the sovereign rule of God over all; then he says, "Now therefore, our God, we thank Thee, and praise Thy glorious name" (I Chron. 29:13). He says in Psalm 9:1-2, "I will give thanks to the Lord with all my heart; I will tell of all Thy wonders. I will be glad and exult in Thee; I will sing praise to Thy name, O Most High."

When we give thanks to God, we should be as specific as possible in reference to the favors he has bestowed. The Bible offers some examples of men who thanked God for particular blessings. King Hezekiah offered a prayer of thanks after God promised to heal his illness and add fifteen years to his life: "It is the living who give thanks to Thee, as I do today; a father tells his sons about Thy faithfulness" (Isa. 38:19). King David apparently has an incidence of healing in mind in these words of gratitude in Psalm 30:1-4:

> I will extol Thee, O Lord, for Thou hast lifted me up, and hast not let my enemies rejoice over me. O Lord my God, I cried to Thee for help, and Thou didst heal me. O Lord, Thou hast brought up my soul from Sheol; Thou hast kept me alive, that I should not go down to the pit. Sing praise to the Lord, you His godly ones, and give thanks to His holy name.

Jonah's heart was filled with gratitude after the great fish gave him an unexpected and unlikely deliverance from drowning. In the very stomach of the fish he thanked God: "I called out of my distress to the Lord, and He answered me. I cried for help from the depth of Sheol; Thou

1. Friedrich Heiler, *Prayer: A Study in the History and Psychology of Religion*, tr. Samuel McComb (New York: Oxford University Press, 1932), p. 271.

didst hear my voice. . . . Those who regard vain idols forsake their faithfulness, but I will sacrifice to Thee with the voice of thanksgiving" (Jonah 2:2, 8-9). David thanked God for another kind of deliverance, namely, from his enemies and from King Saul in particular: "Thou dost even lift me above those who rise up against me; Thou dost rescue me from the violent man. Therefore I will give thanks to Thee, O Lord, among the nations, and I will sing praises to Thy name" (II Sam. 22:49-50).

It is fairly easy to be moved to gratitude and thanksgiving for such stand-out blessings as those experienced by Hezekiah and Jonah and David. But the Bible tells us to be "always giving thanks for all things in the name of our Lord Jesus Christ" (Eph. 5:20). "In everything give thanks; for this is God's will for you in Christ Jesus" (I Thess. 5:18). We are to give thanks for *everything* that God's providence sends into our experience. This includes the ordinary things, such as our daily food. Jesus sets the example for "saying grace" prior to the feeding of the five thousand: "Jesus therefore took the loaves; and having given thanks, He distributed to those who were seated" (John 6:11). Thus we give thanks for our meals. But there are many other ordinary things that we take for granted which ought to be acknowledged as "good and perfect gifts" from God, if we indeed are blessed with them. For example, we could name our general good health, freedom from pain, antibiotics, anesthesia, electricity, refrigerators, telephones, a bird's song, and warm clothing. The list is endless; but it does us much good to go over the list in our minds and to express our thanks to God for his provision of them all.

When God says that we should give thanks in *everything,* this includes even the hard times and the dark side of life: the tragedies, the sufferings, the accidents, the nuisances, the worries of life. These too have come to us at least by God's permissive will, and we know that his wisdom and power will bring good out of them. Thus James can exhort us to "consider it all joy, my brethren, when you encounter various trials, knowing that the testing of your faith produces endurance" (James 1:2-3). It is not easy to be thankful in such situations, but a reflective and submissive heart can see God's smiling face behind the frowning providence. Matthew Henry was once robbed of his purse. He is said to have written this in his diary: "Let me be thankful first because I was never robbed before; second, because, although they took my purse, they did not take my life; third, because, although they took my all, it was not much; fourth, because it was I who was robbed and not I who robbed."

When we have considered the magnitude of God's providence we will have no difficulty in obeying this instruction from God's word: "Oh give thanks to the Lord, call upon His name; make known His deeds among the peoples" (I Chron. 16:8). We will joyfully reply, "I will give thanks to the Lord according to His righteousness, and will sing praise to the name of the Lord Most High" (Ps. 7:17).

Praise

Responsive prayer also includes the element of praise, a concept very similar to and often associated with thanksgiving, as the quotation just given from Psalm 7:17 illustrates. They are similar in that each can be a response to God's providence. They differ, however, in that thanksgiving is to a degree self-descriptive, while praise describes the divine glory and majesty reflected in his providential acts. Whereas the former expresses our legitimate feelings of gratitude, the latter calls attention to God's own greatness.

The Bible again provides numerous examples of such praise, including the following general statement from Psalm 66:1-4:

> Shout joyfully to God, all the earth; sing the glory of His name; make His praise glorious. Say to God, "How awesome are Thy works! Because of the greatness of Thy power Thine enemies will give feigned obedience to Thee. All the earth will worship Thee, and will sing praises to Thee; they will sing praises to Thy name."

Revelation 15:3-4 gives a similar general hymn of praise: "Great and marvelous are Thy works, O Lord God, the Almighty; righteous and true are Thy ways, Thou King of the nations. Who will not fear, O Lord, and glorify Thy name? For Thou alone art holy; for all the nations will come and worship before Thee, for Thy righteous acts have been revealed." Psalm 145:1-7 is a model of such praise:

> I will extol Thee, my God, O King; and I will bless Thy name forever and ever. Every day I will bless Thee, and I will praise Thy name forever and ever. Great is the Lord, and highly to be praised; and His greatness is unsearchable. One generation shall praise Thy works to another, and shall declare Thy mighty acts. On the glorious splendor of Thy majesty, and on Thy wonderful works, I will meditate. And men shall speak of the power of Thy awesome acts; and I will tell of Thy greatness. They shall eagerly utter the memory of Thine abundant goodness, and shall shout joyfully of Thy righteousness.

More specific prayers of praise include a remembrance of God's daily and seasonal visitation to bring rain and harvest: "Thou dost visit the earth, and cause it to overflow; Thou dost greatly enrich it; the stream of God is full of water; Thou dost prepare their grain, for thus Thou dost prepare the earth" (Ps. 65:9; see 65:10-13). Similar praise to God for his providential care for his creatures is found in Psalm 104:24-30. Specific praise for God's intervention in history to help his people is found in Moses' song of the Exodus:

> . . . The Lord is a warrior; the Lord is His name. Pharaoh's chariots and his army He has cast into the sea; and the choicest of his officers are drowned in the Red Sea. The deeps cover them; they went down into the depths like a stone. Thy right hand, O Lord, is majestic in power, Thy right hand, O Lord, shatters the enemy. And in the greatness of Thine excellence Thou dost overthrow those who rise up against Thee; Thou dost send forth Thy burning anger, and it consumes them as chaff. . . . Who is like Thee among the gods, O Lord? Who is like Thee, majestic in holiness, awesome in praises, working wonders? (Exod. 15:3-7, 11).

Psalm 77:11-20 also recounts this mighty act of deliverance in praise to the Deliverer.

These words from Isaiah 25:1 typify the response of praise: "O Lord, Thou art my God; I will exalt Thee, I will give thanks to Thy name; for Thou hast worked wonders, plans formed long ago, with perfect faithfulness."

Complaint

A third form of prayerful response to providence, found not infrequently in Scripture, is that of complaint or questioning directed to God on account of the painful or difficult experiences dealt to us by providence. This is not to be equated with expressions of doubt or angry bitterness or even hatred toward God. It is rather an honest questioning, born out of finitude and often despair; it is, as Heiler says, "a passionate wrestling with God, manifested in accumulated complaints, reproaches, and interrogations."[2] It is a sincere cry for God to make plain the promise of Romans 8:28.

We are not surprised to find this kind of prayer on the lips of Job. He says,

> . . . I will not restrain my mouth; I will speak in the anguish of my spirit, I will complain in the bitterness of my soul. Am I the sea, or the sea

2. Ibid., p. 241.

> monster, that Thou dost set a guard over me? . . . Wilt Thou never turn Thy gaze away from me, nor let me alone until I swallow my spittle? Have I sinned? What have I done to Thee, O watcher of men? Why hast Thou set me as Thy target, so that I am a burden to myself? (Job 7:11-12, 19-20).

"Why then hast Thou brought me out of the womb? Would that I had died and no eye had seen me!" (Job 10:18). "Why dost Thou hide Thy face, and consider me Thine enemy? Wilt Thou cause a driven leaf to tremble? Or wilt Thou pursue the dry chaff?" (Job 13:24-25).

There were times when the psalmists felt deep distress that caused them to utter similar complaints to God. "Why dost Thou stand afar off, O Lord? Why dost Thou hide Thyself in times of trouble?" (Psalm 10:1). "How long, O Lord? Wilt Thou forget me forever? How long wilt Thou hide Thy face from me? How long shall I take counsel in my soul, having sorrow in my heart all the day? . . . Consider and answer me, O Lord, my God" (Ps. 13:1-3).

> How long, O Lord? Wilt Thou hide Thyself forever? Will Thy wrath burn like fire? Remember what my span of life is; for what vanity Thou hast created all the sons of men! What man can live and not see death? Can he deliver his soul from the power of Sheol? Where are Thy former lovingkindnesses, O Lord, which Thou didst swear to David in Thy faithfulness? (Ps. 89:46-49).

As Habakkuk observed the depths of wickedness and injustice to which God had allowed his people to sink, his heart was filled with questions concerning this state of affairs:

> How long, O Lord, will I call for help, and Thou wilt not hear? I cry out to Thee, "Violence!" yet Thou dost not save. Why dost Thou make me see iniquity, and cause me to look on wickedness? Yes, destruction and violence are before me; strife exists and contention arises. Therefore, the law is ignored and justice is never upheld. For the wicked surround the righteous; therefore, justice comes out perverted (Hab. 1:2-4).

God's reply—that he was going to correct the situation by sending the Babylonians upon his people for punishment—stirred even deeper questions in Habakkuk's mind. "Why dost Thou look with favor on those who deal treacherously? Why art Thou silent when the wicked swallowed up those more righteous than they?" (Hab. 1:13). After the Babylonians came, Jeremiah was confronted with the spectacle of Jerusalem besieged and destroyed; and he echoed Habakkuk's questions after the fact:

> . . . See, O Lord, and look! With whom hast Thou dealt thus? Should women eat their offspring, the little ones who were born healthy? Should priest and prophet be slain in the sanctuary of the Lord? On the ground in the streets lie young and old, my virgins and my young men have fallen by the sword. Thou hast slain them in the day of Thine anger, Thou hast slaughtered, not sparing (Lam. 2:20-21).

Perhaps the most significant example of this type of prayer is found in Psalm 22:1-2, "My God, my God, why hast Thou forsaken me? Far from my deliverance are the words of my groaning. O my God, I cry by day, but Thou dost not answer; and by night, but I have no rest." This is significant because Jesus quotes these opening words while hanging in agony on the cross: "My God, My God, why hast Thou forsaken Me?" (Matt. 27:46). This shows the reality of his own human nature and of his suffering, and it shows that this kind of prayer is not an improper response to providence when it is spontaneously wrenched from a pious heart in the midst of great distress.

What is most important is to see that the prayer of complaint and questioning is never the final response to providence for the believer. It is fleeting and momentary, yielding to the dominant expressions of trust and submission as seen in the next section.

Submission

The final prayer element that is elicited by God's providential work we may call submission. In the face of God's absolute wisdom, goodness, and power, what else can we do but express our willingness to accept whatever his providence sends or allows to come our way? This is not just a passive resignation, a bending of the back to receive the whip. It is a confident trust in the one who sovereignly rules over all, a sense of dependence upon his mighty arm, a willing submission to his will. It is seen in its highest expression in Jesus' prayer in Gethsemane: "My Father, if it is possible, let this cup pass from Me; yet not as I will, but as Thou wilt" (Matt. 26:39). A little later he prayed, "My Father, if this cannot pass away unless I drink it, Thy will be done" (Matt. 26:42). This perfect submission to the Father's will is not diminished on the cross, even though the cry of Psalm 22:1 is torn from his lips in his suffering. When the moment of his death came, he uttered another prayer of complete submission: "Father, into Thy hands I commit My spirit" (Luke 23:46). When David penned the original cry of forsakenness in Psalm 22:1-2, he followed it immediately with these words of trust:

> . . . Yet Thou art holy, O Thou who art enthroned upon the praises of Israel. In Thee our fathers trusted; they trusted, and Thou didst deliver them. To Thee they cried out, and were delivered; in Thee they trusted, and were not disappointed (22:3-5).

Habakkuk likewise, in the midst of his questioning of God's providential dealings with Israel and Babylon, does not lose his basic trust in God: "Art Thou not from everlasting, O Lord, my God, my Holy One? We will not die. . . . Thine eyes are too pure to approve evil, and Thou canst not look on wickedness with favor" (Hab. 1:12-13). At the end of his brief prophecy he utters what is perhaps the most eloquent affirmation of submission found in Scripture:

> Though the fig tree should not blossom, and there be no fruit on the vines, though the yield of the olive should fail, and the fields produce no food, though the flock should be cut off from the fold, and there be no cattle in the stalls, yet I will exult in the Lord, I will rejoice in the God of my salvation. The Lord God is my strength, and He has made my feet like hinds' feet, and makes me walk on my high places (Hab. 3:17-19).

Time and again the psalmists address God as Rock, Fortress, Shield, and Refuge, which are all expressions of trust and dependence. "I will say to the Lord, 'My refuge and my fortress, my God, in whom I trust!'" (Ps. 91:2). "The Lord is my rock and my fortress and my deliverer; my God, my rock, in whom I take refuge; my shield and the horn of my salvation, my stronghold and my refuge; my savior, Thou dost save me from violence" (II Sam. 22:2-3). The psalm that stands out as a prayer of submission to God's will is Psalm 31, whence Jesus drew his final words from the cross:

> In Thee, O Lord, I have taken refuge; let me never be ashamed; in Thy righteousness deliver me. Incline Thine ear to me, rescue me quickly; be Thou to me a rock of strength, a stronghold to save me. For Thou art my rock and my fortress; for Thy name's sake Thou wilt lead me and guide me. Thou wilt pull me out of the net which they have secretly laid for me; for Thou art my strength. Into Thy hand I commit my spirit; Thou hast ransomed me, O Lord, God of truth. . . . But as for me, I trust in Thee, O Lord, I say, "Thou art my God." My times are in Thy hand . . . (Ps. 31:1-5, 14-15).

What we have seen here thus far is that a great deal of prayer, as evidenced by the examples from the Bible itself, would not be possible were it not for the reality of God's providential working in nature and history and the worshiper's perception of its bearing on his own life. All of the forms of prayer noted here—thanksgiving, praise, complaint, and submission—are expressions of the believer's heart after he has reflected upon what God has done and is doing in his world. They are all valid forms of prayer, though complaint is not essential and would most certainly be an exceptional kind of prayer for most of us. The other prayer elements discussed here, however, are not only worthy but would seem to be essential to a healthy prayer life. Hence the necessity for a sensitivity to divine providence.

PROVIDENCE AS A RESPONSE TO PRAYER

We have seen that providence affects our prayers, but it is just as true to say that our prayers affect providence. This is what we mean when we say that God answers prayer. This leads us into a discussion of the most common yet the most controversial form of prayer, namely, petition.

Prayer as Petition

Probably the first thing that comes to our minds when we think about prayer is petition or supplication, or calling upon God to do something for us. Such petitionary prayer is, as Buttrick puts it, "prayer which asks God to change things."[3] We realize that this is not the only form of prayer, but most of us accept petition as natural and as a kind of prayer expected and invited by God. Not everyone has this view of prayer as petition, however. For various reasons individuals both within and outside the bounds of Christendom have declared that petition is an improper form of prayer. It is said, for example, that such prayer is selfish, particularly when we call upon God to give us things that we need or think we need.[4]

For another example, in his book comparing evangelical theology with liberal theology, Richard Coleman asserts that at least some liberals do not accept the idea that God is personally involved in the on-going world; the universe is basically impersonal and religiously neutral. Thus "the liberal cannot logically expect God to intervene for

---

3. George A. Buttrick, *Prayer* (New York: Abingdon-Cokesbury Press, 1942), p. 70.

4. Mario Puglisi, *Prayer*, tr. Bernard M. Allen (New York: Macmillan, 1929), p. 88; cited in George Buttrick, *Prayer*, p. 70.

the sake of some good."[5] This means that prayer cannot be considered as "an appeal to God to change our external situation."[6] What, then, is the function of petition? It is basically a device by which we energize ourselves to go out and accomplish those things for which we have prayed. As Robert Raines puts it, prayer "is not calculated to move the arm of God, but rather, to make ourselves available to him that our arms may be moved by him; . . . not that our will be done by him but that his will be done in and through and despite us."[7] Thus, as Coleman says, the one who prays is transformed by prayer, and he in turn transforms the world.[8] "The purpose of prayer is to push us deeper into Christian involvement."[9] "When the liberal prays to God he does not intend to move him to intervene or to change his external circumstance. The liberal prays for justice, healing, comfort, peace, thinking that these things will be accomplished if he does them."[10] Prayer becomes a kind of psychological pep talk addressed to oneself.

In his monograph on prayer, Friedrich Heiler has noted that philosophers over the centuries have been quite critical of prayer in the form of asking God for things. Besides the problem of selfishness, it is claimed that petition to God is a sign of weakness on man's part, or else an inexcusable presumptuousness.

> It seems petty, repellent, and unmanly for a man not to reconcile himself to his fate, but defiantly to pray for the fulfillment of his momentary wishes and cravings. In the judgment of Kant "it is at once an absurd and presumptuous delusion to try by the insistent importunity of prayer, whether God might not be deflected from the plan of His wisdom to provide some momentary advantage for us."[11]

But these are not the most serious philosophical objections to petitionary prayer, according to Heiler. The most serious problem lies rather in the philosophical concept of God. A prayer-answering God is a primitive concept of deity, according to the philosopher. It presupposes that God is anthropomorphically personal, that he is really present in the

---

5. Richard J. Coleman, *Issues of Theological Warfare: Evangelicals and Liberals* (Grand Rapids: Eerdmans, 1972), p. 151.

6. Ibid.

7. Robert A. Raines, *The Secular Congregation* (New York: Harper, 1968), p. 128; cited in Richard Coleman, *Issues of Theological Warfare*, pp. 151-152.

8. Richard Coleman, *Issues of Theological Warfare*, p. 152.

9. Ibid., p. 155.

10. Ibid., p. 156.

11. Friedrich Heiler, *Prayer*, p. 89.

world, that he is changeable, and that we can have personal communion with him. But rational philosophical thought destroys these presuppositions.[12] Prayer thus is reinterpreted into something like the following:

> . . . a mere recollection of God or the symbol of a pious disposition, a humble and grateful mood, a trusting and loving heart. The element in prayer which is objectionable to the philosopher, the thought of an influence brought to bear on God is accordingly set aside, the objective metaphysical character of prayer is obliterated, and the significance which is admitted is purely subjective and psychological.[13]

Heiler himself rejects the philosophical approach, since he recognizes the personality and the presence of God.[14] Nevertheless he rejects the petitionary element of prayer in favor of prayer as a kind of mystical communion with God. It is "a living relation of man to God, a direct and inner contact, a refuge, a mutual intercourse, a conversation, spiritual commerce, an association, a fellowship, a communion, a converse, a one-ness, a union of an 'I' and a 'Thou.'"[15] For a formal definition, prayer is "a living communion of the religious man with God, conceived as personal and present in experience, a communion which reflects the forms of the social relations of humanity."[16]

Such an aversion to petitionary prayer is quite foreign to biblical teaching and example. From beginning to end Scripture presents to us the picture of men and women praying to God, asking him to intervene into the course of human affairs and to give them the desires of their hearts. This includes prayer for what many would consider the lowliest of blessings, namely, those that fall within the category of the physical. Even Jesus, in the "model prayer," taught us to pray, "Give us this day our daily bread" (Matt. 6:11). John prayed that his friend Gaius might "prosper and be in good health" (III John 2). Abraham prayed that God would remove the plague of barrenness he had sent upon Abimelech's household (Gen. 20:17). The barren Hannah prayed fervently that God would give her a son (I Sam. 1:10ff.). There are also several examples of prayers for the healing of physical sickness. When God punitively struck Miriam with the disease of leprosy, Moses cried out, "Oh God, heal her, I pray!" (Num. 12:13). David prayed

12. Ibid., pp. 95-98.
13. Ibid., p. 99.
14. Ibid., p. 357.
15. Ibid.
16. Ibid., p. 358. Italics omitted.

for God to heal his and Bathsheba's child (II Sam. 12:16ff.). King Hezekiah prayed that God would heal him and not let him die (II Kings 20:2-3).

There are also many examples of petition that can be classified as prayers for God to intervene either to protect from trouble or to deliver from trouble. When the Israelites were enslaved in Egypt, they cried out to God for help (Exod. 2:23). When King Hezekiah found that Sennacherib's army was threatening to overrun Jerusalem, he prayed that God would protect the city and deliver it from the enemy's hands (II Kings 19:15-19). When Peter was in prison, the church prayed fervently for him (Acts 12:5, 12). Even Jesus prayed for deliverance from the ordeal of the cross: "My Father, if it is possible, let this cup pass from Me" (Matt. 26:39). Both Ezra and Nehemiah prayed for protection from Israel's enemies (Ezra 8:21-23; Neh. 4:9). The Psalms are filled with examples of such prayers for protection and deliverance: "Give ear to my words, O Lord, consider my groaning. Heed the sound of my cry for help, my King and my God, for to Thee do I pray" (Ps. 5:1-2). "Contend, O Lord, with those who contend with me; fight against those who fight against me. Take hold of buckler and shield, and rise up for my help" (Ps. 35:1-2). "Be pleased, O Lord, to deliver me; make haste, O Lord, to help me. Let those be ashamed and humiliated together who seek my life to destroy it; let those be turned back and dishonored who delight in my hurt" (Ps. 40:13-14). "Deliver me from my enemies, O my God; set me securely on high away from those who rise up against me. Deliver me from those who do iniquity, and save me from men of bloodshed" (Ps. 59:1-2). See also Psalms 6:1-7; 38:21-22; 69:13-15; 140:1-4.

On several occasions, after God had announced his desire to mete out providential punishment, prayers of intercession were offered up to him. Abraham interceded for Sodom (Gen. 18:23ff.). Moses prayed that God would not destroy Israel for their idolatry (Exod. 32:11-13) and their rebellion (Num. 14:19). Samuel also prayed for God to spare a repentant Israel from the hands of the Philistines (I Sam. 7:5-9). Even Jesus interceded for those who were nailing him to the cross: "Father forgive them; for they do not know what they are doing" (Luke 23:34).

Many other petitions are recorded in Scripture, requesting God to act on behalf of his people or his work. Solomon prayed for God to bless the newly-built temple (I Kings 8:23-53). Elijah prayed for fire from heaven to consume his offering (I Kings 18:36-37). Nehemiah prayed for success in his plans to rebuild Jerusalem (Neh. 1:4ff.). The apostles prayed for God to guide the lot that would determine the replacement for Judas (Acts 1:24).[17]

We can readily see that there is no way to deny the propriety of petitionary prayer without tearing apart the very fabric of biblical piety. This is all the more evident when we see how often we are *commanded* to pray in the form of petition. Jesus says, "Ask, and it shall be given to you; seek, and you shall find; knock, and it shall be opened to you" (Matt. 7:7). He told the parable of the persistent widow to show "that at all times" everyone "ought to pray and not to lose heart" (Luke 18:1). He gave instructions to pray for certain specific things. "The harvest is plentiful, but the laborers are few," he said; "therefore beseech the Lord of the harvest to send out laborers into His harvest" (Luke 10:2). In view of the approaching destruction of Jerusalem with its attendant calamities, he instructed his followers to be on the alert and to be "praying in order that you may have strength to escape all these things that are about to take place" (Luke 21:36).

Other commandments to pray are found in the epistles. Paul tells the churches to pray for him and his mission (Col. 4:2-3; II Thess. 3:1-2). He urges that petitions be offered up for all men, but especially "for kings and all who are in authority, in order that we may lead a tranquil and quiet life in all godliness and dignity" (I Tim. 2:1-2). James instructs those who are sick to call for the elders, who should pray for their healing (James 5:14-16). "The effective prayer of a righteous man can accomplish much," he says (James 5:16). In Philippians 4:6 Paul spells out very clearly what God expects of us in the way of prayer: "Be anxious for nothing, but in everything by prayer and supplication with thanksgiving let your requests be made known to God."

All of these examples and commandments imply not only that petition is a valid and expected form of prayer, but also that God can and will respond to such prayers if it pleases him to do so. In other words, "God answers prayer." This fact is affirmed over and over in Scripture. "I have called upon Thee, for Thou wilt answer me, O God; incline Thine ear to me, hear my speech" (Ps. 17:6). "Delight yourself in the Lord; and He will give you the desires of your heart" (Ps. 37:4). "O Thou who dost hear prayer, to Thee all men come" (Ps. 65:2).

17. We have concentrated here mainly on prayers that would affect God's providential involvement in the world. Petitions of other kinds have not been included, e.g., prayers for forgiveness (Ps. 51; Ps. 130:1-4; Matt. 6:12; Luke 18:13; Acts 8:22) or for aid in holy living (Pss. 19:14; 25:4-5; 86:11; 143:10; Matt. 6:13; Eph. 3:16; Col. 1:9; 4:12; I Thess. 5:23).

> The eyes of the Lord are toward the righteous, and His ears are open to their cry. . . . The righteous cry and the Lord hears, and delivers them out of all their troubles. The Lord is near to the brokenhearted, and saves those who are crushed in spirit (Ps. 34:15, 17-18).

"Then you will call, and the Lord will answer," says Isaiah; "you will cry, and He will say, 'Here I am'" (Isa. 58:9). Jesus says, "Again I say to you, that if two of you agree on earth about anything that they may ask, it shall be done for them by My Father who is in heaven" (Matt. 18:19). He promised his apostles, "Truly, truly, I say to you, if you shall ask the Father for anything, He will give it to you in My name. Until now you have asked for nothing in My name; ask, and you will receive" (John 16:23-24).[18] James says that the only reason we do not have some things is that we do not ask; he then says that if we ask with the wrong motives we still will not receive that for which we ask (James 4:2-3). Finally, I John 5:14-15 assures us, "And this is the confidence which we have before Him, that, if we ask anything according to His will, He hears us. And if we know that He hears us in whatever we ask, we know that we have the requests which we have asked from Him."

In accordance with these many promises of answered prayer, the Bible records many occasions when God did answer specific requests by his people. He answered Abraham's prayer for Abimelech's household (Gen. 20:17). He heard the cries of Israel in bondage, and planned their deliverance (Exod. 3:7-8). He heeded Moses' intercessory prayers for Israel (Exod. 32:14; Num. 14:19), and likewise those of Samuel (I Sam. 7:9). He gave Hannah her son (I Sam. 1:19), and Elijah his fire (I Kings 18:38). In response to Solomon's lengthy prayer regarding the new temple, God said, "I have heard your prayer and your supplication, which you have made before Me; I have consecrated this house which you have built by putting My name there forever" (I Kings 9:3). To Hezekiah God said, "Because you have prayed to Me about Sennacherib king of Assyria, I have heard you" (II Kings 19:20). Regarding his prayer for healing God said, "I have heard your prayer, I have seen your tears; behold, I will heal you" (II Kings 20:5). The Lord answered Ezra's prayer for safety (Ezra 8:23) and Daniel's prayer for the correct meaning of the king's dream (Dan. 2:19-23). He let the lot fall on Matthias (Acts 1:26), and he delivered Peter from prison (Acts 12:7ff.).

---

18. It is often overlooked that this is not a general promise but is part of Jesus' private session with his apostles on the eve of his death.

It is quite obvious, then, that prayer as petition is a proper part of our total prayer life. God asks us to call upon him, and he promises to hear us and respond to us. This does raise some questions about the nature of God and the nature of providence, however, which must be discussed in the following sections.

Petition and the Nature of God

If we can make our requests known to God, and if he responds to such requests, this has certain very important implications with regard to the *kind* of God he is. It would seem that a prayer-answering God would have to be of a certain nature, with certain very specific attributes. In this connection certain difficulties arise that must now be considered.

Does Prayer Change God?

One of the biggest problems raised in the minds of many people in this connection is that if God answers prayer, then somehow he must change. If my prayer causes God to do something he would not have done otherwise, then he must have changed his mind or his plan or his heart; *something* about God has to change. Or so it is said. Exodus 32:14 would seem to confirm this: "So the Lord changed His mind about the harm which He said He would do to His people," in response to Moses' intercession for them.[19] Heiler contends that what he calls "primitive prayer," of which raw petition is the primary form, presupposes the changeableness of God.[20] But both traditional metaphysical philosophy and traditional theology agree that God must be unchangeable. So how can we say that God answers prayer without somehow diminishing the nature of God?

The answer to this problem lies in the foreknowledge of God. Since God is unlimited by time, he has known from eternity every prayer that men would freely offer. Thus in his own eternal and unchangeable decisions about everything he would and would not do in the course of this world's history, he was able to decide which prayers he would answer and which he would not answer from the very beginning. There is, then, no need for God to change his plans in response to our petitions. He has always known about these petitions, and he has always

19. A complete discussion of the whole subject of God's unchangeableness, including this passage, will be given in the next volume on God the Redeemer.

20. Friedrich Heiler, *Prayer*, pp. 56, 96-98.

known what he has planned to do about them. Thus the problem of answered prayer is similar in many ways to the problem of predestination, and the solution is the same. Answers to prayer are prearranged according to foreknowledge, just as faithful believers are predestined to glory according to foreknowledge.

Anyone who believes in true foreknowledge should see this connection at once and should have no difficulty dismissing the idea that petition changes God. William Doty states it very clearly: "We are certain that God 'foresees' all that will happen in human history, and in fact foresaw it from the very beginning." Thus "He also foresaw the prayers of the faithful and was able to take them into account in His ordering of material and human existence, as well as in His disposition of graces and gifts in the historical order."[21] Jean Daujat agrees: "Our prayer and the event obtained in answer to it are both equally present to the sight of God at the same time and if one says that the event is 'foreseen,' then one must also say that the prayer is 'foreseen'." Thus prayers do not change God's decisions, "but, when he decides, our future prayers are present to him because all things are present to him."[22] As C. S. Lewis says, "We have long since agreed that if our prayers are granted at all they are granted from the foundation of the world." He says that "our prayers are heard . . . not only before we make them but before we are made ourselves."[23] Thus, says Lewis, though we may pray for a healing today, if God in eternity decided to grant it, he has already set in motion the causes necessary for its accomplishment. "Our prayers, and other free acts, are known to us only as we come to the moment of doing them. But they are eternally in the score of the great symphony."[24]

This raises the interesting question of whether it is proper to pray for events that we know are already in the past. The answer would seem to be yes, as long as we do not already know the actual outcome of that event. If God sees our prayers from all eternity, then he can take account of that prayer even if it occurs historically after the thing prayed for. Daujat says it thus: "One can even pray for something that is already past and done if we do not know how it has actually turned out, because at the moment when the event in question did occur

---

21. William L. Doty, *Prayer in the Spirit* (New York: Alba House, 1973), pp. 31-32.

22. Jean Daujat, *Prayer*, tr. Martin Murphy (New York: Hawthorn Books, 1964), pp. 29-30.

23. C. S. Lewis, *Letters to Malcolm: Chiefly on Prayer* (London: Geoffrey Bles, 1964), p. 69.

24. Ibid., p. 142.

our future prayer was present to the sight of God."[25] An example would be hearing a news report about an airplane crash, and knowing that a friend or family member was on that particular plane. If the news report said there were no survivors, then it would not be proper to pray for the safety of the loved one (assuming the report is accurate). But if the report said only half the passengers survived, then it is proper to pray that the loved one is among them. This prayer, like all others, would be seen in eternity and *already answered* if God chooses to answer it at all. It should be noted that this is not the same question as whether God can change the past. In view of God's complete foreknowledge and his ability to take everything into account before making any of his decisions, there would never be a need for him to change the past even if it were possible (which does not seem to be the case anyway).[26]

Does Prayer Influence God?

Because of foreknowledge, prayer does not change God. But because of foreknowledge, prayer does *influence* God. He takes into account our foreseen prayers and decides to do certain things just because of these prayers. Thus prayer has a real effect on the course of nature and history. Coleman says that the "conviction that prayer affects events and circumstances as well as the one praying" is one of the things that distinguish the evangelical from the liberal.[27] As Strong puts it,

> Since prayer is nothing more nor less than appeal to a personal and present God, whose granting or withholding of the requested blessing is believed to be determined by the prayer itself, we must conclude that prayer moves God, or, in other words, induces the putting forth on his part of an imperative volition.[28]

The only one who has any real difficulty with this idea among Bible believers is the Christian determinist. Because of his view that a sovereign God cannot react to or respond to *anything*, he cannot really say that our prayers influence God to act in a certain way. In fact, he cannot truly say that God answers prayers at all, since the very concept of

---

25. Jean Daujat, *Prayer*, p. 29.
26. See Ronald Nash, *The Concept of God* (Grand Rapids: Zondervan, 1983), pp. 44-47, for a discussion of this point.
27. Richard Coleman, *Issues of Theological Warfare*, p. 157.
28. Augustus H. Strong, *Systematic Theology*, 3 vols. in 1 (Valley Forge, Pa.: Judson Press, 1907), p. 435.

"answer" implies reaction. Pink cites these words from John Gill: "When God bestows blessings on a praying people, it is not for the sake of their prayers, as if He was inclined and turned by them; but it is for His own sake, and of His own sovereign will and pleasure."[29] Blamires says something along the same line. He declares that God "is not the kind of God who is laboriously pressed into action by human prayer, stirred from passivity by ideas submitted from below. If we pray to him as that kind of God, then we pray to him as something he is not. He is an initiating God."

> The work is already afoot. God initiates: man fits in with his plan—or he does not fit in. We speak of God's answer to prayer, and what an unfortunate phrase it is. How much damage it can do, used so frequently and glibly. As though the rhythm of divine activity on earth usually started with man. As though man were the initiator, conceiving a desirable course of action, bringing it to God's notice as one might send a letter to an M.P., and then waiting for a favourable response—hoping, as we say, that the idea will be adopted. . . .[30]

How, then, does the determinist account for the abundant biblical data concerning answered prayer? That is really not too difficult for him. Since God determines everything, he determines the ends he desires as well as all the *means* necessary to their accomplishment. If a prayer is in some sense a means to an end, then God has determined that there will be such and such a prayer. He determines the prayer as well as the answer to the prayer. The prayer originates from God in the same way that the answer does. As Blamires says, we pray to God, thinking that our idea will be adopted. But "if we have a good idea—a really good, unselfish idea—then indeed he gave it to us. It was his before it was ours."[31] Here is Pink's statement of this point:

> . . . Prayer is *not intended* to *change* God's purpose, nor is it to move Him to form fresh purposes. God has decreed that certain events *shall* come to pass, but He has also decreed that these events shall come to pass through the means He has appointed for their accomplishment. . . . God has decreed the means as well as the end, and among the means is prayer. Even the prayers of His people are included in His eternal decrees. . . .[32]

29. Arthur W. Pink, *The Sovereignty of God,* revised ed. (London: Banner of Truth Trust, 1961), p. 118. He does not give the reference for Gill.

30. Harry Blamires, *The Will and the Way: A Study of Divine Providence and Vocation* (London: S.P.C.K., 1957), p. 30. An "M.P." is a Member of Parliament.

31. Ibid.

32. Arthur Pink, *The Sovereignty of God,* p. 116.

This way of thinking is necessary only if one has decided that unconditionality is the only view consistent with the sovereignty of God. We have already discussed this point at length and have shown that this is a false idea. God has freely created beings with truly free wills, and he has placed himself in the position of reacting to their choices. The whole concept of prayer as petition is a perfect example of this fact. Man does pray, and God does make his decisions in part just because of these prayers. Doty remarks that "the influence of prayer cannot be ruled out as an important factor" in God's providence. "In some mysterious way His causality is at work, and our prayers may have a part in its working."[33] The awesome conclusion is, as Thiessen says, "that God does some things only in answer to prayer."[34] As Fosdick says, some things are contingent on man's praying.[35] "The notion of asking God," says Baelz, "suggests that God may act in some specific way in answer to man's prayer, and that this activity, consequent upon man's request, may cause something to happen in the world which might otherwise not have happened."[36] To put it another way, there may be times when our prayers are the *only* reason why something happens the way it does. How important prayer is, then, even for the little things!

What Kind of God?

When we pray to God and ask him to do certain things in his wise providence, we are assuming certain things about the nature of such a God who can hear and answer prayer. First of all we are assuming that he is a *personal* God with whom communication is possible.[37] As

33. William Doty, *Prayer in the Spirit*, p. 32.

34. Henry Clarence Thiessen, *Introductory Lectures in Systematic Theology* (Grand Rapids: Eerdmans, 1949), p. 187.

35. Harry Emerson Fosdick, *The Meaning of Prayer* (New York: Association Press, 1915), p. 64.

36. Peter Baelz, *Prayer and Providence: A Background Study* (New York: Seabury Press, 1968), p. 58; see p. 115. Baelz has gone to another extreme, though, in the following statement: "Nevertheless, in pursuing this ultimate purpose he takes note of man's response or failure to respond. He is in dialogue with man. And if the dialogue is in any sense genuine and the encounter real, it seems that he must wait upon human response and in some relative but real sense be dependent on it" (p. 61). In this idea that God must "wait upon human response" he does not take account of foreknowledge. His statement is quite inadequate.

37. For a discussion of the meaning of personhood as it applies to God, see Jack Cottrell, *What the Bible Says About God the Creator* (Joplin, Mo.: College Press, 1983), pp. 234ff.

Buttrick says, "it is not in human nature to discuss life with a wall, or to plead earnestly with a fog."[38] When we talk to God, we talk to him as a person. We expect him to hear and understand and to be sympathetic. We expect him to be able to respond personally to our entreaties.

A second assumption is that God is a God of *power*, that he is *able* to do what is necessary to answer our prayers. Since much prayer involves the natural world as such, as in prayers regarding the weather or healing, we must assume that God is in complete control of his universe, that it is subject to his sovereign rule. Prayer, then, is calling upon God to use his almighty power.

Third, when we bring our petitions before God we are assuming that he is *present* with us in such a way that he can hear the most softly-whispered prayer and even the unspoken prayers of the heart. We do not worry that Elijah's taunting of the prophets of Baal applies to us: "Call out with a loud voice, for he is a god; either he is occupied or gone aside, or is on a journey, or perhaps he is asleep and needs to be awakened" (I Kings 18:27). When we pray we know that God is here and thus he hears.

Finally, prayers of petition assume the *goodness* of God. We would not even make an attempt to call upon God for help if we did not believe that he really cares about us and cares about what we need and what burdens lie upon our hearts. We do not expect him to ignore us or to laugh in our face or to tease us, since he loves us and wants what is good for us. Thus we feel comfortable bringing our requests to him.

Of course, these assumptions concerning the nature of God are valid; God *is* personal, powerful, present, and good. Thus our petitions are not in vain.

Petition and Natural Law

Some find it difficult or impossible to accept the validity of petitionary prayer because of their understanding of natural law. In a deistic world view, for instance, petition would be meaningless because God has set up the laws of nature to operate efficiently without any further interference from himself. By his own decision he declines to intervene for any reason, including the answering of prayer. Likewise physical determinism has no place for answered prayer, since it considers the interlocking web of natural causes and natural effects to be inviolable.

---

38. George Buttrick, *Prayer*, p. 59.

Everything is fixed by the very nature of natural law; thus we cannot hope to change anything by our prayers. As Fosdick states this particular objection, "In a world where there is a cause for every effect and an effect for every cause, where each event is intermeshed with every other and all move by inevitable consequence from what has gone before, it seems absurd to expect God to change anything in answer to our call."[39] Everything seems to be fixed by "the unbroken reign of law," by an "inexorable regularity immune from personal control."

> . . . We predict sunrise and sunset to the second and they never fail. We plot the course of the planets and they are never late. The achievements of our modern world rest on the discovery that we can rely on the same things happening under the same conditions, always and everywhere. When we figure strain on a bridge we know that the laws of mechanics will not shift overnight. . . . What is the use of praying in a world like that?—"Stern as fate, absolute as tyranny, merciless as death; too vast to praise, too inexorable to propitiate; it has no ear for prayer, no heart for sympathy, no arm to save."[40]

The world must remain wholly predictable if science continues to function. "But if God alters the course of events in answer to prayer, then the world will be unpredictable."[41] Thus prayer is "unscientific."[42]

This particular objection to petitionary prayer is in essence the same as the principal objection to miracles. It misunderstands both the nature of natural law and the nature of answered prayer. Regarding the former, it wrongly sees the laws of nature as an "inexorable steel framework" for the universe, as Buttrick puts it.[43] There is room for variability and flexibility even with their limits. Fosdick points out that man himself exercises some control over them, as when he pumps water up a hill or causes a heavy metal vessel to float or even to fly. "Here too is revealed the fact that persons while they can never break nor change laws, can utilize, manipulate, and combine the forces which laws control to do what those forces by themselves would not accomplish." And certainly if man can do this, God is able to do much more.[44] There is no need to deny the reality of natural law, as Buttrick comes close to doing,[45]

39. Harry E. Fosdick, *The Meaning of Prayer*, p. 102.
40. Ibid., pp. 102-104.
41. C. S. Lewis, *Letters to Malcolm*, p. 56.
42. George Buttrick, *Prayer*, p. 73.
43. Ibid., p. 74.
44. Harry E. Fosdick, *The Meaning of Prayer*, pp. 104-105.
45. George Buttrick, *Prayer*, pp. 85ff.

in order to insure God's control over nature. He is free to work apart from natural law, as he does in miracles; or he is free to manipulate it within its normal bounds, as he does in special providence. But neither kind of work destroys the validity or even the regularity of natural law itself.

This is seen all the more clearly when we understand the nature of answered prayer itself. Some seem to be under the impression that every time God answers a prayer, that is a miracle. Sometimes this idea is encouraged by a misuse of the term *miracle*. Buttrick is guilty of this when he describes "doing what natural law of itself could never do" as a miracle. For instance, digging up a small tree and planting it in another spot: "This is a miracle!"[46] This is an unfortunate use of the term, since it obscures the vital distinction between miracle and special providence. The fact of the matter is that *special providence* is the normal mode for answering prayers, not miracle. It is true that in Bible times God sometimes responded to prayer with a miracle, but it is most likely that God's miraculous interventions into the world ceased after the first generation of the church. But miraculous intervention is not essential for answered prayer. As we have seen, special providence itself is a supernatural intervention of God into the natural processes of the world, but it works within natural law rather than working outside it. This is how prayer is answered, as Strong says: "by new combinations of natural forces . . . so that effects are produced which these same forces left to themselves would never have accomplished."[47] Coleman understands this point and gives the following example:

> . . . In other words, even if God does work through natural means, he takes the initiative to guide those processes, whether mental or physical, toward a definite goal. In the case of a man at the point of death, God can reverse the processes at work and begin others which will put him back on the path of regaining his life and health. In one instance it may be a new will to live, in another the sudden resurgence of some physiological resources, in a third a combination of both, but in each instance God is the initiator. It does not matter whether God acts indirectly or directly, immediately or later, naturally or miraculously; what matters is that God does act on behalf of the petitioner.[48]

---

46. Ibid., p. 87; see pp. 92-93.
47. A. H. Strong, *Systematic Theology*, p. 434.
48. Richard Coleman, *Issues of Theological Warfare*, p. 157.

God's foreknowledge of our prayers makes this all the more simple for him, as he can begin to modify the natural processes even before the prayers are offered in anticipation of them.

We should remember that there is no *need* for a miracle if God can answer prayer just as effectively through special providence. As Doty says, "We can't expect God to intervene in some miraculous way, that is to say in a manner surpassing the normal powers of nature, when He already has adequate instruments to carry out His will." "Occam's Razor" should be applied to the miraculous, says Doty: "Miracles are not to be multiplied without sufficient reason." There is "little basis for contending that our prayers are being answered by God less favorably or not at all if He sends a competent physician to cure our relative rather than performing a miracle."[49] This point is illustrated by a current humorous story in which a man is trapped on his roof in the midst of a gigantic flood. But he is not worried, because he believes in prayer. He prays earnestly for God to rescue him. As he prays, a boat approaches his perch and offers him a ride to safety. He refuses, expressing his confidence that God will answer his prayer and rescue him. Later a helicopter and then another boat come by, but they too are sent away. Finally the man perishes in the flood. In heaven he complains to God that his prayers were not answered. God replies, "I don't know what you are talking about. I sent you two boats and a helicopter; what more could you ask?"

Petition and the Will of God

If God hears and answers prayer, why does so much prayer go unanswered? One reason may be that the petitioner is not asking in the name of Christ (John 16:23-24).[50] That is, he is not praying as a Christian to the God of the Bible, the God of our Lord Jesus Christ. Or it may be that he is praying from selfish motives (James 4:3). But often the answer to this question has to do with the will of God. I John 5:14 says, "This is the confidence which we have before Him, that, if we ask anything according to His will, He hears us." What does this mean, "according to His will"? We have seen that one aspect of God's will is his preceptive will, or his laws and commandments. Perhaps John has this in mind: we cannot expect God to answer our prayers

49. William Doty, *Prayer in the Spirit*, p. 33.

50. Though this passage is addressed to the apostles in particular, the principle would seem to be valid for all prayer.

if that would aid and abet our sinning against his will. Imagine that someone buys a lottery ticket and prays for God to let him be a winner. Can we expect God to give tacit approval to gambling by honoring such a prayer? Or maybe winning the lottery would only engender pride and greed in the heart of the ticket-holder; thus the all-knowing and holy God could not be expected to contribute to this by answering the prayer.

But there is another important aspect of the will of God that is relevant here, namely, his purposive will, that which is accomplished by his desire and his decision. This has to do with the purposes God is working out in his world. If God has decided to do a thing, then he will not deviate from it and cannot be influenced to abandon it. We know the general outline of his purposive will from Scripture, but we may not know how a particular thing relates to it. We only know that God is working out his purposes, and nothing can hinder him. Most likely, when I John 5:14 says that we must ask "according to His will," this is what he has in mind. God measures every prayer in accordance with the things that he has purposed to do. If the prayer is in conflict with this will of God, then certainly he will not answer it. For example, God had already determined to take the life of David's and Bathsheba's baby to punish David for his sins; thus his prayers for the baby to be spared were not according to God's will (II Sam. 12:18). Doty makes this point:

> . . . Can we really expect God to grant us a favor here and now which He foresees will not fit into development of fuller union with Him, or which may in some way violate His providential plan for the promotion of the spiritual good of others? In other words, can we really expect God to grant petitions in such a way as to work against Himself? The answer, I think, must obviously be no . . . .[51]

Fosdick says, "If a prayer is left unanswered it is not because the reign of law prevents. It is because there are vast realms where God must not substitute our wish for his plan."[52]

Thus it should be obvious that prayer is not designed to change the very purposes of God, contrary to the following quotation cited by Pink: "The possibilities and necessity of prayer, its power and results, are manifested in arresting and *changing the purposes of God* and in

51. William Doty, *Prayer in the Spirit,* p. 63.
52. Harry E. Fosdick, *The Meaning of Prayer,* p. 109. Italics omitted.

relieving the stroke of His power."[53] But this is surely a false representation of prayer. As Fosdick says, true prayer never says, "Thy will be changed"; it says, "Thy will be *done*."[54] Such is the example of Jesus in Gethsemane. Though he prayed for the cup of suffering to be removed from him, he obediently said, "Yet not My will, but Thine be done" (Luke 22:42). That is, may God's purpose be accomplished; and if answering this prayer would mean thwarting that purpose, may this prayer *not* be answered.

This limitation imposed upon prayer by the will of God is an important one. It keeps us from trivializing prayer and from treating God himself like a puppet whose strings we can manipulate at will. As Doty says,

> . . . Prayer is not an automatic miracle-worker whereby we can accomplish anything we choose (no matter how outlandish or incredible) simply by the process of expressing a petition to God. If that were so, then we would all be miracle-workers, no one would ever die, we would never have any problems or difficulties, pain would cease, uncertainties would be eliminated, poverty, hunger and natural calamities would be averted, and the whole world would be converted to Christ tomorrow, or rather today.[55]

This may sound very desirable, and in fact it is; but if it could be accomplished automatically by prayer, that would nullify the integrity of God's creation-plan. God made creatures with free will, and his plan is that they should both exercise their wills and reap either the ill or the good that their decisions generate. Prayer is not a substitute for reality.

Since we usually do not know God's purposive will as it relates to individual aspects of our existence, we cannot know in advance what is according to his will and what is not. Thus we cannot tailor our prayers so that nothing is included in them that is contrary to his will. We must simply go ahead and pray in accordance with the desires of our hearts, and let God sort out what is not in accordance with his purposes. Why a particular prayer should *not* correspond to his will may be a mystery that we will never understand. As Doty says,

> . . . At times it is difficult to see how this or that particular favor would interfere in any way with the spiritual advancement of anyone. In fact,

53. Arthur Pink, *The Sovereignty of God*, p. 112. He does not identify the source.
54. Harry E. Fosdick, *The Meaning of Prayer*, p. 66.
55. William Doty, *Prayer in the Spirit*, p. 62.

> it often seems to the pray-er that his petition would very much advance his own spiritual growth as well as that of others. But we must remember that God sees the whole picture and we do not. He anticipates our temptations and those of others . . . . We cannot know or understand the sequence of events, the effects which even good gifts may have eventually on ourselves or on others; we cannot know how good gift "A" may in some way militate against good gift "B," which is often of greater importance. God alone can know these things, and since He is all good and all wise, we must abandon ourselves to His goodness and His wisdom.[56]

This is probably the key to contentment with regard to our prayers. Rather than agonize over the possible flaws in our prayers that may be hindering their effectiveness, we should simply trust the wisdom of God and surrender to his will. In Buttrick's words, "If we knew why some prayers are granted and some are denied we would have the wisdom of God."[57]

CONCLUSION

What we have attempted to show in this chapter is that providence and prayer go hand in hand, or perhaps hand in glove. Prayer intermeshes with providence, finding both its roots and its fulfillment there in the constant working of God in the world. As one reflects upon the providence of God, he cannot help but find his prayer life maturing and deepening. Seldom does one find such ready and available nourishment for that which needs so desperately to grow.

---

56. Ibid., p. 63.
57. George Buttrick, *Prayer*, p. 94.

Chapter Eleven

THE PROBLEM OF EVIL

Throughout this volume we have stressed God's sovereign control over nature and history: how he infallibly works out his purposes through and in spite of his free-will creatures, how he sovereignly permits or prevents that which he does not purpose, how he provides for and protects his people and causes all things to work together for their good, how he hears and answers prayer. We have emphasized the attributes of God which make such providence possible and which give it a desirable and trustworthy character, namely, his power and knowledge and goodness and wisdom. We have shown how our Sovereign Ruler is worthy of all our praise and thanksgiving and wonder and trust.

But there is a problem here. Over the majestic beauty of this entire landscape of providence, a shadow falls. In the midst of this grand and harmonious symphony of all the works of God, a sour note appears. In the great drama of the universe there is a villain. It is usually called "the problem of evil." It is called a problem because it brings into question the whole theistic interpretation of reality. The ugliness and dissonance of evil cause many to wonder whether there really is a God who created this world and who rules over it in power, wisdom, and goodness. In fact, the existence of evil has long been the primary argument against the existence of such a God. As one writer puts it,

> . . . The primary charge brought against religion, and particularly the Christian religion, in the modern period has been its failure to deal adequately with the problem of evil. Innocent suffering both as a result of natural calamity and human malevolence is presumed to count decisively against the existence of a benevolent and omnipotent God. A "God of love" such as Christians profess to worship, surely would not permit such wanton destruction of human life as represented by the Lisbon earthquake or the Holocaust.[1]

Thus we cannot conclude our study of the providence of God without an examination of the problem of evil. If what we have said up to this point is true, how can we explain the existence of so much evil in the world? That is the question that will be discussed in this chapter.

THE NATURE OF THE PROBLEM

Before we turn to a consideration of the proposed solutions to the problem of evil, we must first make sure we understand the problem.

---

1. Robert H. King, review of *The Traces of God* by Diogenes Allen, *Princeton Seminary Bulletin*, New Series (No. 3, 1982), 3:336.

In this context there are two kinds of evil, moral and natural. Moral evil is the sin or wickedness which originates in the hearts of free moral creatures (human beings and fallen angels) and which expresses itself in their sinful actions. Examples include greed, hatred, selfishness, deceit, stealing, lust, and envy. Natural evil (sometimes called physical evil) is that which originates from natural processes or the perversion thereof. Examples would be genetic defects, diseases, insanity, famine, suffering, and death; also any natural event—flood, lightning, earthquake, tornado, hurricane—that results in suffering or death.[2] Sometimes moral evil and natural evil may be combined into a single event. For example, an act of murder is a moral evil on the part of the murderer which results in a natural evil (i.e., death) for the victim. Other examples are torture; rape; spouse and child abuse; and drug or alcohol abuse that results in birth defects, injury, or death for others. The problem is, how is it possible for all of these things to take place in a universe over which an all-good and all-powerful God sovereignly rules?

In examining this problem it is important to distinguish between the *origin* of evil on the one hand, and the possible *uses* of evil on the other hand. This is important especially in reference to God's role in the matter. Did God originate or cause evil to exist in the world, or does he simply make use of it now that it is here? If God did not cause evil to exist but simply adapts it to his purposes once it has come into existence, then the "problem of evil" is vastly more simple than otherwise. However, if one acknowledges that God does use evil (e.g., to punish or to chastise), but also says that God *designed* the universe so that it necessarily contains evil, *just so* he could use it for these purposes, then the problem is much more difficult. In other words, evil is a problem mainly when God is seen as being responsible for its origin.

Also, it is important to see that the problem of evil has to do with the origin of evil as such, rather than the cause of a particular instance of evil. Most people do not reflect upon evil as a problem until a specific incident occurs. For instance, a baby dies from a serious birth defect. This triggers a chain of questions: "Why did this happen? Why did God do this to us? Why did God punish this innocent baby? Did God really make my baby die? If he could have prevented it, why didn't he?"

2. I believe the predator-prey relationship, as well as death itself, is natural in the animal kingdom and should not be included in the category of evil. Thus the suffering and death of which I speak here are limited mostly to human beings. I say "mostly" because there are times when animals may experience unnatural pain and suffer untimely deaths because of the evil that exists in the world.

These are serious and valid questions, but the problem of evil goes much deeper than this. It asks, "Why is there such a thing as human death in the first place? Why are there such things as birth defects at all? Did God make the world with such things already built into its structure?" The former set of questions cannot even be considered until the latter set is answered.

A final point of clarification is the distinction between evil as a practical problem and evil as a theoretical problem. On the practical level the main problem of evil is how to cope with it, how to live with it, how to overcome it. Where it came from is not a real problem, except insofar as knowing its origin will help us to know how to overcome it or eliminate it.

In many major religions, the problem of evil takes this practical form. In Hinduism, for example, the main emphasis is on physical evil rather than moral evil; the problem is to explain why men suffer so the suffering can be avoided. In order to understand this, it is necessary to ask about the origin of evil. This question has nothing to do with justifying the ways of God with men; it is asked only in the interest of being able to avoid suffering. The answer, according to Hinduism, is that suffering is due to the nature of the universe as diverse and differentiated. Ultimate reality (Brahman) is ONE. When the ONE becomes manifested in the universe, it can only be in multiplicity and diversity. This necessarily results in conflicts and tensions. Suffering arises out of this.[3] More specifically, suffering arises from our fixation upon or attachment to the realm of diversity, which is not ultimately real.[4] When such attachment occurs, it perpetuates itself via the laws of karma and samsara (the wheel of rebirth, or reincarnation).[5] The only way to escape suffering, then, is to develop a complete detachment from this realm of diversity and focus on Brahman.[6] Buddhism takes a similar approach. It says that suffering is due to desire or craving or thirst after the ever-changing and decaying things of the world. Only when one is able to conquer such desire will suffering cease.[7] In both cases evil is viewed as a practical problem, not a theoretical one. Once one has the answer concerning how to avoid suffering, there is no further difficulty.

---

3. John Bowker, *Problems of Suffering in the Religions of the World* (New York: Cambridge University Press, 1970), pp. 203, 205, 210-211.
4. Ibid., pp. 212-214.
5. Ibid., pp. 195ff.
6. Ibid., p. 224.
7. Ibid., pp. 239ff.

In Christianity, however, as in Judaism and Islam to a somewhat lesser extent, the existence of evil is a theoretical problem as well as a practical one. It becomes such only when evil of a particular kind exists alongside a particular view of God. That view of God is the one found in traditional Christianity and the one presented in this book. It is the view that God is all-wise, all-good, and all-powerful. The problem is this: how is the existence of such a God consistent with the existence of evil? The usual statement of the problem is that the following three assertions cannot all be true at the same time: "God is all-good." "God is omnipotent." "Evil exists." Here is a simple statement of the issue as put into the words of a skeptic: "You say that God is both omnipotent and perfectly good. If so, there ought not to be any evil in the world, since your God would both be able to prevent it and want to prevent it. But there is evil in the world; so either there is no God, or he is not omnipotent, or he is not perfectly good."[8] David Hume notes that Epicurus's old questions are still unanswered: "Is he willing to prevent evil, but not able? then is he impotent. Is he able, but not willing? then is he malevolent. Is he both able and willing? whence then is evil?"[9] As we can see, the question is no longer just the practical problem of how to deal with suffering. It shifts to the question of what kind of God really exists, anyway? How can we reconcile the existence of an all-good, omnipotent God with the existence of evil? This is sometimes called the problem of theodicy. This term comes from the Greek words for God (*theos*) and justice (*dikē*), and literally means the justification of God, or the justification of God's ways with men. We might also say that it is the problem of justifying our belief in a particular kind of God, namely, the God of the Bible.

It was said earlier that a theoretical problem exists only when a *certain kind* of evil exists alongside this view of God. This kind of evil includes one or both of the following. First, it includes what is called indiscriminate evil or undeserved evil, i.e., the suffering of innocent people. It may well be that no problem would exist if the only people who suffered were the wicked. After all, they deserve it. This would be consistent even with the existence of a benevolent, omnipotent God. Indeed, it is a view sometimes held by unthinking people, such as Job's friends. But—as in Job's case—this answer does not always suffice.

8. Brian Hebblethwaite, *Evil, Suffering and Religion* (New York: Hawthorn Books, 1976), p. 60.

9. David Hume, *Dialogues Concerning Natural Religion*, part X, ed. Norman Kemp Smith (Indianapolis: Bobbs-Merrill, 1947), p. 198.

Sometimes the wicked *do* suffer; but sometimes the innocent suffer, too, as in the case of infants in particular (and even animals, as some would point out). Often the opposite is the case as well: the wicked who deserve to suffer seem to thrive and prosper. Such an indiscriminate distribution of suffering does not seem consistent with the view of God mentioned above.

In the second place, the existence of such a God is difficult to reconcile with the existence of *so much* suffering in the world, sometimes called gratuitous suffering. Peterson calls this "the most serious formulation of the evidential problem of evil."[10] It emphasizes the existence of pointless, useless suffering, such as these kinds listed by Ramm:

> . . . (1) Babies, children, and animals may suffer terrible pain, but because they have no real mind, there is no spiritual good that can come from their suffering. (2) Suffering in an adult over a limited period of time may increase his spirituality, but when the suffering is prolonged indefinitely, no more spiritual growth takes place. (3) Degenerative diseases of the brain or nervous system destroy the sufferer's mind so that he is unable to gain good from suffering. (4) The pain a person has may be so intense that the person is too numbed to do any kind of thinking or meditating that would increase his spirituality. (5) Two or more diseases may strike the same person, and if to treat one is to excite the other, the person is likely to become too confused to do any kind of thinking that would be of spiritual profit.[11]

Hebblethwaite cites a passage from *The Brothers Karamazov* that captures the essence of this problem perhaps as no other scene can. He describes this encounter between two of the brothers:

> . . . There is a scene, which no one who has read the book can ever forget, in which Ivan visits his brother Alyosha in the monastery where Alyosha is a novice, and talks to him about his inability to accept God's world, because of the terrible wickedness and suffering it contains. He describes a number of instances of quite gratuitous cruelty and suffering—the mindless lashing of a worn-out horse by a drunken peasant, the pleasure taken by marauding Turks in blowing out a baby's brains in front of its mother, the case of a child who accidentally injured a Russian general's favourite hound, was stripped and made to run, and had the hounds set on him to tear him to pieces before his mother's eyes. 'I recognize in all humility' says Ivan, 'that I cannot understand why the

10. Michael Peterson, *Evil and the Christian God* (Grand Rapids: Baker Book House, 1982), p. 73.

11. Bernard Ramm, *The God Who Makes a Difference: A Christian Appeal to Reason* (Waco: Word Books, 1972), p. 120.

> world is arranged as it is.' He understands that men have been given freedom; but, he asks, is it worthwhile? Is God's purpose worth the tears of one tortured child? Even universal forgiveness and harmony in the future will not make it worth such sufferings. So he hastens to give back his entrance ticket. 'It's not God that I don't accept, Alyosha, only I most respectfully return Him the ticket.' And he clinches the argument by challenging his brother: 'Tell me yourself, I challenge you—answer. Imagine that you are creating a fabric of human destiny with the object of making men happy in the end, giving them peace and rest at last, but that it was essential and inevitable to torture to death only one tiny creature . . . and to found that edifice on its unavenged tears, would you consent to be the architect on those conditions? Tell me, and tell the truth.'
>
> 'No I wouldn't consent,' said Alyosha softly. . . .[12]

Here, then, is the problem starkly presented. How can we say that the world which actually exists, with all its indiscriminate and gratuitous evil, exists according to the sovereign providence of an all-good, all-powerful God?

SOME INADEQUATE ANSWERS

Theists have always had to wrestle with the problem of evil. It is not surprising that centuries and even millennia of speculation about it have produced a number of answers, some of which are quite inadequate when weighed in the light of Scripture. In this section we shall examine a few of these inadequate answers which nevertheless enjoy some popularity in our day.

God Is Not Omnipotent

We will recall that there are three propositions which are said to be incompatible, i.e., all three of them cannot be true at the same time. They are as follows: God is omnipotent; God is benevolent; evil exists. One approach to the problem of evil has been simply to deny one of the propositions. Since it is almost impossible to deny the last one, many are suggesting that perhaps we should deny one of the first two. Consequently there are those who explain the problem by denying that God is omnipotent. Proponents of this view realize that they are going

12. Brian Hebblethwaite, *Evil, Suffering and Religion*, p. 5.

against centuries of traditional theology. For the most part, however, they are not only willing to do this but are actually saying that a God whose power is limited is actually consistent with authentic biblical teaching and the Christian gospel.

The system of thought that provides a made-to-order framework for this approach to evil is process philosophy and its derivative, process theology. This twentieth-century creation of Alfred North Whitehead begins with the idea of a finite God who co-exists with the world and is limited by it. Neither God nor the world is absolute; both are involved in an eternal process of change and development. Though one side of God's nature is unaffected by this change, the other side is thoroughly involved in it. His very reality undergoes a constant evolution. As Mellert describes this view,

> . . . He is constantly changing as he includes more and more reality in his consequent nature. Indeed, he is constantly being changed by that reality. What we do on earth makes a difference to the very reality of God. What we are and how we become affects what God is and how he is to become.[13]

Thus "God is not an all-powerful, arbitrary ruler of the earth. In fact, he is powerless before the freedom of each individual moment. For in this sense he is no different from every other actual entity."[14]

One reason why this philosophical system is so appealing today is that it does seem to offer a way to solve the problem of evil. This is one reason why many are adapting traditional Christian theology to fit into its framework. One author who attempts to do this with specific reference to the problem of evil is David Griffin.[15] Griffin declares that the starting point for process theodicy is the denial of creation *ex nihilo*. This is of course inherent in every version of process thought. As Griffin understands it, "God's creation of our world did not involve the absolute beginning of finite existence but rather the achievement of order out of a pre-existing chaos."[16] From this beginning point a solution to the problem of evil is possible. In order to arrive at a solution, Griffin says, "the rejection of *creatio ex nihilo* is fundamental."[17] He continues,

---

13. Robert B. Mellert, *What Is Process Theology?* (New York: Paulist Press, 1975), p. 46.

14. Ibid., p. 47.

15. See David R. Griffin, *God, Power, and Evil: A Process Theodicy* (Philadelphia: Westminster Press, 1976); also "Creation out of Chaos and the Problem of Evil," *Encountering Evil: Live Options in Theodicy*, ed. Stephen T. Davis (Atlanta: John Knox Press, 1981), pp. 101-119.

16. David R. Griffin, "Creation out of Chaos," p. 101.

17. Ibid., p. 104.

> . . . In fact, the problem of evil is uniquely a problem for those theistic positions that hold the doctrine of omnipotence implied by the doctrine of creation out of nothing. For, the problem of evil can be stated as a syllogism validly entailing the non-existence of deity only if deity is defined as omnipotent in the sense of having no essential limitations upon the exercise of its will. And it is precisely omnipotence in this sense that the speculative hypothesis of *creatio ex nihilo* is designed to support.[18]

Thus having rejected creation from nothing, Griffin feels free to reject the concept of omnipotence. God's power is not absolute, but is rather shared with the universe. The universe has an inherent power of its own and is not completely subject to God. God's power over the universe is more of the nature of the power of *persuasion*, and the universe does not always go as he wants. Thus it sometimes produces evil, and God cannot really do anything about it. We should note that such autonomy applies not only to free moral beings, but even to the inanimate elements and particles of nature. Thus both natural evil and moral evil are the result of God's weakness or inability to prevent it.[19]

This approach to evil has considerable popular appeal, with or without the supporting framework of process theology. This is illustrated by the fact that in the early 1980's one of the general best-selling books was Harold Kushner's *When Bad Things Happen to Good People*.[20] His basic thesis is that although God is good, he simply is not omnipotent. Thus the world sometimes gets out of his control. Evil runs wild, and he cannot do anything about it.

The fact that this book was a best-seller shows that people are open to this explanation of the problem. However, in view of the Bible's teaching concerning the omnipotence of God and his sovereign control over all of nature and history, this is simply not an option open to the Bible believer. It is an inadequate solution.

God Is Not Good

If really pressed to surrender either the omnipotence or the goodness of God, most would probably opt to give up the former. They would

---

18. Ibid. This is of course a complete misrepresentation of the doctrine of creation *ex nihilo*. It is not a "speculative hypothesis," as I have shown in *What the Bible Says About God the Creator* (Joplin, Mo.: College Press, 1983; pp. 105ff.). Also, this doctrine was not "designed to support" omnipotence. Omnipotence is rather the presupposition of creation from nothing, and is supremely demonstrated by it. (See ibid., pp. 292-305).

19. See David R. Griffin, "Creation out of Chaos," pp. 105ff., 111ff.

20. Harold Kushner, *When Bad Things Happen to Good People* (New York: Schocken Books, 1981).

rather have a good God who is weak than a strong God who is harsh. This is why very few take this next approach to the problem of evil, namely, the denial of the absolute goodness of God. Most of those who feel constrained to give up the goodness of God just give up the idea of God altogether.

Nevertheless there are some who suggest this as the best approach to the problem. They do not deny the existence of God, nor do they reject his omnipotence. But they assert that he is not as good as we are inclined to think he is. How can he be, since he allows so much evil to exist in the world?

The book entitled *Encountering Evil,* edited by Stephen Davis, contains five essays on the problem of evil, with five authors describing their own ways of approaching it. Two of the five argue for a less-than-good God. One of these writers is Frederick Sontag, who grants that "the nature of God is our chief problem."[21] There is so much gratuitous evil in the world, climaxed by the Jewish holocaust, that we must simply reconceive what God is like. When we think seriously about it, we are led to question his goodness.

> God has purposefully placed us in a situation of less than optimal advantage and subject to more waste and destruction than any purpose can account for. We have not been given good odds for success. This does not prove that there is no God but simply that we are dealing with a God capable of harshness more extreme than some people would use. . . .[22]

In reference to the holocaust in particular, Sontag asks, "What kind of God is compatible with such an experience of waste and destruction and the degradation of human life? . . . If one lives beyond such a total death experience, a new view of life and God is bound to result. Most obviously, all easy and sweet views of God disappear."[23] "Does this mean that Christians must abandon all notion of God as loving or as entering into human life to share it? Not necessarily, but it certainly means that our notions of love must be rethought."[24]

The other essay is by John K. Roth, and it takes basically the same approach as Sontag, with an even stronger denial of God's goodness.

21. Frederick Sontag, "Anthropodicy and the Return of God," *Encountering Evil: Live Options in Theodicy,* ed. Stephen T. Davis (Atlanta: John Knox Press, 1981), p. 141.
22. Ibid., p. 142.
23. Ibid., p. 148.
24. Ibid., p. 149.

"Most people want a totally good God or none at all," Roth observes. But again, such events as the Jewish holocaust will not allow it. "Such a wasteful God cannot be totally benevolent. History itself is God's indictment."[25] "History refutes more than it confirms God's providential care," he says.[26]

> Everything hinges on the proposition that God possesses—but fails to use well enough—the power to intervene decisively at any moment to make history's course less wasteful. Thus, in spite and because of his sovereignty, this God is everlastingly guilty and the degrees run from gross negligence to murder. . . .[27]

If we shout our protests loudly enough, Roth thinks, perhaps God will sooner or later be moved to intervene for us in a more favorable way.[28]

No doubt Sontag and Roth are quite serious in their recommendation that we revise our notion of God's goodness, but it is still difficult to read what they are saying without shuddering. More importantly, we cannot read such views as this without recognizing at once that they are completely ruled out by the Bible's teaching concerning the goodness of God. This, too, is an inadequate approach to the problem of evil.

God Deliberately Caused Evil

Neither of the views presented above necessarily makes God the originator of evil. The former view says that evil just happens, and God is too weak to prevent it. The latter view says that evil just happens, but God doesn't care enough to prevent it. Neither has to attribute the evil to God as its source. There is another approach to the problem of evil, however, that says that God himself is the *cause* of evil's existence in the world. He has included it in the overall design of things for a specific purpose. It is here because he wants it here.

Interestingly, those who take this approach usually adhere to the traditional view of God as all-good and all-powerful. They do not want to reject either of these aspects of God's nature. Thus they say that God—the traditional God of theism and Christian faith—had a legitimate reason for creating a world with evil in it. In fact, they go so far as to

---

25. John K. Roth, "A Theodicy of Protest," *Encountering Evil: Live Options in Theodicy*, ed. Stephen T. Davis (Atlanta: John Knox Press, 1981), p. 11.
26. Ibid., p. 17.
27. Ibid., p. 16.
28. Ibid., pp. 18ff.

say that evil is actually *necessary* for God to be able to carry out his purposes for mankind.

Two versions of this view deserve to be mentioned here. The first may be described only briefly. It is the idea that God had to include evil in the world as a necessary *contrast* to all the good in his creation, so that we may be able to *appreciate* the good. How could we appreciate beauty if we never saw anything ugly? How could we appreciate light if there were no darkness? Would Bach mean as much to us if we had never heard Alice Cooper? Would we really enjoy pleasure if we never experienced pain? So goes the argument.

In my judgment this view has several basic weaknesses. In the first place, it cannot really be proved, since no one has had the opportunity to *try* to appreciate a world with only good in it, with no evil to contrast with it (except for Adam and Eve for a brief period). Hence, how can we say that an appreciation of the good would be impossible? Indeed, I can imagine that it *would* be possible. (Let us remember that those who say the opposite are only imagining, also.) Chocolate fudge would delight the palate whether or not one had ever tasted vinegar or alum. A mother does not have to lose a child in order to experience the great joy of her baby's dependent love. We will not have to remember all the evils and sufferings of this life in order to make heaven enjoyable.

The second weakness of this view is that it cannot account for the apparent excess of evil that actually exists. If this were its purpose, surely we could get the point without being subjected to the extreme degree of suffering that often occurs.

A third problem is that whatever plausibility this view has applies only to natural evil (e.g., suffering) and not to moral evil. But any adequate solution to the problem must take account of both.

Finally, there does not seem to be any biblical support for this idea. Nowhere is there any suggestion that God thought we needed this kind of contrast in order to appreciate his good creation. Such an idea is a purely philosophical speculation, and an inadequate one at that.

But there is a second version of this view that God deliberately caused evil, and it must be taken much more seriously. It is sometimes called the "soul-building" view. The idea is that God deliberately caused evil to be present in the world because it is necessary for man's spiritual growth. It rightly assumes that God desires to make creatures who will be mature persons of fully-developed character, creatures who will freely serve both God and their fellow men. The problem, however (according to this view), is that moral perfection cannot be created *ex nihilo*; it must be developed. But since such growth is impossible apart from the experience of evil, it thus becomes necessary for God to include evil in the world by his own deliberate decision and purpose.

Brief explanations of two versions of this view will now be given. First we will consider the position of John Hick, who is probably the most prominent proponent of this approach to the problem. Hick begins with very traditional assumptions. Unlike the first two views described above, he desires to retain the classical view of God as all-good and all-powerful. Also, he assumes that God desires creatures who will freely choose to love him and to do good. Once these ideas have been accepted, says Hick, we then have two options with regard to the explanation of evil. One of these he calls the Augustinian view, since Augustine seems to be the first to give it a coherent form. This is the view that the original pair, Adam and Eve, introduced evil into the world of their own free choice. They were created in a state of perfection with free wills. But they chose to sin, causing the Fall; and evil became a reality. But Hick believes that this view is quite unacceptable since it begins with the idea that Adam and Eve were created in a state of maturity and perfection, which Hick regards as an impossibility. Moral character is not creatable; it must be developed. Thus he rejects the Augustinian view and any view which contains the idea of a Fall from a state of original perfection.[29]

The other option, the one Hick prefers, is called the Irenaean theodicy. It is named after Irenaeus, though this early Christian theologian did not personally hold to this view. Its central feature is the concept of an evolutionary development of man which excludes any kind of Fall. As Hick says, it "hinges upon the creation of humankind through the evolutionary process as an immature creature living in a challenging and therefore person-making world."[30]

An essential part of this world is moral evil. Since mankind arose from the animal kingdom, it begins with a basically animal nature. Since the essence of animality is self-interest, mankind thus began with an innate selfishness, which is the essence of all moral evil. But this is not all bad; in fact, it is good, because it provides a way for man to develop character. As he comes to recognize this selfishness for what it is, he formulates within his own mind a set of higher ideals which he then

---

29. John Hick, "An Irenaean Theodicy," *Encountering Evil: Live Options in Theodicy*, ed. Stephen T. Davis (Atlanta: John Knox Press, 1981), pp. 40ff. See also his major study of this issue, *Evil and the God of Love* (New York: Harper and Row, 1966), pp. 175ff.

30. John Hick, "An Irenaean Theodicy," p. 40.

pursues. But it is not easy, as he has to fight against the built-in tendency to self-interest. But when he succeeds, he can say that he has finally become what God had in mind for him in the first place, a morally mature being in God's own image. Thus "our sinful world is the matrix within which God is gradually creating children for himself out of human animals."[31]

It is also necessary for a character-building world to be filled with natural evils, for "a world in which there can be no pain or suffering would also be one in which there can be no moral choices and hence no possibility of moral growth and development." Why is this so? Because a morally wrong act is by definition an act that brings harm to someone else. But if harm (pain and suffering) is environmentally impossible, then no action would be morally wrong; and no man would ever face the challenge of overcoming the temptation to harm someone else. Thus no growth would occur.[32] Thus it was necessary for man's environment to contain all the elements that it does in terms of natural or physical evil, including diseases, accidents, and natural disasters. God's very purpose for man

> . . . requires that their environment, instead of being a pain-free and stress-free paradise, be broadly the kind of world of which we find ourselves to be a part. It requires that it be such as to provoke the theological problem of evil. For it requires that it be an environment which offers challenges to be met, problems to be solved, dangers to be faced, and which accordingly involves real possibilities of hardship, disaster, failure, defeat, and misery as well as of delight and happiness, success, triumph and achievement. For it is by grappling with the real problems of a real environment, in which a person is one form of life among many, and which is not designed to minister exclusively to one's well-being, that one can develop in intelligence and in such qualities as courage and determination. And it is in the relationships of human beings with one another, in the context of this struggle to survive and flourish, that they can develop the higher values of mutual love and care, of self-sacrifice for others, and of commitment to a common good.[33]

It is especially important that such disasters and suffering be distributed indiscriminately, "because only in such a world can mutual caring and love be elicited."[34]

---

31. Ibid., p. 45.
32. Ibid., pp. 46-47.
33. Ibid., p. 48.
34. Ibid., p. 50.

An interesting feature of Hick's view is that this world is only one stage of the total person-making process. Since progress on this earth is usually minimal and always incomplete, there must be further stages of growth following bodily death. In the end all will achieve the goal of perfecton, i.e., there will be universal salvation. "Without such an eschatological fulfillment, this theodicy would collapse."[35]

It is quite obvious that certain features of Hick's Irenaean theodicy—the very ones he considers indispensable—must be rejected by Bible-believers. These include especially the evolutionary, no-Fall development of man, and the continuation of the process in the after-life with everyone ultimately being saved. Thus this view as Hick formulates it is not a serious option for Bible-believing Christians. It must be rejected as inadequate.

But there is another version of this view which does not require these objectionable features. In fact it is presented by a theologian who is firmly committed to the Bible as the inerrant word of God, namely, Norman Geisler. He begins with what seems to be a dilemma. On the one hand, we must assume that a totally good God must always do his best. But on the other hand, it is obvious that this world is not the best of all possible worlds, since it has so much evil in it.[36] "The dilemma seems most painful for theism. God must do His best and yet this world He made is not the best. Is there any way out? Only one: this is not the best of all possible worlds, but it is the best of all possible ways to achieve the best of all possible worlds."[37] The best possible world, of course, is heaven; but the best and only way of achieving it is to begin with this world where evil necessarily exists.

Geisler agrees with Hick that "it is impossible for God to create directly a world with achieved moral values of the highest nature."[38] Moral maturity is something that must be developed through a person's own experiences and choices. This requires exposure to moral evil. Thus Geisler says,

> . . . A sinless heaven is better than an evil earth, but there was no way for God to achieve a sinless heaven unless He created beings who would sin and did sin in order that out of their sin He could produce the best

---

35. Ibid., p. 51.

36. Norman L. Geisler, *Philosophy of Religion* (Grand Rapids: Zondervan, 1974), pp. 325-327. (For another discussion of this subject by Geisler, see *The Roots of Evil* [Grand Rapids: Zondervan, 1978].)

37. Norman L. Geisler, *Philosophy of Religion*, p. 326. Italics omitted.

38. Ibid., p. 366.

> world where beings could sin but would not sin. An imperfect moral world is the necessary precondition for achieving the morally perfect world. . . .[39]

Less-than-perfect moral worlds would have been possible for God to make, but we must remember that his nature demands that he produce only the best possible world; and "a world with evil is a morally necessary prerequisite to the most perfect world possible."[40] Why is this so? Basically for the same reason given by Hick, namely, that certain virtues are attainable only in a world where sin occurs. These include courage, fortitude, mercy, patience, and forgiveness.[41] Surely there can be no higher virtues than these,

> . . . and without the presence of evil, the greatest lessons in life will never be learned. Jesus was said to have "learned obedience through what He suffered" and thereby was "made perfect" (Heb. 5:8). . . . In the final analysis obedience to God is the ultimate lesson to learn. And the very best way to learn it is by disobedience to God. For if God never permitted actual disobedience, how would man ever *learn* from experience (and experience is the best way men learn) that obedience is better than disobedience? . . . [42]

"The presence of evil is in fact a necessary condition for the maximization of moral perfection for free creatures."[43]

Geisler explains the presence of physical evil in the same way: it is the best way to achieve the best possible world. Some virtues essential to the latter are possible only if evil is present in the form of suffering and misery and pain. Some are acquired by enduring suffering, e.g., patience, trust, courage, and hope. Others are acquired only by interacting with others who are suffering, e.g., sympathy, mercy, and selfless love. "In brief, some virtues would be totally absent from a world without physical evil."[44]

Although Geisler's version of the soul-building approach to evil has some important differences from Hick's view, it shares some of the same weaknesses that make both versions inadequate. We will now

---

39. Ibid., p. 326.
40. Ibid., p. 352.
41. Ibid., pp. 361, 363.
42. Ibid., pp. 363-364. Note that this line of reasoning would require Jesus to be disobedient, too.
43. Ibid., p. 365.
44. Ibid., p. 389.

offer several comments and criticisms which, except for the first two, apply to both Hick and Geisler.

The first comment is directed only toward Hick's argument. It is simply to point out that there is a *non sequitur* gap between two of his principal premises. First, he says that moral character can be developed only through a process. Second, he says that evolution provides this process. But an important shift of meaning has taken place here. In the former statement the moral character of each *individual* is in view, while in the latter statement the development refers to that of the human *race*. When Hick speaks of such things as "growth of moral insight," "gradual assimilation of higher ideals," and "intellectual development,"[45] he is referring to the latter. As a matter of fact, in an evolutionary process there would be very little development of the individuals near its beginning. And, as unlikely as it may seem, even those near its end would develop very little personally, since they would begin on a much higher level, having inherited the results of all the preceding ages. Hence it would seem that the only process is the macrocosmic one, with individuals benefiting very little if at all from evolution, if the process of individual development is what is at stake. The prominent place given to evolution in Hick's scheme appears to be cultural accommodation more than anything else.

The second comment is directed only to Geisler. His argument contains a significant ambiguity with regard to the origin of evil. On the one hand, he puts repeated emphasis on the idea that God only *permitted* evil to occur. "Permitting evil is the best way to produce the best world," he says.[46] "Unless an imperfect world is permitted . . . , the perfect world cannot become a reality."[47] He specifically distinguishes between permitting and performing: "The theist does not say that a good end justifies God's *performing* evil acts, but it only justifies God's *permitting* such acts."[48] The problem is that Geisler's argument requires him to say much more than this. It requires him to say that evil—both moral and natural—is a *necessary* means for the accomplishment of God's purpose for man. Geisler affirms that moral evil is a "necessary precondition," a "morally necessary prerequisite," a "necessary condition" for achieving the best world.[49] A sinless world "could not fulfill

45. John Hick, "An Irenaean Theodicy," pp. 45, 47.

46. Norman L. Geisler, *Philosophy of Religion*, p. 352. See p. 361: "Permitting an evil world is the best way to achieve the morally best world."

47. Ibid., p. 362. See also pp. 366, 377.

48. Ibid., p. 395.

49. Ibid., pp. 326, 352, 365, 376.

the requirements" for the best world.[50] The same is true of physical evil: it is necessary to maximal moral perfection.[51] It seems to me that the concepts of permission and necessity are incompatible. If evil is truly necessary for God's purposes, then he must do more than merely permit it to occur. He must deliberately design the world so that it will necessarily occur. It is part of his purpose. At least twice Geisler states his solution in very different (and much more acceptable) terminology when he speaks of the necessity of the *possibility* of evil: "Only by producing the possibility of evil can God produce the best possible world."[52] Also, "if God is responsible only for the *possibility* of evil, not its *actuality*, then the antitheist cannot validly conclude that God is responsible for all the actual evil in the world."[53] This is true, but this is not really Geisler's position. His view does not depend on the mere possibility of evil; it requires its actuality. Thus the fact is that he leaves himself open to the very criticism that he deplores, namely, that God is responsible for the existence of evil in the world.

This leads to a third comment, which applies (as do the rest) to both Geisler and Hick. It is more of a question: is evil the *only* way to achieve the virtues that are essential to the highest moral character? Feinberg asks whether moral evil in particular must be present, and he answers no. "So long as there are situations which test one's character and develop it by means of such testing, a soul can be built by overcoming difficulties, but none of those tests which must be faced need stem from the presence of moral evil."[54] All that is really needed is the *possibility* of moral evil, which would make temptation real and the conquest of it a character-building experience. Geisler did mention this, but he cannot integrate it into his system. Feinberg also questions whether physical evils are necessary for spiritual growth.[55]

Another point is whether actual development of all the so-called highest virtues is really necessary for the fulfillment of God's purposes for man. It would seem more appropriate to say that a fully-mature moral character *would* express these virtues *if* the circumstances called for it. But if no circumstance ever arose to call forth the virtue

50. Ibid., p. 377.
51. Ibid., p. 387.
52. Ibid., p. 380.
53. Ibid., p. 329.
54. John S. Feinberg, *Theologies and Evil* (Washington, D.C.: University Press of America, 1979), p. 114.
55. Ibid.

of sympathy or forgiveness, this would not leave some kind of gap in a person's character. One might ask the parallel question, whether the characteristics of grace and forgiveness must necessarily be exhibited by God in order for him to be God in the fullest sense of the word. But since such things are called forth only by the existence of sin, a yes answer would mean that a sinful world is necessary for God's own sake, i.e., for the necessary expression of all sides of his nature. But such a conclusion seems groundless. God does not *have* to show his forgiveness *unless* the circumstances exist that call for it. If there had never been any sin in God's universe and therefore no need for forgiveness, God would still be just as much God as he is now. I think the same is true of man. If he had never sinned, the absence of such virtues as could develop *only* in connection with sin (or natural evil, for that matter) would not detract from his character.

A fifth point is whether it is true that moral character is uncreatable. Both Hick and Geisler affirm this, and Hick's system is quite consistent with such an affirmation. The concepts of an evolutionary origin and an open-ended after-life go hand in hand with it. But can a Bible believer (such as Geisler), who believes in the creation of Adam and Eve as responsible adults and in the full sanctification of believers by fiat at death, really take this position? The fact is that many saints die before they have progressed very far into the development of the Christian virtues. But most Protestants reject the purgatorial concept, which would allow for the completion of the process after death. They prefer rather to think that God bestows full sanctification—a mature moral character—upon each deceased saint as a gift. This seems to be the point of Hebrews 12:23, which speaks of "the spirits of righteous men made perfect." Thus the idea that such character is achieved *only* by experience, and the experience of evil at that, does not seem to be required by Scripture.

A sixth point is that the soul-building approach to evil might justify the presence of a little suffering or a little bit of sin, but it cannot really account for the presence of the enormous amount of gratuitous and catastrophic evil that actually exists (at least as some understand it). Why would God need so much evil to teach man patience? Couldn't we learn how to show mercy with a little less suffering around us? We may recall that Ramm mentions five kinds of pointless, useless suffering that actually exist.[56] Then he says,

56. See above, p. 383.

> In such cases the pain and suffering is so great that no spiritual or moral or religious growth is possible. Therefore any explanation of evil at this point is self-refuting because the very nature of the case prevents spiritual growth. It is therefore maintained that in situations like these it cannot be said that God is good, for there is terrible evil which he could prevent and doesn't; and the possibility of the sufferer to gain in spirituality is impossible because he is in no condition to do the thinking or reflecting that would increase his spirituality.[57]

So it seems that the soul-building concept is inadequate to explain the kind of evil which actually exists.

A few other miscellaneous comments are in order. It is sometimes pointed out that the experience of suffering, especially if it is of the gross kind, often has a negative effect on human character, leading to bitterness and estrangement from God rather than spiritual growth. Also, it is sometimes suggested that this view is a denial of the third part of the three-pronged dilemma (God is all-good, God is all-powerful; evil exists). The so-called evil that exists is not genuine but only apparent, since it is a necessary means to a higher good.[58] Finally, this view seems to confuse the questions of the origin of evil and the use of evil. It is true that once evil is in existence it can be *used* as a means of character building, regardless of how it came to exist. But this view focuses on the *origin* of evil as such. It makes soul-building the very rationale for evil's existence, and thus places the full responsibility for its origin upon God.

THE FREE-WILL ANSWER

In the preceding section we have examined the major approaches to the problem of evil which are inadequate in the light of Scripture and reason. Two of them attempt to solve the problem by altering the nature of God, denying either his benevolence or his omnipotence. The third approach retains the traditional view of God and attempts to show that an all-good, all-powerful God could have a sufficient rationale or even a necessary reason for deliberately including evil in his creation. We have found all of these views to be inadequate. The view that we are proposing in this chapter agrees that the traditional view of God must be maintained, i.e., God's goodness and power must not be denied or diminished. But we do not agree that God deliberately caused evil

57. Bernard Ramm, *The God Who Makes a Difference*, p. 120.
58. See David R. Griffin, "Creation out of Chaos," p. 103.

out of any kind of necessity for fulfilling the purposes of his creation. The most that we can say is that in the world that God created, evil was a *possibility* but not a necessity. This is an old, old view in Christianity, the one Hick calls the Augustinian view. It is usually called the free-will defense. It says in essence that God created the world with neither moral evil nor natural evil existing in it. But he did create free-will beings for whom moral evil was a possibility. In the exercise of their freedom these beings introduced moral evil into the world, with natural evil following from it as its consequence. This view will now be explained in detail.

Explanation of the View

Throughout this book we have stressed the reality of human free will. Man was created with the ability to consider the options and to make his own choices with respect to his behavior. Though God foreknows his choices, he does not predetermine them. Why did God make free-will creatures? The Bible does not give an explicit answer to this question. We infer from other teaching in Scripture that God's chief purpose and desire were to have creatures who would love, serve, and glorify him of their free choice and not by coercion or manipulation. We infer this, for example, from the fact that the first and greatest commandment is that we should love God with all our hearts and minds (Matt. 22:37). The fact that this is the most important thing that we can do suggests that it is what God desires from his creation more than anything else. Giving his creatures free will was a necessary means to this end.

The existence of evil, however, was not essential for God to receive free worship and love from his creatures; therefore the world as originally created contained neither moral evil nor physical evil. It was all "very good" (Gen. 1:31). The fact that human beings (and angels before them) were created with free will, though, means that there was the *possibility* of or *potential* for evil. For if man is to have the ability freely to choose to love God, he must also be given the capacity to choose to hate and reject God. Thus in a sense the creation of free-will beings entailed a risk. But God was willing to risk the free choice of evil in order to have freely-chosen love and worship. Here is the extent of God's responsibility for evil: he is responsible for its possibility, but not its actuality. He made the free creatures who had the potential for choosing evil.

The rest, of course, is history. His creatures did choose to do evil. And as a consequence of this free choice, all the evil that exists in the world has come into existence, the natural as well as the moral. It is not difficult to see how moral evil is the result of free will. Angels and men were created with the capacity to sin; some of the angels and the first human beings exercised that capacity under the permissive will of God, and moral evil became a reality. Alvin Plantinga explains it this way:

> . . . A world containing creatures who are significantly free (and freely perform more good than evil actions) is more valuable, all else being equal, than a world containing no free creatures at all. Now God can create free creatures, but He can't *cause* or *determine* them to do only what is right. For if He does so, then they aren't significantly free after all; they do not do what is right *freely*. To create creatures capable of *moral good*, therefore, He must create creatures capable of moral evil; and He can't give these creatures the freedom to perform evil and at the same time prevent them from doing so. As it turned out, sadly enough, some of the free creatures God created went wrong in the exercise of their freedom; this is the source of moral evil. The fact that free creatures sometimes go wrong, however, counts neither against God's omnipotence nor against His goodness; for He could have forestalled the occurrence of moral evil only by removing the possibility of moral good.[59]

Why did God want to do it this way? Is this the "best of all possible worlds"? No, but as Geisler says, it is the best *way* to the best possible world. But unlike Geisler, I deny that the actual existence of evil is necessary as the best way to the best world. All that are necessary are free choice and thus the possibility of evil.

But what about natural evil? Free will can explain the presence of moral evil in the world, but how do we explain evils such as birth defects, disease, and death? The answer is that free will *is* the ultimate origin of natural evils. Natural evils are present in the world because of sin, and sin is present because of free will. This point must be explained very carefully. Even though it is a very important truth, it is easily misunderstood. Here is the best way to say it: all physical evils are ultimately the consequence of sin, but they do not all derive from sin in the same way.

What are the ways in which physical evils derive from moral evil (sin)? First and most important, the very introduction of sin into the pristine

---

59. Alvin Plantinga, *God, Freedom, and Evil* (Grand Rapids: Eerdmans, 1977), p. 30.

world by the first couple instilled an element of corruption into the entire cosmos that will remain until the second coming of Jesus. Thus much of the evil that is in the world today can be traced directly back to the sin recorded in Genesis 3:1-6. While it may be in part a natural consequence of sin, it is specifically described as a divine curse in Genesis 3:14ff. The curse includes pain in childbirth (3:16), uncooperative fields (3:17-19), and physical death (3:19). Bodily death is described as a judicial penalty upon the entire human race as the result of the sin of its first representative pair in Romans 5:12-18, while Romans 8:10 adds that "the body is dead because of sin."[60] That is, because of sin in general, not because of some specific sin. Since physical death is often preceded by and caused by various diseases and defects and accidents, we may reasonably assume that these too are present in the world because of sin. Romans 8:20-22 shows how general and widespread this corruption is throughout the entire cosmos:

> . . . For the creation was subjected to futility, not of its own will, but because of Him who subjected it, in hope that the creation itself also will be set free from its slavery to corruption into the freedom of the glory of the children of God. For we know that the whole creation groans and suffers the pains of childbirth together until now.

This passage also indicates that the creation will be redeemed or set free from this corruption, no doubt through the final purification out of which come the new heavens and new earth (II Peter 3:10-13).

What these passages show is that nature today is not the way God made it in the beginning. It has been distorted by sin's presence; evil is now built into its very fabric. This is how we may explain so many of the individual instances of suffering that occur around us, including birth defects, disease, death, and even natural disasters. They happen because sin has distorted nature, and the sin happened through a free-will decision of our first parents.

In this connection it should be pointed out that man's capacity for pain, and even pain itself to some degree, are not evils in and of themselves. Philip Yancey has pointed out the fact that the body's pain mechanism is necessary as a warning system to keep us from injuring ourselves.[61] For instance, the brief pain experienced from touching a hot

60. See Jack Cottrell, *His Truth* (Cincinnati: Standard Publishing, 1980), pp. 45-46.

61. Philip Yancey, *Where Is God When It Hurts* (Grand Rapids: Zondervan, 1977), pp. 21-39. See also Philip Yancey, "Pain: The Tool of the Wounded Surgeon," *Christianity Today* (March 24, 1978), 22:12-16.

stove prevents us from burning ourselves much more seriously. Thus the capacity for pain is absolutely essential for the kind of life we live in this finite world. Though it is "the gift nobody wants," Yancey thinks that it may be "the paragon of creative genius."[62] There is a great difference, however, between the capacity for pain and momentary warning pains on the one hand, and the prolonged agony suffered by the victims of certain diseases on the other hand. While the former may be natural and good, the latter is surely the result of sin's distortion of nature. It is not God's work, but is part of the "slavery to corruption" that permeates the fallen world.

A second way that physical evil derives from moral evil is even more direct. Sometimes a person's own sins cause him to suffer many kinds of pain and even untimely death. A person may contract lung cancer through smoking or venereal disease through promiscuity. He may go through all kinds of suffering and eventually destroy himself through drug abuse or alcohol abuse. He may injure or kill himself in an accident because of recklessness or the violation of traffic laws. Thus many instances of suffering are self-caused through the free-will choice of sin. James 1:15 sets forth this principle: "When lust has conceived, it gives birth to sin; and when sin is accomplished, it brings forth death."

A third way that physical evil results from moral evil is similar to the previous one. Sometimes one individual's sins are the direct cause of suffering and misery in others. A drunken driver injures an infant in an automobile accident. A jealous wife shoots her husband. A sadistic bigot tortures an innocent victim. A greedy teen-ager mugs an elderly person. A covetous head of state starts a war. A heartless terrorist blows up a building. An evil leader undertakes genocide. The examples are endless, but in each case the suffering endured by one person is the result of a sinful act on the part of another person.

In the fourth place, sometimes physical evil is caused by the supernatural intervention of Satan or a demonic spirit. Through manipulation of the weather, men, and disease, Satan inflicted misery and death upon Job and his household. Evil spirits may sometimes be the cause of disease (see Luke 13:11-16; Matt. 9:32-33), and through possession they may inflict harm (Matt. 17:14-18; Mark 5:5). Whether such things still occur today is a matter of dispute, but the biblical examples show that it is possible.

Finally we would note that God himself may use natural evils as a means of chastising or punishing people. In this book we have seen

62. Philip Yancey, *Where Is God When It Hurts*, pp. 21, 23.

many examples of this in tracing God's special providence in the lives of the peoples of the Old Testament times. We saw how God inflicted such things as drought, insect plague, disease, and death upon various ones. As Job 37:13 reminds us, God can manipulate the weather for purposes of correction. Yes, God has done and may still do such things as these, but the important point is this: God does not cause natural evils as part of his original purpose for man and the universe; rather, he does so only as a reaction to or response to sin. If there were no more evil demanding correction, chastisement, or punishment, then God would not bring about such things. Thus even the God-inflicted natural evils stem ultimately from the presence of moral evil in the world.

Thus we see that evil in both its forms is the consequence of free will, i.e., the free-will choices of men and some angels to sin against God. It is not a necessary element of God's creation. But given the existence of free-will beings, it was from the beginning a possibility. As everything actually turned out, it was a possibility that became a reality.

Objections to the Free-will Answer

There are some problems with the free-will defense that must be dealt with briefly. First, some say that this can explain the origin of moral evil, but not natural evil. Davis mentions this objection but says that it is invalid in view of the fact that Satan can cause evil in the world. He calls this the "luciferous defense."[63] Davis' response to this objection is accurate but incomplete. As we have just seen, there are at least five different ways in which natural evil derives from moral evil. The objection truly is invalid.

A second objection argues that an omnipotent God could have created free-will beings who would always do right and never sin.[64] If free-will love and worship are so important to God, and if he can do anything, then he should have made free-will beings but simply determined that they would never sin. As Flew states the objection, "If it really is logically possible for an action to be both freely chosen and yet fully determined

63. Stephen T. Davis, "Free Will and Evil," *Encountering Evil: Live Options in Theodicy*, ed. Stephen T. Davis (Atlanta: John Knox Press, 1981), pp. 74-75. He gets his material from Alvin Plantinga, *God, Freedom, and Evil*, p. 58.

64. See Antony Flew, "Divine Omnipotence and Human Freedom," *New Essays in Philosophical Theology*, ed. Antony Flew and Alasdair MacIntyre (London: SCM Press, 1955), pp. 152-153.

by caused causes, then the keystone argument of the Free-will Defence . . . cannot hold."[65] It is important to see that when stated in this form, the objection is valid. *If* an action can be both free and determined at the same time, then an omnipotent God could simply have determined that all free acts would be morally good. But we must point out that Flew is arguing from the determinist definition of free will, which we have already shown to be invalid.[66] A free-will being, created so that he cannot sin or will not sin by design, is a contradiction. Some would argue, though, that heaven is supposed to be exactly this sort of situation. When God perfects the saints (Heb. 12:23) and confirms them in their holiness, will it not then be impossible for them to sin? And will they not remain free-will beings? This is a difficult point to answer, but we may point out that there is a difference between creating a free-will being so that he can never sin, and confirming in holiness a free creature who has already demonstrated his preference and desire for that state by his free acts.

But let us change the wording of the objection just slightly. Instead of saying that God could create free-will beings who *cannot* sin—which is a contradiction, could we say that God could create free-will beings who in fact *do* not sin? There seems to be no logical contradiction to this. It is logically possible that God could create a world of free creatures which in fact never choose to sin. Not sinning is always a possibility for free-will beings, just as sinning is. So why did God not create such a world? It would surely be the best of all possible worlds.[67] In response we may say that this objection operates from a misconception of divine foreknowledge in relation to creation. The idea seems to be that God in his infinite foreknowledge could line up all the possible worlds that could ever be, then select any one of them to create. An all-good and all-powerful God would surely have chosen the possible world where the free creatures never sin.[68] The problem with this conception of things is that true foreknowledge is foreknowledge of an *actual* world, not just a *possible* world. God knows (not foreknows) all the possible worlds which could result from the creation of free-will beings, but he does not *fore*know the realities of the actual world until he has

65. Ibid., p. 153.

66. See above, pp. 223-224.

67. See Alvin Plantinga, *God, Freedom, and Evil*, pp. 32-33, for a description of this point.

68. This is similar to the determinist explanation of how God could create free-will beings whose free choices are all determined in advance. See p. 178 above.

committed himself to the creation of that particular world. Before[69] committing himself to the creation of our world, he knew that sin would be a *possibility* because of the presence of free will, but he did not know *whether* sin would occur or *how much* evil would actually come about until he decided to bring this specific world into existence.[70] Since this world was to be inhabited by free creatures, it was logically possible that they would choose never to sin. But in fact they chose otherwise. Such is the risk of creating free-will beings.

One may ask, then, whether this *is* the "best of all possible worlds." The answer is yes, with regard to its *form,* i.e., it is a world wherein free creatures may choose to love and honor God. But with regard to its *content*, it is not the best, since these free creatures have in fact made sinful choices as well as good ones. But this is something that even an omnipotent God could program neither in nor out without contradicting the very nature of free will. Thus this objection to the free-will defense is invalid.

A third objection is that free-will worship cannot possibly be worth the excessive amount of evil that exists in the world. It is not necessarily wrong for God to desire the love of creatures who freely choose to serve him, but is it worth the price? Two things may be said in response. First, this objection would have more force if God himself were directly responsible for all the evil that exists, if he himself needed it to accomplish his purposes and designed the world to include it. This is why the objection has validity against the soul-building view, as noted above; but it loses its force against the free-will view because in this view man is responsible for evil, not God. Second, this objection like the second one above assumes that God foreknew all the evil that would come into existence in this world even before he made the decision to create it. If this were so, then the complaint would be more relevant. But as we have already indicated, God's commitment to create this particular world preceded his foreknowledge of the kinds of choices that would be made. Thus God was not committing himself to a world that he knew would be so full of gratuitous evil. Of course, he knew that such would be *possible,* but apparently felt that it was worth the risk.

We do not claim to have solved all the problems relating to the presence of evil in the world in conjunction with the existence of an

---

69. The term is used in a logical sense, not chronological.

70. For a fuller discussion of the decision to create, see the section on the primacy of creation in Jack Cottrell, *What the Bible Says About God the Creator,* pp. 179-183.

all-good and omnipotent God, but the free-will answer does seem to be the best approach to the problem. It gives a reasonable explanation for evil's existence while maintaining the integrity of God's power and the integrity of his love.[71]

PROVIDENCE AND EVIL

Given the existence of evil in the world, and given the free will choices of creatures as its origin, just how does it fit into God's providential control of all things? Now that it is a part of his world, he cannot just ignore it. One thing is sure: evil does not lie outside the sovereignty of God. But how can we explain his sovereign control over it? We can do so by relating it to the concept of the will of God in two ways. First, some instances of evil fall within the purposive will of God and are caused by him; second, the remaining instances are allowed to occur by virtue of his permissive will.

Evils Caused by God

Even though God did not originate evil and did not desire it to be a part of his universe, now that his free-will creatures have made it a reality he uses it for his purposes when appropriate. This means that sometimes he causes specific instances of evil to happen. This does not apply to moral evil or sin, but only to natural evils; and it applies to only a small percentage of these. The point is that there are times when God, through his special providential control of the processes of nature, brings about a particular ill or disaster.

We must remember that all the instances of natural evil caused by God are responses to sin. This may take the form of *judgment* upon sin. In a real sense, human death in general was imposed by God upon the whole race as a penalty growing out of Adam's sin. The transgression of the one resulted in *condemnation* for all, says Paul (Rom. 5:15-18), and this condemnation must include at least physical death. But here we are concerned with the fact that at times God has intervened in the historical process to cause the deaths of specific individuals as a judgment upon the sin in their own lives. A number of these have been

71. For more complete presentations of the free-will defense, see the works of Alvin Plantinga, especially *God, Freedom, and Evil.* See also Edward P. Myers, *The Problem of Evil and Suffering* (West Monroe, La.: Howard Book House, 1978); and Michael Peterson, *Evil and the Christian God.*

mentioned in the course of our study; we may recall for example King Ahab (I Kings 22:34) and Ananias and Sapphira (Acts 5:1-10). God's providential judgments have also taken forms other than death, such as pestilence and disease (II Kings 15:5; I Chron. 21:7, 14; II Chron. 21:18-19).

At other times God's providential causation of calamities has been not for the purpose of punishment but for the purpose of *correction* or chastisement. This, too, is a response to sin; the goal is to turn people away from sin and to cause them to repent and return to God. We will remember, for example, that God can control the clouds for the purpose of correction (Job 37:13), e.g., to bring about a drought (James 5:17; Amos 4:7-8). He can destroy crops by such means as insect plagues (Amos 4:9; Joel 1:4ff.). He can elicit repentance by causing a windstorm (Jonah 1:4) or a disease (Num. 12:10). In other words, God can *use* evil and suffering in specific instances to serve his purposes in relation to sin, now that they are in existence.

The examples cited are of course taken from the biblical records. We know that God caused certain natural evils in Bible times. But does he still do so today? Perhaps so; but without special revelation to interpret providence for us, there is no way to be sure. When certain natural disasters strike, we may wonder and we may speculate. We may offer our tentative opinions as to the meaning of a particular event such as a tornado or flood, and we may draw some lessons from them in the way of correction. But there is no basis for dogmatism regarding the meaning of a particular calamity. Thus a believer who is experiencing disaster or suffering must not torture himself with such questions as "What have I done to deserve this?" or "Why is God punishing me?" He must take comfort in Romans 8:28. If God's hand is in it, it has a good purpose, and we must trust him to bring that good purpose to pass.

Evils Permitted by God

It is safe to say that most of the evil in the world is not caused by God but is allowed to happen according to his permissive will. This is in keeping with his commitment to the relative independence of his creation, including the relative independence of the natural processes and creaturely free will. This applies to all moral evil, including the first sins in the Garden of Eden. God allows man the integrity of free choice. When evil is chosen, he allows the evil consequences that flow from it to pour out their cup of suffering upon mankind. This includes all the ways pointed out above in which moral evil results in natural suffering: the corruption of nature, personal suffering from one's own sins, suffering from someone else's sins, and Satanic interference. The great majority of evil in the world is from these sources, as God chooses not to intervene and prevent it.

Thus in the face of personal calamity and suffering it is probably improper to ask, "Why is God doing this to me?" In all likelihood God himself is *not* doing it; it is probably the result of somebody's free-will choice, either directly or indirectly. A baby born with a birth defect, for example, may be suffering the consequence of his mother's smoking or drinking during her pregnancy. Or the genetic flaw may go back much further, perhaps even to the garbling of nature that occurred with Adam's sin.

In view of the sovereignty of God's permissive will, it *is* proper to ask, "Why did God *allow* this to happen?" This is so because nothing happens without God's foreknowing it and deciding not to prevent it. To say that God permits something to happen means that he *could* have prevented it if he had chosen to do so, if he had had a good reason for doing so. It is true, then, that God could have prevented this birth defect or that accident or that disease. When a saint of God in the throes of undeserved suffering cries out, "Why is God allowing this to happen?" I confess that this is one of the most difficult questions to answer. We may offer two considerations, however. First, we must remember that the possibility of evil is the price of free will. Now that creaturely freedom has made evil a reality, there is no turning back. God cannot overrule every evil choice of man and every evil consequence therefrom without contradicting his own purposes in creating beings with free will. This is part of the price we pay for freedom, and which God himself pays for creating us thus. When a child lies suffering from an incurable illness and his parents stand beside him in grief, do we think that God suffers any less than the child or his parents? Yet God has decided that having creatures with free will is worth the price of suffering, even the suffering of sacrificing his own Son on the cross. If we cannot penetrate the mystery of a particular experience of suffering, at least we can appreciate the fact that God is suffering with us and in his wisdom and goodness has judged the final result to be worth it.

The second thing to remember is that God has promised that all things will work together for good to those who love him and are called in accordance with his purpose (Rom. 8:28). Thus even the suffering which he permits can be used for the benefit of those who experience it or for the benefit of those whose lives are touched by it. For example, though God did not design suffering for this purpose, he can use it to help build Christian character. Paul says, "And not only this, but we also exult in our tribulations, knowing that tribulation brings about perseverance; and perseverance, proven character; and proven character, hope" (Rom. 5:3-4). James adds, "Consider it all joy, my brethren, when you encounter various trials, knowing that the testing of your faith produces endurance. And let endurance have its perfect result, that you may be perfect and complete, lacking in nothing" (James 1:2-4). Also, the one who has suffered affliction is then able to minister to others who are going through the same kind of suffering. It enables us to comfort them and show them mercy. Paul says,

> Blessed be the God and Father of our Lord Jesus Christ, the Father of mercies and God of all comfort; who comforts us in all our affliction so that we may be able to comfort those who are in any affliction with the comfort with which we ourselves are comforted by God. For just as the sufferings of Christ are ours in abundance, so also our comfort is abundant through Christ. But if we are afflicted, it is for your comfort and salvation; or if we are comforted, it is for your comfort, which is effective in the patient enduring of the same sufferings which we also suffer . . . (II Cor. 1:3-6).

Another fulfillment of Romans 8:28 is that a certain affliction may multiply our opportunities for and effectiveness in witnessing to the love of God in Christ Jesus. For example, if Joni Eareckson had not suffered a severe injury in an accident, would she have influenced even a fraction of the people who have been touched by her story?[72] Probably not. These are just some examples of the kinds of positive benefits that can accrue from suffering to those who trust themselves to God's sovereign providence.[73]

This may be one reason why God does not always answer our prayers for protection and deliverance from evil. Sometimes he does protect and deliver us, of course; so we should never fail to pray for

---

72. See Joni Eareckson, *Joni* (Grand Rapids: Zondervan, 1976); Philip Yancey, *Where Is God When It Hurts*, pp. 111ff.

73. For other suggestions see Virgil Hurley, "Good Uses of Adversity," *Christian Standard* (June 18/25, July 2, 1978), 113:7-8/4-5/4-5; and Ken Idleman, "Why God Permits Suffering," *Christian Standard* (October 24, 1976), 111:13-14.

God's special providence in these matters. But sometimes he does not intervene; rather he allows the affliction to occur or to continue. In these cases we must trust that the wisdom of God has discerned a higher good that will come from the affliction, such as one of those mentioned above. Perhaps we ourselves will observe or experience this higher good; perhaps it will take place without our ever being aware of it. After all, he sees the whole pattern of providence while we see only small parts of it, often just the darker parts. In such cases there is no alternative to trusting the goodness and wisdom of the Sovereign Ruler of the universe. The following time-tested lines by William Cowper capture this spirit of trust perfectly:

> God moves in a mysterious way His wonders to perform.
> He plants His footsteps in the sea and rides upon the storm.
>
> Ye fearful saints, fresh courage take; the clouds ye so much dread
> Are big with mercy, and shall break in blessings on your head.
>
> Judge not the Lord by feeble sense but trust Him for His grace.
> Behind a frowning providence He hides a smiling face.
>
> His purposes will ripen fast, unfolding every hour;
> The bud may have a bitter taste, but sweet will be the flower.
>
> Blind unbelief is sure to err, and scan His work in vain;
> God is His own interpreter, and He will make it plain.

Chapter Twelve

OUR RESPONSE TO PROVIDENCE

In this volume we have attempted to expound the biblical data concerning the doctrine of providence, i.e., the work and nature of God as the Sovereign Ruler over creation. We have explored the several aspects of his work in connection with the on-going world, including general providence, special providence, and miracles. We have seen how God maintains complete control over his creatures while preserving the integrity of their relative independence. We have set forth the Bible's teaching concerning the character or attributes of God which are particularly demonstrated and magnified by the works of providence. We have seen how the whole of reality is embraced within the will of God in one sense or another. We have seen how predestination is consistent with human freedom and how answered prayer is consistent with divine immutability, the key to both being God's foreknowledge. We have seen how the existence of evil fits into the sovereign rule of a God who is both all-powerful and benevolent. And we have also seen how this view of providence is quite unique, being not at all akin to the non-biblical alternatives of indeterminism, self-determinism, and determinism.

Consideration of the all-inclusiveness and all-sufficiency of God's sovereign rule should lead us to certain specific responses. Though many of these have already been touched upon in the preceding chapters, it seems appropriate to conclude this volume with a summary statement of them. What attitude or state of mind should come over us in the face of the realization that the Almighty God does indeed rule the universe in goodness, wisdom, and power?

WORSHIP

The first responses to providence fall under the general heading of worship. When we reflect upon the wonders of God's sovereign working in nature and history, we should be filled with an attitude of worship that takes at least three different forms. In the first place, an awareness of providence should inspire us with a sense of *awe* and *reverence* before the Lord. "Stand and consider the wonders of God," says Job 37:14. Indeed, the heavens declare his glory, and their expanse shows forth the work of his hands (Ps. 19:1). Even ordinary things like rainfall and harvest bear witness to him (Acts 14:17). Thinking about the way galaxies of stars are hurtling through space, watching fields of wheat grow into golden oceans, watching in fascination as lightning writes its signature across the midnight sky, trying to imagine the sound and the fury of a Vesuvius or a Krakatoa, observing blossoms unfold via time-lapse photography: such phenomena in themselves are capable of evoking wonder even in the heart of an agnostic or atheist. But when we place them all in the context of divine providence and realize that they are the works of the Lord God, the Sovereign Ruler of the universe, the wonder they inspire is not only magnified beyond measure but is also directed as worship toward the God who is their author.

The second worshipful attitude evoked by providence is *humility*. The mind and skills of human beings have produced some truly awesome works down through the centuries, from the pyramids to St. Louis' Gateway Arch, from the Panama Canal to space shuttles. Some of these works have been labeled the "wonders of the world" and have engendered much pride in human accomplishment. But the psalmist puts this into perspective when he says, "When I consider Thy heavens, the work of Thy fingers, the moon and the stars, which Thou hast ordained; what is man . . . ?" (Ps. 8:3-4). When placed alongside the works of God, even man's most significant achievements are relatively puny; and man's pride rightly gives way to a worshipful humility.

It is not that man's works are meaningless and amount to nothing, for they are often quite remarkable. But obviously they pale in comparison with the works of God. Also, it must be emphasized that whatever man accomplishes is done under the sovereign permission and control of the God who rules over all things. How can even the greatest artists and thinkers and engineers boast when they realize that their skills and abilities are the gifts of God's providence? "For who regards you as superior? And what do you have that you did not receive? But if you did receive it, why do you boast as if you had not received it?" (I Cor. 4:7). It is only by God's goodness and power that anyone is able to achieve anything: "You ought to say, 'If the Lord wills, we shall live and also do this or that'" (James 4:15). Through his providential control of all things he is able to seal the hand of every man and magnify the works of his own hands (Job 37:7).

In view of all this, perhaps we can say that man's greatest work is to bow humbly before the Sovereign God and to acknowledge him as the Lord of the universe. As Pink says, "A true recognition of God's sovereignty humbles as nothing else does or can humble, and brings the heart into lowly submission before God."[1]

1. Arthur W. Pink, *The Sovereignty of God*, revised edition (London: Banner of Truth Trust, 1961), p. 123.

The third attitude of worship inspired by reflection upon God's providence is *gratitude*. Gratitude has to do with *gifts*; we are grateful for the things *given* to us. Also, since giving is something that only persons can do, gratitude cannot be an impersonal, abstract feeling but must be directed toward another person, the giver. In light of the doctrine of providence we can easily see that God is the great *Giver* (James 1:17), the one to whom we must be thankful. Thus the reality of providence causes us to bow before God in gratitude for his many gifts: "Bless the Lord, O my soul, and forget none of His benefits" (Ps. 103:2). The true focus of gratitude, however, is not the gifts but the Giver. More important than the things he gives us is the fact that he is a loving and wise Father who *wants* to bless his children and who is truly concerned about their welfare. This is why we worship our Ruler in the spirit of gratitude.

FREEDOM

The second response to God's providence is the attitude of freedom. The realization that God is in complete control of the universe gives us a true peace of mind as it frees us from all kinds of tensions. We will mention three of these in particular. In the first place, we have a *freedom from pressure*. Stress or pressure is common in today's fast-paced world of high goals and imminent deadlines and multiple responsibilities. But these things in themselves do not cause us to feel pressure. Pressure does not arise simply from having a lot to do; it arises from thinking that everything depends upon us, that we have to accomplish everything all by our selves, that the whole load lies upon our shoulders alone. A consciousness of God's providence, especially his ability to answer prayer and to intervene on our behalf to give us help and strength, relieves us from this kind of stress. We realize that everything in fact does *not* depend upon us alone, and that God is in complete control of all things. We recall the words of Zechariah 4:6 and feel a tremendous freedom: "'Not by might nor by power, but by My Spirit,' says the Lord of hosts."

In the second place, we have *freedom from fear*. When we are truly convinced that God loves us and that his sovereignty rules over all, we no longer need to fear anything that could happen to us in this world. God is in charge, and he will see that all things work together for good for those who love him (Rom. 8:28). Thus as Psalm 91:5-6, says, "You will not be afraid of the terror by night, or of the arrow that flies by day; of the pestilence that stalks in darkness, or of the destruction that lays waste at noon." Jesus tells us not to fear those who can kill the body but cannot touch the soul (Matt. 10:28). "If God is for us, who is against us?" (Rom. 8:31). Everything is in the hands of the God who so "wondrously reigneth." Such marvelous providence, says Sherlock, convinces us "how perfectly we are in God's hands, and how secure we are in his protection—what little reason we have to be afraid of men whatever their power, how furious soever their passions are."[2]

Finally, an understanding of providence gives us *freedom from worry*. Worry is a way of thinking about the unknown, and it may be directed toward the future or the past. It is a fear that the future will not turn out the way we want it to or the way we think it should. It is a fear that something dreadful may have already occurred in circumstances about which we have not yet been informed. It involves imagining and dwelling upon undesirable yet possible scenarios with regard to things that are important to us. A mother worries when her daughter is late getting in from a date. Has she had a bad accident? Has she run away from home? Has she been attacked? A father worries about paying his bills. Will there be unexpected expenses? Will he be laid off from his job? Will the electric company accept partial payment if necessary? A teenager worries about whether he passed his exams. A writer or editor worries about meeting his deadline. A college graduate worries about finding a job. The examples are endless.

How may we be freed from such anxieties and negative fantasizing? The providence of God is the answer. When we accept the reality of God's providential control over all things, we can learn to leave the unknown in his hands. He who knows all things and with whom nothing is impossible is also good and wise; we have no reason to doubt or to brood. The Sovereign Lord cares about us and he cares for us, and because of this we are invited to cast all our anxieties upon him (I Peter 5:7). This is the very point Jesus is making in his definitive rebuttal of worry in Matthew 6:25-34:

> For this reason I say to you, do not be anxious for your life, as to what you shall eat, or what you shall drink; nor for your body, as to what you shall put on. Is not life more than food, and the body than clothing? Look at the birds of the air, that they do not sow, neither do they reap, nor gather into barns, and yet your heavenly Father feeds

2. William Sherlock, *A Discourse Concerning the Divine Providence* (Pittsburgh: J. L. Read, 1848), p. 58.

> them. Are you not worth much more than they? And which of you by being anxious can add a single cubit to his life's span? And why are you anxious about clothing? Observe how the lilies of the field grow; they do not toil nor do they spin, yet I say to you that even Solomon in all his glory did not clothe himself like one of these. But if God so arrays the grass of the field, which is alive today and tomorrow is thrown into the furnace, will He not much more do so for you, O men of little faith? Do not be anxious then, saying, "What shall we eat?" or "What shall we drink?" or "With what shall we clothe ourselves?" For all these things the Gentiles eagerly seek; for your heavenly Father knows that you need all these things. But seek first His kingdom and His righteousness; and all these things shall be added to you. Therefore do not be anxious for tomorrow; for tomorrow will care for itself. Each day has enough trouble of its own.

It should be noted that this is not a cold-hearted resignation to fate (as in the often-heard advice, "There's no need to worry over things you can't do anything about"); it is rather a recognition that a loving and personal God is in charge of the universe.

TRUST

The final group of responses to providence may be considered under the general heading of trust. It is one thing to assert an academic or intellectual belief in God's sovereign lordship; it is another thing to really believe that it is so, and that one's own life is firmly fixed in the heart of God's love. We can quote Romans 8:28 backwards and forwards, but until we are really and truly convinced that it actually applies to us, we do not yet know the meaning of providence. Faith is more than assenting to the truth of propositions; it is also personal trust in the personal God. This is true no less in the way we cope with day-to-day circumstances than in the way we receive our eternal salvation. We must trust in the God of providence as well as in the God of redemption.

The first element of trust is a consciousness of *dependence* upon God for our daily provisions and for our very existence. Whether we are aware of it or not, we *are* dependent upon him, "for in Him we live and move and exist" (Acts 17:28). An understanding of providence simply makes us *aware* of that dependence. It enables us to look beyond impersonal nature and natural law as the power that sustains us, to the personal God who provides us with every good thing and every perfect gift (James 1:17). As Sherlock says,

> Our trust in God signifies our absolute dependence on the wisdom, and power, and goodness of God to take care of us; it is committing ourselves to God, putting ourselves absolutely into his hands, with a full persuasion that he will do what we desire, or do what shall be better for us; that he will answer our requests, or deny them with greater wisdom and goodness than he could grant them.[3]

The second element of trust is *submission*, which comes when we realize that whatever happens is the will of God at least in the sense of permission if not in the sense of purpose. We learn to live and to pray in complete submission to his will, even as Jesus did as he faced Calvary: "Father, if Thou art willing, remove this cup from Me; yet not My will, but Thine be done" (Luke 22:42). Such an attitude is especially important in the face of adversity. Eli exhibited this attitude when the young Samuel told him what God had revealed to him, namely, that he was about to bring judgment upon Eli's two sons because of their wickedness. Though his heart must have been breaking, Eli fully trusted God's decision as he said, "It is the Lord; let Him do what seems good to Him" (I Sam. 3:18). As Pink says, "Wonderful submission! Sublime resignation!"[4] A similar example is King David, at the time he was forced to flee from Jerusalem for safety during the rebellion of his own son Absalom. He meets Zadok the priest and a group of Levites who are carrying the ark of the covenant, and he says to them, "Return the ark of God to the city. If I find favor in the sight of the Lord, then He will bring me back again, and show me both it and His habitation. But if He should say thus, 'I have no delight in you,' behold, here I am, let Him do to me as seems good to Him" (II Sam. 15:25-26). Pink makes this comment:

> . . . Here, too, the circumstances which confronted the speaker were exceedingly trying to the human heart. David was sore pressed with sorrow. His own son was driving him from the throne, and seeking his very life. Whether he would ever see Jerusalem and the Tabernacle again he knew not. But he was so yielded up to God, he was so fully assured that *His* will was best, that even though it meant the loss of the throne and the loss of his life, he was content for Him to have His way—"let Him do to me as seemeth good unto Him."[5]

The immortal words of Job breathe the same spirit of submission: "The Lord gave and the Lord has taken away. Blessed be the name of the Lord" (Job 1:21).

---

3. Ibid., pp. 320-321.
4. Arthur W. Pink, *The Sovereignty of God*, p. 129.
5. Ibid., pp. 147-148.

We must be careful not to mistake submission to providence for the spirit of quietism, which makes no attempt to avoid adversity or to alter the undesirable circumstances which befall us. When such things occur we have not only the right but also the responsibility to set things right insofar as we are able to do so. Sherlock offers this example: "If a thief breaks open my house, or robs me upon the road, submission to providence does not hinder me from pursuing and taking him, and recovering my own of him, and bringing him to punishment, if I can."[6] If a person loses his job, this does not mean that he should not look for another one. The person who becomes ill by all means ought to seek medical attention to aid his recovery. The point of submission is this: once we have done everything we can to change or to better our situation, but still the adversity persists, then we can only say, "Thy will be done." We submit to God's providence in patience and without complaining or murmuring, just as Habakkuk did when he learned from God that the Babylonian hordes would soon be invading and plundering his land:

> I heard and my inward parts trembled; at the sound my lips quivered. Decay enters my bones, and in my place I tremble. Because I must wait quietly for the day of distress, for the people to arise who will invade us. Though the fig tree should not blossom, and there be no fruit on the vines, though the yield of the olive should fail, and the fields produce no food, though the flock should be cut off from the fold, and there be no cattle in the stalls, yet I will exult in the Lord, I will rejoice in the God of my salvation. The Lord God is my strength, and He has made my feet like hinds' feet, and makes me walk on my high places (Hab. 3:16-19).

The final way in which trust responds to providence is *confidence,* i.e., a firm confidence that God is in control and that the future will turn out in accordance with his purposes. This is especially important in view of the many opposing philosophies and forces which are constantly working against God and his purposes. There are so many times when the enemies of God seem to be prevailing, when the forces of evil and the very gates of hades seem to have the upper hand. These are the times that tempt us to doubt and to cry out, "Where is the God of justice?" (Mal. 2:17). When this happens, it is an incomparable blessing to be able to reflect upon the providence of God and upon the sovereignty of his rule over the universe. In light of all we know about his providential control, we can trust the future into his hands with the utmost confidence.

---

6. William Sherlock, *A Discourse Concerning the Divine Providence,* p. 310.

The last book of the Bible, the book of Revelation, was written precisely for this purpose, namely, to assure us that God is in control of universal history and will bring all things to a just end. This point is made through a series of visions, each of which develops the same theme in a different way. First a situation is established in which Satan's forces seem to be victorious and the people of God are the objects of persecution and injustice. The circumstances are such that even the faithful may begin to wonder whether God is really in charge. But then the vision is brought to a climax by the eschatological intervention of God; Jesus returns to rescue his people and bring the wicked to judgment. God *is* in charge; the presumptuous principalities and powers of this world are no match for the sovereign lordship of the Creator and Ruler of the universe. This is the basis of our confidence even in the face of adversity, and it is well summed up near the end of one of the apocalyptic visions in the words of Revelation 11:15:

> "THE KINGDOM OF THE WORLD HAS BECOME THE
> KINGDOM OF OUR LORD, AND OF HIS CHRIST;
> AND HE WILL REIGN FOREVER AND EVER."

Bibliography

Adler, Margot. *Drawing Down the Moon: Witches, Druids, Goddess-Worshippers, and Other Pagans in America Today*. Boston: Beacon Press, 1979.

Altizer, Thomas J. J. *The Gospel of Christian Atheism*. Philadelphia: Westminster Press, 1966.

______________, and William Hamilton. *Radical Theology and the Death of God*. Indianapolis: Bobbs-Merrill, 1966.

Ambrose. "Exposition of the Christian Faith," *A Select Library of Nicene and Post-Nicene Fathers of the Christian Church*, Second Series, ed. Philip Schaff and Henry Wace; Volume X, *St. Ambrose: Select Works and Letters*, tr. H. De Romestin et al. Grand Rapids: Eerdmans reprint, 1979. Pp. 199-314.

Anderson, J. Kerby. *Genetic Engineering*. Grand Rapids: Zondervan, 1982.

Augustine. "The City of God," tr. Marcus Dods. *Basic Writings of Saint Augustine*, Volume II, ed. Whitney J. Oates. New York: Random House, 1948. Pp. 1-663.

Baelz, Peter R. *Prayer and Providence: A Background Study*. New York: Seabury Press, 1968.

Baepler, Richard. "Providence in Christian Thought," *The Caring God: Perspectives on Providence*, ed. Carl S. Meyer and Herbert T. Mayer. St. Louis: Concordia Publishing House, 1973. Pp. 45-66.

Banerjea, Jitendra Nath. "The Hindu Concept of God," *The Religion of the Hindus*, ed. Kenneth W. Morgan. New York: Ronald Press, 1953. Pp. 48-82.

Barth, Karl. *Church Dogmatics, Volume II: The Doctrine of God, Part 1*, ed. G. W. Bromiley and T. F. Torrance, tr. T. H. L. Parker et al. Edinburgh: T. & T. Clark, 1957.

______________. *Church Dogmatics, Volume III: The Doctrine of Creation, Part 3*, tr. G. W. Bromiley and R. J. Ehrlich. Edinburgh: T. & T. Clark, 1961.

Basak, Radhagovinda. "The Hindu Concept of the Natural World," *The Religion of the Hindus*, ed. Kenneth W. Morgan. New York: Ronald Press, 1953. Pp. 83-116.

Basinger, David, and Randall Basinger. "Science and the Concept of Miracle," *Journal of the American Scientific Affiliation* (December 1978), 30:164-168.

Bavinck, Herman. *The Doctrine of God*, ed. and tr. William Hendriksen. Grand Rapids: Eerdmans, 1951.

Behm, J. "προνοέω, πρόνοια," *Theological Dictionary of the New Testament*, ed. Gerhard Kittel, tr. G. W. Bromiley. Grand Rapids: Eerdmans, 1967. IV:1009-1017.

Berkhof, Louis, *Systematic Theology*. London: Banner of Truth Trust, 1939.

Berkouwer, G. C. *Divine Election*, tr. Hugo Bekker. Grand Rapids: Eerdmans, 1960.

______________. *The Providence of God*, tr. Lewis B. Smedes. Grand Rapids: Eerdmans, 1952.

Bhagavad-gita As It Is, tr. A. C. Bhaktivedanta. New York: Collier Books, 1972.

Birks, T. R. *The Bible and Modern Thought.* Cincinnati: Curts and Jennings, 1861.

Bjornstad, James, and Shildes Johnson. *Stars, Signs, and Salvation in the Age of Aquarius.* Minneapolis: Bethany Fellowship, 1971.

Blamires, Harry. *The Will and the Way: A Study of Divine Providence and Vocation.* London: S.P.C.K., 1957.

Bloesch, Donald G. *Essentials of Evangelical Theology, Volume One: God, Authority, and Salvation.* San Francisco: Harper & Row, 1978.

Boettner, Loraine. *The Reformed Doctrine of Predestination.* Grand Rapids: Eerdmans, 1932.

Boice, James Montgomery. *Foundations of the Christian Faith, Volume I: The Sovereign God.* Downers Grove, Ill.: InterVarsity Press, 1978.

Bonhoeffer, Dietrich. *Letters and Papers from Prison,* enlarged edition, ed. Eberhard Bethge, tr. Reginald Fuller et al. New York: Macmillan, 1972.

Bowker, John. *Problems of Suffering in the Religions of the World.* New York: Cambridge University Press, 1970.

Brother Lawrence. *The God-Illuminated Cook: A New Edition of The Practice of the Presence of God,* ed. Robin Dawes et al. Callicoon, N.Y.: Lifesavers Library, 1975.

Brown, Colin. *Miracles and the Critical Mind.* Grand Rapids: Eerdmans, 1984.

Bruce, Alexander Balmain. *The Miraculous Element in the Gospels.* 2 ed. London: Hodder and Stoughton, 1890.

______________. *The Moral Order of the World in Ancient and Modern Thought.* London: Hodder and Stoughton, 1899.

Brunner, Emil. *The Christian Doctrine of Creation and Redemption: Dogmatics, Volume II,* tr. Olive Wyon. Philadelphia: Westminster Press, 1952.

______________. *The Christian Doctrine of God: Dogmatics, Volume I,* tr. Olive Wyon. Philadelphia: Westminster Press, 1950.

Bultmann, Rudolf. *Jesus Christ and Mythology.* New York: Charles Scribner's Sons, 1958.

______________. "New Testament and Mythology," *Kerygma and Myth: A Theological Debate,* ed. Hans Werner Bartsch, tr. Reginald H. Fuller. New York: Harper Torchbook, 1961. Pp. 1-44.

Buswell, James O., Jr. *A Systematic Theology of the Christian Religion.* 2 vols. Grand Rapids: Zondervan, 1962.

Buttrick, George A. *Prayer.* New York: Abingdon-Cokesbury, 1942.

Cahn, Steven M. "Chance," *The Encyclopedia of Philosophy,* ed. Paul Edwards. New York: Macmillan, 1967. II:73-75.

Calvin, John. "A Defence of the Secret Providence of God," *Calvin's Calvinism,* tr. Henry Cole. Grand Rapids: Eerdmans, 1956. Pp. 207-350.

______________. *Institutes of the Christian Religion,* ed. John T. McNeill, tr. Ford Lewis Battles. 2 vols. "Library of Christian Classics," Volumes XX-XXI. Philadelphia: Westminster Press, 1960.

______________. "A Treatise on the Eternal Predestination of God," *Calvin's Calvinism,* tr. Henry Cole. Grand Rapids: Eerdmans, 1956. Pp. 1-206.

Campbell, Alexander, and N. L. Rice. *A Debate on the Action, Subject, Design and Administrator of Christian Baptism.* Lexington, Ky.: A. T. Skillman & Son, 1844.

Carnell, Edward John. *An Introduction to Christian Apologetics: A Philosophic Defense of the Trinitarian-Theistic Faith.* Grand Rapids: Eerdmans, 1948.

Carson, D. A. *Divine Sovereignty and Human Responsibility: Biblical Perspectives in Tension.* Atlanta: John Knox Press, 1981.

Chafer, Lewis Sperry. *Systematic Theology.* 8 vols. Dallas: Dallas Seminary Press, 1947.

Chandler, Russell. "Disciples Debate Community and Unity," *Christianity Today* (November 10, 1967), 12:54-56.

Chantry, Walter J. *Signs of the Apostles: Observations on Pentecostalism Old and New.* 2 ed. Carlisle, Pa.: Banner of Truth Trust, 1976.

Charnock, Stephen. *The Existence and Attributes of God.* Grand Rapids: Kregel reprint, 1958.

Chatterjee, Satis Chandra. "Hindu Religious Thought," *The Religion of the Hindus,* ed. Kenneth W. Morgan. New York: Ronald Press, 1953. Pp. 206-261.

Childe, V. Gordon. *Man Makes Himself.* New York: New American Library Mentor Books, 1951.

Christlieb, Theodore. *Modern Doubt and Christian Belief,* tr. G. H. Venables and H. U. Weitbrecht. New York: Charles Scribner's Sons, 1903.

Clark, Gordon H. *Biblical Predestination.* Nutley, N.J.: Presbyterian and Reformed, 1969.

______________. *From Thales to Dewey: A History of Philosophy.* Boston: Houghton Mifflin Company, 1957.

______________. "The Sovereignty of God," *The Trinity Review* (November-December 1982). Pp. 1-4.

Clement of Rome. "To the Corinthians," *The Apostolic Fathers,* ed. J. B. Lightfoot and J. R. Harmer. Grand Rapids: Baker, 1962. Pp. 13-41.

Coleman, Richard J. *Issues of Theological Warfare: Evangelicals and Liberals.* Grand Rapids: Eerdmans, 1972.

Coles, Elisha. *God's Sovereignty.* Grand Rapids: Baker, 1979 reprint of 1831 edition.

Collins, James. *God in Modern Philosophy.* Chicago: Henry Regnery, 1959.

Copleston, Frederick. *A History of Philosophy, Volume I: Greece and Rome.* New revised edition, in two parts. Garden City, N.Y.: Doubleday Image, 1962.

______________. *A History of Philosophy, Volume IV: Descartes to Leibnitz.* Garden City, N.Y.: Doubleday Image, 1963.

______________. *A History of Philosophy, Volume V: Modern Philosophy, the British Philosophers, Part I: Hobbes to Paley.* Garden City, N.Y.: Doubleday Image, 1964.

Cornford, F. M. *From Religion to Philosophy.* New York: Harper Torchbook, 1957.

Cottrell, Jack. *The Bible Says.* Cincinnati: Standard Publishing, 1982.

____________. "Conditional Election," *Grace Unlimited*, ed. Clark Pinnock. Minneapolis: Bethany Fellowship, 1975. Pp. 51-73.

____________. "Conditional Election," *The Seminary Review* (Summer 1966), 12:57-63.

____________. *His Truth.* Cincinnati: Standard Publishing, 1980.

____________. "The Jews in Prophecy," *Christian Standard* (October 14, 1979), 114:22-24.

____________. "The Predestination of Individuals," *Christian Standard* (October 4, 1970), 105:13-14.

____________. *What the Bible Says About God the Creator.* Joplin, Mo.: College Press, 1983.

Cox, Harvey. *The Secular City.* Revised edition. New York: Macmillan, 1966.

The Creeds of Christendom, ed. Philip Schaff. 4 ed., 3 volumes. New York: Harper and Brothers, 1919.

Custance, Arthur C. *The Sovereignty of Grace.* Phillipsburg, N.J.: Presbyterian and Reformed, 1979.

Daane, James. *The Freedom of God: A Study of Election and Pulpit.* Grand Rapids: Eerdmans, 1973.

Dabney, R. L. *Syllabus and Notes of the Course of Systematic and Polemic Theology.* 5 ed. Richmond, Va.: Presbyterian Committee of Publication, 1871.

D'Abro, A. *The Rise of the New Physics.* 2 vols. New York: Dover Publications, 1952.

Dandekar, R. N. "The Role of Man in Hinduism," *The Religion of the Hindus*, ed. Kenneth W. Morgan. New York: Ronald Press, 1953. Pp. 117-153.

Daujat, Jean. *Prayer.* tr. Martin Murphy. New York: Hawthorn Books, 1964.

Davis, Stephen T. "Free Will and Evil," *Encountering Evil: Live Options in Theodicy*, ed. Stephen T. Davis. Atlanta: John Knox Press, 1981. Pp. 69-83.

DeCaro, Louis A. *Israel Today: Fulfillment of Prophecy?* Nutley, N.J.: Presbyterian and Reformed, 1974.

Dick, John. *Lectures on Theology.* 2 vols. in 1. New York: R. Carter and Brothers, 1878.

Dickinson, Curtis. "The Sovereign," *The Witness* (May 1969), 9:1-2.

Diemer, Johann H. *Nature and Miracle*, tr. Wilma Bouma. Toronto: Wedge Publishing Foundation, 1977.

Diogenes Laertius. "Life of Zeno," tr. C. D. Yonge, *Essential Works of Stoicism*, ed. Moses Hadas. New York: Bantam Books, 1961. Pp. 1-47.

Doty, William L. *Prayer in the Spirit.* New York: Alba House, 1973.

Dunham, Barrows. *Man Against Myth.* Boston: Little, Brown, 1948.

Eareckson, Joni. *Joni.* Grand Rapids: Zondervan, 1976.

Ensign, Grayson H., and Edward Howe. *Bothered? Bewildered? Bewitched? Your Guide to Practical Supernatural Healing.* Cincinnati: Recovery Publications, 1984.

Epictetus. "The Manual," tr. George Long, *Essential Works of Stoicism*, ed. Moses Hadas. New York: Bantam Books, 1961. Pp. 83-101.

Feinberg, John S. *Theologies and Evil.* Washington, D.C.: University Press of America, 1979.

Ferre, Nels F. S. *The Christian Understanding of God.* New York: Harper & Brothers, 1951.

Fisk, Samuel. *Divine Sovereignty and Human Freedom.* Neptune, N.J.: Loizeaux Brothers, 1973.

Flew, Antony. "Divine Omnipotence and Human Freedom," *New Essays in Philosophical Theology*, ed. Antony Flew and Alasdair MacIntyre. London: SCM Press, 1955. Pp. 144-169.

Forster, Roger T. and V. Paul Marston. *God's Strategy in Human History.* Wheaton: Tyndale House, 1974.

Fosdick, Harry Emerson. *The Meaning of Prayer.* New York: Association Press, 1915.

Friesen, Garry, with J. Robin Maxson. *Decision Making & the Will of God: A Biblical Alternative to the Traditional View.* Portland, Ore.: Multnomah Press, 1980.

Geisler, Norman. *Miracles and Modern Thought.* Grand Rapids: Zondervan, 1982.

____________. *Philosophy of Religion.* Grand Rapids: Zondervan, 1974.

____________. *The Roots of Evil.* Grand Rapids: Zondervan, 1978.

____________, and J. Yutaka Amano. *The Religion of the Force.* Dallas: Quest Publications, 1983.

Gienapp, John C. "Providentialism and Evolutionary Biology," *The Caring God: Perspectives on Providence*, ed. Carl S. Meyer and Herbert T. Mayer. St. Louis: Concordia Publishing House, 1973. Pp. 217-240.

Gilkey, Langdon. "The Concept of Providence in Contemporary Theology," *The Journal of Religion* (July 1963), 43:171-192.

Glover, Ruth. "Lilliputian or Leviathan," *Christian Standard* (June 10, 1984), 119:15.

Godet, Frederick. *Commentary on the Epistle to the Romans*, tr. A. Cusin. Grand Rapids: Zondervan, 1956 reprint of 1883 edition.

Goodavage, Joseph F. *Astrology: The Space Age Science.* New York: New American Library Signet Books, 1966.

Greene, William Chase. *Moira: Fate, Good, and Evil in Greek Thought.* Gloucester, Mass.: Peter Smith, 1968.

Griffin, David R. "Creation out of Chaos and the Problem of Evil," *Encountering Evil: Live Options in Theodicy*, ed. Stephen T. Davis. Atlanta: John Knox Press, 1981. Pp. 101-119.

____________. *God, Power and Evil: A Process Theodicy.* Philadelphia: Westminster Press, 1976.

Gruenler, Royce. *The Inexhaustible God: Biblical Faith and the Challenge of Process Theism.* Grand Rapids: Baker, 1983.

Hamilton, William. *The New Essence of Christianity.* New York: Association Press, 1961.
Hargraves, Archie. "Go Where the Action Is," *Social Action* (February 1964).
Harkness, Georgia. *The Providence of God.* Nashville: Abingdon, 1960.
Hartshorne, Charles, and William L. Reese, eds. *Philosophers Speak of God.* Chicago: University of Chicago Press, 1953.
Hasker, William. *Metaphysics: Constructing a World View.* Downers Grove, Ill.: InterVarsity Press, 1983.
Hebblethwaite, Brian. *Evil, Suffering and Religion.* New York: Hawthorn Books, 1976.
Heiler, Friedrich. *Prayer: A Study in the History and Psychology of Religion,* tr. Samuel McComb. New York: Oxford University Press, 1932.
Heim, Karl. *The Transformation of the Scientific World View,* tr. W. A. Whitehouse. New York: Harper and Brothers, 1953.
Helms, Randel. "On Miracles," *Free Inquiry* (Spring 1984), 4:44-46.
Hendriksen, William. *Israel in Prophecy.* Grand Rapids: Baker, 1968.
Henry, Carl F. H. *God, Revelation and Authority, Volume VI: The God Who Stands and Stays, Part Two.* Waco: Word Books, 1983.
Hesse, Mary. "Miracles and the Laws of Nature," *Miracles: Cambridge Studies in Their Philosophy and History,* ed. C. F. D. Moule. New York: Morehouse-Barlow, 1965. Pp. 33-42.
Hick, John. *Evil and the God of Love.* New York: Harper and Row, 1966.
______________. "An Irenaean Theodicy," *Encountering Evil: Live Options in Theodicy,* ed. Stephen T. Davis. Atlanta: John Knox Press, 1981. Pp. 39-52.
Hodge, Archibald Alexander. *Evangelical Theology.* London: Thomas Nelson and Sons, 1890.
______________. *Outlines of Theology.* New York: Robert Carter and Brothers, 1876.
______________. *Popular Lectures on Theological Themes.* Philadelphia: Presbyterian Board of Publication, 1887.
Hodge, Charles. *Systematic Theology.* 3 vols. Grand Rapids: Eerdmans reprint, n.d.
Holmes, George F. "Leibnitz," *Cyclopedia of Biblical, Theological, and Ecclesiastical Literature,* ed. John M'Clintock and James Strong. New York: Harper and Brothers, 1894. V:332-337.
Hoover, Arlie J. *Dear Agnos: A Defense of Christianity.* Grand Rapids: Baker, 1976.
Houston, James M. *I Believe in the Creator.* Grand Rapids: Eerdmans, 1980.
Howard, J. Grant, Jr. *Knowing God's Will—And Doing It!* Grand Rapids: Zondervan, 1976.
Hughes, H. Maldwyn. *The Christian Idea of God.* London: Duckworth, 1936.
Humanist Manifestos I and II. Buffalo: Prometheus Books, 1973.
Hume, David. *Dialogues Concerning Natural Religion,* ed. Norman Kemp Smith. Indianapolis: Bobbs-Merrill, 1947.

____________. "An Enquiry Concerning Human Understanding," *Hume: Theory of Knowledge*, ed. D. C. Yalden-Thomson. New York: Thomas Nelson and Sons, 1951. Pp. 1-176.

Hurley, Virgil. "Good Uses of Adversity," *Christian Standard* (June 18/25, July 2, 1978), 113:7-8/4-5/4-5.

Huson, Paul. *Mastering Witchcraft: A Practical Guide for Witches, Warlocks, and Covens.* New York: G. P. Putnam's Sons, 1970.

Huxley, Aldous. *Brave New World.* New York: Bantam Books, 1953.

Huxley, Julian. *Evolution in Action.* New York: New American Library Signet Books, 1953.

____________. *Religion Without Revelation.* New York: New American Library Mentor Books, 1957.

Idleman, Ken. "Why God Permits Suffering," *Christian Standard* (October 24, 1976), 111:13-14.

James, William. "The Dilemma of Determinism," *The Will To Believe and Other Essays in Popular Philosophy.* New York: Longmans, Green, and Co., 1896. Pp. 145-183.

Jenkins, David E. *Guide to the Debate About God.* Philadelphia: Westminster Press, 1966.

Johns, Kenneth D. *Election: Love Before Time.* Phillipsburg, N.J.: Presbyterian and Reformed, 1976.

Ketcherside, W. Carl. "The Dynamic of God," *Christian Standard* (July 31, 1983), 118:12-13.

____________. "The Hand of God," *Christian Standard* (August 7, 1983), 118:10-11.

____________. "No Credibility Gap," *Christian Standard* (August 28, 1983), 118:10-11.

King, Robert H. Review of *The Traces of God* by Diogenes Allen, *Princeton Seminary Bulletin,* New Series (No. 3, 1982), 3:336-337.

Kirk, John. *The Cloud Dispelled: Or, The Doctrine of Predestination Examined.* New York: N. Tibbals and Co., 1860.

König, Adrio. *Here Am I! A Christian Reflection on God.* Grand Rapids: Eerdmans, 1982.

The Koran, tr. George Sale. London: Frederick Warne and Co., 1890.

Kushner, Harold. *When Bad Things Happen to Good People.* New York: Schocken Books, 1981.

Laubach, Frank C. *The Game with Minutes.* Syracuse, N.Y.: New Readers Press, 1960.

Lee, Francis Nigel. *Communist Eschatology.* Nutley, N.J.: Craig Press, 1974.

Leupold, H. C. *Exposition of Ecclesiastes.* Grand Rapids: Baker reprint, 1966.

Lewis, C. S. *The Abolition of Man.* New York: Macmillan, 1947.

____________. *Letters to Malcolm: Chiefly on Prayer.* London: Geoffrey Bles, 1964.

____________. *Miracles: A Preliminary Study.* 2 ed. New York: Macmillan, 1960.

Lightner, Robert P. *The First Fundamental: GOD*. Nashville: Thomas Nelson, 1973.

Lloyd, G. E. R. "Leucippus and Democritus," *The Encyclopedia of Philosophy*, ed. Paul Edwards. New York: Macmillan, 1967. IV:446-451.

Luther, Martin. *The Bondage of the Will*, tr. J. I. Packer and O. R. Johnston. Old Tappan, N.J.: Fleming H. Revell Co., 1957.

____________. "Luther's Small Catechism," *The Creeds of Christendom*, 4 edition, ed. Philip Schaff. New York: Harper and Brothers, 1919. III:74-92.

MacIntyre, Alasdair. "Freud, Sigmund," *The Encyclopedia of Philosophy*, ed. Paul Edwards. New York: Macmillan, 1967. III:249-253.

____________. "Pantheism," *The Encyclopedia of Philosophy*, ed. Paul Edwards. New York: Macmillan, 1967. VI:31-35.

MacKay, Donald M. *The Clock Work Image: A Christian Perspective on Science*. Downers Grove, Ill.: InterVarsity Press, 1974.

Mackie, J. L. "Evil and Omnipotence," *God and Evil: Readings in the Theological Problem of Evil*, ed. Nelson Pike. Englewood Cliffs, N.J.: Prentice-Hall, 1964. Pp. 46-60.

Macquarrie, John. *Principles of Christian Theology*. New York: Charles Scribner's Sons, 1966.

MacRae, Allan A. "*'ōlām*," *Theological Wordbook of the Old Testament*, ed. R. Laird Harris et al. Chicago: Moody Press, 1980. II:672-673.

Marcus Aurelius. "To Himself," tr. George Long, *Essential Works of Stoicism*, ed. Moses Hadas. New York: Bantam Books, 1961. Pp. 103-205.

Mark, Alexandra. *Astrology for the Aquarian Age*. New York: Essandess, 1970.

Mascall, E. L. *Christian Theology and Natural Science*. New York: Ronald Press, 1956.

Mauro, Philip. *The Hope of Israel*. Swengel, Pa.: Reiner Publications, 1970.

McBrien, Richard P. *The Church in the Thought of Bishop John Robinson*. Philadelphia: Westminster Press, 1966.

McGarvey, J. W. *Evidences of Christianity*. Nashville: Gospel Advocate reprint, 1956.

Mellert, Robert. *What Is Process Theology?* New York: Paulist Press, 1975.

Miller, William McElwee. "Islam," *Religions in a Changing World*, revised edition, ed. Howard F. Vos. Chicago: Moody Press, 1961. Pp. 61-90.

Monod, Jacques. *Chance and Necessity: An Essay on The Natural Philosophy of Modern Biology*, tr. Austryn Wainhouse. New York: Alfred A. Knopf, 1971.

Montgomery, John W. *History and Christianity*. Downers Grove, Ill.: InterVarsity Press, 1965.

____________. "Science, Theology and the Miraculous," *Journal of the American Scientific Affiliation* (December 1978), 30:145-153.

Moore, George Foot. *History of Religions, Volume II: Judaism, Christianity, Mohammedanism*. New York: Charles Scribner's Sons, 1919.

Muller, H. J. *Proceedings of the Eighth International Congress of Genetics.* Lund, 1948.

Mullins, E. Y. *The Christian Religion in Its Doctrinal Expression.* Philadelphia: Judson Press, 1917.

Myers, Edward P. *The Problem of Evil and Suffering.* West Monroe, La.: Howard Book House, 1978.

Nash, Ronald. *The Concept of God.* Grand Rapids: Zondervan, 1983.

Nash, Stephen. "Is Physical Healing an Intended Benefit of the Atonement?" *The Seminary Review* (September 1981), 27:111-121.

"One Man with God," *The Presbyterian Journal* (December 28, 1966), pp. 9-10.

Orr, John. *English Deism: Its Roots and Its Fruits.* Grand Rapids: Eerdmans, 1934.

Outler, Albert C. *Who Trusts in God: Musings on the Meaning of Providence.* New York: Oxford University Press, 1968.

Packer, J. I. *Knowing God.* Downers Grove, Ill.: InterVarsity Press, 1973.

Pannenberg, Wolfhart. "Dogmatische Thesen zur Lehre von der Offenbarung," *Offenbarung als Geschichte,* ed. Wolfhart Pannenberg. 3 ed. Göttingen: Vandenhoeck and Ruprecht, 1965. Pp. 91-114.

Peterson, Michael. *Evil and the Christian God.* Grand Rapids: Baker, 1982.

Phillips, J. B. *Your God Is Too Small.* London: Epworth Press, 1952.

Pieper, Francis. *Christian Dogmatics,* tr. Theodore Engelder et al. 4 vols. St. Louis: Concordia Publishing House, 1950.

Pink, Arthur W. *The Sovereignty of God,* revised ed. London: Banner of Truth Trust, 1961.

Piper, John. *The Justification of God.* Grand Rapids: Baker, 1983.

A Plan of Union for the Church of Christ Uniting. Princeton: Consultation on Church Union, 1970.

Plantinga, Alvin. *God, Freedom, and Evil.* Grand Rapids: Eerdmans, 1977.

Pohle, Joseph. *God: The Author of Nature and the Supernatural,* ed. Arthur Preuss. St. Louis: B. Herder, 1912.

______________. *Grace Actual and Habitual,* ed. Arthur Preuss. St. Louis: B. Herder, 1949.

Pollard, William G. *Chance and Providence: God's Action in a World Governed by Scientific Law.* New York: Charles Scribner's Sons, 1958.

Pond, Enoch. *Lectures on Christian Theology.* Boston: Congregational Board of Education, 1867.

Pontifex, Mark. *Freedom and Providence.* New York: Hawthorn Books, 1960.

Pope, William Burt. *A Compendium of Christian Theology,* 3 ed., 3 vols. Cleveland: Thomas and Mattell, n.d.

Puglisi, Mario. *Prayer,* tr. Bernard M. Allen. New York: Macmillan, 1929.

Rachleff, Owen S. *Sky Diamonds: The New Astrology.* New York: Hawthorn Books, 1973.

Rahman, Fazlur, "Islamic Philosophy," *The Encyclopedia of Philosophy,* ed. Paul Edwards. New York: Macmillan, 1967. IV:219-224.

Raines, Robert A. *The Secular Congregation.* New York: Harper, 1968.

Ramm, Bernard. *The Christian View of Science and Scripture.* Grand Rapids: Eerdmans, 1956.

______________. *The God Who Makes a Difference: A Christian Appeal to Reason.* Waco: Word Books, 1972.

______________. *Protestant Christian Evidences.* Chicago: Moody Press, 1959.

Raymond, Miner. *Systematic Theology.* 3 vols. Cincinnati: Walden and Stowe, 1877.

Read, David H. C. *Whose God Is Dead? The Challenge of the New Atheism.* Cincinnati: Forward Movement Publications, 1966.

Rengstorf, Karl H. "σημεῖον," *Theological Dictionary of the New Testament,* ed. Gerhard Friedrich, tr. Geoffrey W. Bromiley. Grand Rapids: Eerdmans, 1971. VII:200-269.

Reymond, Robert L. "*What About Continuing Revelations and Miracles in the Presbyterian Church Today?*" Phillipsburg, N.J.: Presbyterian and Reformed, 1977.

Richardson, Alan. *Christian Apologetics.* London: SCM Press, 1947.

______________. *The Miracle-Stories of the Gospels.* New York: Harper and Brothers, n.d.

Roth, John K. "A Theodicy of Protest," *Encountering Evil: Live Options in Theodicy,* ed. Stephen T. Davis. Atlanta: John Knox Press, 1981. Pp. 7-22.

Rushdoony, Rousas. *The Mythology of Science.* Nutley, N.J.: Craig Press, 1967.

Russell, Bertrand. "A Free Man's Worship," *Mysticism and Logic.* Garden City, N.Y.: Doubleday Anchor, n.d. Pp. 44-54.

Schaaffs, Werner. *Theology, Physics, and Miracles,* tr. Richard L. Renfield. Washington, D.C.: Canon Press, 1974.

Schaeffer, Francis. *Back to Freedom and Dignity.* Downers Grove, Ill.: Inter-Varsity Press, 1972.

The School of Faith: The Catechisms of the Reformed Church, tr. and ed. Thomas F. Torrance. London: James Clarke and Co., 1959.

A Secular Humanist Declaration. Buffalo: Prometheus Books, 1980.

Seneca. "On Providence," *The Stoic Philosophy of Seneca,* tr. Moses Hadas. Garden City, N.Y.: Doubleday Anchor, 1958. Pp. 27-45.

______________. "On Tranquility of Mind," *The Stoic Philosophy of Seneca,* tr. Moses Hadas. Garden City, N.Y.: Doubleday Anchor, 1958. Pp. 75-106.

Shank, Robert. *Elect in the Son.* Springfield, Mo.: Westcott Publishers, 1970.

Shedd, William G. T. *Dogmatic Theology.* 3 vols. Grand Rapids: Zondervan, 1969 reprint of 1888 edition.

Sheed, F. J. *Communism and Man.* New York: Sheed and Ward, 1949.

Sherlock, William. *A Discourse Concerning the Divine Providence.* Pittsburgh: J. L. Read, 1848.

Simpson, George Gaylord. *The Meaning of Evolution.* New Haven: Yale University Press, 1949.

Skinner, B. F. *Beyond Freedom and Dignity.* New York: Alfred A. Knopf, 1972.

Smith, Charles R. "How To Miss God's Will," *Spire* (Winter 1982), 10:3-4.

Sontag, Frederick. "Anthropodicy and the Return of God," *Encountering Evil: Live Options in Theodicy,* ed. Stephen T. Davis. Atlanta: John Knox Press, 1981. Pp. 137-151.

Speer, Robert E. *The Light of the World.* West Medford, Mass.: Central Committee on the United Study of Missions, 1911.

Starhawk. *The Spiral Dance: A Rebirth of the Ancient Religion of the Great Goddess.* San Francisco: Harper & Row, 1979.

Staton, Knofel. *How To Know the Will of God,* revised edition. Cincinnati: Standard Publishing, 1979.

____________. *Spiritual Gifts for Christians Today.* Joplin, Mo.: College Press, 1973.

Steuer, Axel D. "The Supposed Incoherence of the Concept of God," *Is God GOD?,* ed. Axel D. Steuer and James E. McClendon, Jr. Nashville: Abingdon, 1981. Pp. 86-107.

Stone, Sam. "Knowing God's Will, Part Three: Man Should Choose God's Will," *The Lookout* (April 13, 1980), 92:3-4.

Strauss, James D. "God's Promise and Universal History," *Grace Unlimited,* ed. Clark H. Pinnock. Minneapolis: Bethany Fellowship, 1975. Pp. 190-208.

Strong, Augustus. *Systematic Theology.* 3 volumes in 1. Valley Forge: Judson Press, 1907.

Swinburne, Richard. *The Coherence of Theism.* Oxford: Clarendon Press, 1977.

Taylor, Richard. "Determinism," *The Encyclopedia of Philosophy,* ed. Paul Edwards. New York: Macmillan, 1967. II:359-373.

Teske, Romand H. "Omniscience, Omnipotence, and Divine Transcendence," *The New Scholasticism* (1979), 53:277-294.

Theophilus. "To Autolycus," tr. Marcus Dods. *The Ante-Nicene Fathers,* Volume II, ed. Alexander Roberts and James Donaldson. New York: Charles Scribner's Sons, 1913. Pp. 89-121.

Thielicke, Helmut. *The Evangelical Faith, Volume One: Prolegomena, The Relation of Theology to Modern Thought Forms,* tr. and ed. Geoffrey W. Bromiley. Grand Rapids: Eerdmans, 1974.

Thiessen, Henry Clarence. *Introductory Lectures in Systematic Theology.* Grand Rapids: Eerdmans, 1949.

Thittila, Maha Thera U. "The Fundamental Principles of Theravada Buddhism," *The Paths of Buddhism,* ed. Kenneth W. Morgan. New York: Ronald Press, 1956. Pp. 67-112.

Tillett, Wilbur Fisk. *Providence, Prayer and Power.* Nashville: Cokesbury Press, 1926.

Torrance, T. F. *Divine and Contingent Order.* New York: Oxford University Press, 1981.

Vahanian, Gabriel. *The Death of God: The Culture of Our Post-Christian Era.* New York: George Braziller, 1961.

Van Buren, Paul M. "Speaking of God," *Is God GOD?*, ed. Axel D. Steuer and James W. McClendon, Jr. Nashville: Abingdon, 1981. Pp. 55-82.

Vos, Geerhardus. *Biblical Theology: Old and New Testaments.* Grand Rapids: Eerdmans, 1948.

Warfield, Benjamin B. *Miracles: Yesterday and Today, True and False.* Grand Rapids: Eerdmans, 1965 reprint of 1918 edition entitled *Counterfeit Miracles.*

______________. "The Question of Miracles," *Selected Shorter Writings of Benjamin B. Warfield,* ed. John E. Meeter. Nutley, N.J.: Presbyterian and Reformed, 1973. II:167-204.

Waring, E. Graham, ed. *Deism and Natural Religion.* New York: Frederick Ungar Publishing Co., 1967.

Weidner, Revere Franklin. *Theologia, or the Doctrine of God.* New York: Revell, 1902.

Wendel, Francois. *Calvin: The Origins and Development of His Religious Thought,* tr. Philip Mairet. New York: Harper and Row, 1963.

Wesley, John. *Sermons on Several Occasions.* 2 vols. New York: G. Lane and C. B. Tippett, 1845.

Wiley, H. Orton. *Christian Theology.* 3 vols. Kansas City, Mo.: Beacon Hill Press, 1940.

______________ et al. "The Debate Over Divine Election," *Christianity Today* (October 12, 1959), 4:3-6, 14-18.

Williams, Colin W. *New Directions in Theology Today, Volume IV: The Church.* Philadelphia: Westminster Press, 1968.

Williams, William G. *An Exposition of the Epistle of Paul to the Romans.* Cincinnati: Jennings and Pye, 1902.

Wolfson, Harry A. *The Philosophy of the Kalam.* Cambridge: Harvard University Press, 1976.

Wykstra, Stephen J. "The Problem of Miracle in the Apologetic from History," *Journal of the American Scientific Affiliation* (December 1978), 30:154-163.

Wynkoop, Mildred Bangs. *Foundations of Wesleyan-Arminian Theology.* Kansas City, Mo.: Beacon Hill Press, 1967.

Yancey, Philip. "Finding the Will of God: No Magic Formulas," *Christianity Today* (September 16, 1983), 27:24-27.

______________. "Pain: The Tool of the Wounded Surgeon," *Christianity Today* (March 24, 1978), 22:12-16.

______________. *Where Is God When It Hurts?* Grand Rapids: Zondervan, 1977.

Zaehner, R. C. *Hinduism.* 2 ed. New York: Oxford University Press, 1966.

Zolar. *The Encyclopedia of Ancient and Forbidden Knowledge.* Los Angeles: Nash Publishing, 1970.

Zwingli, Huldreich. "On the Providence of God," *The Latin Works of Huldreich Zwingli,* tr. Samuel M. Jackson, ed. William J. Hinke. 3 vols. Philadelphia: Heidelberg Press, 1922. II:128-234.

Index of Bible Names

Index of Names

Index of Scriptures

Leviticus

Numbers

Deuteronomy

(Deuteronomy)

Joshua

Judges

I Samuel

(Ezra)

Nehemiah

Job

(Job)

New Testament

Matthew

(Matthew)

Mark

Luke

(Galatians)

Ephesians

(Ephesians)

Philippians

Colossians

I Thessalonians

II Thessalonians

I Timothy

Index of Subjects